The ARCHAEOLOGY *of the* MEDIEVAL ENGLISH MONARCHY

JOHN STEANE

B.T. Batsford Ltd. London

First published 1993

Typeset by Best-set Typesetter Ltd, Hong Kong
and printed in Great Britain by
Butler and Tanner, Frome, Somerset

Published by B T Batsford Ltd
4 Fitzhardinge Street, London W1H 0AH

A CIP catalogue record for this book is available from the British Library

ISBN 0 7134 7246 4

Contents

Illustrations

Cover illustration:
Details from Richard Smirke's painting of the mural from St Stephen's Chapel, Westminster. See Fig. 89.

Title page:
The seal of Edward I. See Fig. 7.

Foreword

By HRH Prince Richard of Gloucester

The advance of modern technology has enabled archaeologists to deduce a great deal more information from the artifacts that they unearth than could their predecessors. It is not only the speed with which computers can supply information, but also the immensely powerful microscopes that can identify where things have originated and further processes that can date objects so much more accurately.

The use of these techniques to identify objects with certainty, removes much of the speculation about the distant past and provides a firm framework, from which historians can make the more interesting speculations as to why historical personalities may have behaved the way they did.

This country has always been rich in historical documents, much studied and reported on in the vast bibliography that can be extracted from libraries. However, the work of archaeologists provides further reference points to enable us to seek to answer the questions that interest us today, rather than only those that the chroniclers chose to write about at the time.

It is the archaeologist's skill to deduce a great deal from very little – like Sherlock Holmes – it comes from knowing what to look for and how to compare it with previous discoveries. They are then able to demonstrate to the public how to read the evidence – very often the very landscape we see in front of us – as proof of occupation by particular groups of people at a certain period.

I first met John Steane, the author of this book, when he was Headmaster of Kettering Grammar School. He spent six summers excavating a deserted medieval village at Lyveden on my farm in Northamptonshire. Here he found and published his excavation of an industrial site which extended our understanding about the technology of the medieval pottery industry. His sixth formers were involved in the excavations and a number went on to become professional archaeologists. He enlarged his interests to include the whole man-made environment when he wrote *The Northamptonshire Landscape* (Hodder and Stoughton 1974). At this point he switched careers and joined the Oxfordshire Museum Service as its second County Archaeological Officer. He continued to foster the study of archaeology in schools as a member of the Council for British Archaeology's Schools Committee. But his developing interests brought him increasingly in contact with the medieval English monarchy. He had written on the royal fishponds of Northamptonshire as early as 1970 and subsequently made forays into the subjects of parks, forests and hunting. His interests in royal government were given expression in Chapter One of *The Archaeology of Medieval England and Wales* (Croom Helm, London 1984). He surveyed royal fishponds across the country in an article of 1988.

The present book attempts what I think no one has tried to do before. Traditionally the subject has been the preserve of historians who have used the incomparable wealth of documents and chronicles at their disposal. Here a survey is made of the material evidence for the activities and lifestyle of the medieval monarchy. The new facts coming from excavations are combined with a meticulous study of the buildings which remain above ground. The few artifacts which have undeniable royal associations are also scrutinised. The result is a vivid and at times unusual reconstruction of the lives of perhaps the most prominent element in medieval society.

The eye of an excavating archaeologist has joined with the historical researcher to answer exactly those questions that we would most like to know about the medieval monarchy, but which the contemporary chroniclers could not or dared not tell us.

A medieval King had not the complicated machinery of a modern state to help him share the responsibility for the future of his people. His success as a King depended on his ability as a general, as well as an administrator and a moral leader. How much time he could afford to devote to his own interests of, maybe, hunting, music and architecture, or raising an heir capable of succeeding to his responsibilities, depended on his other abilities and the economic fortunes of his times. Much of what was achieved was done by bluff, for the monarch's resources were only marginally greater than many of his more powerful subjects.

Shakespeare's histories speculate on the ambitions of these characters and the fates which brought them success or failure, but it is the archaeologist who can make the clearest distinction between the similarities and the differences between then and today.

The ruins of castles, abbeys and palaces found in all corners of the country mark the passing of this age, they also provide a sense of the significance of the past, not as just an inevitability, but monuments to exceptional individuals, who rose to prominence and influenced their communities for good or evil. I hope this book will provide many insights and bring a greater sense of understanding of the past and the way our present came to be created as a consequence of people and the conflicts of their ideas and beliefs.

Preface

Archaeology as a technique for shedding light on past human societies and activities has made major contributions during the last forty years to our understanding of medieval England. Material aspects of the medieval landscape such as field systems, forests, chases, parks, warrens, marshland, waste, villages and towns, roads and tracks have all been profitably studied (Cantor 1982, Rackham 1986). It is now some time since the pages of medieval economic, social and political historians were based exclusively on documentary sources. It is increasingly being realized that substantial, if fragmentary and scattered, remains of the medieval past lie buried or are upstanding throughout the country. English archaeologists have pioneered new techniques such as dendrochronology, the study of timber joints in buildings and the analysis of pottery, which all allow greater precision for dating structures.

Archaeological progress in the study of the medieval period, however, reflects twentieth-century preconceptions and obsessions. Ours is the century of the common man and much energy has been expended in reconstructing rural peasant life by studying medieval settlement. The doings of kings, nobles, barons and clerks no longer dominate the historical stage. The modern fashion for accumulating consumer goods has led students into spending perhaps a disproportionate amount of time in describing and analysing such common artifacts as pottery, knives and shoes (McCarthy and Brooks 1988, Cowgill *et al.* 1987, Grew and de Neergaard 1988). The current interest in ecology has fuelled the historical study of woodland and hedgerows (Rackham 1980, Hooper 1974). A further characteristic of the modern age which continues to excite and divide men is class. Social division is detected in the multifarious patterns of buildings, costume, accessories and food residues which appear in excavation reports. Most of these matters are discussed in my *The Archaeology of Medieval England and Wales* (Croom Helm 1984).

The mechanisms of political power are another favoured topic of the 1980s and 1990s. This book has arisen out of a reconsideration of Chapter One of the work just cited. I felt that the activities and preoccupations of kings, their families and their courtiers had been given inadequate treatment by medieval archaeologists (Clarke 1984, Hinton 1983). Royalty received scant attention in the *Research Objectives in British Archaeology* issued by the Council for British Archaeology (Thomas 1983). This dolefully claimed that the large corpus of excavated sites included only two royal palaces (Yeavering and Cheddar). Unknown, apparently, to its contributors were the excavations of medieval and Tudor palaces in the years just preceding and after the Second World War; such royal houses included Clarendon, Eltham, Greenwich, Whitehall, Bridewell, Nonsuch and the Tower of London.

The trouble was that the CBA's research priorities seem to have been topographical rather than political or social. Discrete categories of monuments within the landscape, such as moated sites and castles, were considered worthy of further study. The material apparatus of rulers responsible for government, expressed in highly symbolic artifacts such as crowns, croziers, seals and thrones, was not. Here then was a gap which needed to be filled.

One result of declining interest in organized religion and the reluctance of our generation to face up to the inevitability of death is that the medieval royal passion for the foundation of religious communities seems to our eyes an alien activity. However, the royal tombs of the English kings continue to exercise a mesmeric attraction to the thousands of tourists trampling through Westminster Abbey and St George's, Windsor.

For the purposes of this book I have defined the 'Middle Ages' as the period 1060–1547. Despite the exaggerated attempts in recent years to promote the idea of continuity between the late Anglo-Saxon kingdom and its Norman successor, these dates mark two decisive events, the Norman Conquest, and the break with Rome at the Reformation. Since the latter event occurred in the middle of Henry VIII's reign, I have continued to draw on examples up to 1547. Henry VIII seems to me to be far more 'medieval' than 'Renaissance'.

'England' is an artificial power bloc of royal, baronial and ecclesiastical estates, rights and claims during this period. I was tempted to deal more equally with 'England and France' but for the four years 1985 to 1989 family preoccupations meant that I did no foreign travelling. Hence the references to France and Spain and the Netherlands, all areas of great interest and influence on the medieval English kings, are brief and fleeting. I am grateful to my daughter, Anna, for living in the south of France and for encouraging me to visit her and my grandson. If there is a revised edition this is the direction in which I would shape the book.

I believe it is most important to visit and record one's own observations of each monument. The bulk of the photographs, apart from aerial views, are by the author.

I have attempted a synthesis; two major aspects, however, I have left for other books – the archaeology of government (that is to say law, justice, prisons, coinage) and the art of war.

John Steane
Oxford
May 1992

Acknowledgements

I acknowledge the help of many friends, colleagues and students in the writing of this book, which has taken five years squeezed into a busy life of museum work. It is dedicated to the memory of my mother, Edith, who in her sixties and seventies was still lecturing on the monarchy and the capital on behalf of the City of London Society. I owe to her my early love of visiting ancient buildings. She unfailingly provided me with travelling costs from her limited resources and trusted me from the age of twelve to get there on my own.

I thank Professor Martin Biddle of Hertford College, Oxford, for inspiring me with his lectures, lending me the typescript of his book on the Winchester Round Table, and showing much enthusiasm towards the projects of his fellow students; Howard Colvin for writing the bulk of the medieval and early Tudor volumes of *The Kings Works*, an incomparable quarry for the would-be medieval archaeologist: its majestic scholarship, scrupulous accuracy and unpretentious style make it a pleasure to use; Professor Karl Leyser of All Souls College, Oxford, to whom I am indebted for my (limited) understanding of early medieval European history; Dr Tom James for reading Chapter 4, for allowing me to read his *The Palaces of Medieval England* in advance of publication and for accompanying me on a number of visits; Dr Gerald Harriss of Magdalen College, Oxford, for reading and suggesting improvements to Chapter 2; the President and fellows of Magdalen College for allowing a former demy to spread the papers of Chapter 7 over the tables of the McFarlane Library and for hospitality on a number of occasions; the staffs of the Bodleian, Ashmolean, Magdalen College and History Faculty Libraries for their unfailing courtesy in providing books and articles.

I am grateful for the secluded facilities of St Deiniols Library, Hawarden, Wales where much of this book was written; to F.E. Thompson and Hugh Chapman for facilitating the permission of the Society of Antiquaries to photograph books and objects in the Society's possession; to Professor Sheppard Frere for loans of books; to Julian Munby for books and many ideas connected with Westminster; to Dr Ian Goodall for a loan of his thesis; to my aunt, Mrs Rich, for accompanying me to Nonsuch; to Trevor Rowley, Deputy Director of Oxford University Department for External Studies for organizing a conference on palaces in 1989; to Dr John Blair of Queens College who has again read and commented critically and I hope fruitfully on the whole book; to Brian Durham of the Oxford Archaeological Unit for sharing his ideas on palaces; to Dr Paul Stamper, Brian Dix and Bob Croft, former students of Kettering Grammar School, for providing me with up-to-date information about archaeology of Shropshire, Northamptonshire and Somerset respectively; to Arthur McGregor and John Cherry for allowing me to study the objects in their care in the Ashmolean Museum; to my brother, Christopher, for an abiding interest in building materials and for information on French cathedrals; to Georgina Stonor for her mine of knowledge and enthusiastic support; to Dr Martin Henig for sharing his massive scholarship with me; to my daughter Kate for recent references to the city of Lincoln; to my niece, Mary Anne, for the loan of her dissertation on Charlemagne and Aachen; to Mr Foster, formerly Clerk of Works at Westminster Abbey for making accessible the upper parts of that building; to James Bateman, Carol Anderson and Martin Brown of the Oxfordshire County Museum Services for encouragement and support; to Cynthia Bradford and Vernon Brooke for help with photographs, to Lisa Toogood, Elsebeth Wulff, and Samantha Hatzis for typing the successive drafts of the manuscripts; to Jennifer Mossop, Audrey Cruse and Elaine Fullard for accompanying me on many expeditions: two pairs of eyes are better than one. Finally, I am grateful for the prompt and efficient services of Tony Seward and Sarah Vernon-Hunt and to Peter Kemmis Betty, who has encouraged the writing of the book in its later stages.

CHAPTER ONE
Symbols of power

The European Middle Ages are dominated by the concept of kingship. The Norman, Angevin, Plantagenet, Capetian and Hohenstaufen dynasties lend their names to periods in English, French and German history. The politics of the period are virtually synonymous with the attempts of rulers to fulfil monarchical ambitions by means of marriage, diplomacy or war. Kings were also constantly expanding their influence into the spiritual sphere and thus conflicting with churchmen as well as barons. The ideal medieval king meant different things to different sections of the people who made up the kingdom (Barraclough 1957). He was a leader of his magnates in war; a priest-king protecting the interests of the church, appointing bishops and abbots; an administrator and tax-gatherer upholding and supported by the interests of the class of royal officials, the *ministeriales*. He was also a judge, the fount of law, and was likely to satisfy his more lowly subjects if he was prepared to distribute justice, however sternly, with an even hand.

This irradiation of monarchy throughout society was helped in England by a number of circumstances. Historical accident produced three 'strong' kings in succession: William I, William II and Henry I, who created or improved institutions too powerful to be destroyed by the 20 years' anarchy of Stephen's reign. Henry I, by begetting 30 bastards and systematically slotting them into positions of political importance in his dominions consolidated his family's grip on widely scattered possessions (Given-Wilson 1988, 61). Henry II cemented alliances by marrying his children to other ruling houses throughout Europe. The concept of primogeniture, the unresisted acceptance of the heir to the throne, usually the king's eldest son, had become the norm as far as England was concerned by the end of the thirteenth century. Edward I succeeded his father almost immediately in 1272 although he was absent on crusade; he was sufficiently assured of the succession to postpone his coronation until 1274. Edward II was the first king to date his regnal years from the day after his father's death. In this way continuity was assured; a close bond was forged between the royal dynasty and the royal office. This was demonstrated symbolically by the fact that the arms of the Plantagenet dynasty (Latin *plantagenista* = broom), 'Gules three lions passant guardant or' became the arms of the kingdom of England. The identification of the king with the nation meant that his achievements became the achievements of England – Edward I's conquest of Wales, and Edward III's military victories over the French at Crécy, 1346, and Poitiers, 1356.

Concurrently, the rapid development of effective departments of government meant that strong monarchical administration was carried on despite periods of royal weakness and crisis. Royal government could survive minorities such as Henry III's (1216–27), and baronial revolts (those of Simon de Montfort 1258–65 and Thomas of Lancaster 1321–2). Kingship as an institution emerged unscathed through the reigns of such flawed characters as Henry III and Edward II.

Archaeology provides a window into the contemporary perceptions of monarchy. Kingship was surrounded and bolstered by ceremonies and symbols, many of which have left structural and artifactual vestiges. The most significant was the ceremony of coronation whereby the king was invested by the Archbishop of Canterbury with spiritual power as

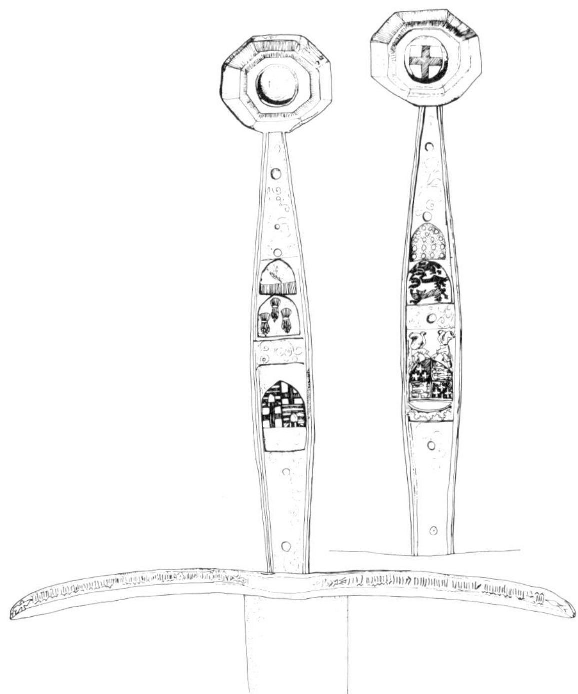

1 *A royal sword now in the British Museum. This is northern German in manufacture and dates to the mid-fifteenth century. It was carried before the Prince of Wales and bears the royal arms on the principal side of the grip and the pommel as well as those of Wales, Cornwall, and St George. On the other side are those of Mortimer quartering Burgh. It may have been used by the eldest son of Edward IV, created Prince of Wales and Earl of Chester in 1471. Alternatively, it may have been used by the son of Richard III, Prince Edward, 1473–84, invested as Prince of Wales and Earl of Chester in 1483.*

God's anointed, like the kings of Israel before him. Henceforward the anointed king was set apart from his subjects, at least on a par with, and to some extent superior to, churchmen. His periodic crown wearings reminded recalcitrant subjects of this divine stamp of approval. The effect of such ceremonies was strengthened by the dissemination of the royal coinage and of seals attached to documents, carrying images of the royal *persona* to every part of the land. Palaces were painted and churches filled with glass and images, further powerful projections of royal power. Apart from the crown and sceptre the third most potent symbol of royal power was the sword (Fig. 1). Kings were recorded on a number of occasions as giving the sword from their own sides as a mark of special favour. With the sword the king knighted his followers. The chivalric code was reflected in the 'Matter of England', the tales of King Arthur and his Round Table. The cult of personality which backed their political pretensions was further fostered by the fact that medieval kings spent their lives in progresses throughout their dominions, characterized by conspicuous consumption; and when they died their obsequies were carried out on a magnificent scale and their bodies buried under tombs of great splendour. This chapter will survey four main aspects of these symbols of power: portraits and images, seals and regalia.

Portraits of kings

If by portraits we mean realistic and recognizable representations of the faces of people, then this genre can hardly be said to have started before the medieval period had largely run its course. For one thing, only the rulers in the twelfth and thirteenth centuries were represented in art in any numbers; they were shown, monarchs and bishops, loaded with the symbols of their office – crowns, sceptres and so on. Their faces lack personal features, and without their beards, sceptres and crowns could easily be mistaken for those of saints; yet by means of the symbols the identifications are made clear. It seems that at this time the symbols of power were more potent than the idea of portraiture. There are, however, qualifications to be made. Some kings acquired attributes which were taken up by artists and repeated. Such is the long beard which is found in representations of Edward the Confessor. He is depicted on his coins, on his great seal and on the Bayeux Tapestry with a long beard, unlike any of his predecessors or successors (Whittingham 1974, 99). Even in the fifteenth-century glass at Great Malvern he is shown with flowing white hair and a beard (Rushforth 1936, 123–4).

The Norman conquerors, however, are shown as clean-shaven in the near-caricatures of their rulers stamped on their coins and embroidered on the Bayeux Tapestry. Some full-face coins of William I show him with long moustaches. The impression of his great seal is unfortunately too indistinct to settle the question of whether the Bayeux Tapestry or these coins are correct in this detail (Wyon and Wyon 1887, 5–7). Clearly, if we are not even sure whether the Norman kings were bearded or shaven we are not going to get very much nearer to solving the question of their personal appearance.

During the twelfth century the idea of the portrait had still hardly germinated in western Europe. The image of the ruler, on the other hand, was strongly rooted in the visual scene; rulers had themselves been interpreted by artists in wall paintings, sculptures, bronzework and manuscripts as incarnations of justice. They are shown very much as Christ was depicted on the sculptured tympana over the doorways of great churches, seated in judgement on thrones, bearded, crowned, holding swords and sceptres. Their icons demonstrate little humanity and less individuality. The last thing one would call these solemn and soulless representations of monarchy is portraiture. Towards the middle of the century funeral monuments began to take the form of sculptured effigies. The first of these to survive in Italy were the papal effigies. It is possible that Henry I and Stephen were similarly commemorated but their monuments have been destroyed. The earliest monumental effigies in England are those of Roger and Jocelyn, bishops of Salisbury (d. 1139 and 1184 respectively) (Shortt 1958–9, 217–19). Those of the Angevin kings and queens at Fontévrault followed soon after. They are shown as *gisants*, stretched out as in death, remote, statuesque and withdrawn; surrounded by and clothed with the symbols of earthly power, devoid of individuality.

The thirteenth century, however, saw a move in two directions: the monuments to the dead begin to be idealized, and there is a tendency towards realism, though hardly naturalism, before the end of the century. One reason for this in England must be the great increase in artistic patronage during the reign of Henry III. There are no less than 19 references in royal records to the making of royal portrait images (this includes king, queen and members of the immediate royal family in stone, glass and metalwork) during his reign, 1216–72 (Whittingham 1974, Appendix 2). Three instances may be cited of the idealization of royal portraits. Eleanor of Castile's effigy in Westminster Abbey shows her as a considerably younger woman than the matron who had born Edward I's 15 children. Edward II's alabaster effigy at Gloucester is another idealized version. It is an example of a very common feature of the mid-fourteenth century – that men had to be represented at the perfect age of about 33 (the supposed age of the crucified Christ) – as they hoped to appear at the General Resurrection (Gardner 1940, 24). Edward III, when commemorating the death of his children, Blanche of the Tower and William of Windsor (Fig. 2), had effigies made of well-grown striplings of the age of 10 despite the fact that both had died as babies (Tanner 1953, 34). An example of the somewhat uncertain move towards realism is the generalized portrait effigy of Henry III at Westminster – its rather lack-lustre handling may be due to the clumsiness of the bronze-founder (Plenderleith and Maryon 1959, 87–8).

Royal portraiture took a marked step forward in the latter part of Edward III's reign, with the French effigy of Queen Philippa of Hainault, who died in 1369 (Noppen 1931). This is no idealized woman but the realistic portrayal of a plain, rather stout, middle-aged lady, whose alabaster image still succeeds in arousing our sympathies.

The advent of realism coincides with the use of the death-mask. This has been first traced in the case of Edward III, whose death-mask it is thought was employed to make the head of the king's effigy used for the funeral celebrations (Howgrave-Graham 1961, 160–1). Henceforward there is a real possibility that when we are looking at a royal monument or a royal portrait we are gazing at a more or less accurate delineation of royal features. At this stage, however, portraiture was only regarded as an additional means of identification. It still took second place to heraldry and nomenclature. The male members of the royal family depicted in the fourteenth-century St Stephen's Chapel wall paintings (see Fig. 89) were shown wearing heraldic surcoats, and all the figures were labelled with their names; portraiture functioned here only as a kind of 'belt and braces' means of identifying figures represented on large-scale public paintings. The famous Westminster Abbey portrait of Richard II is in a sense labelled by means of the crowned letter Rs patterning the royal robe (Hepburn 1986, 91).

2 *Effigies of William and Blanche, children of Edward III in Westminster Abbey, London. These children were still babies when they died but are portrayed in idealized form as ten-year-olds.* (Photograph: RCHM England.)

While the funeral effigy of Edward III may give us an accurate delineation of his face, the icon which the bronze founder made of his royal visage is shown wrapped in an enormous beard which inevitably obscures some of the lower features of his face. It may well be that epochs of beardlessness went with periods of realistic portraiture (Whittingham 1974). Certainly, we have a clearer idea of Richard II's face because he chose to sport a comparatively meagre forked beard which is combined with a long narrow nose and hooded eyes on the Westminster picture and the tomb effigy.

The unsigned and undated panel portraits of the later Plantagenets have recently been subjected to dendrochronological analysis (Fletcher 1974, 250–8) which provides a date, *c.*1518–23, for the painting of the portrait in the Royal Collection at Windsor Castle of Henry V and confirms that it was painted at the same time as the two other portraits in the Royal Collection showing Henry VI and Richard III (Hepburn 1986, 27). They are all identical in size and a comparison of the patterns of the tree rings from the boards which make them up indicates that the main board of all three panels was cut from the same tree.

Despite the fact that Henry V's portrait was painted nearly a hundred years after his death it is thought to be a close copy of a contemporary Gothic votive painting. The king's face may be slightly stylized but it comes through as recognizably youthful, firm and determined; he is 25 years old, long-featured, handsome, and with more than a touch of the *dévot*. The Royal Collection portrait of Henry VI, on the other hand, tends to bear out contemporary observations that as an adult the king looked naive and childlike; it shows a ruler whose mental health was precarious. In fact 'the Kyng was simple and lad by covetous counseylle . . . the quene with such as were of her affynyte rewled the reaume as her lyked' (quoted by Wolffe 1981, 20).

Dr Fletcher suggests that alone among the works of the later medieval rulers which have survived in the Royal Collection the portrait of Edward IV's queen, Elizabeth Woodville, is an original work dating from *c.*1471–80 (Fletcher 1974, 256). Other lines of evidence, however, such as the costume, the jewellery and the composition suggest that it was a later copy (Hepburn 1986, 56–7). A more likely contemporary representation of Elizabeth and her husband is the excellent stained glass kneeling figures in the north window of the north-west transept of Canterbury Cathedral (Caviness 1981, 251–61). Here are accurately portrayed the same high forehead, large eyes, straight nose and small pointed chin which so captivated Edward IV that he was prepared to set half his kingdom in an uproar in order to marry this bewitching (widowed) commoner. The fact that they are kneeling is significant. The royal family is seen as a human group, taking part in an act of worship. This is far from the God-like figures of royal judges seen three hundred years before.

Edward himself was reckoned to be a handsome man, if somewhat corpulent in his later years. The best of a group of three surviving portraits from the so-called 'Cast Shadow Workshop' shows the king wearing a richly brocaded cloth-of-gold gown; this painting was dated by tree-ring analysis to 1520–35 (Fletcher 1974, 256, 257, Table 2). The oriental-looking cast of the eyes, the straight nose, the small pinched mouth, bear a close resemblance to the standard facial type which appears in late fifteenth-century English alabaster figures. No likeness survives of little Edward V. Richard III, on the other hand has been the subject of a plethora of portraits; he is the first English king for whom there is evidence to suggest that two panel-portraits of him were produced during his lifetime (Tudor Craig 1973, 80–95). Both are known now through later copies, the most important being that in the Royal Collection at Windsor. It is clear that this picture has been tampered with; the right shoulder has been raised in order to suggest that the subject was crook-backed. The eye similarly has been straightened to give it a sinister glint; both doubtless to reflect Tudor smear campaigns. It seems from verbal descriptions that King Richard was a short man, 'of bodily shape comely enough, only of low stature'; he also very likely suffered from an overwhelming sense of anxiety. His face in the portraits shows strain but is toughly determined in contrast to the bland self-confidence of his brother Edward. The body beneath the face is lean, with a thin neck: insofar as both the shoulders are rather drawn up and the head juts forward slightly, the image also reflects Richard's alleged round-shoulderedness (Hepburn 1986, 84–5).

There are a number of paintings of Henry VII but the most celebrated image is that sculptured in bronze for his funeral effigy in Westminster Abbey by the Florentine master, Pietro Torrigiano. This fine posthumous portrait was possibly based on that of the funeral effigy modelled in turn on a death mask. The effigy in Westminster Abbey when repaired after the Second World War, was noted as having 'an open, bold and commanding face, entirely without the crafty and unpleasant expression seen in many inferior portraits' (Howgrave-Graham 1961, 167). When Torrigiano came to work on his other commission, that of a monument to Henry VII's mother, Lady Margaret Beaufort (the great educational benefactress, founder of St John's College, Cambridge), he was separated from his subject by two years and had to work from drawings prepared by the court painter. On 22 June 1513 payment was made 'to Maynarde paynter for makinge the picture and image of the seide ladye . . . 33s 4d'. His contract mentions 'A Tabernacle of copper with an ymage lying at the fote of the same . . . with like pillars' (Scott 1914–15, 365–76). The result is a beautiful gothic effigy of an austere, veiled widow, her hands joined in prayer, in black and gold (RCHM 1924, 68).

Despite the magnificence of the surroundings of Henry VII's chapel and the panoply of the tombs themselves there is a reticence about the effigies of these early Tudors which contrasts with the vainglorious and rumbustious image of the young Henry VIII dominating the European stage on the Field of the Cloth of Gold. Lord Mountjoy wrote to Erasmus in 1509, with singular lack of perception, 'Our King is not after gold, or gems, or precious metals, but virtue, glory, immortality'. We have plenty of verbal descriptions of Henry VIII at different times in his reign to supplement the powerful visions provided by Holbein and other, lesser, artists. A Venetian, writing in 1515, probably was not flattering when he wrote

> *His Majesty is the handsomest potentate I ever set eyes on, above the usual height, with an extremely fine calf to his leg, his complexion very fair and bright with auburn hair combed straight and short, in the French fashion, and a round face so very beautiful, that it would become a pretty woman, his throat being rather long and thick.* (Longford 1989, 209.)

It is surprising that Henry never exploited the full potential of the artists who offered their services to his court. Holbein, one of the greatest international painters of the day, he despatched on foreign missions to paint possible wives for himself. The fact that his aristocratic sitters only allowed the painter limited three-hour sittings contributed to his distinctive flat patterns, elaborate dresses, aloof and inscrutable features (Waterhouse 1953, 8). When Holbein turned to paint the king himself in 1537, he designed a remarkable commemorative group in fresco of Henry VIII and Jane Seymour with Henry VII and Elizabeth of York, on the wall of the Privy Chamber in the Palace of Whitehall. The original perished in the Whitehall Fire in the seventeenth century but a copy had been made; and part of the original cartoon survives at Chatsworth, which shows the image of the king that every schoolboy knows.

The stance is dramatic. The king stands with legs wide apart – where are those fine calves? Small piggy eyes stare out suspiciously over a long straight nose and a narrow cruel mouth; below is a thick neck, an enormous trunk under a slashed, pleated, upholstered set of padded garments which would not be out of place on an American footballer. This cartoon was reused and the subsequent portraits copied and re-copied. Kings avoided sitting for artists.

During his last years, Henry showed signs of further physical and spiritual decline. Whether he was suffering from the complications arising from untreated syphilis (the traditional explanation of his medical problems) or a dreadfully bad diet leading to scurvy (the fashionable modern alternative (Kybett 1989, 19–25)) is not clear. He becomes gross; his eyes practically disappear into his face; he had himself painted huge and towering out of scale above the quivering barber-surgeons, granting a charter to them in 1541 (Ganz 1950, 290). By the time of his death he increasingly saw himself as the embodiment of King David (Tudor Craig 1989, 183–98), a form of self-delusion which gave him a kind of ideological stiffening, useful in the Age of Plunder when values, moral and economic, were collapsing all around him. His daughter, Elizabeth I, exploited the sacred nature of the portrait image (Strong 1963). Together with the royal arms displayed in churches, the Queen's portraits, distributed as presents to nobility and to foreign courts, became universally regarded as emanations of royal power.

Images of kingship

The other main tradition producing powerful images of kingship involved the creation of major representations of rulers in glass, painting or sculpture. This developed contemporaneously in France, England, Spain and Germany in the early Middle Ages. It began with the schematic trees of Jesse depicting the ancestors of Christ, the royal line of David. In *c.*1130 a tree of Jesse was carved over the façade of Nôtre Dame la Grande at Poitiers. Fifteen years later the famous tree of Jesse glass window was made for St Denis Abbey, Paris. This church became one of the mausolea for the Capetian monarchy. The design was imitated shortly afterwards in one of the west windows at Chartres. The Romanesque west front of Lincoln Cathedral is thought to have had a tree of Jesse, since a few sculptured fragments remain (Zarnecki 1964, plates 21, 22a).

The tree could be transmuted into a horizontal scheme with the kings seated under niches. Great rows of sculptured kings integrated into the west fronts of the cathedrals of Paris, Chartres, Amiens and Rheims shed glory on kingship regardless of which kings they were supposed to commemorate – Capetian or of the stock of Judah (Mâle 1972, 168). It is significant that their production coincided with the reign of Philip Augustus (1180–1223) when the French monarchy was emerging from a long period of political difficulties, its prestige newly enhanced. This connection between royal and biblical was deliberately blurred in political life. Both the kings of England and France at this time claimed to have divine powers of healing (Bloch 1973).

The idea of using the west front or an interior screen of a cathedral as suitable places to display the panoply of royal power commended itself to the ruling powers, royal and episcopal, in England. The tree of Jesse theme was adopted in some places but there were two other ways in which rows of kings might be displayed. The first was a chronological scheme whereby a series starts with Anglo-Saxon saints and martyr-kings and works through a number of well-known individual monarchs of outstanding reputation, ending with the king in whose reign the scheme was ordered. The other is one with a more overtly political flavour which became usual in the fifteenth century;

here the choice of monarchs was dictated by their dynastic affiliations. Lancastrian kings chose respectable Lancastrian predecessors, Yorkists avoided those embarrassing to their cause. Clearly, each side regarded these impressive if stagey sculptural demonstrations as valuable visual props to their shaky causes.

Why were kings associated with the west fronts of cathedrals and great churches? It was an oriental and Hellenistic-Roman custom for the ruler to be received in a most solemn way whenever he visited a city or entered his capital. When Christianized, this ceremonial entrance or *adventus* (if by the emperor) was seen as reflecting our Lord's Entry into Jerusalem. The city or the monastery which was approached by the Lord's Anointed became a Jerusalem (Kantorowicz 1958, 72–5). The western entrances of such great churches as Nôtre Dame, Paris, and Canterbury remind us of the façades of holy cities and were the traditional place of royal ingress. At Winchester, Biddle has argued that part of the sequence of crown wearings in Norman England may have involved a ceremony on a balcony on the west front of the Norman cathedral which in turn had replaced the west-work of the old minster dedicated in AD 980 (Biddle 1986, 62–3).

Royal figures appear on the west front of Wells Cathedral (Fig. 3), dating from *c.*1230–55 (Cockerell 1851, 51, Stone 1955, 112). The old choir screen of Salisbury Cathedral dated to *c.*1250 contained a series from Edgar down to Henry III (Wordsworth 1914, 566). Fifty years later the west front of Lichfield Cathedral was designed with sculptured figures of kings of England along the second tier (Dugdale 1846). Exeter Cathedral (Fig. 4) was given a splendid two-storeyed screen of kings by its politically ambitious bishop, Grandisson (1327–69). It is uncertain whether these were English kings, or kings on an unfinished tree of Jesse, but what is undoubted is that they were meant to be a paean in stone in praise of monarchy. A recent archaeological survey (Blaylock and Henderson 1987) (Fig. 5) has been completed which has revealed for the first time the extent of the former brilliant colouring of the scheme, the high quality of the remaining work, its vulnerability and the extent of the various restoration programmes. Lincoln Cathedral has a single row of kings above the Norman portal on its west front, carved in 1350–80 (Fig. 6).

3 *Wells Cathedral. A seated figure of a king on the west front, thirteenth century.* (Photograph: J. M. Steane.)

The kings at both Exeter and Lincoln are shown seated and in many cases their legs are crossed. This positioning of the legs is often seen in representations of rulers. In the Glazier Psalter (Bodleian Library) of *c.*1230, David is shown being crowned; he sits with one leg lifted high over the other in what seems to modern eyes a nonchalant gesture. Such a convention is meant to express dignity and an exalted state. It is equally displayed by monarchs famed for

4 *Exeter Cathedral. The image screen on the west front, the work of Bishop John Grandisson (1327–69), consisting of a lower tier of demi-angel figures supporting a row of mainly seated full figures of kings.* (Photograph: J. M. Steane.)

their wisdom or notorious for their tyranny and wickedness. Cross-legged effigies of knights of the thirteenth century have been claimed to be class signifiers, the variety of their attitudes reflecting their individualism (Tummers 1980, 125–6).

Such elaborate sculptural schemes were the result of episcopal patronage if not direct design; the first time that a king can be proved to have intervened in a great scheme involving sculptured standing kings occurred in Richard II's reign (1377–99). In 1385 £30 6s 8d was paid 'to Thomas Canon Marbler (of Corfe) for making 13 stone images in the likeness of kings to stand in the Great Hall'. This was the Great Hall at the Palace of Westminster which was reconstructed ten years later, evidently incorporating these statues. Although they are relatively crude pieces of sculpture, with their towering crowns, tall upright figures, long faces, wig-like hair and corkscrew beards, holding sceptres and orbs carved in the round, they were to have a profound effect on royal images in the fifteenth century (Stone 1955, 194). Standing figures, moreover, were particularly appropriate for fitting into the multiple long lights of perpendicular windows.

Richard II's tendency towards absolutism and his realization of the uncertainty of his position are revealed by the fact that he felt it necessary to multiply these powerful images of his kingship. At Canterbury, the spiritual centre of the kingdom and first port of call for all foreign visitors entering the country via Dover, he had a great west window glazed with figures of kings. They are again shown standing in their robes of state, crowned, sceptred and orbed. They are in historical sequence; the intention certainly would appear to have been to present them in such a way as to buttress the continuity of royal succession in the face of Lancastrian claims to the throne (Caviness 1981, 282–3).

Political motivation of this nature becomes more overt during the next century. The Lancastrian and Yorkist kings profited from the efforts of time-serving clerics who made available the large advertising spaces offered by the glass windows, west fronts and screens of England's two metropolitan cathedrals, Canterbury and York. Both provide an archaeological commentary on the dynastic fluctuations of the fifteenth century.

5 *Exeter Cathedral. The image screen on the west front. This is from a survey recently made at scale of 1:10 based on the study of existing figures and the most useful previous illustrations of the west front by John Carter whose* Specimens of Ancient Figure Sculpture and Painting in England *was printed in 1794.* (Blaylock and Henderson.)

Henry IV took advantage of the sacred aura offered by the popular martyr-saint St Thomas and willed his body to Canterbury for burial. He had earlier reinstated his supporter, Archbishop Arundel, to his see. The Lancastrian monarchy celebrated its connection with Canterbury visually by providing the subject matter for a series of royal images in the choir screen under construction 1420–50, designed to emphasize its dynastic claims (Stone 1955, 204).

Similarly, when the Yorkist king Edward IV seized power he bound Archbishop Bourchier to him with ties of allegiance and even marriage. The Canterbury connection gave rise to the royal portraits in the north transept window. The change to kneeling figures has taken place. Edward IV and Elizabeth Woodville, with their sons and daughters, are shown as kneeling donors, but there is no reason to suppose that the glass was a royal gift. It was begun as early as 1482 but was still unfinished after Henry VII had come to the throne and may have been completed as a kind of memorial (Caviness 1981, 258–61).

6 Lincoln Cathedral. The screen of kings above the Norman doorway on west front. The screen was probably carved by London artists between 1350 and 1380. Some of the figures are in the mid-century cross-legged attitude and all wear tall crowns and deep tippets of the latter half of the century. (Photograph: J. M. Steane.)

At York there is a screen similar to that at Canterbury containing original statues of 15 kings of England down to Henry VI, dating, it is thought, to *c.*1470–80 (Hope 1916–17, 59–60, Stone 1955, 220). The glass here contains a number of political allusions. The so-called St Cuthbert window 'was erected in order that all the world might see and know of the many kings, princes, and cardinals who came of that noble stock'; including John of Gaunt, founder of that princely line, Henry IV, Henry V, and Henry VII, Humphrey, Duke of Gloucester, and Cardinals Beaufort, Kemp and Langley. The last was the donor of the window (Knowles 1936, 183).

Another interesting variant is the series of kings in the painted glass in the west windows of the Old Library at All Souls' College, Oxford (Hutchinson 1949, 51–4). Here Archbishop Chichele and King Henry VI were co-founders and the iconographic scheme was intended to record the predecessors of the royal co-founders and Henry VI himself. Henry's own religious instincts may be recognized by the inclusion of all the English kings who had been canonized. Constantine, reputed to have been born of an English (i.e. British) mother, who was proclaimed Emperor at York in AD 306, is also there; and the legendary Arthur is added for good measure. Alfred, Athelstan and Edgar, who had done most for the unification of England, are included. The Normans, never popular in the English folk-memory, are conveniently left out. 'Edwardus Martir', that is Edward II, popularly, but never canonically sainted, is present. Edward III's son, John of Gaunt, qualifies by the fact that he assumed for a time the title of king of Castile and Leon by right of his wife Constance, daughter and heiress of Pedro the Cruel. The All Souls' glass is an idiosyncratic example of the English medieval monarchy's perception of its own past, true and legendary.

The great seals of the medieval English kings

Royal portraits were seen by a relatively small number of people. Statues in stone were by their very nature static. A more powerful method of projecting the royal image throughout the land was by the use of seals (Fig. 7).

The increasing use of seals by the ruling class in the early Middle Ages is also an instructive pointer to the developing effectiveness of government. Seals were employed to close up documents to protect them from being read by anyone except the persons to whom they were addressed. As Heslop remarks, a seal acted as the equivalent of the glue on an envelope flap and as an instant indication of the source of the letter (Heslop 1980, 1–17). Just as today's correspondent is alerted by tell-tale crinkles and weak adhesion to the fact that his letter has been steamed open and its contents read by others, so in the twelfth century a broken seal, or one which did not look like that of the sender, set alarm bells ringing. A seal, in addition, served to identify the sender; it was known to be his, and could be sworn to by witnesses. By sealing it, a document could be authenticated. The late Saxon English monarchy realized the advantages of the seal and exploited its opportunities.

Edward the Confessor effected an important development in the use of seals because his royal writs were the first that we know of to be patent sealed, that is sealed open in such a way that the seal did not have to be broken for the letter to be read. This was done by attaching the seal to a thin tongue of the parchment at the base of the sheet. The writ remained authenticated by the seal and as a result it could be usefully preserved among the muniments as evidence. Another feature of importance

7 *The seal of Edward I. This is almost an exact copy of the second seal of Henry III. The King has a long straight sceptre with a dove and is seated on a highly ornamental throne supported by lions. The legend is +* EDWARDUS DEI GRACIA REX ANGLIE DOMINUS HYBERNIE DUX AQUITANIE. *The counterseal shows the king on horseback. The horse is clothed in a caparison charged with the arms of England reversed.* (Impression: Public Record Office; photograph: V. Brooke.)

was that this pendant seal was double sided: Edward the Confessor's seal and counterseal have different designs. The area available for propaganda was thus doubled, while the chances of forgery were lessened. It has been suggested that the designer of the Confessor's seal was the German goldsmith Theodoric, who appears in Domesday Book. Certainly the iconography is closely paralleled in contemporary seals of the Holy Roman Empire (Bauml 1969, Fig. 22).

Ivory and bone were the favoured materials for making seal matrices during the Romanesque period. By the late twelfth century lead, copper alloy and silver and, very occasionally, gold were used. There were several reasons for this. The change-over to metal was probably something to do with the increased wear and tear on seals. Two-sided seals required the use of a seal press to make an impression; this imposed a strain on the material from which they were made. Also, silver and bronze can be both cast and engraved and this means that it is easier to produce deeper, more plastic and more smoothly rounded forms. Prestige was also, doubtless, an issue. Great men and great institutions derived status from seals engraved in precious metal. There is a stylistic change noticeable round about 1180 – from linearity to plasticity and depth. Metal seal matrices were made by goldsmiths. We know, for instance, that Henry III's first great seal was made by Master Walter de Ripa, a goldsmith of London. He was paid in November 1218 with five marks of silver, the weight of the metal used to make a pair of matrices. A month later he was paid 40s for the work, a considerable sum for several weeks' work, which is likely to reflect the satisfaction felt by the 11-year-old king in the design of the resultant seal (Alexander and Binski 1987, 397). The second seal of Henry III was fashioned by Master William of Gloucester, Keeper of the mints of London and Gloucester: clearly, seal-making required similar skills to those of coining (see Fig. 7). In this case it seems that the king himself took a hand in the design since William was instructed to have the dies made in the form enjoined on him and Edward, the king's artistic adviser, by the king himself.

Early in the thirteenth century all dies began to be engraved on flat discs or ovals of metal ranging in thickness from about 3mm to about 7mm. Some matrices, such as those of the great seals, were in two parts of equal size and these would require the use of a seal press. In Canterbury Cathedral one made of copper alloy with an iron handle and an oak base has survived (Alexander and Binski 1987, 399). The style of the miniature capitals and bases on the columns of the press indicates a mid-thirteenth-century date; the screw thread is a masterly piece of accurate casting (Fig. 8). To use such a machine, the wax had to be formed into two thin cakes, each being fitted into its half of the matrix. The two dies were then lined up, being kept in register by pins slotting into rings on the peripheries of the metal discs. The cords or tags of parchment were inserted between the two parts. The press was screwed down, the wax was forced into the dies, and the pressure united the two cakes, trapping the cords between them. Despite the apparent fragility of the material hundreds of such wax impressions attached to medieval documents have survived to the present day (Fig. 9).

Because it is often known precisely when

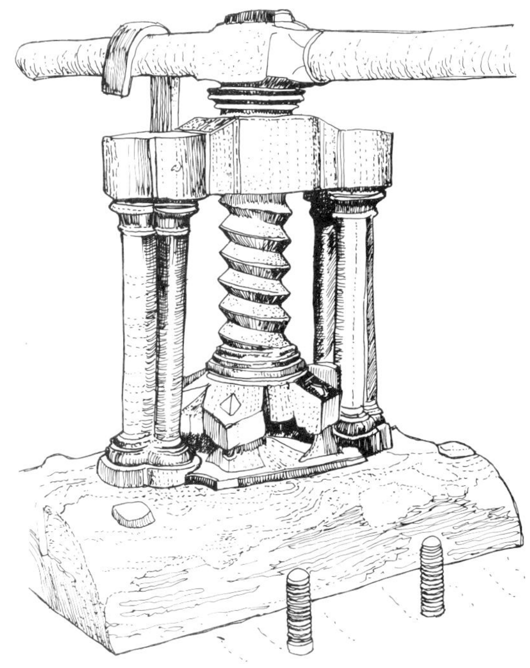

8 *Thirteenth-century seal press from Canterbury Cathedral. The central base plate is 126mm (5in) square and the column height is 191mm (7½in). It was probably made for use with the large two-sided seal of 1232.* (After Alexander and Binski.)

seals were made, they are a valuable aid to dating stylistic changes in metalwork and sculpture. Despite their small compass they frequently mirror artistic developments. The seal of Richard of Cornwall, King of the Romans (1209–72) is a case in point. Here the English seal engraver has borrowed selectively from continental prototypes – such as the seal of William of Holland, King of the Romans – the legend, regalia and throne type. The drapery style of the king's figure displays the looping teardrop fold terminals favoured in contemporary sculpture; angularity has not yet developed. Henry III's second great seal has clearly been greatly influenced by that of Richard, in throne, pose and regalia; it also demonstrates a greater angularity in the drapery folds. Quite often seals seem to lag behind stylistic evolution in the thirteenth century; perhaps an element in their design was a deliberate emphasis on unchanging tradition.

9 *The second Great Seal of Richard I in use c.1197–9. The king is shown enthroned on a backless seat holding a sword and an orb from which spring four sprays. Above are a crescent and a sun, favourite Plantagenet emblems. On the counterseal the king is on horseback: his shield has three lions passant gardant in pale.* (Impression: Public Record Office; photograph: V. Brooke.)

The stylistic changes in the design of fourteenth-century great seals are more radical because they involve more elements. These include the architectural canopy work which spreads over the whole surface of the seal surrounding the figures, the quantity of subsidiary figures introduced, the profuse heraldry and other badges. The main figures are also subject to greater experimentation in pose and proportion. The 1327 seal of Edward III is an excellent example of the developed Decorated Style with

10 The second Great Seal of Edward III, 1327. The architecture of the throne with its ogee arch and wave parapets and the elegance of the king's pose with knees pushed to one side and a bend to the waist show a developed Decorated Style. The two fleurs-de-lis refer to the French royal connection of his mother, Isabella, daughter of Philip IV. It may be the first sign of Edward's claim to the French throne. (Photograph: Dean and Chapter, Durham Cathedral.)

its ogee arch, crocketed finials and the elegance of the king's pose in place of the solid monumentality of the twelfth- and thirteenth-century judgemental figures (Wyon and Wyon 1887, 28) (Fig. 10). Edward's knees are turned to one side and there is a subtle twist to his waist. These features have been traced to the design of the second seal of Louis X of France. By the time the sixth great seal of Edward III was made, the design had become more complex, under the influence of ecclesiastical seal design (Wyon and Wyon, 1887, Plate X). The work of the London seal engraver who made it portrays the king seated in a throne niche with a vault, traceried rear wall and projecting wings, all reflecting the Proto-Perpendicular Style. The architectural framework is peopled with figures of hunched and bearded 'watchmen'. The symmetrical magnificence of these later medieval great seals is brought to a culmination with Edward III's seventh great seal of 1360 (known as the 'Brétigny' seal) (Wyon and Wyon 1887, No. 63). Here the spare spaces were filled with niches containing images of the Virgin and Child, St George and angels flanking the royal figure. The most telling piece of propaganda is in the small figure in a niche above the king's head: it is apparently the presence of God, his pose echoing that of the king. No doubt the intention was to point out that the king governed on earth just as God did in heaven.

The imagery of the royal seals

The imagery of the great seals is an important source of information about medieval concepts of kingship. The main themes are unchanging from the eleventh to the sixteenth centuries and consist of two basic icons: the king as a fount of justice in majesty seated full-face on his throne on the obverse; and the king as a war leader in military gear, on horseback, on the reverse or counterseal. The former dates back to the reign of Edward the Confessor and was probably modelled, as we have noted, on the seal of majesty of the Holy Roman Emperors: the type is first found in the fifth seal of Emperor Otto III. The image of the king is full-face, bearded and crowned, seated with legs wide apart and feet pointed outwards, in classical garb of a full-length tunic and mantle, on a backless throne (Wyon and Wyon 1887, Plate I). On one side Edward is shown holding a sceptre and orb. On the other side Edward is shown holding a sceptre, topped by a dove and a blunt sword, the 'Curtana'. The general pose is paralleled by representations of Christ in Majesty, found on contemporary tympana, wall paintings and manuscript illuminations. The inescapable conclusion is that such an image sums up in visual form the sacral elements of early medieval kingship.

William I adopted this image just as he took over many other features of Anglo-Saxon government, but he added something of his own. As a conqueror he emphasized the military aspects of regality. His kingly and crowned figure is shown grasping – and indeed waving – an unsheathed sword in his right hand and an orb in the left. It is likely that the sword represented was the ducal badge of Normandy, shown on the silver pennies of William I and William Rufus. More significantly he had himself shown on the reverse in full mail armour, lance in one hand and shield in the other, riding a horse from left to right. This mounted symbol of regality continued as a type

11 The seal of Henry II. The king as anointed priest-king, as fount of justice and as war leader. The great extension of titles is also recorded in the inscription. Henry had succeeded to the duchy of Normandy, the earldom of Anjou, Touraine and Maine and, by marriage to Eleanor, the duchy of Aquitaine. (Impression: Public Record Office; photograph: V. Brooke.)

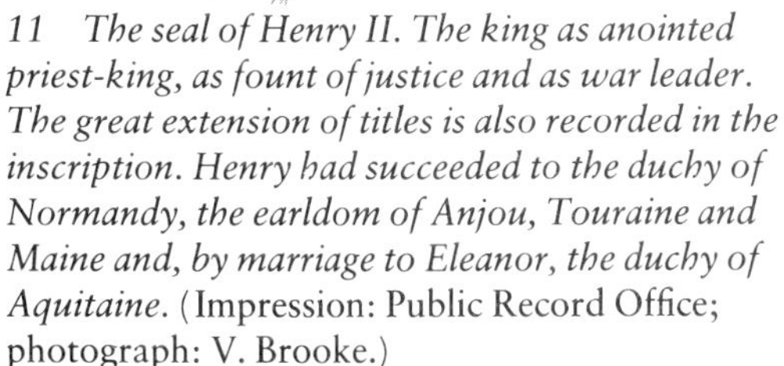

image on great seals throughout the Middle Ages. Its origin has been recently traced far back into the eighth century. The 'ageing figure of Aethelbald on the Repton stone is the oldest known large-scale representation of an English king' (Biddle and Biddle 1989, 291). He is shown sculptured in armour, on horseback, brandishing a sword and shield.

Three of the most important aspects of kingship – the monarch as anointed priest-king, as fount of justice and as war leader – are thus reflected in basic designs of the great seal. Further, the seal was an advertisement of the king's titles and claims to lordship. Since these varied according to political events they were quite likely to change during a long reign, necessitating the withdrawal of the obsolescent seal and the substitution of a new one in which the die-cutter presents the up-to-date situation. An early instance is the fourth seal of Henry I: here the counterseal, with the inscription HENRICUS DEI GRACIA DUX NORMANNORUM, has been added to HENRICUS DEI GRACIA REX ANGLORUM (Wyon and Wyon 1887, 11). Henry I assumed the ducal title after he defeated his brother Robert at the battle of Tinchebrai (1106). Stephen's defeat at Lincoln and capture by his rival Matilda in 1141 led to the loss of his first seal, making necessary the production of a second. There is a considerable increase in size over the first one but the style of workmanship is cruder, a minor indication of governmental disruption. Matilda's seal is of interest: it shows the queen (or empress) seated wearing a crown of three points, with the inscription ROMANORUM REGINA. It is smaller than those of the other English sovereigns and, being without a counterseal, is reminiscent of the seals of the German monarchs of the period. She had, of course, married the Emperor Henry V and returned to England after his death in 1125.

A great extension of titles comes with the acquisition of the Angevin Empire. This is recorded on the seals of Henry II. Henry had succeeded in his mother's right to the duchy of Normandy, in his father's (Geoffrey Count of Anjou) to the earldoms of Anjou, Touraine and Maine, and by marriage to Eleanor to the duchy of Aquitaine (Wyon and Wyon 1887, 15) (Fig. 11). Sometimes there is a gap in time between the acquisition of a lordship and its appearance on a seal. Henry II obtained the Lordship of Ireland in 1181 but it did not appear on a seal until John's reign (1199–1216) (Wyon and Wyon 1887, 20). During the next reign, Henry III suffered humiliating setbacks in his continental policies which are reflected in the seals. By the Treaty of Paris in 1259 he renounced his claim to the duchy of Normandy and provinces of Maine, Anjou and Poitou. The new seal leaves out the titles 'Duke of Normandy' and 'Count of Anjou' (Wyon and Wyon 1887, 22). Also, the sword carried by the figure of the king in majesty had been left out and a sceptre substituted. This was considered to be an inglorious admission that the king had not been successful in war: '*Nam Rex in veteri sigillo suo tenuit et gladium et ceptrum, in novo autem ceptrum sine gladio*' ('for the king held both sword and sceptre as he was depicted on his old seal, but on the new one he is shown holding a sceptre without the sword').

During the thirteenth and fourteenth centuries heraldry increasingly comes into the design of great seals and fortifies the verbal statements of title. Heraldry has the advantage of being a kind of shorthand which can express quite a complicated idea in an abbreviated form (Fig. 12). Edward II for instance used a seal which was precisely the same design as that of his father, Edward I, except that there is an addition of two castles in the field, one on each side of the throne (Wyon and Wyon 1887, 27). This was useful in indicating a change of sovereign: the castles are an allusion to the king's mother, Queen Eleanor, daughter of King Ferdinand III of Castile. Edward III made a similar allusion in his first seal. Here he refers to his mother, Isabella daughter of King Philip IV of France, the arms of France at the time being *semée de lis* (covered with fleurs-de-lis).

The claims of the kings of England to the throne of France in the fourteenth century were boldly displayed in novel designs for the great seal. The first of these was the third seal of Edward III, used from 21 February to 20 June 1340 (Wyon and Wyon 1887, 32). Here Edward III first used the title REX FRANCIAE, and the arms of France are quartered with those of England. Special seals had to be made for the king's use while he was absent abroad (Fig. 13). These later seals of Edward III are remarkable in their sheer repetition of the claim to France. Not only is this in the inscription, but the coats of arms are suspended from little cranes projecting from turrets on either side of the throne. On the obverse the king is shown on horseback galloping to the right, holding a sword in his right hand and with a shield covering the left breast – charged with the arms of France and England quartered. The horse too is caparisoned in flowing robes charged similarly. The Brétigny seal issued in 1360 reflects the fact that the king renounced the title King of France, omitting it

12 Tile from the Chapter House, Westminster Abbey. It is probably the earliest representation of the royal arms. The simple red shield with three gold leopards remained the arms of all English kings down to 1340. (After Clayton.)

13 Edward III's First Great Seal of absence in use July 1338–February 1340. The King is shown enthroned, crowned, holding a long sceptre with a dove and an orb. His feet rest on two lions couchant and guardant. The throne has no arched back but has four pinnacles. The lions on either side are an indication that he was intending to use this seal only for English affairs in his absence for the invasion of France. (Impression: Public Record Office; photograph: V. Brooke.)

from the inscription. On the other hand the quartered arms are provocatively retained on the shield, the surcoat of the king and the caparison of the horse. Nine years later Edward resumed the title and thenceforward used seals again with this designation.

The design of the second seal of Henry IV (Fig. 14), used in the period *c.*1408–13, is an interesting piece of political propaganda (Wyon and Wyon 1887, 44). There are no less than 21 men and animals introduced into its principal face, including St Edmund, King and Martyr, and St Edward the Confessor. It has been plausibly suggested that the seal was engraved with the object of impressing on the popular mind Henry IV's claim to the throne by descent from Henry III. Henry III had been devoted to these two saints: he had named his two sons Edward and Edmund after them. Much of his wealth had been spent in creating a worthy resting place for Edward the Confessor at Westminster Abbey and he was himself buried on the festival of St Edmund in 1272. The banners of St Edmund and St Edward had been carried into battle by Edward I. The introduction of these figures on the great seal of Henry IV could not fail to associate him in men's minds with Henry III. The reality was that Henry IV had won his throne by force of arms and election by parliament; the seal on the other hand suggested that he based his title by descent from Henry III.

The so-called silver seal and counterseal of Henry V are identical with those of the first seal of Henry IV. The changed nature of the king's style following the Treaty of Troyes 1420 reads HENRICUS DEI GRACIA REX ANGLIE HERES REGNI FRANCIE ET DOMINUS HIBERNIE. Henry VI continued to use a separate seal for French affairs. The first seal for this purpose brings the heraldry of the French royal arms up to date: it shows the three fleurs-de-lis which had replaced the field *semée de lis*.

The second seal of Henry VIII has features both of Gothic and Renaissance style. The vestigial traces of Gothic are visible in a debased form in the pointed arch of the canopy and the tracery pinnacles and crockets of the throne. The surrounding of the shields with the garter, the shape of the crowns and the Roman lettering are typical of the Renaissance. The third seal again shows a Renaissance feature in that the sovereign is portrayed realistically. More interestingly the seals are records of the momentous changes taking place in the relations between church and state. The second seal includes in its title *Fidei Defensor*, a compliment conferred in 1521 by a bull of Pope Leo X, to commemorate the king's championship of the papacy. The third seal, however, announces the title '*et in terra ecclesiae Anglicanae, et Hibernicae Supremum caput*', thus signalizing the final breach between the papacy and the king and people of England. The union of the two royal families, York and Lancaster, is symbolized by the presence of a huge double rose behind the image of the king on horseback on the second seal (Wyon and Wyon 1887, 70–1).

14 Henry IV's Second Great Seal, in use c.1408–13. The King is enthroned and crowned holding a sceptre and orb. He is surrounded by no fewer than 21 figures and animals and these include the shields and figures of St Edward and St Edmund thus carrying the minds of his people back to Henry III. Above the King is the Virgin and Child, a king crowned and a martyr holding a palm.

The regalia of the medieval English kings

Kings and priests have been accoutred with unusual headgear, capable of being seen from a long way away, since at least the Roman period. Some 'diadems' and crowns have been found in what are believed to be rural Romano-British shrines. In March 1956 three sheet bronze diadems were ploughed up at Hockwold-cum-Wilton (Norfolk), associated with second- to fourth-century pottery. A year later two more diadems and a crown were found on the same site. The crown consisted of a head-band from which rise four strips meeting at the top of the head. At the apex is a spike or knob and at each junction of the vertical strips of the headband is a medallion bearing a mask. The finds are now in the British Museum and it is thought that such headgear was more likely to be priestly than royal regalia (Twining 1960, 99–100).

In the late Saxon period there are already signs of a desire to link regalia used by kings with the Roman imperial past. An interesting story related that Ethelwulf of Wessex sent his youngest son, Alfred, then five years old, to Rome. The *Anglo-Saxon Chronicle* stated that Alfred was consecrated by Pope Leo IV, and later writers, including Robert of Gloucester, *c.*1270, embroidered the story by alleging that the prince brought back to England regalia bestowed on him on this occasion. In fact, Alfred was not heir to the throne at the time but it does seem as if the Pope confirmed the prince and invested him with the insignia of a Roman consul (Twining 1960, 101).

In the absence of the crowns themselves coinage provides evidence for the nature of the Anglo-Saxon regalia. As early as the seventh century AD there is a portrait on the coin of a Mercian king which is copied from the common coins of Constantine the Great, in which the king is depicted wearing the diadem worn by the Eastern emperors. In fact, it is more likely that the first regalia worn by the Anglo-Saxon kings were not crowns but diadems, but it is not clear what the nature of the distinctive royal head-covering was. The expression that was naturally used is *cynehelm* or kings' helmet and there are also references to *couldon-bag* or circlet of fame, or *coven-beag*, circlet of the elected one. Athelstan was the first king to be portrayed on his coins wearing a crown. Dunstan's biographer tells how the young King Edwy, or Edwin, absented himself from the coronation feast, and Dunstan was sent to fetch him. The royal crown, wrought with gold, silver and precious stones, was found lying neglected on the floor (Twining 1960, 102). Edgar is depicted (Cotton MSS Vespasianus A VIII) wearing a crown with three trefoils, an ornament which had been used by Constantine the Great as an imperial and royal badge, and was to develop in a stylized form into the fleur-de-lis. Another indication of the power of Constantinople is that English kings used the title *Basileus* from the time of Athelstan. Clearly, there was a constant and conscious referring back to the Roman imperial past.

The diadem went on being used up to the middle of the reign of Edward the Confessor. On the first five types of coins issued during the reign the king is shown in the traditional style with a helmet and diadem. By 1057, however, a change has occurred. Edward is now enthroned, wearing the English lily crown, and holding a long sceptre with a cross in his left hand. Edward attempted to have his crown jewels refashioned but was thwarted by the absconding of the goldsmith, Abbot Spearhavoc of Abingdon, with the precious material (Zarnecki *et al.* 1984, 301). The first seal of the Confessor was in use from 1053 to 1065 and shows the king enthroned wearing a crown with three trefoil points. In his right hand is a sceptre surmounted by a trefoil and in his left an orb. On the counterseal he has in his right hand a sceptre with a bird and in his left a sword. The design on the seal closely parallels those of the emperors Conrad II (1034–9) and Henry IV (1056–1108). In Germany the bird was a phoenix adopted from Roman imperial practice.

The great seals and coinage of Edward the Confessor and his Norman and Angevin successors are potential sources of information on the nature of the regalia but need to be treated with caution (Brooke 1916, II, 1). It is likely that regalia depicted on them retained the ancient forms of such charismatic symbols of authority long after they went out of current use. It is reasonable to expect that artists who produced illuminated manuscripts or funeral effigies would have been more up to date (Holmes 1937, 73–82).

For what it is worth, William I is shown on his great seal wearing a closed crown of three points on each of which is a fleur-de-lis. He also holds a sword erect in his right hand and in his left an orb and a cross. It is said that he brought with him his own regalia because he feared that the Anglo-Saxon regalia would not fall into his hands, and a description of the crown from Bishop Wido of Amiens makes it clear that it was a *stemma* – it had an arch or arches – and had been made by a Greek jeweller. Moreover, it was studded with 12 precious or semi-precious stones. Both the number and the nature of the stones had an allegorical meaning found in the Bible. The breastplate of the High Priest and the foundation stones of the Heavenly City are recalled (Twining 1960, 108–9).

Crown wearings were a key political and religious ritual painstakingly pursued by the Norman kings of England (Kantorowicz, 1958). William I made it a rule that there should be three crown wearings a year: on Christmas Day at Gloucester, on Easter Day at Winchester and on Whitsunday at Westminster. On these occasions the barons, leading churchmen and magnates met the king in council (Biddle 1986, 51–2). This custom was already followed in Germany and France and it continued in England until the reign of Edward I who was averse to wearing his crown in public.

William Rufus used his father's seal until about 1096 when a matrix was specially executed for him. On this the crown is shown changed: it is the English lily crown but with five points surmounted by trefoils. New features which appear on Rufus's crown and on crowns in subsequent seals until the reign of Henry II are two strings, tassels or straps which dangle on either side of the royal ears. Such strings or tassels are also seen appended either at the back or to either side of the crown in Anglo-Saxon coinage from the reign of Edgar (957–75). They were prestigious badges. Gervase of Canterbury relates a curious story of how Archbishop Ralph, the successor of Anselm, snatched the crown from the head of Henry I at Windsor. The king had apparently crowned himself! In this way the *ansula* (clasp or straps) was broken.

It seems that from the twelfth century there had been at least two regalia. One was the personal or semi-dynastic regalia belonging to the kings. This was stored in the Tower of London. The other was the regalia of St Edward the Confessor, preserved since the twelfth century under the perpetual custody of the abbots of Westminster (Lightbown 1989, 257). Some of this – the crown, a gold sceptre topped by a cross, two rods, one topped by a dove and one of iron, a great chalice and the accompanying paten – had probably been made for the Confessor and deposited by him in Westminster Abbey either for safe custody, or for perpetual use in all future coronations.

Other kings added to the regalia from time to time. Henry I's daughter Matilda had married the emperor Henry V and on his death kept those ornaments she judged to be her husband's own property. She brought two crowns and a relic of the Apostle St James to England; the latter was given to the Abbey of Reading and the crowns handed to her father Henry I. What happened to these crowns is not known but on Stephen's two seals the regalia shown is similar to that displayed on the later seals of Henry I. On his coins, on the other hand, the crown is the arched lily crown used by Henry I.

Henry II's crown was described as being very massive, and so heavy that it had to be supported when worn, either by two noblemen or by two rods. It could apparently be taken to pieces, there being seven segments in the shape of lilies and a cross was set above the brow, on which there was a large and valuable stone. It is not easy to visualize the crown and it is only very summarily depicted on the coins of Henry II (Allen 1951, xxi). The weight is attested, for one of the duties of the Earl Marshal was to support the crown. Roger de Hoveden, in his account of the coronation of Richard I, mentions that the crown was so heavy that it had to be supported on the king's head by two earls. The king changed it for a lighter one before leaving the church for the coronation banquet. The *Annals of Winchester* state that Richard I was buried in the crown he had worn at Winchester for his second coronation (after he returned from imprisonment and ransoming). He wore it when lying in state but probably a crown of cheaper material was substituted on his tomb, as at the burial of Edward I a century later.

From this time the regalia appear in the increasingly profuse documents of royal administration. The king, by letters patent dated 11 October 1203, acknowledged the receipt at

Caen from John, Bishop of Norwich of '*Regalia nostra, scilicet, magnam coronam nostram, gladium deauratum, tunicam, pallium, dalmaticam, bandricam, sandalia, cirotecas, frettas et calcaria*'. John gave a golden crown to his royal monastic foundation of Beaulieu where it is said to have been made into a shrine or casket. Another of his crowns was found to be in the treasury of Adam de Stratton. John lost his baggage train in the Wash in the last years of his reign but authorities disagree over whether the regalia is likely to have travelled with it (St John Hope 1906, 93–110). When Henry III was crowned at Gloucester on 28 October 1216 he was invested with a simple gold circlet which romantic writers have claimed was his mother's bracelet. By the time he was re-crowned in Westminster Abbey on Whitsunday, 16 June 1220, a considerable amount of regalia had been brought together. It included a golden crown entirely adorned with diverse stones, and also 'a pair of old stockings of red samite with orfrays, and a pair of old stockings embroidered with gold which belonged to King John' (Wickham Legg 1901). This does indeed suggest a rather scratch collection, so maybe much of John's regalia was lost deep in the swampy ooze of the Fens. Henry III had several other crowns; when he went on an expedition to Brittany in 1229 he had a new set of regalia made including a crown. In 1235, his sister Isabella married the emperor and took with her a crown bearing the representation of the four Holy Kings from whom the English claimed descent. An inventory of the jewels belonging to the king was made in 1272 and a large and valuable crown recorded, followed by three crowns of gold enriched with precious stones, valued at £336 13s 4d. Henry III's effigy in Westminster Abbey, made by William Torel in 1291–2, shows him wearing an open crown ornamented with lilies and formerly adorned with imitation precious stones (RCHM 1924, Frontispiece).

What form did the crown of the English monarchy take in the thirteenth and fourteenth centuries? All our sources – seals, coins, manuscript illuminations and funeral effigies – agree that it was of an open type, that is to say a golden circlet elaborately worked and decorated with precious stones or enamels (Holmes 1937, 75). The ornaments along its upper edge were shown as fleurons (as on the seals of Henry I, Stephen, Richard I, Edward I, Edward II, Edward III and Richard II) or, more rarely, crosses (as on the seals of William I, William II, Henry II and Henry VI). Sometimes it would have been made in one piece, at others as a series of separate plaques, soldered or even hinged together. Its essential characteristic was that it was not 'closed' above with anything crossing the top of the head.

Only one English medieval royal crown has survived, the burial crown of Edward I, and this is not readily available for inspection. When Edward I's tomb in Westminster Abbey was opened in 1774, the royal corpse was found dressed in full regalia including robes, crown and sceptres (Ayloffe 1786, 386). The crown had been made specially for the burial. It resembled a piece of stage jewellery and was described as 'an open crown or fillet of tin or latten, charged on its upper side with trefoils and gilt with gold but evidently of inferior workmanship in all respects to that of the sceptres'. Unfortunately for archaeology, it was reburied in the tomb with not even an on-the-spot drawing being made. In the cathedral treasury of Aachen is the crown used by Richard, Earl of Cornwall, when he became Holy Roman Emperor in 1257; *Romanitas* was celebrated by the insertion of classical cameos and intaglios (Clark 1986, 96).

A stunningly beautiful object met the eyes of the bemused visitor at the Royal Academy's 'Age of Chivalry' exhibition in 1987 (Alexander and Binski 1987, 202–3). It was the crown of Blanche, daughter of Henry IV, who married Ludwig III of Bavaria in 1401 (Fig. 15). It may well have belonged to Anne, wife of Richard II, and could have been brought from Bohemia when she married the king in 1382. Whether it was made in Bohemia or in Paris it is one of the finest surviving achievements of the Gothic goldsmith. It consists of 'an elaborate twelve part circlet from which rise twelve golden lilies large and small alternating with beaded edges'. It is richly decorated with sapphires and enamelled flowers in blue, red and white. Diamonds, rubies, pearls and emeralds encrust the whole but do not overpower the pattern; slender and spiky elegance is the keynote. A comparable crown is sculptured on the effigy of Joan of Navarre, queen of Henry IV, in Canterbury Cathedral. Here there is the same alternation of tall and short lilies.

15 A crown of gold set with sapphires, rubies, diamonds, pearls and decorated with enamelling. Height 18cm (7in). One of the finest achievements of the Gothic goldsmith, it was probably made in France c.1370–80. It came to Bavaria as part of the marriage dowry of Blanche, daughter of Henry IV, who married Ludwig III in 1401. It may well have belonged to Anne of Bohemia, wife of Richard II, and if so illustrates well the glittering magnificence of the court of Richard II. (After Alexander and Binski.)

The court of Richard II glittered with splendid jewellery and sumptuous costumes. A glimpse of this may be seen in pictures such as the great panel of Richard II in Westminster Abbey, and the Wilton Diptych (Tomlinson 1974, Plate 32). In the latter Richard, dressed in rich robes, kneels accompanied by three patron saints, Edmund the King, Edward the Confessor and John the Baptist. The king wears a collar of broom pods and a brooch in the form of a hart; his dress of gold tissue is brocaded with medallions of the hart. He is crowned with a light gold circlet with crosses studded with pearls and jewels. At major events in court life such jewels changed hands. An instance of this is Richard II's marriage to his second wife, Isabella of France, a girl of seven. A large number of rich presents were showered on the young queen. These included a crown of eight fleurons and a jewelled eagle from the Duke of Gloucester. The citizens of Dover and Canterbury gave her other crowns and the City of London a jewelled circlet. At Eltham Palace, Richard gave her other presents including a collar of diamonds, rubies and large pearls. A considerable proportion of the king's working capital was locked up in jewellery.

Financial mismanagement and the consequent shortage of cash meant that the Crown frequently had to borrow on the security of the crown jewels. In Edward II's reign the king's great crown was pledged in Flanders to bring in funds from Flemish merchants. In 1378 there was an acquittance for three crowns and other jewels delivered to the Exchequer by William, Bishop of London, and Richard, Earl of Arundel, who held them as pledges for £10,000 lent to the king by John Philpot and other merchants. Crowns were constantly being repaired, modernized or actually broken up by court jewellers, and so were carefully valued in connection with their use as security for royal debts.

Despite this – to modern eyes – rather unseemly trade, the regalia were regarded with reverence. At Edward II's coronation great offence was given because St Edward's Crown, esteemed as a holy relic, was carried in the 'polluted hands' of Piers Gaveston (Holmes 1959, 216). What was objected to was not the honour done to the royal favourite but the dishonour to the Crown. Again, one of the charges levelled against Richard II was that he had taken the regalia to Ireland; it seems to have been understood that the heirlooms of the realm should not leave its shores. Clearly, the crown was of great symbolic significance. At his abdication, according to Froissart, Richard II took off his crown in the Tower of London and handed it to Henry of Lancaster saying, 'Harry, fair cousin and Duke of Lancaster, I present and give to you this crown with which I was crowned King of England, and all the rights dependent on it'. Bolingbroke had the crown and sceptre promptly packed up and taken to the Treasury at Westminster Abbey. Shakespeare shows historical insight, if not strict accuracy, when he portrays Henry IV anxiously treasuring the crown on his deathbed (*Henry IV*, Part 2, IV, 5, 57).

At the beginning of the fifteenth century a decisive change appears to have taken place in the form of the English crown. Froissart, who was probably relying on an eye-witness, described the coronation of Henry IV on 13 October 1399. He described the crown of St Edward, which the Archbishop of Canterbury placed on the king's head, as being 'archeé en croix'. This has been interpreted as a 'closed' crown which had bands of metal crossing usually from one side to another and from back to front so that they met in the middle. Two sculptured representations of the coronation of Henry V in Westminster Abbey, admittedly dating from the following reign, would seem to confirm this use of the closed crown. In one of them the king is sitting in state with an 'imperial' crown with four arches meeting and crossing, topped by a mound and a cross (Holmes 1937, Plate XV, Fig. 2). It has been suggested that Henry V may have had this imperial type of crown made on the occasion of the visit of the Emperor Sigismund to England in 1416; it was important that the crown of the king of England should appear to be of similar status to that of the imperial visitor. Two reasons account for the imperial shape of the crown. It was partly that English kings claimed to rule over several kingdoms and lordships; but more importantly, that they claimed to be subject to no other ruler, only to God (Lightbown 1989, 259).

The arches of such closed crowns were in part utilitarian: they served to strengthen the crown and prevented it from being squashed out of shape. In part they were traditional, harking back to ancient Germanic helmets (and the Anglo-Saxon royal helms) which had metal bands crossing at the top of the head to protect the skull from injury. In part they are purely decorative, the crossed arches serving to support a central cross or a globular jewel over the top of the monarch's head.

Henry V had a battle helmet made with a crown of the arched type which he wore over his bascinet at Agincourt. It is known as 'the golden crown for the Bascinet', was garnished with rubies, sapphires and pearls, and was valued at £679 5s 0d. During the battle it was naturally a highly sought-after target for the high-spirited French nobility. The Duke of Alençon hacked a piece off with his battleaxe and further fleurons were cut away by a French esquire who had sworn (with 17 others) to do this or die in the attempt! It was described as 'broken and depeased in the fielde by the violence of the enimie, and great strokes that he there receaved' (Holmes 1937, 80). A ceremonial helmet, the '*chapel doré*' of the French king, Charles VI (1380–1422), was found in 155 pieces in the 1984 excavations of the Louvre (Fleury and Kruta 1989, 63).

The crown jewels continued to be pledged to raise money for the French wars. The so-called 'Crown Henry', apparently the state crown of Henry IV, was pawned to Thomas, Duke of Clarence. This crown featured pinnacles, each set with six pearls, two sapphires and a square balas (a red spinel resembling a ruby). Another crown of gold set with 56 balases, 40 sapphires, eight diamonds and 47 great pearls was valued at £800 and was handed over to the Mayor of Norwich and others. Clearly, the crown jewels were in the nature of a monetary reserve which could be drawn on in times of royal financial embarrassment. Henry VI was an infant in arms at his accession and there was little point in taking the crowns out of pawn until he was old enough to withstand the rigours of a coronation. A special crown was made for the occasion.

It is well known that Henry VI was personally averse to wearing the magnificent robes of his office. He is nevertheless portrayed in a miniature on the foundation charter of King's College, Cambridge in 1446 as wearing an arched crown with a miniature orb and cross at the point of intersection of the arches at the summit. A similar crown is shown on pilgrim badges sold to devotees of the cult of Henry VI, which grew up at Windsor after his alleged murder in 1471. An inventory of Henry VI's regalia and jewels, dated 13 March in the second year of Edward IV's reign, includes:

> *The Kynges grete crowne of gold which is closed within a little coffin of leather and bound with iron and locked with divers locks and keys and is also sealed without with divers lords seals which is in the King's Great Treasury at Westminster.*

This box sounds very much like the case made

for the jewelled mitre of William of Wykeham, at New College, Oxford (Alexander and Binski 1987, 471). Also mentioned are several fleurs-de-lis or pinnacles deriving from crowns which had been broken up. Edward IV is shown on his great seal as wearing an arched crown. This is confirmed by an illustration in an illuminated manuscript showing Edward IV and his consort, Elizabeth Woodville, receiving a book from Caxton. Both are shown wearing arched crowns (Lambeth Palace Library MS 'Dictes and Sayings of Philosophers').

Richard III is shown on his great seal, wearing an arched crown, as are Henry IV, V and VII in the series of pen and ink sketches illustrating the life of Richard Beauchamp executed between 1485 and 1490 (Dillon and St John Hope 1914). On 22 August 1485 the king was defeated by his rival, Henry Tudor, at Bosworth and slain. The battered crown from Richard's helmet was placed on Henry's head by Lord Stanley. Henry's claim to the throne was none too secure, and Polydore Vergil's description suggests that the episode was a deft piece of political manoeuvring on Stanley's part, intended to put the succession beyond doubt by declaring Henry a king elected, and crowned by his people on the battlefield. Quarries of fifteenth-century glass at Chewton Mendip (Somerset) and Langley Marish (Buckinghamshire) show the crown in a bush with the initials HR or HE (for Henry VII and Elizabeth of York).

The Tudors gloried in pageantry. Speaking of Henry VIII's preparation for his crowning the chronicler Edward Hall wrote:

> *If I should declare what pain, labour and diligence the tailors, embroiderers and goldsmiths took both to make and devise garments for lords, ladies, knights and esquires, and also for decking, trapping and adorning of coursers, jennets and palfreys, it were too long to rehearse.*

The regalia of the Tudors in the 1520s consisted of 'a gold imperial state crown for the king, a gold imperial state crown for the queen, a sceptre of gold topped by a dove and a gold rod for the king, and another smaller gold sceptre for the queen, also topped by a dove, a pair of gold bracelets and a gold orb' (Lightbown 1989, 258). The crown painted by Mytens in his portrait of Charles I is thought to have been made for Henry VIII (Strong 1990, 121). It consisted of a circlet from which rose five fleurons of the usual fleur-de-lis design alternating with five crosses. Each of the fleurons bore a figure: Christ, the Virgin and Child, St George, and two figures which were probably St Edmund and St Edward the Confessor, the two most revered of the sainted kings of England. In this way the iconography of the crown invoked for its wearer the protection of Christ, the Virgin and the especial Saints, two of whom the king could claim as his ancestors. Sir Edward Coke proclaimed that 'the ancient jewels of the crowne are heirloomes, and shall descend to the next successor and are not devisable by testament'. This proved a poor defence when the crown jewels were broken up and sold at the beginning of the Commonwealth (Strong 1990, 119–25).

Another piece of regalia which appears on the earliest great seals is the sceptre. Edward the Confessor is shown holding in his right hand a sceptre ending in a trefoil, and in his left hand an orb. On the counterseal he holds a long sceptre ending in a dove. The sceptre is to the king what the crozier is to the bishop; both symbols spring from a common origin, namely the shepherd's staff or guiding wand of the flock. The dove as an emblem appears again on the second great seal of Henry I which represents him seated with an orb on which is a cross and a dove in his left hand. Sometimes the dove grows to an enormous size as in the second seal of Stephen. It has been plausibly suggested that the design of the sceptre with a dove may have been inspired by the eleventh-century German Imperial eagle-headed sceptre. By the reign of Richard I it had become standard in English coronations. In the treasury of Aachen Cathedral is the sceptre of Richard of Cornwall (1209–72) the brother of Henry III who was the only Englishman to be elected king of the Romans and thus in effect ruler of part of Germany (Alexander and Binski 1987, 208). Richard was crowned in 1257 and in 1262 gave to Aachen Cathedral insignia to be used at all future coronations of the kings of the Romans. These included a gem-encrusted gold crown, vestments, a gilt apple and this sceptre. It is 86cm (34in) long and consists of two hollow rods, silver gilt, with plain knobs in the middle;

at either end, soldered on to the top, is a dove, cast and chased. This slim and elegant imperial insignia was deservedly a centrepiece in the 1987 'Age of Chivalry' exhibition held in London. The sceptre was an indispensable part of the trappings of royalty in the thirteenth century. Despite John's heavy losses in the Wash during the last year of his reign, his successor, Henry III, was soon equipped with a silver gilt rod and a golden sceptre. Edward I in his coffin held in his right hand a 'scepter [*sic*] with the cross made of copper gilt. This scepter is 2ft 6 inches in length, and of most elegant workmanship. Its upper part extends unto and rests on the king's right shoulder' (Ayloffe 1786). The coffin also contained

> *a rod with the dove which is five feet and half an inch in length. The stalk is divided into equal parts by a knob or fillet, and at its bottom is a flat ferule. The top of the stalk terminates in three bouquets or tiers of oak leaves of green enamel, in* alto relievo, *each bouquet diminishing in breadth as they approach towards the summit of the sceptre, whereon stands a ball or mound, surmounted by the figure of a dove, with wings closed of white enamel.*

The sceptre remained an essential attribute of European monarchy until the end of the Middle Ages. Pairs of sceptres were placed in the hands of royal effigies at Westminster Abbey in the thirteenth and fourteenth centuries; they have all been stolen by souvenir hunters. Sceptres also figure on the screens at Canterbury and York. The French royal effigies in St Denis and Royaumont are also equipped with sceptres, often topped by the fleur-de-lis. Gaignière's drawings, made *c.*1700, show John of France, for instance, the son of Louis IX and Margaret of Provence, holding a sceptre with a fleur-de-lis head (Bodleian Library, MS Gough).

The image of late medieval kingship is well summed up in a stained glass panel occupying one of the lights of Great Malvern Priory Church (Rushforth 1936, 123–4, Fig. 54). It represents St Edward the Confessor, a popular subject linking the monarchy with a golden Anglo-Saxon past of martyrs and saintly kings. He stands with flowing white hair and beard, with a tall jewelled crown with a nimbus suggesting similarities with images of God the Father. He wears a brocaded mantle or pallium trimmed with ermine, the form of which is scarcely distinguishable from the robes of an archbishop – the sacral function of kingship is recalled. He holds in his left hand a gold sceptre with a foliated head – the wand of authority and a symbol of peace. With his right hand he offers a kneeling donor a charter with a suspended seal – here the king is seen in his function as lawgiver.

Thrones

The cult of medieval kingship is inseparably linked with the concept of the chair. This can be traced back into Byzantine and classical antiquity and beyond. In sculpture and ivory carvings the emperors or their representatives are shown on curule seats or stools. These are often decorated with lions' heads or feet. A typical instance is the consular diptych of Rufus Gennadius Probus, Consul of Rome AD 530, in London (Victoria and Albert Museum 1927, plate VII). A second tradition was that of episcopal thrones. An early example, which probably originated in sixth-century Alexandria and is now know as the 'Sedia de San Marco', combines an impressive but small alabaster seat with armrests and a high back, with a receptacle for reliquaries. The fact that the decoration imitates basket-work reminds one that such seats were usually made of wood (Buckton, Entwistle and Prior 1984, 98–103). The royal stool became a regular part of the iconography of the late Saxon and Norman kings of England. The Bayeux Tapestry shows Edward the Confessor, Harold and the Duke William of Normandy all sitting on stools reminiscent of those of classical antiquity. The skilled lathe-turners of the eleventh and twelfth centuries improved on this by constructing seats in wood much more akin to modern armchairs for their kings and bishops (Eames 1977, 191–4).

As more sophisticated carpentry techniques evolved, so more ambitious seats of majesty were devised. Henry III was the first king known to have been particularly interested in thrones. In 1245 he wrote to his Keeper of Works *because we recall that you have said that it will be much grander to make the two leopards, which will be on either side of our new chair at Westminster, of bronze rather than of marble or carved, we command you that they should be made of metal as you have suggested and you make the steps in front of the throne of wrought stone.* (Cal. Close R, 1242–7, 293.)

There seems little doubt that he was thinking of the throne of Solomon, mentioned in I Kings 10, 18, and II Chronicles 9, 18. Earthly monarchs in thirteenth-century manuscripts are commonly shown seated on thrones placed on platforms approached by steps ornamented with lions' heads. Henry's introduction of leopards into the design of his throne may well have been intended as a reflection of the lions on the throne of Solomon. This throne with its rich arcading and high back is seen in the later seals of Henry III (Wormald 1988, 61–9).

There was thus a background of interest and technical expertise in making impressive royal seats which Edward I was able to draw upon when he commissioned work to begin on a stately throne late on in the reign.

The coronation chair

It is difficult to conjure up the magnificence of a medieval coronation. Gone now are the regalia, the cloth of gold, the hangings, but fortunately one item still remains, though admittedly much damaged by souvenir hunters and scratched by graffiti. The coronation chair still stands in St Edward's Chapel, Westminster Abbey. It was made by Walter 'the king's painter' by order of Edward I, to contain and display the Stone of Scone brought back as part of the spoils of war from Scotland. Edward had solemnly offered the stone to St Edward the Confessor, together with the golden sceptre and crown of Scotland, on 18 June 1297. It appears that the king intended in the first place to have a chair made of bronze, and work had already started on this magnificent if expensive project (Scott 1863, 122). Adam the king's goldsmith incurred expenses

about a chair of copper which the king had first ordered to be made in the 25th year after his return home from Scotland, for putting on the stone on which the kings of Scotland were crowned found at Scone in the 24th year.

Heavy expenses had thus been incurred on this project before it was stopped on Edward's departure for Flanders in 1297. A wooden model for the chair had been made and templates, moulds and tools bought; the bronze chair had, in fact, been cast and workmen were engaged on the finishing process. On 1 August the king ordered work on the bronze chair to be stopped and a wooden chair was substituted. Probably the gilding process would have added more expenses than the total cost of making and decorating the chair in the cheaper material. The wooden chair was made by Master Walter of Durham between 1 August 1297 and 27 March 1300 (Fig. 16).

16 *The coronation chair, Westminster Abbey, first stage.* (After Percival-Prescott.)

The chair is made of oak planks and designed with grand architectural proportions meant to be seen from afar, as would be necessary if it was to take its place in the abbey at the centre of the coronation ceremony. It has a high plain back finished with a moulding and rising in the middle to an acute angle with carved crockets (Fig. 18). The design is carved rather than applied and the chair is of a curious construction, entirely carved from a number of thick oak panels which run its full height from the base of the quatrefoil tracery to the top of the gable. The original chair had four soaring wooden columns crowned with crocketed finials, one at each corner. Only two stumps of these remain at the rear of the chair. The sides have curved arm-rests with panelled spandrels externally, and below the seat is a box-like space containing the Stone of Scone. This space is now open in the front where the frame has been broken away but there are quatrefoils at the back and sides. At the back of the chair above the quatrefoils is a range of six panels. From recent intensive investigations it seems that there have been two systems of painted decoration (Percival-Prescott 1957). Walter of Durham's scheme involved painting the recessed compartments of the four high corner posts in white and gold with inscriptions in vermilion. Small painted shields filled the spandrels of the external arcading here, as well as in the small roundels on the surface.

Only a few decades after its making an entirely different scheme of decoration was applied to the chair. The whole of it was covered (except the parts already painted) with a thick layer of gesso. This was applied over an undercoat containing white lead. The subsequent gilding of the gesso was probably carried out with glair (white of egg). Upon this gold surface a pattern was then 'pounced', i.e. pricked upon it with a blunt instrument, before the ground and gilding lost its elasticity (Fig. 17). This had evidently been done with

17 *The coronation chair, Westminster Abbey. The decoration pounced on arms of chair.* (After Percival-Prescott.)

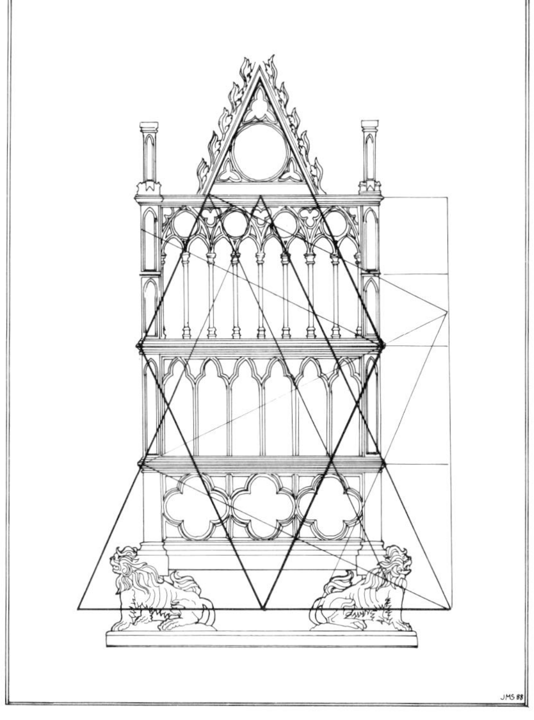

18 *The coronation chair, Westminster Abbey. The geometry and elements in the design.* (After Percival-Prescott.)

great care because the dots as they were made had not penetrated through the gold to show the gesso underneath. Within the arcaded panels are areas of diapered decoration which alternate between grotesques and ornate foliage patterns. Particularly fine are a lion's head with winged eyebrows and a grotesque strutting bird with large clawed feet, long beak and a cloth wrapped round its neck. A decoration of vine leaves and grapes can be found in one of the foliage diapers, the other consisting of leaves and nuts. There are the much damaged remains of the figure of a king, possibly St Edward the Confessor, on the back of the chair. Only the lower part of a heavy robe with a bordered hem and a foot with a long pointed toe remain; the foot rests on the back of a lion whose mane, tail and clawed feet are visible. The drawing is bold and of superb quality. The artist has not been inhibited by the difficulties of the medium. The glazed lustre decorations noted by Brayley in 1823 have almost completely disappeared but careful study of the surface of the chair indicates that the technique involved the placing of a clear saturated glaze on top of thin beaten tin. Traces of gold, amber, red and crimson can be seen. On this richly coloured base gilded patterns were executed in leaf gold. The whole was then covered with pieces of clear or coloured glass.

The decoration of the chair has suffered excessive damage over seven hundred years. The present ruined condition of the gesso possibly originated in the repeated tacking and nailing on of coverings on the occasion of coronations. A large number of tacks and nails show up vividly on X-ray photographs, particularly in the interior.

The custom of covering the chair with precious material started early, and evidently it was customary for the populace after a coronation to sweep up the nave and rip pieces of the precious cloth from the chair as mementoes. Names, dates and initials were carved on the chair by the boys of Westminster School who habitually made nocturnal incursions into the abbey for almost a century. The pinnacles were sawn off for the coronation of George IV; the shields in the quatrefoiled tracery were stolen at the same time. Probably the gesso suffered its most serious damage in 1887 when in preparation for the Jubilee the Office of Works removed the chair from the abbey and toned down the large part of the chair with dark-brown semi-transparent paint, at the same time smothering with brownish-black paint the few remaining glazed lustres and white lead pastes. When confronted with this barbaric treatment the wretched officials scraped it off again. It is difficult to know which process did the greater damage. Finally the chair was a target for attack by suffragettes in 1913. They hung on it a 'dorothy bag' packed with explosives and nuts and bolts which detonated, blowing off a pinnacle and leaving deep gashes in the side. The chair is still the subject of concern because the response of the wood to variations in the humidity of its surroundings causes the gesso to move and flake. This has now been corrected by placing a suitable moisture-insulating material between the ground and the chair and by coating the internal surfaces of the base of the chair with a hot wax-resin mixture to retard the absorption of moisture.

In the later Middle Ages a more hierarchically-minded power structure demanded the production of a 'chair of estate' which was placed on steps in a palatial presence chamber; over it was a canopy of state. The figure of King Herod in the scene of the Massacre of the Innocents in fifteenth-century glass at St Peter Mancroft, Norwich, is seated on such a chair of estate. He is similarly shown while presiding over the feast where Salome danced, at Gresford (Anderson 1971). The early sixteenth-century glass at Fairford (Gloucestershire), which may be a royal donation, also shows King David judging the Amalekite under a canopy of state (Wayment 1984, plate CCI). The English Tudor kings had a similar chair of estate at Hampton Court and the Scottish kings likewise at Stirling (Baillie 1967). Even if the monarch was absent reverence was still paid to this symbol of power.

CHAPTER TWO
Burials of the medieval royal family

Royal burials were of great significance during the Middle Ages. When the king died a political vacuum occurred, because the *persona* of the king was indistinguishable from the state. The functions of government were suspended for a time. Feudal society was so volatile that, if chaos was to be avoided, extreme speed was required by the successor to seize the crown. One thing needed to be demonstrated beyond all doubt, namely, the death of the monarch. Hence the importance afforded to a public funeral. This is why royal corpses lay in state and were carried on exposed biers. Sometimes they were carried on long journeys before reaching a burial place. The public nature of the royal funeral had a second function. If the king had died under dubious circumstances, his subjects could have their suspicions of foul play allayed by inspecting the body. On a number of occasions (the deaths of Richard II, Henry VI, Edward IV), the bodies of kings suspected of being murdered were laid out in St Paul's Cathedral or Westminster Abbey; people filed by to view the face or body bare from the waist upwards (Stanley 1911, 101).

The public ritual occasioned by a royal death accorded with views about death held throughout medieval western society (Ariès 1976, 12). Death became a ceremony, and the dying man's bedchamber a public place to be entered freely by parents, friends and neighbours. Cemeteries, too, were public places but the remains of the more wealthy dead were placed in mausolea near the saints, or in churches close to altars. The practice of sepulture by division (dividing up the body and burying the parts in different places) is linked with this concern for public participation. Monks, canons and the communities they served vied with one another to obtain royal bones (Hallam 1991, 11). The desire to profit from prayers by any means, at all times, and in a number of places led to the ready willingness on the part of royal defuncts to arrange in advance for the dismemberment of their corpses; the heart might be deposited in one church, the entrails in another and the body elsewhere (Brown 1981).

The places chosen for royal burial reflected the complex and constantly changing economic, political and religious preoccupations of the monarchy. The Anglo-Saxon kings of Wessex, for the most part, were buried at Winchester where they had been crowned and where one of their principal houses stood. Perhaps a more potent reason, however, was proximity to the relics of powerful and intercessory saints such as St Swithin. The saintly Edward the Confessor was buried in his refounded abbey at Westminster but this was not seen as a precedent to follow for another 206 years. The Norman Conqueror died while warring in France and was buried in one of his own monastic foundations. Rufus was assassinated in Hampshire and interred at Winchester. His successor died across the Channel but was brought back to England to be buried at his newly-founded monastery of Reading, planned perhaps to be a family mausoleum. The Angevin kings demonstrated where the centre of their interests lay by switching their place of burial to Fontévrault, in the heartland of Anjou. John, of course, had lost his continental possessions and had his own (religious) reasons for favouring Worcester.

It was not until Henry III's reign that the three basic royal events, coronation, residence and burial were united in one place, Westminster. Throughout most of the fourteenth and early fifteenth centuries, kings (apart from Edward II who had no choice) favoured burial at Westminster. The reason was, to begin with, the attraction of the cult of St Edward the Confessor, combined with the convenience of proximity to the royal palace and seat of government. Gradually, a dynastic aura developed as successive Plantagenets were interred there. The Lancastrian usurper, uneasy at the presence of the bodies of his political opponents, opted for Canterbury where St Thomas Becket's bones offered powerful intercession. Henry V, more secure, returned to Westminster Abbey which was now becoming overcrowded with royal tombs, packed around the shrine of St Edward. The Yorkists during the fifteenth century founded their own family mausoleum in the collegiate church at Fotheringhay (Northamptonshire). When Edward IV became king, he refounded St George's Chapel at Windsor Castle in which he prepared his tomb and thus began a tradition of an alternative place to the coronation church. Henry VII added a great extension to Westminster Abbey to contain the tombs of the Tudor dynasty. He was anxious to share in the power emanating from such a sacred locus.

Norman royal burials

The Duchy of Normandy remained central to the political interests of the Norman Conquerors of England for at least a hundred years after Hastings. William I was killed there while defending these interests and significantly, he was not buried at Rouen or Falaise where his ancestors lay, but at Caen where he had founded two splendid abbeys. His controversial marriage with Matilda (Douglas 1989, 76–7) had been allowed by Pope Nicholas II in return for a promise that the duke and his wife should each build and endow a monastic house at Caen; St Stephen's Caen contains William's tomb. His son, William Rufus, met a bloody end while hunting in the New Forest and was unceremoniously brought to Winchester and buried in the new cathedral. The presence of such a sacrilegious unbeliever, carried off violently and unshriven, invited divine wrath, and, according to contemporaries, caused the fall of the central tower seven years later. A tomb in which William's bones are alleged to have rested 'under a playne flat marble stone' no longer exists. One was investigated in 1868 but no satisfactory connection was proved with Rufus; in fact, according to W. St John Hope, the tomb in question was that of Bishop Henry of Blois.

The third Norman king, Henry I, also died in Normandy, this time in the chief city, Rouen. 'The Normans kept his intestines and the rest of his body the English carried away to a tomb in the Abbey of Reading.' Reputedly, the body was sewn up in a bull hide. Reading Abbey had been founded by the king and endowed with a wonder-working relic, the hand of St James. Presumably the king was buried as close as possible to the saintly member but one seeks in vain in the shapeless flinty ruins of Reading Abbey for any vestige of the 'tomb and effigy' of the founder which were mentioned in 1398 when Richard II agreed to confirm the charters of the abbey provided that they were repaired within a year.

The fourth Norman king, Stephen, is reported to have been buried in his monastic foundation at Faversham (Kent). Faversham's original plan included a specially enlarged choir, designed as a burial church, although it was shortened later due to lack of funds (Hallam 1990, 12). The abbot of Faversham told Cromwell in 1536 that Stephen and the body of his queen and son were 'buried in honourable sepulture' in the abbey; this did not save it and them from the destruction which overwhelmed the monasteries (Brown, Colvin and Taylor 1963, 478).

The Angevin connections: Fontévrault and Worcester

The focus of attention of the Angevin monarchs shifted southwards to the centre of France to correspond with the great growth of their continental dominions. Fontévrault is on the southern border of Anjou in the department of Maine-et-Loire, 14.5km (9 miles) south-east of the town of Saumur. In the forest a double monastery with an abbess had been founded and strongly patronized by Fulk the Fifth, Count of Anjou, whose daughter Matilda was one of the nuns. This lady was the aunt of Henry II who gave the monastery many benefactions. Here the Angevin kings and queens were buried (Hallet 1902, 265, Boase 1971, 1–10).

The study of the royal tombs at Fontévrault

owes much to an antiquarian draughtsman Charles Stothard, who in 1816, after the Revolution and Napoleonic wars, found them vulnerable to neglect and decay (Stothard 1817, 19). The abbey had been converted into a prison and he discovered in a cellar belonging to it, the effigies of Henry II and his queen, Eleanor of Guienne, Richard I, and Isabella of Angouleme, queen of John: '. . . these valuable effigies . . . were subject to continual mutilation from the prisoners who came twice a day to draw water from the well'. They were eventually rehabilitated and restored by the French, despite their reluctance to honour royalty, particularly that of the national enemy. For a time there was a possibility they might come to England, a thank offering by Napoleon III to Queen Victoria in return for the ashes of Napoleon (Boase 1971, 9).

Henry II, when seriously ill in 1170, had announced to his horrified courtiers that he intended to be buried in the tiny church of Grandmont, the mother church of the ascetic Grandmontine order. His barons maintained that this would be against the dignity of the realm. He actually died at Chinon, 19 years later, worn out by waging ceaseless wars against his rebellious sons. His body was carried to Fontévrault where 'he lay in state robed in royal splendour, wearing a gold crown on his head, gauntlets on his hands and a gold ring on his finger, holding the sceptre in his hand, with gold braided shoes and spurs on his feet, girded with his sword and his face uncovered.' When his eldest surviving son Richard went to attend the corpse, it was said that blood gushed from the dead king's nostrils as a sign of anger with his faithless son (Stothard 1817, 6).

The freestone effigy, the oldest to survive of any medieval English king, appears to be a faithful representation of the dead ruler as described by Matthew Paris. This is not to say that it is to be regarded as a portrait. As in all twelfth-century sculptures of kings, the symbols of majesty outweigh the accurate depiction of physiognomy. The face (in Stothard's description) shows high cheek bones, projecting lips and chin. The mantle is fastened by a fibula to the right shoulder but the badges of authority are damaged; the right hand on which was the great ring is broken; the crown similarly is cracked. Stothard recorded that the image was brightly painted: the cushion under the king's head was a deep reddish chocolate; the dalmatic was crimson starred with gold; the mantle similarly; the boots were green ornamented with gold and there were gold spurs.

By the side of Henry's effigy is a similar monument to his quarrelsome, energetic and power-seeking wife. Eleanor of Aquitaine is shown with her head on a blue cushion, in a white tunic with gold banded and criss-crossed patterning, and wrapped in a blue cloak with crescents powdering it.

Henry II had the misfortune to survive his eldest son. The so-called 'Young king Henry' had been unruly and violent in life but his body was a prize much competed for by monks and canons, anxious to house the prestigious royal remains. After his death, the citizens of Le Mans kidnapped the cortège on its way through their town and buried him in their cathedral. The citizens of Rouen to whom he had promised his body for burial threatened to raze Le Mans to the ground. The king had to intervene in the unseemly business and his son was exhumed and moved to Rouen for burial.

The disposing of different organs of the bodies of royal personages for separate burial is one of the characteristics of the early medieval monarchy of England and France. This practice eventually roused grave opposition within the church and in 1299 Boniface VIII issued his bull *Detestande Feritatis*, denouncing the custom (Brown 1981, 221). In the meantime Richard I, with his dying breath, directed that his mortal remains be split three ways. His body was to be interred at the feet of his much wronged father. He bequeathed his brain, blood and viscera to the Poitevins, a veiled insult referring to their treacherous conduct to him in the past. His heart was sent to the canons of Rouen 'en remembrance à amour' (Way 1842, 210).

The special veneration in which the heart was held was connected with the belief that it was the seat of the affections and certain of the higher emotions such as courage and piety (Bradford 1933). The first accredited heart burial in western Europe was that of Robert d'Arbrissel, the founder of the order of Fontévrault (d. 1117). Devorgilla, the founder of Sweetheart Abbey, was buried with her husband's heart in a casket. The crusades spread the cult. It was a two-way traffic. Some people died on crusade and their hearts, easily portable objects, were posted home. William de Warenne, Earl of Surrey, killed by the Turks in 1148, was buried in the Middle East but his heart was sent to England to be interred in Lewes Priory (Sussex). Others made arrangements for their hearts to be sent to the Holy Land. Edward I in 1307 willed that his heart be sent to Palestine but there is no record that this command was carried out.

Richard I's heart burial was excavated at Rouen in 1838. It was found that the stone effigy of the king was two feet below the surface, with all the cavities of the drapery and other parts of the figure filled up with cement and the hands and feet levelled to create a flat pavement. Painting and gilding had survived, however, and the heart itself was discovered enclosed within two boxes of lead with the inscription HIC COR: RICARDI: REGIS: ANGLORUM. The redoubtable organ 'once remarkable for its physical capacity, as by its moral development, withered . . . to the semblance of a faded leaf' (Way 1842, 206, 211).

The circumstances of John's death and funeral were unusual. Despite the fact that he had apparently proposed that his body should rest in his Cistercian foundation of Beaulieu Abbey (Hampshire), his last days were spent in continuous campaigning and journeying in the Midlands (St John Hope 1906). He crossed the Fens and lost part of his baggage train, including, it is alleged, his regalia and jewels. Despite the onset of dysentery, he struggled on, strapped to a litter made from a hurdle because he was unable to ride his own horse, and eventually arrived at Newark Castle. Here he was confessed, received the Eucharist from the Abbot of Croxton and died. His intestines were entombed in Croxton Abbey. Four fully-armoured knights accompanied the king's body across Midland England to the cathedral at Worcester. As Stanley puts it, 'with that union of superstition and profaneness so common in the religious belief of the Middle Ages, he was anxious to elude after death the demons whom he had so faithfully served in life' (Stanley 1911, 103). In fact, John was ensuring exactly what other kings did before and since: proximity to powerful saintly intercessors, in this case Saints Wulfstan and Oswald. For good measure he had given orders for his body to be wrapped in a monk's cowl. This solution much aggrieved the monks of Beaulieu who enlisted Henry III's help to write to the Pope, asking for John's body to be transferred to them. They were ignored (Hallam 1990, 11).

John's tomb is in the centre of the chancel at Worcester. It is now in two units (Pafford 1958, 58–60). The chest was opened on 17 July 1797 and several observations were made of the earliest medieval royal skeleton to come down to us. The skull was found reversed and presented what anatomists call the *foramen magnum* or aperture through which the spinal marrow passes. The upper jaw lay near the elbow. There was no sign of a crown but in place of it was found the celebrated monk's cowl which fitted the head closely and was buckled under the chin with straps. The body had been covered with a crimson robe of strong texture reaching from neck to feet. The king's left arm was bent towards his breast and his hand was found grasping a sword in the same gesture as on the tomb. The sword was very corroded; the scabbard was better preserved. A covering of the legs was found tied round the ankles.

The disarray of the bones of the upper part of the body is probably to be explained by the disinterment of the heart which was sent 60 years later to Fontévrault to be buried among John's Angevin predecessors. The effigy was placed there by his son, Henry III, after a lapse of some years. It is carved in grey Purbeck marble, the dark shell-filled limestone which polishes to a gleaming finish. Its head is supported by two small figures of bishops, no doubt representations of Saints Wulfstan and Oswald. Stothard studied the effigy carefully and detected more signs of colour than are now visible (Stothard 1817, 14–16). The king was portrayed as wearing a dalmatic of crimson lined with green, the neck and cuffs edged with gold, with a jewelled border. His tunic was yellow or cloth of gold, girt with a belt; on his hands were jewelled gloves. There was a ring on the middle finger of his right hand. He wore red hose and golden spurs; his feet were shod in black shoes and gold spurs; they rest on a lion. The king is shown supporting a sceptre in his right hand and grasps a sword in his left. Recent attempts to rehabilitate John's evil reputation will have received a measure of support from this impressive icon, the product of the king's dutiful son, Henry III.

The cult of St Edward the Confessor

Henry III (1216–72) associated himself in life and death with his royal and saintly predecessor, Edward the Confessor, who was the cult figure not only of the monastery of St Peter at Westminster but also of the Plantagenet monarchy itself. During the period 1066–1269 a series of steps had already been taken to raise the status of the Saxon king. Edward had been buried before the high altar; William the Conqueror, who claimed to be his designated successor, was crowned at the side of the royal tomb and presented two palls as coverings before reconstructing the tomb at great expense. In 1101, Gilbert Crispin caused the tomb to be opened; the body was found to be incorrupt and Gundulf, Bishop of Rochester, tried and failed to pull out a hair of the king's yellow beard! Abbot Laurentius secured the Pope's agreement to canonization in 1163 and the saint was transferred to a higher tomb with a rich feretory (a shrine, richly adorned, in which relics were kept) by Henry II, with Thomas Becket assisting. A ring, said to have been given to Edward by St John the Evangelist, was removed and kept as a relic, and the royal vestments, presumably rich samples of *opus anglicanum* (English embroidery, which enjoyed a high reputation) were made into three copes by order of the abbot. These actions and events, however, pale into insignificance when compared with Henry III's ambitious plans for his royal patron saint.

Henry had in mind nothing less than the complete restructuring of the Confessor's Abbey. The rehousing of the shrine of the saint was seen as the climax of the rebuilding programme. It began as early as 1241 when, according to Matthew Paris, the king ordered picked goldsmiths from London to make a shrine of the purest gold to receive the royal remains. This work went on for over twenty years and it was not until 1269 that both church and shrine were ready for the saint's translation to the new resting place behind the high altar, the source of sacerdotal power which the anointed king claimed to share.

Detailed archaeological studies have been made of the remains of the shrine which still stand in the choir (O'Neilly and Tanner 1966, 129–55) (Fig. 19). It was a composite structure

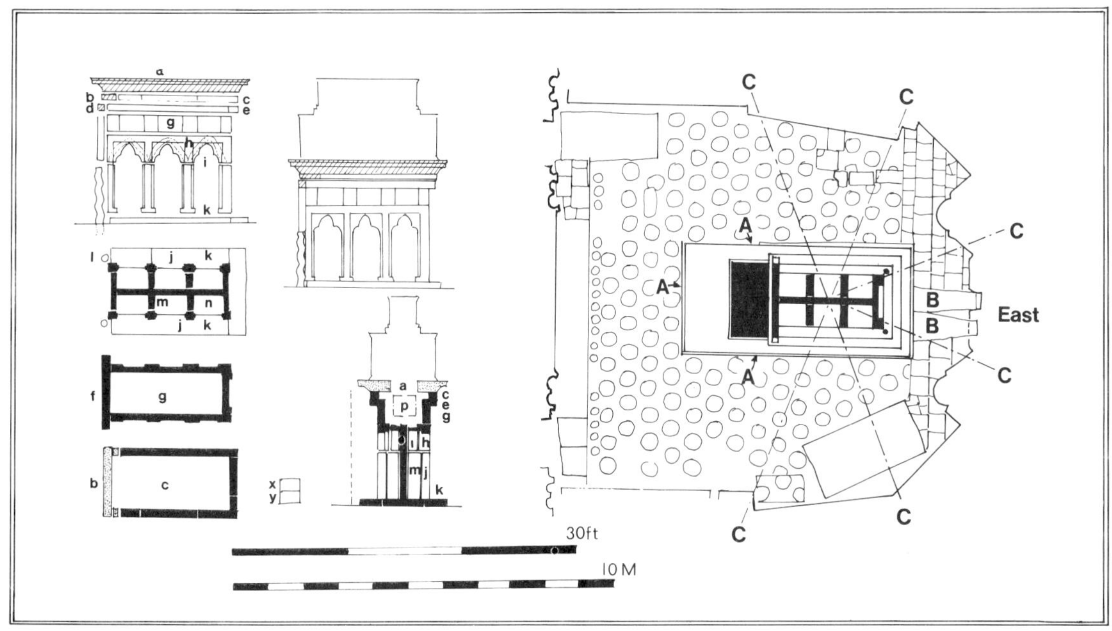

19 *The shrine of St Edward the Confessor, Westminster Abbey, showing the constructional details (see O'Neilly and Tanner, 1966). Plan of chapel: (A) Cosmati floor. (B) Valence tombs; the radiating point of apse vaulting ribs (C) occurs over the central point of shrine.* (After O'Neilly and Tanner.)

consisting of four parts. It rested on a base of stone or marble which was pierced with trefoil-headed arches or openings into which crippled or diseased pilgrims were allowed to creep so as to be as close as possible to the sacred relics. In this it was similar to the first tomb-shrine of St Thomas Becket in the crypt at Canterbury. On top was the 'feretory' itself, a wooden, ark-like chest covered with gold and silver plates, enriched with jewels and enamels, enclosing the body of the saint. Over the shrine was a movable cover which was hoisted up by ropes and a counterweight attached to the vaulting above to display the riches to the faithful and to hide and safeguard them when necessary. The fourth component was an altar at the west end of the shrine. It appears that the Confessor's shrine was taken down completely at the Reformation and hastily and inaccurately set up again by Abbot Feckenham, who was installed during the Marian Reaction. Nearly all the pieces, are still there – an extraordinary survival.

20 A reconstruction of the shrine of St Edward the Confessor, Westminster Abbey, as it probably existed before 1539. The canopy is partly raised, revealing the ornate feretory. See also Fig. 102. (After O'Neilly and Tanner.)

The shrine was evidently originally placed on four steps (Fig. 20), since it was noticed that there was a gap between the edge of the Cosmati work (glass mosaic work of Roman craftsmen) and the present position of the base. The marble base has been wrongly reassembled, a conclusion reached from a minute survey of the Cosmati decoration. Although much of the glass mosaic has been picked out, the matrices are cut into the surface of the marble and it is possible to reconstruct the very distinctive and beautiful designs. The present canopy is considered to be early Renaissance in style but pre-Reformation in date. This surprising claim is supported by the observation that such a complex piece of carpentry with glass decorations was made to accommodate the feretory and since this latter had vanished as the first victim of Henry VIII's despoliation of the shrine, the canopy must pre-date its removal. O'Neilly and Tanner argued that the altar which was sited at the west end of the shrine was removed bodily and can be found in its new guise as a tomb blocking an arch in the south ambulatory. The 'Fayre godly shrine of Seynt Edward in marble' is still in fact, to all intents and purposes, 'in the myddes of the chappell'.

Westminster Abbey: a mausoleum of the Plantagenet Kings

The idea of creating a royal burying place at Westminster Abbey has been attributed to Edward I. It is not difficult to understand why he was attracted to it. The soaring vaults, gleaming grey Purbeck marble columns, new-worked Caen stone and brilliantly painted white surfaces with red masonry patterns of his father's inspired work were freshly finished and less than twenty years old. The Confessor's tomb was in place. It seems likely that the inspiration for linking the Confessor's chapel with royal tombs came from France. In the church of St Denis, Paris, Louis IX had com-

21 The tomb of Henry III in Westminster Abbey. This is in the chapel of St Edward the Confessor, and is made of Purbeck marble, with Italian marble inlay and marble and glass mosaic by Peter the Roman. The effigy was made by William Torel and lies under a timber tester. (Photograph: RCHM England.)

missioned a set of 16 effigies of his ancestors (Erlande-Brandenburg 1984). The idea of commemorating long dead ancestors did not commend itself to the more practical and hard-headed English king. Instead he erected splendid tombs for his uncle, his wife and his father. Moreover, he filled the Confessor's chapel with the trophies of his successful wars – the Stone of Scone was trundled in from beaten Scotland and a fragment of the true cross presented by a Welsh renegade was suspended in triumph. He arranged for his little son Alfonso (who in the event predeceased him) to hang up before the shrine the golden crown of Llewelyn, the last Welsh prince. All this reflected the confidence of a would-be chivalrous and an actual autocratic king in the destiny of his line. For the next four hundred years, pilgrims, mingling with the kings' subjects, came to gaze at the shrine of St Edward surrounded by the most impressive array of monarchical monuments to be found in Europe.

On 16 November 1272, Henry III died during his eldest son's absence on crusade and was buried on the feast of St Edmund, King and Martyr, in Westminster Abbey. His body was fittingly decked out with the richest clothes and the royal crown and was laid in the coffin occupied by Edward the Confessor's remains until their translation in 1269. There it remained for some years before being reburied in a new tomb to the north side of the Confessor's chapel. Edward, according to the chronicler Rishanger, brought precious stones from France to beautify his father's tomb (Fig. 21). The monument itself is of Purbeck marble with Italian marble inlay and marble and glass mosaic by Peter the Roman (RCHM 1924, 29). This has nearly all been robbed on the south side but the slots which housed the mosaic tesserae still delineate the design. The three trefoil-headed niches on the south side of the tomb are similar to those of the Confessor's shrine. The effigy was made by William Torel and is similar in technique to that of Eleanor of Castile. It is crowned with a fleuron crown from which the jewels have been plundered; the face is noble, idealized and bearded, the hands formerly held sceptres while cushions and shoes are diapered with leopards. Henry had in his earlier years, when at the ancestral burial place in Anjou, promised that his heart should be deposited at Fontévrault. The abbess happened to be in England at the time of the removal of Henry's body to its new tomb and the heart was delivered into her hands for reburial in the Plantagenets' foreign home.

Archaeological examination of the tomb, of a rather half-hearted nature, was made in Dean Stanley's time (Stanley 1880, 317–22). The effigy, and the plate on which it lay, were hoisted up to the triforium for cleaning and the Purbeck marble blocks beneath them were found to be three in number, held together by iron cramps. There were no fastenings to connect the effigy and its bed with the marble beneath; the weight of each part was quite sufficient to make them immovable without the use of some special appliance – indeed the combined efforts of nine Victorian navvies were needed to shift them! Beneath the marble bed was a coffin of oak covered all over, top, sides and ends, with cloth of gold. It was woven in two alternating patterns consisting of striped stars and eight-foils. The chains whereby the coffin had been lowered into the tomb were intact and in place. The coffin measured 6ft 1½in (1.87m) long, 1ft 10½in (57cm) wide at the head and 1ft 9in (53cm) wide at the foot. Unfortunately, at this point the hearts of the investigators failed them; they rather lamely concluded that they did not have enough historical reasons for proceeding and desisted from further probing. Henry III lies there undisturbed. We have no notion how well preserved his mortal remains are.

Edward I and Eleanor of Castile

Edward I had shown filial piety in honouring his dead father. His motives in commemorating his first wife arose from deep grief as well as family feeling. When Queen Eleanor of Castile died on 28 November 1290, he ordered a monumental display more splendid and more elaborate than that accorded to any other medieval English king or queen. It seems that the affection in which Edward held his first wife was the result of one of the few happy unions enjoyed by the medieval monarchy. Normally, such dynastic marriages were purely business affairs aimed at cementing political alliances and building up power blocks. Eleanor was the only daughter of five children born to Ferdinand of Castile and Leon by his second wife, Jeanne de Dammartin. The heraldry of Castile and Leon would figure prominently in her monuments. Eleanor had married Edward I on 1 November 1254, traditionally at the Cistercian monastery of Las Huelgas near Burgos. It is not difficult to understand the sources of their mutual regard. Eleanor between 1255 and 1284 had borne Edward 15, perhaps 16 children, including 11 daughters and four or five sons. She was an energetic and vital personality who enjoyed her frequent travels by the side of the king. She had accompanied him on crusade in the 1270s and her life had been spent in constant movement from one residence to another. These royal progresses were the only way for a king or queen to be seen by most of their subjects. She shared with the king her interest in religion and they visited religious shrines together. Her almsgiving also seems to have been on the same generous scale as that of her husband. From 25 April 1289 to 28 November 1290 she provided meals for no less than 9306 paupers at a cost of three half pennies per meal. This was less than the number fed by the king but together they must have contributed in no small way to the relief of the poor of the kingdom. This public display of piety contrasts with the reputation she gained as a greedy acquirer of other peoples' manors (Parsons 1990, 27).

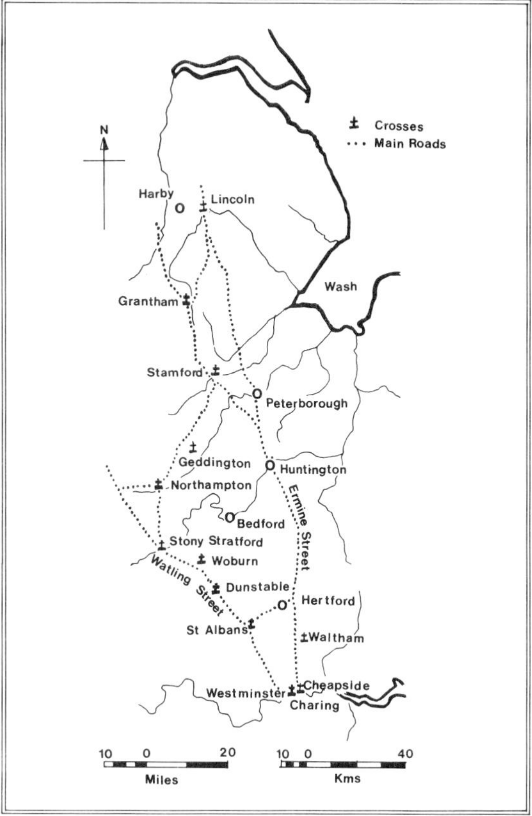

22 Distribution map of Eleanor Crosses. Only three survive today (Northampton, Geddington and Waltham) but fragments are known from Lincoln and Cheapside. (After Brown, Colvin, Taylor.)

The last four years of her life were marred by increasing ill health. Already in 1286 she had resource to the old custom of *mensura*; a wax candle of her own height was sent to be burned before the shrine of her favourite saint to beg intercession for a return to health. She seems to have suffered from a quartan fever which may have been a malarial infection. She accompanied the king on his expedition to Gascony and was there three years. In early 1290 there are signs that she sensed that she was unlikely to be cured. In February, a court goldsmith, William de Farendon, was paid £6 8s 4d for making 'images of the Queen's likeness when she fell sick'. In the same month the queen gave £100 to have a chapel prepared for the burial of her heart at the Dominican Friary in London. Despite this, she did not alter the hectic pace of her life. She was with the king almost constantly throughout the year, accompanying him to Nottinghamshire for the parliament held at Clipston, 27 October–11 November. The court physician, Master Peter of Portugal, was sent for by the queen on 23 September and syrups and other 'medicinalia' were bought at a cost of 13s 4d at Lincoln. Eleanor died in the house of Sir Richard de Weston at the little Nottinghamshire village of Harby. The spate of royal writs which up to this point in time had been continuous ceased for five days (Hunter 1842, 170).

The corpse of the queen was taken to Lincoln where the entrails and heart were removed for separate burial (Stevenson 1899, 11). The *Liber* which records the household accounts of Eleanor of Castile in 1290 has two curious entries referring to the evisceration and embalming processes. A bushel of barley (*pro uno bussello ordei*) was to be placed in the queen's body and six ells of cloth and a pound of incense were also provided. The queen's viscera were buried in the choir of Lincoln Cathedral where the king raised a replica of her Westminster tomb. The embalmed body was taken in stately progress from Lincoln to Westminster in 12 stages. At each place where the bier rested for the night the king ordered a memorial cross to be constructed (Fig. 22). This was not the first instance of public memorial crosses placed on highroads. Henry III ordered the sheriff of Surrey to cause 'a fair strong cross' to be erected (*fieri*) at the cross roads (*quadrivio*) outside the gate of Merton towards Carshalton (Surrey) in memory of William, late Earl of Warenne (*Cal Lib R.* 1226–40, 474). Eleanor's resting places (from north to south) were Lincoln, Grantham, Stamford, the royal manor of Geddington, Delapré Abbey (Northampton), Stony Stratford, Woburn, Dunstable, St Albans, the royal abbey of Waltham, West Cheap in the City of London and the royal mews at Charing. At Westminster Abbey and Lincoln Cathedral splendid tombs were constructed.

Of the 12 Eleanor crosses, three survive today: those at Waltham, Northampton and Geddington, but there are fragments of those at Lincoln and Cheapside. John of Battle was given the task of building five of the crosses. He had been undermaster from 1278 to 1280 at Vale Royal Abbey. The cross at Hardingstone which gleams yellow and fretted on the hill above Northampton is the only one of his crosses still standing (Fig. 23). It has an octagonal base in three tiers. The solid lowest tier is decorated with arch and gable motifs separated by pinnacles. Within the arches are shields of arms of Ponthieu (Eleanor succeeded to the county of Ponthieu in Picardy in 1279), Castile, Leon and England. There are also open books which one imagines were once inscribed or painted. The open middle tier rises from an elaborate projecting foliated cornice and here are four tabernacles housing statues of the queen. The ogee arch makes its first appearance in England on a monumental scale in the arches over the statues. The main decorative motifs which enrich the monument are cusping, blind tracery and foliage. It is thought that Edward attached most importance to the crosses raised in London. The craftsmen responsible for these were both referred to in the accounts as master (*magister*). Master Richard of Crundale made the cross at Charing and Master Michael of

23 *The Eleanor Cross at Hardingstone (Northamptonshire). The work of John of Battle it has an octagonal base in three tiers. Within the arches are shields of arms of Ponthieu, Castile, Leon and England; there are also open books. Above are four images in canopied niches. The top is broken off.* (Photograph: J. M. Steane.)

Canterbury that raised at Cheapside. The former cost over £700 and the latter £226 13s 4d. One reason for the large sums lavished on them is the costliness of the materials. Fragments were discovered in 1838 during the reconstruction of a sewer in Cheapside (Fig. 24). They show that a comparatively luxurious material, Purbeck marble, was used and that the formula adhered to by Michael of Canterbury was of a plinth decorated with two-light traceries framing shields of arms suspended from knots of foliage. The same feature can be seen on the surviving crosses at Waltham and Hardingstone.

The cross at Geddington (Northamptonshire) has the same elements but adapted to a triangular plan (Fig. 25). The slender shaft covered with delicate diapering is perfectly adapted to its purpose. On its stepped base it overlooks the centre of the small village which had a lodge much frequented by the Plantagenet kings when they hunted in Rockingham Forest. It survived virtually unscathed under the upkeep of successive Dukes of Buccleuch until 1915, when it was transferred to the State. Only the steps around the base had been replaced. The honey-coloured, open-structured and fossiliferous Weldon limestone of which it was made had

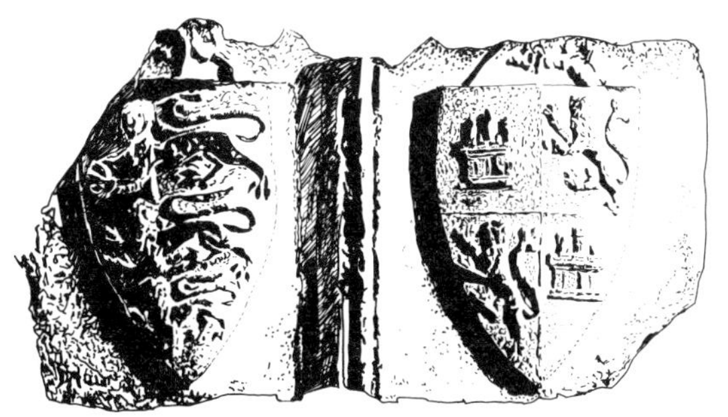

24 *Fragments of an Eleanor Cross from Cheapside. Michael of Canterbury, the designer of St Stephen's chapel, Westminster, was responsible for the design. At £300 it was second only in cost to that of Charing. These two fragments (height 96cm and 54cm (38in and 21½in)) show a lavish use of Purbeck marble. From the Museum of London.* (After Alexander and Binski.)

25 *The Eleanor Cross erected near the royal hunting lodge shortly after 1294 at Geddington (Northamptonshire). It is triangular and covered in diaper work with the shields of England and Castile. Above are three figures in three niches with canopied pinnacles merging into a recessed hexagonal star.* (Photograph: J. M. Steane.)

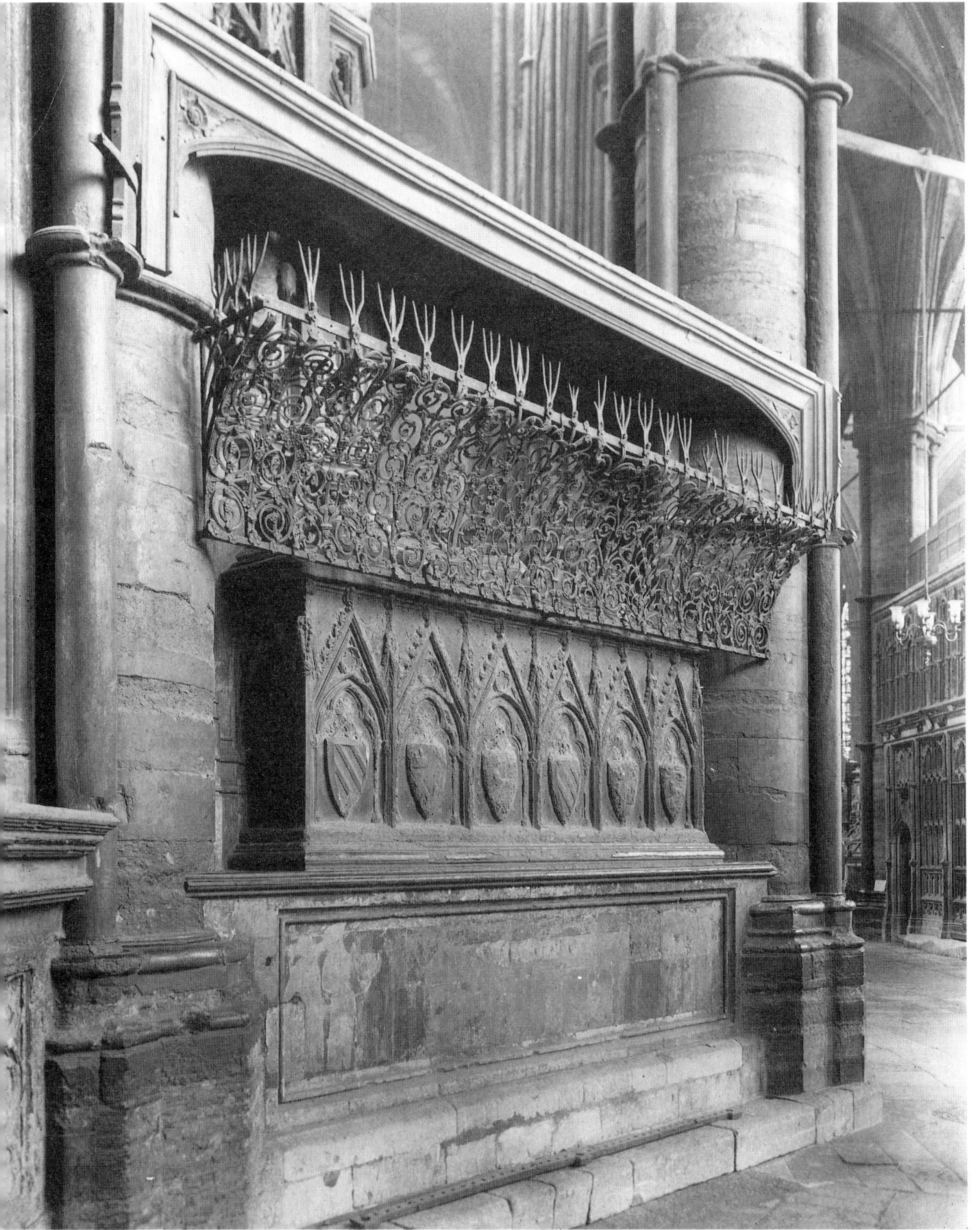

proved extremely durable. Recently cleaning of the architectural framework of lichen growth and sulphation has revealed that the thirteenth-century builders used darker, harder limestone in bands for the construction of the most exposed areas at the top of the base shaft and above the canopies (Smith 1988, 8–10). The gables of the canopies were found to have suffered considerable decay. Eltoline tissue and polyvinyl alcohol were used to support the delicate exfoliating areas before restoration work could be attempted. Loose debris was removed and the voids filled with mortar; lichen then could be removed. Vulnerable areas such as the finials were capped with mortar. The figures, fashioned of a finely grained, possibly French, limestone were found to be sound despite an inevitable loss of surface. The sulphate deposits had formed a skin which it was felt better to leave intact because it was preserving fine carved detail and possible traces of paint. It is highly likely that the monument was originally painted. In this way modern conservation techniques, allied to the high-quality craftmanship shown by the original builders, have ensured the continuing life of this most evocative symbol of thirteenth-century grief.

The bereaved king expressed his mourning not only in stone but metal, and the quality and magnificence of the crosses was matched by the care expended on the two principal tombs of the queen at Lincoln and Westminster. The Lincoln monument was the subject of a drawing made by Sir William Dugdale, prescient of its imminent destruction in the Civil War; it was evidently virtually identical to the one which survives at Westminster Abbey. A full-scale reconstruction/restoration was made in the late nineteenth century, and modern visitors can get a fair impression of the original appearance. The two effigies, and one of the king's father Henry III, were made by the same Master William Torel. The full-sized gilt-bronze effigy of Eleanor of Castile at Westminster has long braided hair and is crowned with an open crown with fleurons. She wears a long gown, kirtle and mantle (Fig. 27). The crown and edge of the garments have holes for added jewellery which has now gone. The queen's left hand holds the cord of her gown (in a similar pose to that of her statue in the Waltham cross) and her right hand probably once held a sceptre. Under the queen's head are two superimposed cushions diapered with the arms of Castile and England. The casting of bronze effigies of such a size was a task unknown before in England; it was carried out in a shed set up in the abbey churchyard (Plenderleith and Maryon, 1959). The *cire perdue* process, which was normally used for making large bells, required a large quantity of wax. The casting of such large objects was evidently still a relatively unrefined technique and the metal was unusually thick, between 4.5cm (1¾in) and 10cm (3¾in); 350 florins were bought from the merchants of Lucca for the gilding. The metal itself was supplied by William Sprot and John of Ware.

26 The tomb of Eleanor of Castile in Westminster Abbey. The coats of arms are of Ponthieu, Leon and Castile and England. A further panel below originally housed wall paintings. (Photograph: RCHM England.)

The iron grille over the tomb of Queen Eleanor at Westminster was made by a provincial smith, Thomas of Leighton, in 1293–4 for £12 (Fig. 26). He had already made the decorative ironwork on the doors of the churches at Turvey and Leighton Buzzard in Bedfordshire. The grille was designed to prevent access by intruders across Eleanor's effigy to the Confessor's shrine and is a most elegant and accomplished piece of ironwork. The stamped scrolls are riveted to iron bars, and rosettes are attached to the lower edge of the frame. Many of the stamped designs used in his earlier works are found on the Eleanor grille but elements of the design also figured on a similar grille from St Denis, Paris, now lost.

A number of features in both the crosses and the effigy in fact recall contemporary French work. The cord-holding gesture for instance is found on a series of French royal effigies at St Denis. Precedents for the Eleanor crosses are found on the other side of the channel. Similar monuments were raised on each spot where the coffin of Philip Augustus rested on the way to his burial in 1223 (Erlande-Brandenburg 1968). These 'montjoies', each containing statues of the French king, were imitated when similar crosses were set up to mark the funeral procession which carried the bones of St Louis from Paris to St Denis. It has also been suggested by Colvin that 'the idea of the royal

27 The effigy of Queen Eleanor of Castile in Westminster Abbey. She wears a gown, kirtle and mantle, had long hair and is crowned; her left hand holds the cord of the gown and the right once carried a sceptre. Her head rests on two superimposed cushions, diapered with the arms of Castile. The crown and the edges of the garment have holes for added jewellery. Made by William Torel, goldsmith. (After Alexander and Binski.)

mausoleum round the Confessor's shrine in Westminster Abbey may have owed something to the example of St Louis'. The French king had commissioned in 1263–4 a series of 16 effigies of his ancestors in the abbey church of St Denis (Erlande-Brandenburg 1984). Mere imitation does not explain the power and glory of the Westminster monuments. They were the expression of Edward I's consciousness of dynastic greatness.

So far we have considered the commemoration of the queen in silent stone and metal. Much more impressive to contemporaries, and indeed to all who frequented the churches, chapels and abbeys concerned, was the generous provision made for the perpetual celebration of memorial services. A chantry was founded at Harby and a priest employed to sing masses for the queen's soul; another at Elynton; another at the house of the preaching friars in London where the queen's heart was deposited. The most grandiose arrangements were reserved for Westminster Abbey. Here Edward I made a princely gift of three Warwickshire manors, as well as lands in Essex, Kent and Buckinghamshire, to the abbot and convent (Harvey 1977, 31). The condition was that they should celebrate the anniversary of the queen's death every year on the eve of Saint Andrew the Apostle, singing Placebo and Dirige with nine lessons, one hundred wax candles weighing 12lb each being then burned round the tomb. All the bells were to be rung and convent was to sing solemnly for her soul's health. Eleanor's tomb became a place to visit, and pilgrims coming to the nearby shrine of St Edward could buy little leaden badges with the arms of Leon and Castile stamped on them (Mitchiner 1986). Such a splendid commemoration service and the accompanying weekly almsgiving continued for 250 years and ceased only at the Reformation.

Edward I

Edward I was taken mortally ill in 1307 at Burgh-on-Sands on his way to fight the Scots once more. One chronicler suggested that his last wish was for his flesh to be boiled away from his bones so that they could then be carried with the army on every expedition into Scotland. Another said that on his deathbed he enjoined the earls, who gathered round him, to send his heart to the Holy Land, attended by 140 knights. In fact, these wishes were ignored. His undutiful son, Edward, caused his father's body to be carried whole to Westminster Abbey and the king was interred in a plain Purbeck marble chest without effigy or ornament. The simple inscription was added in the sixteenth century: *Edwardus Primus Scottorum malleus hic est 1308* [the date should be 1307] *pactum serva* (RCHM 1924, 29). The tomb, as Dean Stanley points out, was not always so rude as it now appears. There are still traces of gilding on its black Purbeck sides and a massive canopy of wood overshadowed it. Moreover, regular and elaborate ceremonies were enacted round the tomb, involving the Exchequer in considerable expense to pay for the wax candles burning 'round the body of the lord Edward; formerly King of England, of famous memory'.

In 1774 the tomb was opened at the instigation of Daines Barrington, Vice President of the Society of Antiquaries, in the presence of the Dean, John Thomas, and a selected group of observers, including Richard Gough (Ayloffe 1786, 377–8). Contrary to expectation, the king's body was found to be almost intact; it was wrapped in a large waxed linen cloth, clothed in vestments, including a tunic of red silk damask, on which lay a stole decorated with gilt filigree quatrefoils adorned with transparent glass, between which a large quantity of small white beads was powdered. Over this was worn the royal mantle of rich crimson satin fastened on the left shoulder with a gilt ring-brooch ornamented with red and blue stones. The long shanks which gave him his surname were concealed in the cloth of gold. After only an hour the Dean insisted that the tomb be closed again without removing any of the contents. Unfortunately, a very inadequate visual record was made because Barrington had not thought it necessary to bring Basire (the Antiquaries' draughtsman); only Gough made 'rude sketches' which were afterwards worked up and leave most questions unanswered. Walpole's allegation that pitch was then poured in on the corpse to seal it from further violation is unfounded. Walpole was not even present, and in any case he had a 'frenzied irk' against the Society of Antiquaries at the time. What is sad is that the crown, sceptre and robes were all returned to the tomb and we thus lost sight of the most complete set of medieval regalia in the western world (Beard 1933, 188–93).

Edward II and Edward III

The deposed Edward II is thought to have been murdered in September 1327 at Berkeley Castle, Gloucestershire (Moore 1888, 215). Adam of Murimuth, a contemporary, wrote 'Although many abbots, priors, knights and burgesses of Bristol and Gloucester were summoned to inspect the body whole, and thus looked at it superficially, it was widely rumoured that the king had been cunningly killed'. This was done, allegedly, by the insertion of a plumber's soldering iron heated red hot, guided by a tube inserted into his bowels. On 21 December a solemn funeral was held for Edward at Gloucester Abbey, selected because it was the most important monastic house near Berkeley. In any case, the hostility of the Londoners to the régime of Isabella and Mortimer made a funeral at Westminster Abbey too dangerous. Isabella is said to have had the heart removed from the corpse and placed in a silver vase which was later buried in her own coffin, but this was seen as not an avowal of love but an admission of guilt and remorse. Edward III encouraged the glorious commemoration of his singularly unsaintly father for reasons of politics rather than filial piety. The Gloucester monks fabricated a story that the king's body was refused burial by several neighbouring monasteries, frightened of Mortimer's revenge. Whatever the

28 The effigy of Edward II in Gloucester Cathedral is of alabaster, and is London work of c.1330. The tomb chest is made of Purbeck marble with ogee-arched recesses. The canopy consists of two stages of ogee-headed arches with close cusping at the sides of the arches and is made of fine-grained oolite from the Cotswolds. (As seen in Sandford, F., Genealogical History of the Kings of England, 1707; Photograph: J. M. Steane.)

circumstances, it proved a remarkably good spiritual and economic investment for them; a cult grew up which partly financed a great rebuilding programme at Gloucester with pilgrims' offerings.

Traces of the pilgrims are seen in crosses cut into the surrounding stonework of the tomb, and into the bracket inserted into the side of the tomb chest to carry a golden chest presented by Edward III after his deliverance from a stormy sea crossing. The tomb has a richly carved Purbeck marble base articulated with ogee-headed niches divided by buttresses (Fig. 28). The effigy itself, the earliest important English example made from alabaster, was intended to emulate contemporary French royal effigies in marble. The whole is covered with towering tabernacles of complex plan shooting up to triple pinnacles, and gives the impression of a shrine rather than a tomb. The wooden coffin was opened in great secrecy for two hours on 2 October 1855 but not the leaden one which presumably contained a body. It has to be added, however, that some doubt remains as to whether this traditional account of Edward's death is the correct one. A letter written by an Italian cleric who held various English benefices between 1336 and 1343 alleges that Edward II escaped his tormentors and wandered round Europe after fleeing from Berkeley. He is supposed to have been buried in Saint Alberto de Butro (Cuttino and Lyman, 1978).

Edward III's funeral monument in Westminster Abbey is of particular interest, partly because of the magnificence of the design of the tomb and the recumbent effigy and the quality of their execution (Fig. 29). It is probably the best preserved of the medieval royal tombs. It can also claim to be an early attempt at portraiture. There is a strong likelihood that the head of the effigy was modelled on a death mask and that we can thus gaze on the face of the victor of Crécy. This was only realized when the royal funeral effigies were undergoing restoration after damage by water during the Second World War (Howgrave-Graham 1961, 160–1). Such funeral effigies were made specifically to be borne in the funeral procession. They were afterwards given to the Abbey and not very well stored or looked after by the monks. Edward's effigy, made by Stephen Hadley in 1377, is the earliest of those remaining. By 1949, the plaster head was in a terrible state: a considerable part of the nose and large areas of plaster about the head and the right side of the face had rotted completely. Stabilizing fluid was injected and cleaning fluid applied. The result was that under the dirt of centuries were revealed coloured cheeks, eyes, lips and a dark band of colour over the head, chin and sides of the face where there had been a wig, beard and whiskers. A curious asymmetry in the mouth and a dead, abnormal, flattened appearance above the left eye was noticed and attributed to the fact that the face might be a death mask. It is known that Edward had suffered a stroke a short time before his death which deprived him of speech and caused a down-drawn twist on the left side of the mouth. The head of the bronze effigy seems to have been closely modelled on this.

From those observations it is possible to outline the procedure followed on the death of a king from the fourteenth century onwards (Ariès 1981, 170). Once the monarch had expired, there was the urgent task of making a negative mould or death mask from the dead face up to a line well forward from the ears (Howgrave-Graham 1961, 162). While the effigy makers hastened on with their work, the body was opened and the viscera and other parts removed, often for independent burial elsewhere. After a short period of ceremonial exposure (the lying-in-state) the body was embalmed and cired (covered in wax) or enclosed in lead and coffined. The effigy was made of wood and straw, the death mask was fastened to it, provided with hair (in Edward's case the hair of a small brown dog was used for his eyebrows) and robed. It was laid on a bed of state with elaborate ceremonial, surrounded by burning candles and masses were chanted over it (Ariès 1981, 165–6). The coffin and the representation were carried with solemn pomp to the burial church where they lay in state

29 The tomb of Edward III in Westminster Abbey. The bronze effigy shows a heavily bearded king. The two sceptres the king is holding are missing. Below are Edward's children acting as 'weepers'; there are also enamelled shields of arms. Made by Stephen Hadley in 1377. (Photograph: RCHM England.)

accompanied with dirges, offerings and other rites. The 'weepers' or small figures of Edward's children are displayed on the sides of the tomb. The monks at Westminster then received the funeral effigy and the permanent tomb in stone and metal took over as the focus of commemoration.

The final use of the effigy was to provide a model for the maker of the tomb image; Stone reckons that of Edward III was probably the work of John of Liège (Stone 1955, 192). From an inspection of the underside of the Westminster royal effigies when they were cleaned prior to being returned to their places in the Abbey after the Second World War, much was learned of their method of manufacture. The casting technique of Edward III's effigy involved an original model in wax, clay or plaster built on a wooden framework. The whole figure was then covered with a plaster piece-mould. This, in turn, was covered with a plaster casing or 'mother-mould'. The sections of the piece-mould were taken off, piece by piece, and replaced in the 'mother-mould', allowing the original model to be set aside to be used if accidents happened. Varnish and grease were applied to the surface of the piece-mould and it was lined with wax; more wax was now pressed over to build up a sufficient thickness for reproduction in bronze, and lugs and strengthening pieces were fixed. Siliceous refractory material was used to build the under-half of the mould. The surface of the wax cast was now revealed by inverting the work and removing the mother-mould and the piece-mould. The sculptor was able to set about touching up the modelling of the effigy before the siliceous mould was constructed over it. The wax was now removed and the effigy cast in bronze. This was an expert piece of work in the case of Edward III's effigy; the metal is 12mm (½in) to 19mm (⅜in) thick and the head is about 9mm (¾in) thick. The hands were cast separately. Two things remained to be done: the surface was chased, filed and scraped and finally gilding amalgam was applied. The gold was between five and fifteen thousandths of an inch thick (Plenderleith and Maryon 1959).

The image lies on a stone tomb of Purbeck marble with six canopied niches on each long side for the figures of the 12 children of Edward III as 'weepers'. They are in attitudes of impassive calm and create a grand if rather cold mood. The enamelled shields, most of which survive, give a touch of polychrome heraldic magnificence. The king lies on top, a solemn figure with his hair and beard straight and ordered, echoed by the dignity and simplicity of the draperies, under an elaborately carved and fretted tester with cusped ogee arches, crocketed pinnacles and a rich ribbed vault.

Harmony within the royal family was unusual in the first half of Edward III's reign and this is mainly attributable to the tranquil personality of the king's wife, Philippa of Hainault. She prepared her tomb during her lifetime and employed a fellow-countryman, John de Liège, who had risen in reputation at the court of the French king Charles V. He received £133 6s 8d from the Exchequer in 1367 for the white marble effigy.

Philippa is portrayed as a woman of 50, with the stocky thickening figure of someone who had borne her husband 11 children in 15 years. She is shown with a reticulated head-dress, tight bodice laced in front, buttoned sleeves and a loose cloak. One hand is broken off and the other is mutilated. The head rests on a draped cushion formerly supported by angels, and the feet rested on two lions. The tomb itself is of dark marble overlaid with niches, with canopy work of white alabaster. These have nearly all been demolished on the south side but Sandford's engraving shows that below them was a row of heraldic shields. It seems that the niches formerly contained 30 statuettes of different personages connected with the queen by relationship or marriage. The end of the tomb, protected from vandals by the superimposed work of Henry V's chantry, has preserved two weepers with accompanying shields which show the quality of the work. Froissart states that on her deathbed she said to the king:

> *I ask that you will not choose any other sepulchre than mine, and that you lie by my side in the Abbey of Westminster.*

Richard II and Anne of Bohemia

On the death of his beloved queen, Anne of Bohemia, at the Manor of Sheen on 7 June 1394 Richard was grief-stricken. He ordered his Clerk of Works, John Gedney, to raze the

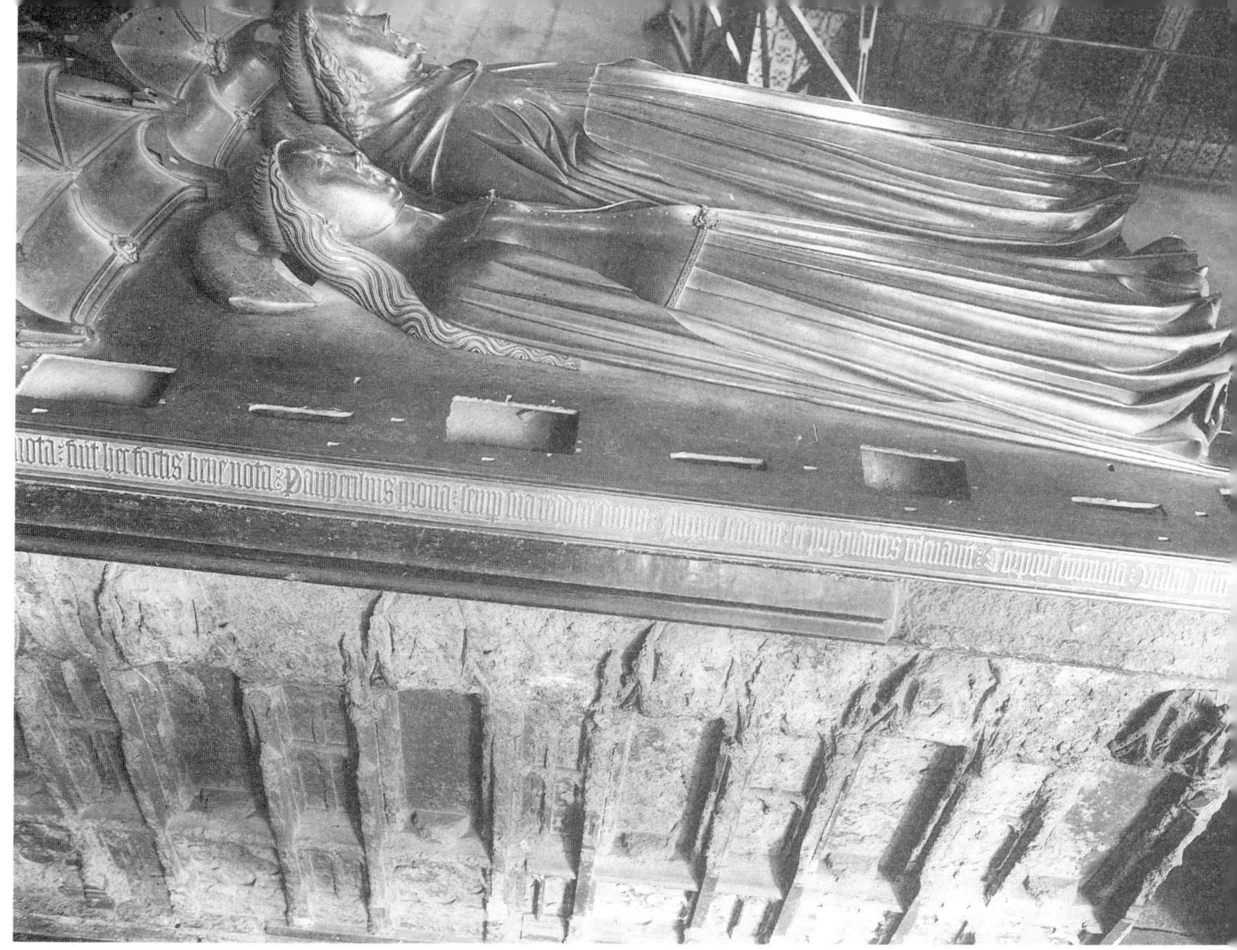

30 The tomb of Richard II and Anne of Bohemia in Westminster Abbey, made in 1394–5, the stone work by Henry Yevele and Stephen Lote, the effigies by Nicholas Broker and Godfrey Prest. The tomb-chest was of Purbeck marble. The gilded bronze plate, the pillows and the effigies have exquisite engraved decoration with fleurs-de-lis, lions, the white hart of Richard II, eagles, leopards, ostriches and broom-pods. (Photograph: RCHM England.)

manor to the ground, 'a romantically morbid gesture' (Colvin). When he came to create a suitable tomb he had, however, two motives in mind. He was determined to have a memorable monument made for both himself and his queen in Westminster Abbey. He was also clearly seeking to enhance his own regal dignity. The tomb was to be of the same height as that of Edward III. Both of them tower above the ambulatory, well out of the reach of the sacrilegious fingers of their subjects. Contracts survive with leading craftsmen for a marble tomb with gilt copper images of Richard and Anne. The Purbeck marble base of the tomb was to be fashioned by Henry Yevele and Stephen Lote according to a *patron* (pattern or design) already made by the masons and sealed by the Treasurer of England. Nicholas Broker and Godfrey Prest, 'citizens and coppersmiths of London', undertook to make gilt copper images of the king and queen 'lying on their backs, crowned, with their right hands joined, sceptres in their left hands and a ball and cross between them'. In addition, there were tabernacles at their heads, two lions at the king's feet, an eagle and a leopard at the queen's, 12 images of saints, eight more of angels and divers scutcheons of arms engraved and enamelled with their proper charges. The tomb remains, but stripped of all these appurtenances of royalty save the two effigies (Fig. 30).

The effigies were probably finished by March 1396, when the king stood the coppersmiths a drink. Richard's effigy was skilfully cast in bronze about 1cm ($\frac{2}{5}$in) thick with the head made separately. The craftsmen, however, had difficulties with Anne's effigy. When it was examined after the Second World War it was noticed that it was about 2.5cm (1in) thick and had evidently had to be recast in part with fresh metal being poured into the mould for the front of the body (Plenderleith and Maryon 1959). It is surprising that the king, interested as he was in aesthetic matters, passed work of such an unsatisfactory standard. Both effigies are powdered with the letters A and R and the badges or devices of the king and queen: the tree stock, sunburst, Plantagenet broom-pod and chained and couchant hart for Richard (Fig. 31), and knots and chained collared ostriches for Anne. The ostrich was a heraldic emblem of Bohemia. It stands erect, collared and chained, and the article in its beak is a nail, suggesting its fabulous powers of digestion, emblematic of the appetite of a valiant warrior for the cold iron of the battlefield (Nichols 1842, 321–59).

31 Details of pattern incised into the surface of the dress on the effigy of Richard II (see Fig. 30), showing sunburst behind cloud and white hart. (Photograph: Warburg Institute.)

The circumstances surrounding Richard II's death are obscure. He was last seen alive in his place of imprisonment after the deposition, Pontefract Castle. He may have been put to death or he may have starved himself to death. The tradition is that he died of violence (Jacob 1961, 27). His death was certainly convenient to the new regime in one sense: the abdication could be seen to have been followed by a vacancy to the throne. The council had Richard's body conveyed to London and put it on public exhibition at various places where the funeral cortège stopped. The body lay for two days in St Paul's where Henry Bolingbroke attended a solemn service and even acted as a pall-bearer. It was then quietly removed to King's Langley (Hertfordshire) where it was handed over to the Black Friars, the late king's confessors, and was buried. There it remained until 1413 when Henry V, perhaps remembering personal kindnesses he had received at the hands of the dead king, and conscious certainly of a need to mollify Richard's supporters, had the body reinterred in the magnificent tomb Richard had prepared for himself and his first wife in Westminster Abbey.

The questions arise: are the effigies portraits or heavily idealized representations of their subjects? They show the king and queen holding hands, evidently united in death as in life. Richard is portrayed with a beard and moustache, a fashion he apparently affected from *c.*1386 onwards (Whittingham 1971). The unfortunate king's weakness but also artistic sensibility are recalled by the haunting oval face with its narrow lidded eyes. A closer portrait of Anne is to be found in the wooden head now in the undercroft museum at Westminster, the only surviving piece of the royal effigy. Its condition before cleaning and restoration was deplorable; it was nearly black, with only a dim suggestion of eyes, the base of the lost nose was splintered and spongy. The hair appears to have been dark brown. The proportions, however, are more likely to be correct than those of the effigy, where the heads are cast oversize and the figures are too short. The plundered state of the tomb of Richard II and Anne of Bohemia belies the fact that it was the most costly of the fourteenth-century royal tombs – the total bill coming to £933 6s 8d.

Two attempts were made, in the eighteenth and nineteenth centuries, to undertake physical examinations of what lay inside the tomb (Stanley 1880, 309–27). The first was a disgraceful affair, an irregular investigation which the antiquaries involved made by thrusting their hands through the vacant holes in the side of the tomb and pulling the royal bones about. The Dean of the day put a stop to it and closed the holes which had resulted from the removal of metal shields by earlier souvenir hunters.

The second, performed in Dean Stanley's time, was more systematic but not a great deal more informative. On looking in, there was seen on the floor the broken and rotten boards of coffins, and bones, apparently in great disorder, especially two skulls which lay towards the foot of the grave. The bones proved to be those of a man and a woman. The skull of the king 'agrees with his well known character, and with the general appearance of his portrait in the Abbey . . . there is no mark of the battle axe on the skull'. It was noted that the volume of the brain cavity was rather small. A number of objects included a wooden staff, a pair of scallop-edged brown leather riding gloves, a double rose in lead, fragments of a silk pall and some small twigs. Similar twigs had been found on opening Henry IV's tomb at Canterbury Cathedral and were thought to be of magical significance. Some of the artifacts were clearly the result of visitors inserting them through the five holes – these include marbles, knives and copper coins. On the boarding of the ceiling above the tomb were several considerable droppings of wax from the wax lights which had formerly been placed above the tomb, and several of the boards where charred. The surprising find was a pair of plumber's shears with a trade-stamp of the Plantagenet fleur-de-lis – which is likely to have been left by the plumber who assisted in the interment of 1413, sealing the lead coffin.

Henry IV and Joan of Navarre

Henry usurped the throne at the age of 33; he arrived with a reputation for athletic prowess and boundless energy, a man who had distinguished himself in the formalized aggressions of the tournament, and had travelled widely as a pilgrim, crusader and political exile. He died after a succession of chronic and debilitating illnesses at the age of 46. It used to be thought that he was struck down by leprosy, an indication of divine anger at his execution of Archbishop Scrope of York, which turned out to have been a political error of the greatest magnitude. A modern study reckons that it is more likely that he was carried off by a circulatory complaint such as coronary heart disease, precipitated by stress (McNiven 1985, 767). There are several stories about the circumstances of his death. During his last illness he lay in the Jerusalem Chamber, part of the abbot's lodgings at Westminster Abbey. Stothard relates that a marked characteristic of his ruling passion appeared 'in his desiring the crown so indirectly gained to be placed on a pillow at his bed's head. He clung to the splendid bauble with the fondness of a child for a favourite toy'. In his will he sought a burial in Canterbury Cathedral; proximity to the powerful intercession of the bones of St Thomas Becket and a lack of enthusiasm for mingling with the usurped regalities of his Plantagenet predecessors perhaps explain this. Another tale states that while his body was being conveyed from Westminster towards Canterbury down the Thames estuary, a violent storm arose which was only allayed when the crew cast the royal corpse into the waters. It was alleged that a chest covered with a cloth of gold was buried in place of the king.

The archaeological investigation carried out in Canterbury Cathedral on 21 August 1832 revealed that in truth the king lay within. The workmen sawed through the lid of the coffin. 'Immediately under this elm board was a quantity of haybands filling the coffin and upon the surface of them lay a very rude small cross, formed by merely tying twigs together . . . under was a leaden case or coffin moulded in some degree to the shape of a human figure.' They next cut through layers of leather wrappers, 'when, to the astonishment of all present, the face of the deceased king was seen in complete preservation. The nose elevated, the cartilage even remaining, though on the admission of the air, it sank rapidly away and had entirely disappeared before the examination was finished. The skin of the chin was entirely of the consistence and thickness of the upper leather of a shoe, brown and moist; the beard thick and matted and of a deep russet colour.'

Unfortunately, at this point the investigation was terminated. Curiosity seems to have been overwhelmed by a sense of guilt at the profanity.

The monument over the grave lies on the west side of the Trinity Chapel in which stood the shrine of Thomas Becket. It was opposite the monument of the Black Prince. The design is similar to those of Edward III and Richard II but the craftsmen (who may have come from London) are unknown in name. The chief unusual feature is that the material is alabaster, painted and gilded. The effigies of the king and queen are crowned, robed and formerly bore in their hands sceptres, the other symbols of royalty, now broken away. Henry IV's widow, Joan of Navarre, had spent an adventurous period as Queen dowager during her son's reign, being accused of witchcraft and suffering imprisonment for a time before returning to favour at court. She died in 1437. The queen has round her neck a collar of SS, an ornament repeated on other parts of the tomb. This is thought to be an abbreviation of the king's favourite motto 'soverayne'. An inscription including this word, with an eagle surmounted by a crown adorns the cornice round the canopy of the tomb.

Henry V

Before departing on the expedition which was to lead to his victory at Agincourt, Henry V made arrangements in his will for burial at Westminster. In fact, he did not die in battle but lived a further seven years, successfully conquering France before succumbing to dysentery at Vincennes in 1422. His servants, recognizing the contagious nature of his disease, refused to go near him. He died in the heat of August, so rapid action was required to prevent decomposition. His entrails were removed and placed in a lead pot which his retainers at Vincennes took to the great abbey nearby at Saint Maur des Fosses; here the liquid was poured into the holy ground of the cemetery and the pot buried under the church. In June 1989, *The Times* newspaper reported that local archaeologists had found the vessel and the tissue in the contents was about to be scientifically examined for traces of dysentery. Permission from the authorities at Westminster was to be sought to obtain matching tissues from Henry V's grave.

Both Paris and Rouen had offered large sums of money for the privilege of burying him, but his known preference for Westminster prevailed and the most sumptuous funeral arrangements were made. The eviscerated body was boiled in aromatics, put in a lead coffin and brought back to England via Paris where a solemn service was held. A long procession then accompanied the body of the king through Rouen to Calais and from Dover to London. This was headed by James I, King of Scots, as chief mourner, and followed by Henry's widow, Catherine of Valois. At each stage, at Canterbury, Ospringe (the royal hospital), Rochester and Dartford, funeral services were celebrated. The chronicler Walsingham describes the cortège: 'an image very like in stature and face to the dead king, arrayed in a long and ample purple mantle furred with ermine, a sceptre in one hand, and a round gold ball infixed in the other; with a gold crown on the head over the royal cap and the royal sandals on his feet.' The obsequies were performed in the presence of Parliament, first at St Paul's, and then at the Abbey.

On arrival at the Abbey the doors of the church were flung open and the procession entered, the chariot with the coffin, followed by the mourners, being drawn by four horses up the new nave, now nearly completed by the munificence of the dead king, to the entrance to the choir. The coffin was then deposited on a temporary hearse railed in by barriers covered with black cloth, and 60 poor men with great wax torches stood round about it. The horses, their trappings, four saddles, a sword, 'cote armour', banners and the ornaments of the boiled leather representation of the king were all handed over to the sacrist. In this way, on 7 November 1422, the body of the Conqueror of France was interred with all pomp and ceremony.

A place was made for the tomb and chantry chapel of Henry V by removing the relics previously housed to the east of the shrine of St Edward the Confessor. The tomb platform is of Caen stone lined with Purbeck marble, and the tomb itself has a series of recesses on its long sides. On the top lies the oak bed and figure of the king's effigy. This consists of a narrow frame of oak board about an 2.5cm (1in) thick carrying a deep and solid block of oak 12.5cm

(5in) thick with a plain chamfered edge probably for a long rhyming inscription such as that on the tomb of Edward Prince of Wales at Canterbury. The core of the effigy is a solid block of oak. The head and the hands are lost but were probably originally separate castings, as no doubt were the sceptres held in the same position as on Edward III's tomb. Recently, resin replacements have been fixed. The king is in the gown, hooded tippet and mantle that formed the parliamentary robes. This woodwork was entirely covered by a close fitting suit of silver-gilt plates. As Colvin notes, the executors of the king had reverted to thirteenth-century practice by commissioning an effigy consisting of a wooden core plated with silver gilt rather than one cast of more solid and lasting metal. As early as 1467, thieves had made off with some of the ornaments and the remainder were robbed one January night in 1546.

Henry V had also ordered a separate chantry to be erected where masses might be offered up for his soul's health for ever (St John Hope 1914). This remarkable structure was planned to stand over the tomb at a higher level, spanning the ambulatory with a bridge; access was by two spiral staircases rising from the east end of the Confessor's chapel. The master mason was John Thirsk, who had been responsible for the rebuilding of the nave of the Abbey since 1420–1. Materials were assembled in 1438 and it took some years to build, judging from the complexity of the structure and elaboration of the decoration. The latter includes tier upon tier of statues under triple-canopied niches, narrative reliefs of the coronation and the king in battle, and heraldic devices. Crowning the whole structure was an upper chapel with cupboards for relics and an altar where the officiating priest could be seen high up by people down below in the Abbey. As Stanley says, 'it towers above the Plantagenet graves beneath, as his empire towered above their kingdom'. Aloft on a beam, as above the Black Prince's tomb, were hung the soldier-king's accoutrements, his large emblazoned shield, his saddle and his helmet. They have been taken down now and lodged in the undercroft museum. Replicas, as at Canterbury, should be placed there to recall the brilliant military exploits of the victor of Agincourt.

Henry VI

This inept, devout and unfortunate king appears to have pondered deeply the location and nature of his sepulture. In the reign of Henry VII there were still alive old officers and workmen of Westminster Abbey who could remember the numerous visits paid by the king to the Abbey at all hours of the day and night to fix the place of his burial. On one occasion he climbed the steps to the chantry of his father and spent an hour surveying the whole chapel. He eventually made up his mind: the master mason of the Abbey, John Thirsk by name, was summoned, and took an iron instrument and traced the circuit of the grave on the pavement. The monument was ordered, but nothing was done 'because of the grete trouble that then dyd folowe'. These great troubles included his alleged murder in the Tower on 21 May 1471.

According to John Warkworth, the chronicler, 'he was chestyde and brought to Paulys and his face was opyne that every manne myghte see hyme; and hys lyinge he bledde on the pament there, and afterward at the Blake Fryres was broughte and ther he blede new and fresche'. He was then taken by boat and buried without much ceremony at Chertsey Abbey. Richard III, hearing that miracles were being done, had the body transferred to Windsor where it was honourably buried. Despite Henry VII's expressed intention of removing it to Westminster (against the strenuous opposition of the canons of Windsor and the Abbot of Chertsey) it remains at Windsor to the south of the high altar. An archaeological investigation was mounted on 4 November 1910 (St John Hope 1911) and the rotted remains of a tapering coffin were found within a brick-lined grave, 2.25m (7ft 5½in) to 1.04m (3ft 5½in) (at head) and 1m (3ft 2in) at the foot. Within the coffin was a lead chest which was cut open. The remains inside appeared to be those of a man about the king's age, and belonged to someone who might have died a violent death judging by some blood-clotted hair. The care with which the bones had been gathered and enclosed in a leaden chest deposited in a place of honour suggests that they were those of a person of some importance. It is possible that they were placed in a full-sized coffin in order to support the reputation of the incorruptibility of the body, in line with attempts by contemporaries to see Henry as a saint and martyr.

Edward IV

Fotheringhay Church (Northamptonshire) takes its place alongside Westminster Abbey and St George's Chapel, Windsor, as one of the great mausolea of the families which ruled medieval England. In 1377 Edward III had given the manor and castle of this piece of Midland England to his youngest son Edmund Langley. Here the college of the Annunciation of the Blessed Virgin Mary and All Saints was founded by Edmund Langley first duke of York. When Edward, second duke of York perished at Agincourt, his body was taken to the collegiate church for burial. Richard Plantagenet, third duke and father of Edward IV, slain at Wakefield in 1460, is also buried in the sanctuary, as is his wife, Cecily who died in 1495. The two Renaissance monuments were raised in pious memory of her ancestors by Queen Elizabeth I. The fourth duke of York became King Edward IV and he donated the chalice-shaped pulpit decorated with the royal shield of arms. The church dominates the landscape rising like a galleon at sea, over the flat meadows next to the river Nene. It is one enormous lantern with huge perpendicular windows filling the wall space. Although shorn of its choir it is still a magnificent fragment recalling Yorkist glories.

Edward IV died at Westminster in April 1483 and his funeral was celebrated in St Stephen's chapel and in the Abbey. A detailed description has come down to us: 'First the corps was laide upon a burde, all naked saving he was covered from the navyll to the kneys.' This was to enable 'the lords spiritual and temporal then being in London or nere thereabout' to view the body. 'And then he was sered and so brought into the chapell on the morne after, where was songen thre solempne masses.' When the corpse was borne into the Abbey it was accompanied by an effigy. 'And in that herse about the corps and the clothe of gold above said there was a personage like to the similitude of the king in habet royall, crowned with the crown oon his hede, holding in the one hand a septur and in the other hand a ball of silver and gilt with a crosse patte.' (Gairdner 1861, 3–10.)

The King had, nevertheless, in the will drawn up in 1475, already made it clear that he wished to be buried at Windsor. Here, in the vast St George's chapel whose building he had furthered so impressively, he ordered his tomb to be prepared with pharaonic thoroughness. His body was to be placed beneath a stone 'wroght with the figure of Dethe with Schochyns of oure Armes and writings convenient aboute the bordures of the same remembring the day and yere of our decease, and that in the same place or nere to an Autre bee made metely for the tome as herafter we shall devise and declare.' It was to be a two-staged tomb because in addition to the cadaver or *memento mori* there was to be 'a vaulte of convenient height . . . and . . . upon the said vaulte . . . a Chapell or a Closet with an Autre convenient and a tumbe to bee made and sett there and upon the same Tumbe an Image for oure figure, which figure we will bee of silver and gilte or at the lest coopre and gilt.' He evidently had in mind an effigy to rival his predecessors' at Westminster but brought up to date with figures of death, a late medieval obsession. Thirty-three casks of touchstone, black marble found in the Low Countries, were shipped to London. Edward's body was interred in the vault he had prepared but the two-tiered tomb was never completed. A pair of iron gates, designed originally to separate the vault with its chapel above from the choir, were made by the principal smith, John Tresillian, who worked on the chapel from 1477 onwards at the high rate of 10d a day. We hear of 'a great anvile' made by Tresillian and subsequently sent to Windsor. The result was a pair of superb iron gates suspended from openwork Gothic towers, also fashioned in iron. They have now been moved to the north side of the Presbytery.

The reasons for Edward's desire to replace Westminster by Windsor as a royal mausoleum are open to speculation. The first and most obvious is that there was literally no more room in the Confessor's chapel; Henry V had taken the last available space and Henry VI was hard put to find room. Henry VII solved the problem by building his great chapel on to the east end of the Abbey, but in the meantime, Edward IV had constructed his own sumptuous chapel at Windsor. Westminster, too, had unfortunate memories, the sanctuary there having sheltered his wife and children during the Wars of the Roses. It may be that the Yorkists preferred to distance themselves from their Lancastrian rivals and to set up a new power base. Certainly, Windsor from now on was an alternative. The only Yorkist buried in the Abbey was little Margaret, a child of nine months who was laid in the altar end, afore St Edward's shrine.

The princes in the Tower

In the north aisle of Henry VII's chapel at Westminster there is a white marble monument supporting an urn or sarcophagus, designed by Sir Christopher Wren, and made to contain certain bones found in the Tower of London in 1674. These, King Charles II was convinced, 'by the most certain indications', were those of the Princes murdered in the Tower: Edward V and his brother Richard, Duke of York, the sons of Edward IV and Elizabeth Woodville. In view of the considerable mystery surrounding the deaths of the princes, it was decided in 1933 to open the urn and to subject the bones to scientific examination (Tanner and Wright 1935, 1–26). Wright came to the conclusion that they belonged to two human beings and were the bones of children differing some two to three years in age. The eldest child was still at the age of puberty since the elements forming the sockets of shoulder and hip joints showed no signs of fusion. The study of the teeth indicated that the younger of the children was about ten years old and the older child between the ages of twelve and thirteen. There was some evidence for consanguinity (the presence of Wormian bones of unusual size and of almost identical shape in the lambdoid sutures of both the crania), also for tooth suppression in both children. The elder had extensive disease affecting almost equally both sides of the lower jaw, originating in or around the molar teeth. This would have affected the general health of the little prince (if the bones are of the princes). Wright further noticed a large red stain reaching from below the orbits to the angles of the lower jaw. He thought that this lent support to the traditional account of the brothers' death, suffocated under a feather bed and pillows 'kept down by force hard unto their mouths'. Wright suggested that the bodies had been placed in the elm chest in which they were found; it appeared that Edward, the elder, lay at the bottom, on his back with a slight tilt to his left, with Richard above him face to face. There was much more of Edward's skeleton present than Richard's. Presumably, lying deeper, it was less disturbed.

There are a number of problems with the evidence, not taken account of by Wright (White 1959, 32–9). There is no proof that the bones placed in the marble urn in 1678 were identical with those dug out in 1674. Some of the bones, in any case, were given away. There is no mention at the time of any bones of animals or birds and yet when the urn was opened in 1933, a large variety, including fish, duck, chicken, rabbit, sheep, pig and ox were found. White came to the conclusion that a number of the original bones, including those appropriated by Ashmole, were given away or sold as relics. When these bones were called for to be interred in the Abbey, the persons in whose charge they were, hurriedly collected any bones they could lay their hands on. On submitting the Wright report to further experts 20 years later, it was adjudged that it was impossible to determine the sex of the children. Also, the theory of the stain being the result of suffocation was rejected. Further, the ages of the children were thought to be too precisely determined. On the other hand, it must be admitted that it would have been a remarkable coincidence if two other boys of the same age had been buried in the Tower; also, according to the circumstantial evidence of Moore, the bodies of the two princes were buried at the foot of a staircase in the Tower, 'at the stayre foote, metely depe in the grounde under a great heape of stones'.

The evidence of the bones is important because if it is accepted that they are likely to be those of the princes, their age becomes crucial to the questions of when they were murdered and by whom. There are two serious reasons for considering that Richard III was the likely murderer. The disappearance of the boys while they were in his care seems unquestioned. Following the execution of Hastings after they had been seen 'shooting and playing in the garden of the Tower', they were 'holden more straight'. Mancini stated that the two princes were withdrawn into the inner apartments of the Tower proper and were seen more rarely behind bars and windows until eventually they ceased to be seen altogether. Also, Richard III had every reason for regarding the boys as a threat to his safety even after he had persuaded Parliament to bastardize them. If we accept the evidence of their age and the identification of the bones, it certainly points towards the responsibility for the murders being Richard III's. On the other hand, it is odd that when Henry Tudor seized the crown, the Act of Parliament attainting Richard III which he caused Parliament to pass made no mention of the princes. The relations between the boys' mother, Elizabeth Woodville, and Richard III seem to have been friendly. Richard at first allowed the boys' sisters to live with their mother and put no restraint on their freedom. The obvious explanation is that the girls were no threat to their uncle so long as the brothers were alive. Henry VII, on the other hand, had every reason for liquidating them. He proposed to unite the crowns of Lancaster and York. He obtained an Act repealing Richard's which had bastardized Edward IV's children. Only by so doing, and by killing the sons, could he make Elizabeth represent the house of York. It is not surprising that a number of historians have concluded that the whole matter is not proven.

Richard III

Three things are noteworthy about the death and burial of Richard III. In the first place he was vanquished in battle and literally lost the crown on the battlefield of Bosworth. The story goes that it was found hanging on a hawthorn bush by the turncoat Lord Stanley, who presented it to the victorious Henry Tudor. Sandford describes how it was set upon the triumphant head of King Henry as he kneeled down and gave God thanks for the victory, whereupon they all cried again, 'King Henry, King Henry'. Secondly, the death of Richard was advertised by his being stripped naked, thrown across a horse and carried to Leicester. Here at the Newarke, within the precincts of the Lancastrian collegiate foundation of the Annunciation of Our Lady, it was exposed to the gaze of the populace. No Yorkist sympathizers could doubt that the former ruler had been slain (Baldwin 1986, 21). Thirdly, the actual place of burial is uncertain. The Grey Friars were charged with the responsibility and in Polydore Vergils' words

> *buryed two days after without any pompe of solmne funerall in th abbay of monks Franciscanes at Leicester.*

Henry VII in 1495 arranged for a Nottingham alabasterman, Walter Hylton, to build a memorial over the grave for £50. At this date such a sum would have been sufficient to buy a full-scale three-dimensional alabaster effigy. Holinshed records in 1577 that it incorporated 'a picture of alabaster representing his [Richard's] person', but it is unclear whether it took the form of a recumbent effigy or was incised on the tomb slab. It was unfortunately defaced at the dissolution of the Friary by Henry VIII and by the eighteenth century Sandford graphically describes

> *his grave overgrown with weeds and nettles . . . very obscure and not to be found, only the stone coffin, wherein his corpse lay was made a drinking trough for horses at a common inn.*

This tale is discounted by Baldwin who considers that it is most unlikely that such a coffin ever formed part of King Richard's tomb. He thinks that the grave lies beneath the northern (St Martin's) end of Grey Friars Street, or the buildings that face it on either side. In fact, King Richard still probably lies in the place of honour, among the foundations of the long-vanished choir.

Henry VII and Henry VIII

Henry VII was an obsessive note-taker.

> *He was a prince, sad, serious, and full of thoughts and secret observation, and full of notes and memories of his own hand, especially touching persons.*

So says Bacon (Longford 1989, 206). It is not surprising that such a systematic man made detailed arrangements for the funerals and commemoration of his wife and himself. His wife, Elizabeth of York, had predeceased him, dying in the Tower on 11 February 1502/3. Services were conducted by bishops on three successive days, and on the tenth a chariot drawn by six horses draped in black velvet drew the corpse to Westminster Abbey. A funeral effigy was a prominent part of the obsequies. It was recorded as follows:

> *a ymage of personage lyke a quene/ clothed in ye very robes of estate of ye quene having her very ryche crowne on her hed here about her shoulder/hir scepter in her right hand/and her fyngers well garneshed wt ryngs of golde and prsyous stones and on every end of ye chayne on ye cofres kneled a gentleman hussher by all the way to Westminster.*

We are told that the corpse was censed, taken from the chariot together with the effigy and the banners of Our Lady, and 'with great folk bearing them these were wt the procession convey'd to the herce'.

When the remains of the royal effigies at Westminster were examined after the Second World War a number of points of interest with regard to that of Elizabeth of York emerged. The head and bust, although nearly black and damaged (the nose was missing and the boards split), were recognizably the same as mentioned in the accounts as 'Twy waynscotts called Regall' (boards of soft wood imported from the Baltic, hence called Riga boards). Also the hand was found to be made of pear wood doubtless what was referred to as 'a pece of peretre tymbre . . . 8d'. The arm is the first example known of a movable joint to facilitate dressing the effigy. When the filthy textile adhering to the bust was cleaned it was found to be a piece of splendid gold satin. The face itself had been described as having 'a pleasant and slightly roguish, or boy-like air' (Howgrave-Graham 1964, 165–9).

On 22 April 1509, Henry VII lay dead in Richmond Palace, killed by the consumption which had already carried off his eldest son, Arthur (Scarisbrick 1988, 7).

On Wednesday 9 May the old king's embalmed body was drawn by chariot to St Paul's, where John Fisher preached a funeral oration:

> *His politic wisdom in governance was singular, his wit always quick and ready, his reason pithy and substantial, his memory fresh and holding . . .*

The splendour of Henry VII's funeral impressed contemporaries. It included an effigy referred to as 'the king's Pyctour' which cost £6 12s 8d to make, apart from the robes. Parts of this survived Second World War damage but it was found that the body had entirely disintegrated into a confused mass of plaster, canvas, hay and wood. The hay was analysed and twelve plants were sorted, including spring clover blossom, autumn vetch pods in seed, with fragments of bedding straw, all evidently derived from fodder via the royal stables.

The head, on the other hand. although decayed, could be plausibly reconstructed with the help of a new nose, the dimensions of which were taken from a fine Italian terracotta portrait head in the Victoria and Albert Museum. The face was a uniform dark grey; possibly the colour of the dead face of the king was intended. Henry VII had abundant hair, if Torrigiano's image can be believed; the effigy had a mixture of bright red and grey human hair. A suggestion that it may have come from the king's head seems far-fetched (Howgrave-Graham 1961, 167).

Henry VII's chapel at Westminster was designed from the first to be a mausoleum for the king and his successors. His will directed that his tomb as well as the 'Grate in manner of a closure' was to be 'in the myddes of the same chappell before the high altir in such a distaunce from the same as is ordered in the plot made for the same chapell and signed with our hande'. The layout of the chapel and the design of the tomb went through a complicated series of alterations. To begin with the chevet or apse was designed to hold the shrine of Henry VI after his canonization. It was Henry VIII's decision to put his father and mother *behind* the high altar, an unusual position for the founder of a chapel. Possibly Henry VIII, as Westlake suggests, intended to appropriate the place of honour before the altar for himself. In the meantime the 'grate' or 'closure of coper and gilte' had been manufactured. It was wholly Gothic in style and is in appearance

> *a little building of brass with open work lattices, traceries and brattishing, with turret-like projections at the corners, all the details sharp and vivid.* (Lethaby)

The first design for the tomb was for one of white marble with only the base of black touchstone. There were to be 19 images: two recumbent (for the king and queen), one kneeling (of the king), a feature which suggests the monuments of the French kings of St Denis, four lords, also kneeling, and 12 'small images' placed round the chest in the traditional manner. This tomb, however, never came to anything and in October 1512 the task was entrusted to Pietro Torrigiano, a Florentine who trained with Michelangelo in the studio of Ghirlandaio. The result was a tomb which Lord Bacon called 'the stateliest and daintiest in Europe' (Fig. 32). It consisted of a chest of black touch-stone on which were recumbent effigies in gilt bronze of the king and queen. The sides were ornamented by niches containing copper-gilt statues of the king's 'avowries' or patron saints. Torrigiano arranged these in pairs surrounded by wreaths carved out of black marble and separated by pilasters of gilded bronze elaborately ornamented with foliage. At the north and south ends are heraldic supporters and devices including a large rose supported by a greyhound and a dragon in high relief. The shield of arms is supported by naked putti. The most original feature of the design is that at each corner, as if suspended in a supernatural fashion, are Renaissance angels with their backs turned on the king and queen but serving to proclaim their royal honour to the world. The gilded bronze recumbent effigies with grand and simple robes have faces and hands which demonstrate an astonishing perfection of modelling. This is one of the earliest Renaissance-style monuments in England and it was to have a profound effect on subsequent royal tomb design.

32 *Tomb of Henry VII and Elizabeth of York in Westminster Abbey, made by Torrigiano, a pupil of Ghirlandaio. The tomb chest with recumbent effigies is in the late English medieval tradition but is in fact a classical sarcophagus; instead of angels or weepers it has putti. The monument is of black and white marble; the figures, of bronze gilt, combine a tender life-likeness with supreme grace of modelling.* (Photograph: RCHM England.)

Henry VIII's increasingly ill health during the last decade of his life has been the subject of numerous medical studies published over the last hundred years. In 1888 A. S. Currie suggested that his sufferings were attributable to syphilis and that the unfortunate obstetric experiences of Catherine of Aragon and Anne Boleyn could have been caused by this disease. In the 1930s it was pointed out in a book published by Frederick Chamberlin that Henry's remarkable and long-lived athleticism (hunting, tennis, jousting) was not the mark of a man whose health was undermined by this sexually transmitted and crippling disease. Moreover, his offspring showed no sign of it. Nor had those great gossip-mongers, foreign ambassadors, breathed a word (Deer, 1989). Still, Henry's well-documented swollen ulcerated legs, a deformed nose, bloated body, frequent colds, constipation, lethargy, forgetfulness, unpredictable mood swings, which could turn him at times into an irascible tyrant, all required explanation. A fresh attempt has led these symptoms to be identified as the classic signs of scurvy caused by massive dietary deficiency (Kybett 1989). Certainly a regime of high protein meals consisting almost exclusively of about five parts beef, two parts venison and the remainder substantially alcohol was harmful enough to produce these effects; red meat such as beef contains almost no B1 and B2 vitamins, very little vitamin A or calcium and no vitamin C. Henry, moreover, followed the best (ill-informed) medical advice of the day and eschewed vegetable, fruit and dairy produce.

Constant ill health plus an inflated idea of his own glory fostered Henry's obsessional interest in creating his own tomb, fitting in its magnificence, during his own life-time. A monument for Henry VIII and his first queen, Catherine of Aragon, was first mooted in 1529, when Torrigiano was indentured to complete it within four years for a payment of £2000. It was to be of white marble and black touchstone like Henry VII's monument but (characteristic of Henry) 'more grettir by the 1111th parte'. The temperamental Italian (who had the distinction of having punched Michelangelo on the nose) baulked at completing the king's project and it was soon eclipsed (as in building matters generally) by a scheme for a tomb of preposterous glory for Cardinal Wolsey. This was modelled by another Italian, Benedetto da Rovezzano, and on the cardinal's fall the materials came into the possession of the king who commandeered them for his own tomb (Colvin, Ransome, Summerson 1975, 219–22). Henry discarded Wolsey's effigy, declined to answer the disgraced prelate's plea to return it to him at York, threw out the cardinalate insignia, and set Benedetto to fashion his own monument during the 1530s. Wolsey's tomb was raised on a podium about 1.52m (5ft) high made of marble or touchstone; a sword, sceptre and two orbs were substituted for the hat, cross and pillars carried by kneeling angels; royal arms were held by pairs of boys at each end, four original corner pillars were replaced by eight or ten taller pillars, and many tall candlesticks were inserted between the pillars. The king's effigy was to be of bronze and gilded. A bronze screen was to surround the whole (St John Hope 1909, 482–3).

By 1546, when the king made his will, the tomb was said to be 'well onward', and was to be erected in the choir of St George's Chapel, Windsor. In the meantime it was under construction in a house belonging to the dean and chapter of Westminster with a third Italian, Nicholas of Modena, working away on it. The tomb was still not finished, however, and Edward VI, in his will, desired his father's tomb to be 'made up'. But the project hung fire. Mary took no action, perhaps an indication of her embarrassment at being sired by a schismatic heretic. Elizabeth hummed and hawed, encouraged surveys to be made by honorific old courtiers like the Marquis of Winchester and then quietly dropped what had become an exceedingly expensive drain on the royal revenues. It was said that over £60,000 had been lavished on it to that date (St John Hope 1913, 484). Apart from the monument being dismantled and taken from Westminster to Windsor nothing further was done, and it remained incomplete in the 'tomb house' at Windsor until the Civil War. Parliament in 1646 ordered the metalwork to be sold, which is how the church of S. Bavon, Ghent, acquired four magnificent bronze candlesticks; a cast of one is in the Victoria and Albert Museum. The marble sarcophagus and its pedestal lasted on *in situ* ultimately to become part of the monument to Lord Nelson, in the crypt of St Paul's Cathedral (Colvin, Ransome and Summerson 1975, 320–2).

CHAPTER THREE
Royal accommodation

The world-wide journeys of the present royal family in which they perform valuable diplomatic and political roles by representing the United Kingdom overseas and by symbolizing the unity of the Commonwealth are descendants of a long tradition of a peregrinatory monarchy. The Norman and Angevin kings of England and parts of France spent their lives on the move, incessantly travelling from one part of their dominions to another. Perhaps 'procession' or 'progress' are better words to use than 'travels'. Such movement was dictated by various circumstances. The problems of supplying a court numbering several hundred persons which quickly ate its way through food rents stockpiled from royal manors might be eased by keeping on the road. It was a vital political requirement for the king to present himself in person at frequent intervals on both sides of the Channel. Only in this way could he impress his will and display his aura at a time when government was at a relatively personal and primitive level.

We are told by the Anglo-Saxon Chronicler that William the Conqueror wore his crown whenever he was in England; at Easter at Winchester; at Whitsuntide at Westminster; at Christmas at Gloucester. On these occasions all the great men of England were assembled about him: archbishops, bishops, abbots, earls, thanes and knights. The practice was carried on by William II and Henry I. Biddle's recent study shows that despite William of Malmesbury's statement to the contrary, such crown wearings continued to be celebrated well into the twelfth century (Biddle 1986, 57). Mobility was also thrust upon the monarch when he played a spiritual role. The royal itinerary was punctuated by liturgical solemnities. The king as a major patron of religious houses found himself frequently attending church dedications and witnessing the translation of saintly relics. Some kings showed great enthusiasm for pilgrimages, which could add considerably to the mileage undertaken in travelling.

One would have thought that English medieval kings would have sought relaxation and repose after such a rackety life. Not a bit of it. Three favourite occupations, jousting, hunting and hawking, involved constant moving about, and demanded widely dispersed accommodation. Whatever other qualities the job demanded, effective monarchy required resources of restless energy which would have worn out lesser men.

Palaces of the Anglo-Norman kings at Winchester, Gloucester and Westminster

The Norman conquerors took over from their Anglo-Saxon predecessors a stock of palaces and houses which they rapidly adapted and adjusted to their needs. Winchester remained in high repute as the ancient capital of Wessex, the location for the shrine of St Swithin and the traditional place of the treasury of the late Saxon monarchy. The old palace of the Anglo-Saxon kings which stood within a few paces of the Old and New Minsters, however, proved inadequate for the needs of the Norman conquerors. William I accumulated the royal landholding here in a number of different parcels, including a strip of built-up land on the south side of the High Street, the cemetery of the New Minster, and part of the Minsters' domestic buildings (Biddle 1976, 293). The new site measured 110m (361ft) each way and is likely to have more than doubled the area of the former palace – 1.2ha (2.9 acres). A few fragments of early Norman masonry are visibly built into the walls, but the site has never been excavated so that nothing is known of the composition or layout of the palace. It was heavily used at first. Of 21 Easters in the Conqueror's reign, ten were spent in France, five in Winchester and the other six in unknown places (Biddle 1986). William II continued to use Winchester as a gathering place after his coronation in 1087, at Easter 1095, Easter 1100, and immediately before his death in August of that year. His charters suggest further visits. Of Henry I's 35 Easters, six were spent in Winchester. In fact, it seems as if the close connection between the city and the ceremonial of the royal court began to wane only during the latter part of Henry I's reign. It is possible that the focus of royal power was already shifting to the castle at the north end of the town. This may well have been a safer location for the royal treasury but cannot have been so convenient for the ceremony of crown wearing. The Angevins confirmed their attachment to Winchester Castle by carrying through considerable alterations and additions there.

At Gloucester the site of the royal palace is rather more uncertain than is the case at Winchester. The Saxon palace is said to have been at Kingsholm in the royal manor of Barton on the north side of the city, on the reputed site of a former legionary fortress. After the Norman conquest the great hall of the castle (on the site of the modern prison) was an alternative place for meetings. Continual references to '*Aula Regis*' make it likely that the old palace continued in use but nothing is known about its size, form or layout.

At Westminster we are fortunate in knowing a great deal about the late Saxon and Norman palaces but we should have learned far more. It is one of the scandals of modern British archaeology that no large-scale archaeological excavation was undertaken to recover the plan of Edward the Confessor's palace when an underground car-park was dug for Members of Parliament in the early 1970s. A narrow strip of low, damp ground, hardly 91.5m (300ft) wide squeezed between the Abbey and the river was, as Lethaby says, 'an extraordinary site on which to rear the chief palace of the kings of England'. Here William Rufus chose to build his great hall in 1097. The walls of Rufus's hall survive below string-course height and prove that it was 73.15m (240ft) long and 20.59m (67ft 6in) wide, making it the largest hall in England and, for its time, perhaps the largest hall in Europe. Its scale certainly impressed contemporaries. When his courtiers thought it was big enough if not too big, Rufus is credited with remarking that 'it was not half large enough'. Another writer reported that the king said, 'it was too big for a chamber and not big enough for a hall'. Boasting apart, there are irregularities of layout which Colvin has explained by suggesting that Rufus's hall was built round an older hall which remained still in use, making it difficult to take accurate measurements from one side to another. The huge width of the hall, in fact, makes it necessary to postulate a double arcade of posts to support the roof although it has to be confessed that no traces of such arcades have yet been found. From discoveries made during repairs in the nineteenth century, R. Smirke restored the great hall and his brother attempted a paper reconstruction of the side wall of the Norman hall which was corrected by W. R. Lethaby in 1906. It seems that the hall was divided externally into 12 bays by shallow pilaster-type buttresses and was decorated with bands of chequered masonry below the parapets of the east and west sides, and by a blind arcade across the base of the north gable (RCHM 1925, 122).

Less is known about the other buildings making up the Anglo-Norman complex at Westminster. St Stephen's chapel is said to have been founded by King Stephen (1135–54); it jutted out towards the river to the east. To the south of this cramped site, and accordingly necessarily in series with the great hall, was the little hall, or lesser hall, which had an undercroft of Norman work. The 'king's chamber' was repaired in Henry II's reign and probably occupied the position of the later 'Painted Chamber'. The Norman Exchequer building was a two-storeyed structure between the great hall and the river; its basement was an assay office and the upper floor served as a court room. Finally there was a quay, known as 'the king's bridge' which provided a landing stage and stressed the importance of the river as a channel of communication.

The Painted Chamber at the Palace of Westminster

During the thirteenth and fourteenth centuries much effort and very considerable resources were employed to bring the royal accommodation up to date. Developments involving the restructuring of the Painted Chamber and St Stephen's Chapel, placed Westminster amongst the most magnificent of royal palaces in western Europe (Fig. 33). The so-called Painted Chamber was on an east-west axis directly south of the twelfth-century foundation of St Stephen's Chapel to which it was eventually linked by an *alura* (a rampart walk), running parallel to the Thames (Binski 1986, 9). The chamber measured internally 24.5m (80½ft) by 7.9m (24ft) with a height of 9.7m (30ft). It was mostly twelfth-century in date but had been brought up to date by Henry III when it was used as a bedroom and audience chamber. The first floor must have commanded a fine view across the river Thames which virtually lapped the foot of its eastern wall. It was lit by large windows in the lateral wall; three on the north and two on the south. Two elegant thirteenth-century windows in the east wall overlooked the river. The flat wooden ceiling of the room was studded with a pattern of lobed paterae, one of which may be seen in Sir John Soane's museum, Lincoln's Inn Fields.

In 1819 the great series of wall paintings that gave the room its name was uncovered. Fortunately they were copied by Charles Stothard and Edward Crocker. Stothard (1786–1821) obtained the post of historical draughtsman to the Society of Antiquaries in 1815. He was famous in his lifetime for his series *The Monumental Effigies of Great Britain*, carefully copied with graduated lines and hand coloured (Stothard 1817). He cleaned the effigies before drawing them; Stothard's drawings are masterpieces of neutral observation and factual representation. He also studied tomb polychromy. He worked in a similar way in the Painted Chamber producing steely and precise line drawings in pencil, then massing in the colours and finally inking in lines. He did a certain amount of discreet restoration. Crocker worked independently of Stothard; his figure drawing is less assured but his palette is richer. Our dependence on these copies is absolute because the paintings themselves were totally destroyed by the fire which consumed most of the palace in 1834. They can be consulted in the Society of Antiquaries' library, London, and at the Ashmolean Museum, Oxford.

The focus of the room was undoubtedly at the east end where the king's state bed was situated (Binski 1986, 36). It was located with its head by the north wall, between the fireplace and the small doorway leading to the attached private chapel. The bed was a piece of state furniture and there was a rich iconographic and decorative programme painted above and around it which mirrored Henry III's love of Edward the Confessor's virtuous kingship. At the head of the bed was a depiction of the coronation of St Edward with the king full face being crowned in the centre and two archbishops and other ecclesiastics on either side. The bird-headed sceptre in Edward's hand is of the same type as that found in the tomb of Edward I. The coronation mural was 1.73m (5½ft) in height and the colour palette is distinctive, using subdued crimsons, olive greens and deep blues. These colours, the decorative motifs, and the architectural details all correspond with those seen on the Westminster Retable.

This depiction of the coronation of Edward the Confessor was in all probability executed in the last years of the reign of Henry III after a fire in the room in 1263. Further paintings of St Edward giving the ring to St John are part of the same scene. Among the most impressive was the series of Virtues and Vices on the window splays of the room opposite the royal bed. The Virtues were larger than life-size figures. *Largesce* (generosity) vanquishes *Covoitise* (covetousness), she is crowned, wears mail armour and sticks a spear into her foe while choking him with coins which stream out from a long purse. Around is brilliant heraldic display: the arms of England and of the Empire (or, more likely, of Richard, Earl of Cornwall d. 1272, Henry's brother and king of the Romans). *Deboneretê* (tranquillity) stands on *Ira* (anger) and switches the writhing vice. She wears a swan badge signifying patience and holds a shield with the arms of England differenced by two bars. In the border are the arms of England and the royal Saints Edward and Edmund (the names of Henry's two elder sons).

What was the significance of all these figures? The evidence is that the king's chamber was put

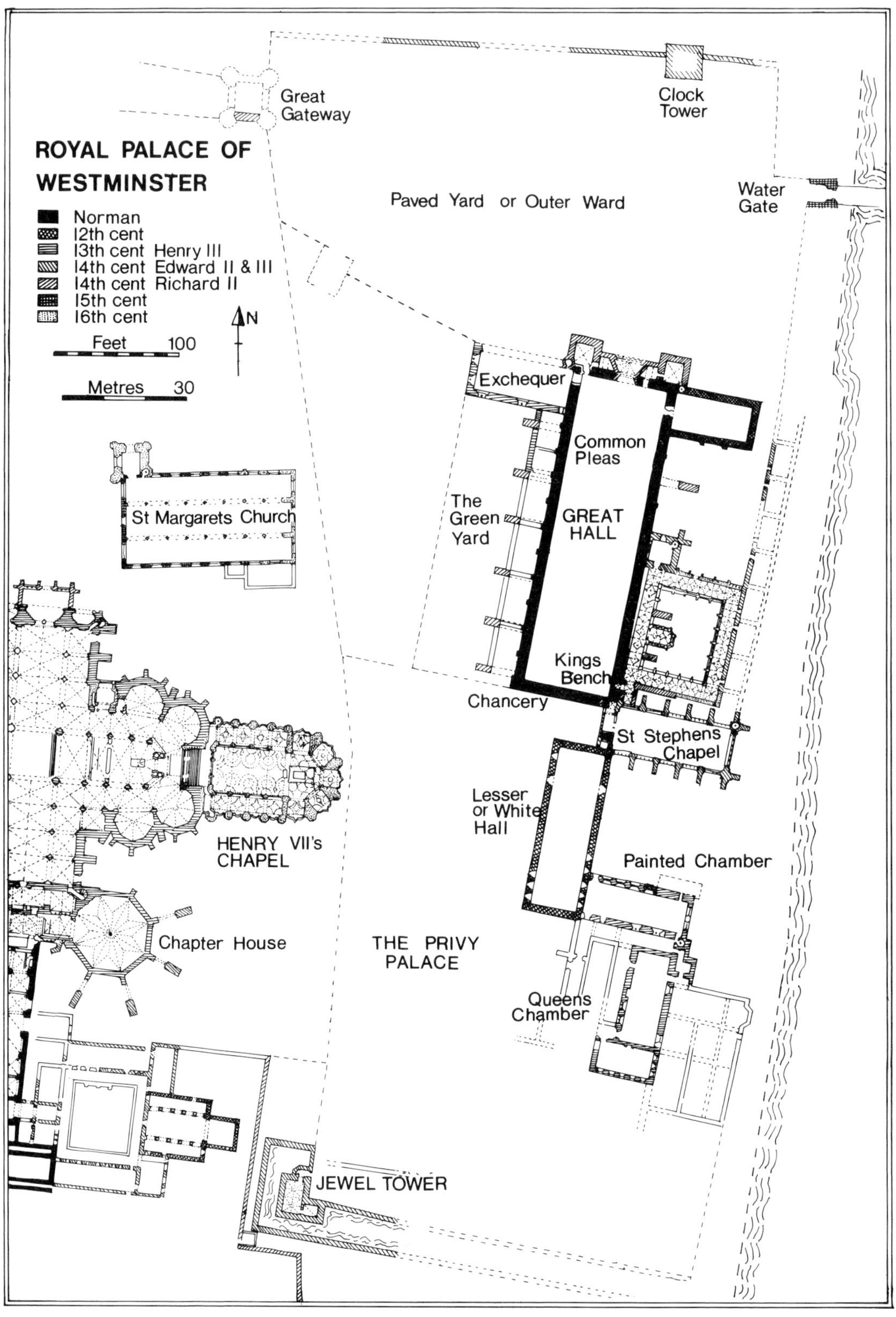
ROYAL PALACE OF WESTMINSTER
Norman
12th cent
13th cent Henry III
14th cent Edward II & III
14th cent Richard II
15th cent
16th cent
N
Feet 100
Metres 30
Great Gateway
Clock Tower
Paved Yard or Outer Ward
Water Gate
Exchequer
Common Pleas
The Green Yard
GREAT HALL
St Margarets Church
Kings Bench
Chancery
St Stephens Chapel
Lesser or White Hall
HENRY VII's CHAPEL
Painted Chamber
Chapter House
THE PRIVY PALACE
Queens Chamber
JEWEL TOWER

to public use, charitable works could be done here and the royal alms-giving displayed on a generous scale. In 1243, for example, some six thousand people were entertained on a biblical scale in the palace, densely packing the great hall, the queen's apartments and the king's chambers. In such an atmosphere the virtuous iconography of the painting and the charitable exhortations of the texts in the rooms are clearly significant. Moreover, the paintings were all part of a programme of decoration which related to the focus of the room, the king's bed. In 1244 it is recorded that it had posts and curtains, implying the existence of a large celour or canopy. By surrounding the royal bed with painted representations of the saint-king, Henry III was physically identifying himself with Edward the Confessor just as later he had himself buried in the old grave of his saintly predecessor (see Chapter 7).

The second group of paintings comprised an extensive series of Old Testament stories arranged round the room in bands, with French inscriptions between them. Binski, who has made a recent study of them, considers that they were executed for Edward I between 1292 and 1297 (Binski 1986, 74). The imagery is unusual and consists of a large cycle of paintings about Judas Maccabeus which is set above paintings concerned with good and bad kings and prophets, illustrating passages from II Kings, Judges and II Maccabees. The choice of Judas Maccabeus is likely to be linked with the heroic Arthurian cycle of legends known to have been much favoured in Edward I's court. Arthur was the type and model of romantic and strong kingship. The narrative scenes are punctuated by small buildings and brilliant displays of arms and heraldry. It has even been suggested that Edward in the Painted Chamber could be seen taking on the *persona* of Judas Maccabeus as liberator; at the very least there may be an allusion to his military prowess in Scotland, or perhaps more decisively, Wales. Another scene brings out a reference to Edward. Abimelech is shown receiving his just deserts when a woman dropped a millstone on his head, fatally wounding him. Edward was apparently reminded of this story when he went, unarmed, too near the walls of Stirling during a siege in 1304. The Jewish people were shown producing despicable tyrants as well as models of chivalry. Edward may have identified with the latter but in one case he behaved like the former. It was in 1290 that the king in his council decreed that all Jews should leave England. The Jews had suffered for decades from arrest, imprisonment and execution. Edward is conceivably 'recounting and mocking Jewish history with a blunt self-confidence' (Binski 1986, 102).

33 Ground-plan of the royal palace of Westminster. The great hall, lower part of St Stephen's Chapel, cloister and Jewel Tower still survive. (After Brown, Colvin, Taylor.)

These elaborate decorative schemes of Henry III and Edward I made the royal apartments in the Palace of Westminster so magnificent as to rival in scale and elaboration those of any other contemporary European monarch. We turn now to developments in the great hall, which towards the end of the fourteenth century was refurbished to a standard which again put Westminster in a class of its own.

The hall of the Palace of Westminster during the Middle Ages

Very little needed to be done in the way of maintenance to the great hall of the king's palace at Westminster during the thirteenth and fourteenth centuries (Brown, Colvin and Taylor 1963, 527). There were periodic renewals of the shingles on the roof, some repairs were probably made after it caught fire in 1315 during a banquet given by the king, and the banners flying from standards fixed to the north and south gables needed attention from time to time. Basically, however, the mighty hall built by Rufus survived intact until Richard II's reign. In the meantime in Europe it was outdone in size by the halls in the Palais de la Cité in Paris (*c.*1301–13) and the Palazzo della Ragione in Padua (*c.*1306) (Alexander and Binski 1987, 506). It remained, however, unmatched in size in England.

During these years the hall seems to have fulfilled a multiplicity of functions (Cooper 1937, 168–223), for instance it was used for coronation festivals after the ceremony in the Abbey. Examples are found as early as the reign of Henry II when the young King Henry, the eldest son of Henry II, was crowned in the presence of his father. Again, Henry III used the hall after his second coronation at Westminster in 1220. This was a re-crowning after his first in 1216 at Gloucester. Receptions were also given in the hall to foreign emissaries. The two ambassadors from the Emperor Frederick who came to ask Henry II for the hand of his sister for their master were received here. Also in 1240 there was a reception for the papal legate's nephew, and the uncle of the queen, Peter of Savoy, was knighted here. A number of Councils were held in Westminster during the reigns of the early medieval kings but it is unlikely that such a large space as the great hall was used for intimate discussions, which were much more likely to take place in the smaller halls and chambers of the palace complex (Cooper 1938, 97–138). It was the place where the much-augmented household of the king lived and slept. It was in addition, as we have seen, the location of much-publicized and large-scale demonstrations of royal charity.

In the later Middle Ages, however, the hall was appropriated for legal business. The southern end was used by the courts of Chancery and Kings Bench. The Lord Chancellor habitually used the marble seat occupied by the king at coronations. Fragments of this seat may be seen at the Jewel Tower, Westminster (see Fig. 85). The Court of Common Pleas was situated half way down on the western side. Events of supreme constitutional significance occasionally took place in Westminster Hall. In 1399 the 'Parliament' met to hear the pronouncement of the abdication of Richard II. Similarly, this was the venue for the proclamation of Edward Earl of March, as King Edward IV, on 4 March 1461. Richard III is also said by Holinshed to have gone to Westminster Hall, sat down on the marble seat and said that

> *he would take upon him the crowne in that place where the king himself sitteth and ministreth the laws, because he considered that it was the chief duty of a king to minister the laws.*

Architecturally the most significant event in the hall's history during the later Middle Ages was the restructuring which took place during the reign of Richard II. 'Richard's refashioning of the secular ceremonial centre of the English Crown was part of an attempt to establish an absolute monarchy.' (Alexander and Binski 1987, 506.) This was accomplished in two main stages. In 1385 13 statues of kings were commissioned from Thomas Canon, one of a well-known family of marblers from the Isle of Purbeck, Dorset. This scheme was to include one statue of each ruler from Edward the Confessor (with whom Richard II identified, as did his predecessor Henry III) to Richard II. Only six were actually set up in niches of Reigate stone in the end wall over the dais; others were kept in store for the time being. When the hall was rebuilt they were added to the north front. Remarkably, nine out of the 15 statues inserted into niches inside the hall remain.

34 Westminster Hall. The core of the lower parts of the walls have survived from Rufus's Hall. The upper parts and the timber roof date from Richard II's reign. (Drawing by J. M. Steane.)

When the decision was taken to remodel the great hall in 1393 it may have been motivated by a realization of the structural weakness of the old building, but the driving power is likely to have been emulation and ambition. The east side of Rufus's hall needed strengthening in 1385–7 when a flying buttress was erected to offset the tendency of the roof to spread. The work of 1393–9 was understated as repair ('*reparacio*') in the accounts. It involved the removal of the Norman posts or columns and the heightening and refacing of the walls,

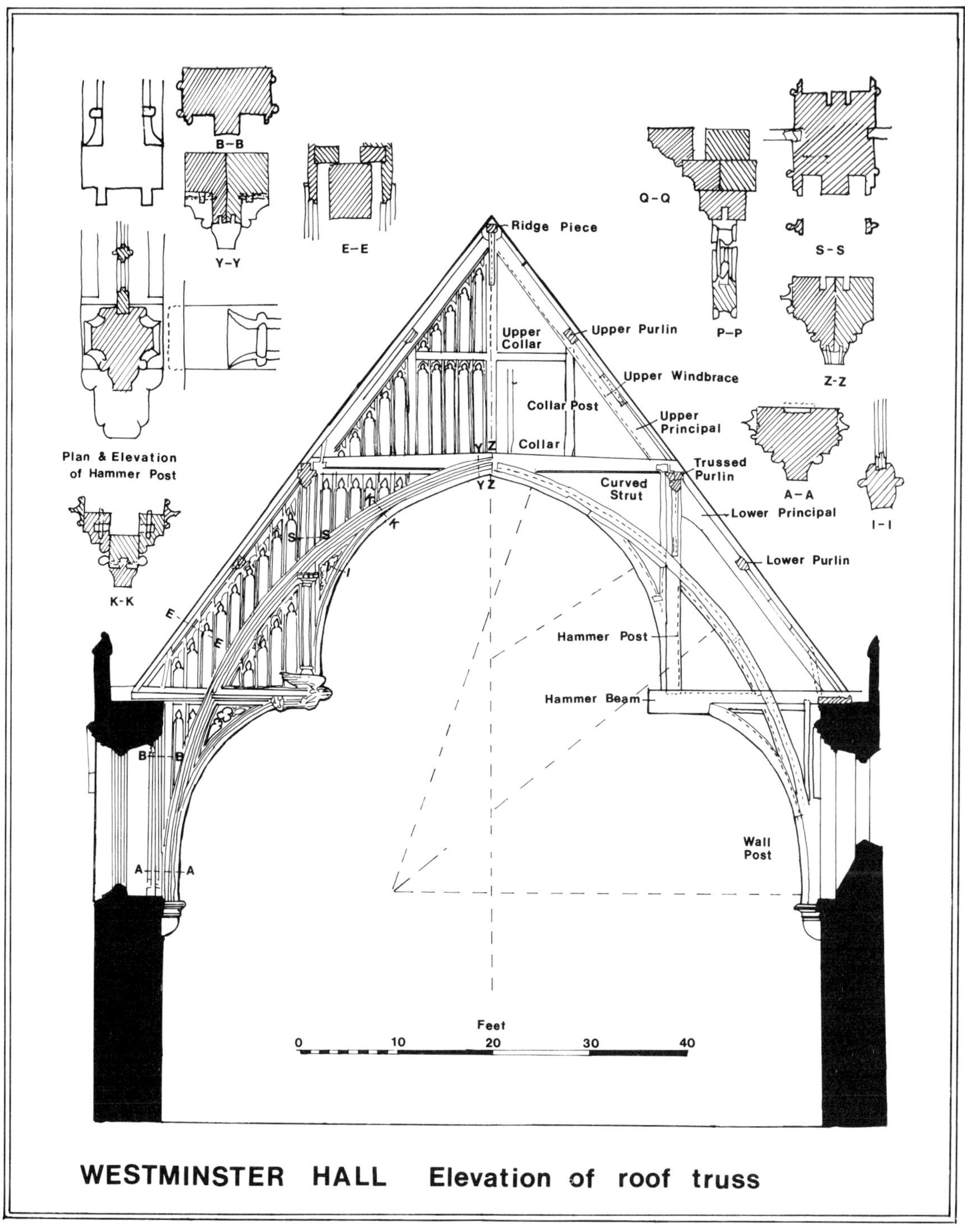

35 Westminster Hall. Elevation of the roof truss and sections through the principal timbers. (After Baines.)

while the Romanesque windows and wall passages were filled in and replaced by traceried windows in the new Perpendicular style. Running along the sill below them was a string-course embellished with carvings of the king's badge, a white hart. Above them a moulded cornice was set to take the new wall plates. Covering the vast space, without any intervention of post or pillar, was a splendid timber roof combining the latest technological developments of hammer beams and arched-braced construction (Fig. 35).

Such an elegant and vigorous conception is unlikely to have sprung into existence without forebears. The principle of supporting posts on hammer beams is illustrated in Villard d'Honnecourt's notebook *c.*1240. The origins of this form of timber roof in England are found in the great timber brackets supporting the roof covering of the kitchen of the bishops' palace at Chichester (*c.*1300), the lantern of Ely Cathedral (1322–42) and the roof of the Strangers' Hall at Winchester (*c.*1320–50). Experiments involving the use of the hammer beams were also being carried out within the royal circle and may have provided a stimulus to the king to outdo them all. At Dartington Hall Richard II's half brother, John Holland, Duke of Exeter, built a hammer beam roof 1388–1400 (Emery 1958, 184–202). The badge of a crowned and chained white hart displayed in the entrance porch was not adopted by the king before October 1390 and would not have been used after his deposition in 1399. So this brings the building very close in date to that of Westminster Hall. Richard's overmighty uncle, John of Gaunt, in the meantime was spanning the 27.43m (90ft) by 13.71m (45ft) space of Kenilworth Castle with another magnificent roof in 1391.

Richard II was fortunate in being served by two master craftsmen, Henry Yevele and Hugh Herland, whose experience and expertise fully matched the aspirations of their patron. Hugh Herland (*c.*1330–1411) had spent most of his life in the royal service and from 1375 was 'disposer of the king's works touching the art of mistery of carpentry', with 12d a day from the Clerk of Works at the Palace of Westminster and the Tower of London during the continuance of the works (Harvey 1984, 137–41). His experience at Rochester and Portchester Castles was enriched by service for William of Wykeham at New College, Oxford and possibly at Winchester College. He acquired a property at Kingston-on-Thames (Surrey), which is significant in view of the importance of that place in the timber trade which served London. When he was put in charge of the reconstruction of Westminster Palace Hall roof he secured for life

> *the little house lying in the outer little ward of the Palace of Westminster . . . for keeping his tools and for making his models and moulds for his carpentry work.*

Yevele provided the patterns and moulds of the masonry. A contract records that two Gloucestershire masons, Richard Washbourne and John Swallow, undertook to make the table or cornice of the wall of Westminster Palace Hall with 26 souses or corbels for the new hammer beam roof (Baines 1914).

While the walls were thus being prepared for the reception of the roof, the great trusses were being put together at a place near Farnham called 'the Frame'. The oak timber is known to have been collected from three sources; the royal woods at Odiham and Alice Holt (Hampshire), the wood of the Abbot of St Albans at Bervan or Barvin, near Northaw (Hertfordshire) and the Surrey woods belonging to William Croyser at Stoke d'Abernon. Because of the great span involved, it was necessary to construct the design in sections. This was done by the sawyers and carpenters while working for 6d a day at Farnham. Other pieces of the roof were paid as task-work. Two angels carrying the shields of the king's arms were made by Robert Brusyngdon for 26s 8d each; others were worked by William Canon for 20s each and the rest for 15s each. Presumably the first were the prototype and the rest copies.

The total weight of timber has been estimated at 660 tons and required considerable organization to move it to Westminster. In June 1395 the sheriffs of Hampshire, Berkshire and Surrey were each asked to send 30 strong wains to 'the Frame' to carry out the timber by road to 'Hamme', a place on the Thames near Chertsey whence it was transported to Westminster by water.

The masonry preparation for the framing took place in 1395–6. During this period the scaffolding and machinery necessary for the raising of the prefabricated trusses was assembled in the hall. From a study of the structure and the documentary sources the sequence of operations after that seems to have been as follows (Courtenay and Mark 1987, 383, fn. 30): after the installation of the masonry corbels and cornice, the lower part of the frame, wall-posts and plates were erected. These were succeeded by the hammer beams, secured from beneath by the pegged tenon of the wall-post in addition to the lower arch brace. Next an operation requiring hoisting gear would have taken place. The hammer posts, lower sections of principal rafters and main collar purlins would have been heaved into position. Finally the great arch rib, constructed in sections, with a continuous outer moulding, was slotted in. An indication that the new roof must have been nearly finished is given in the reference to the purchase of 22 rolls of *wadmole* (a coarse woollen material like felt) 'for covering the hall against the Queen's coronation through lack of lead'. This was the coronation of Richard II's second bride, the young Queen Isabella, daughter of Charles VI of France. A thousand wainscot boards were bought in 1398 for boarding the roof of the hall. This was presumably for fastening the lead to. The final touch to the roof was the completion of two elaborately pinnacled louvres on the ridge which were glazed by Michaelmas 1398. Recent research has clarified the complex support conditions provided by Herland's design (Courtenay 1990, 97).

Steps were taken to ensure that the entrance to this majestic hall was similarly upgraded. The north front with its portal and flanking towers was designed to give the hall a ceremonial entrance like the west end of a cathedral church. Pack thread was used to set out the foundation and masons were soon busy on the doorway and the towers which were described as being 6.1m (20ft) high with battlements, indicating that they projected that distance beyond the parapet of the hall. Elm boarding was used for centering the arch of the great window in the north front and the upper part of the north gable was also under construction, the pinnacle on the gable apex being 9.52m (28ft) higher than the roof itself. The foundations of the north-east tower seem to have given trouble because it was no sooner finished than it began to settle. Ten pounds was spent 'on separating the wall of the new toer at the end of the hall from the old wall of the hall'.

The hall was still unfinished at the deposition of Richard II but the new dynasty lost no time in confirming the appointments of John Godmaston and Hugh Herland as clerk and comptroller of the works of the hall. The porch was vaulted, the towers roofed and the finials of the tabernacles of the niches were set up. To sustain the thrusts of the great arched roof Yevele provided the western wall with six sturdy buttresses, one to each pair of bays, which are surmounted by pinnacles, square in plan with gablets at the feet of the crowning pyramids (Harvey 1944, 60).

By the end of the nineteenth century the roof of Westminster Hall was in a parlous condition. Little had been done in the way of repairs in the seventeenth and eighteenth centuries but radical and not always suitable repairs involving ironwork had been applied in the nineteenth. The causes of the decay were investigated very thoroughly by Frank Baines just before the First World War (Baines 1914, 10). By inserting steel beams in each truss which transferred the weight of the roof away from the timber in distress, he managed to save the structure and thus secure the continuance into the twentieth century of the most magnificent royal work of the Middle Ages.

Royal houses and their distribution

When attempting to understand the reasons behind the distribution of the houses and castles of the early medieval kings the first thing that strikes one is their amazing spread over the whole land (Fig. 36). Colvin registered and mapped the phenomenon in his magisterial study of the King's Works in 1963. It is easy to demonstrate geographically that many, if not most, of the houses used by the Norman and Angevin kings were in areas of permanent afforestation. The unfortified Anglo-Saxon palace at Cheddar (Somerset), amidst the exciting hunting country of the Mendips, went on being used by kings after the Conquest. As the royal forests increased in area and dispersion so did the royal hunting lodges. We hear of a royal hunting lodge at Brill (Buckinghamshire) in Bernwood Forest in the reign of William I. Houses at Brigstock (Northamptonshire) in the forest of Rockingham, and Kinver in the

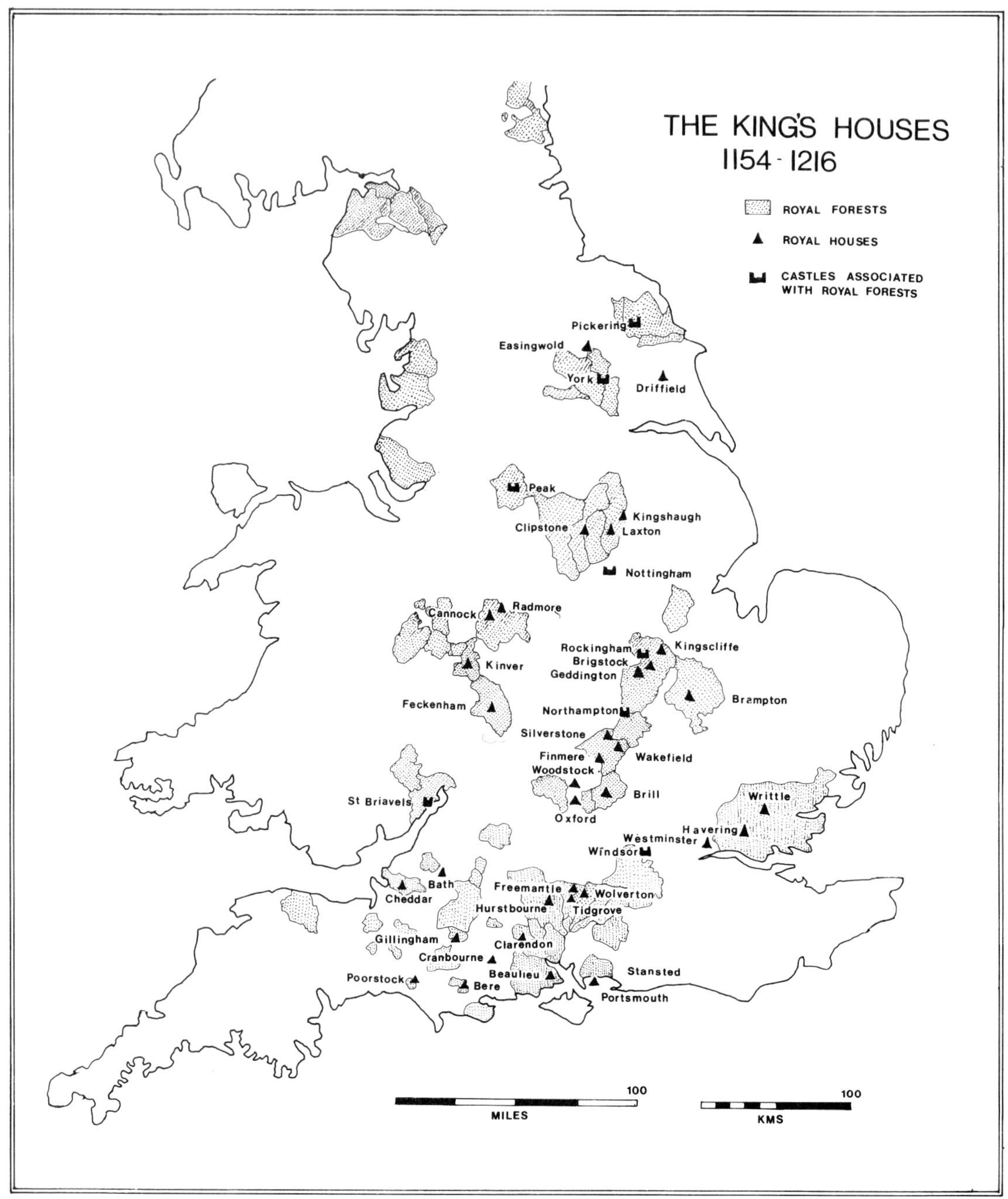

woods of Staffordshire are mentioned in the reign of Rufus. Henry I spent time and issued charters at Clarendon (Wiltshire), Dunstable (Bedfordshire), King's Cliffe (Northamptonshire), Odiham (Hampshire) and Woodstock (Oxfordshire). Henry II added to this number by building hunting lodges at Clipstone (Nottinghamshire), Feckenham (Worcestershire), Wakefield (West Yorkshire) and five other places. Even Richard I, who was abroad for most of his reign built a house at Kinver (Staffordshire) (Brown, Colvin and Taylor 1963, 81–4).

36 Distribution map of the king's houses 1154–1216. The close connection between royal accommodation and the forests is shown. (After Brown, Colvin, and Taylor.)

Another explanatory factor is the personalities and idiosyncrasies of the kings themselves. John, for instance, had an unpleasing propensity for accumulating other people's houses; to the 23 which he had inherited from his brother Richard he acquired five or six more which he took from their rightful owners. He had a predilection for houses in the south-western part of the country. Cheddar he took from the archdeacon of Wells in 1209, Cranbourne (Dorset) and Tewkesbury (Gloucestershire) he illegally retained after his divorce from his first wife, Isabella de Clare, in 1200. He rebuilt the existing house at Gillingham and erected new ones at Bere and Padstock, all in Dorset. He did in fact possess more houses than any other medieval king and it is not surprising that popular tradition attributed more building works to King John and the devil than to any other powerful agency.

Henry III is perhaps the first king who indulged in a building programme of domestic residences largely because he had architectural ambitions. He inherited at least 20 houses from his father. Some he allowed to decay and some he gave away; he handed over Freemantle (Berkshire), to his eldest son, the Lord Edward. He also spent vast sums on Westminster (£10,000), Clarendon (£3600), Woodstock (£3300), Havering (Essex) (£2100) and Guildford (Surrey) (£1800), while extensive building works were carried out at hunting lodges such as Brill, Clipstone, Feckenham, Freemantle, Geddington (Northamptonshire), Gillingham and Silverstone (Northamptonshire).

Edward I's houses were still scattered over the Midlands and the south but the next 200 years saw a complex, shifting pattern of alienation, escheat, wardship and permanent acquisition. Of 20 houses which Edward inherited from his father in 1272 only six were still held by the Crown in 1485. They were Clarendon, Clipstone (Fig. 37), Havering, Windsor, Woodstock and Westminster. But in the meantime 25 others were held and kept by the Crown for periods ranging from five years to over a century. They might be acquired by marriage, gift or purchase, or, in times of rebellion or civil war, by forfeiture and escheat. In the meantime too, royal taste changed. Among the most favoured residences of kings in the fourteenth and fifteenth centuries were Eltham (Greater

37 Clipstone (Nottinghamshire). The remains of a royal hunting lodge in Sherwood. The masonry seen in this view was probably the work of Edward I's reign. (Photograph: J. M. Steane.)

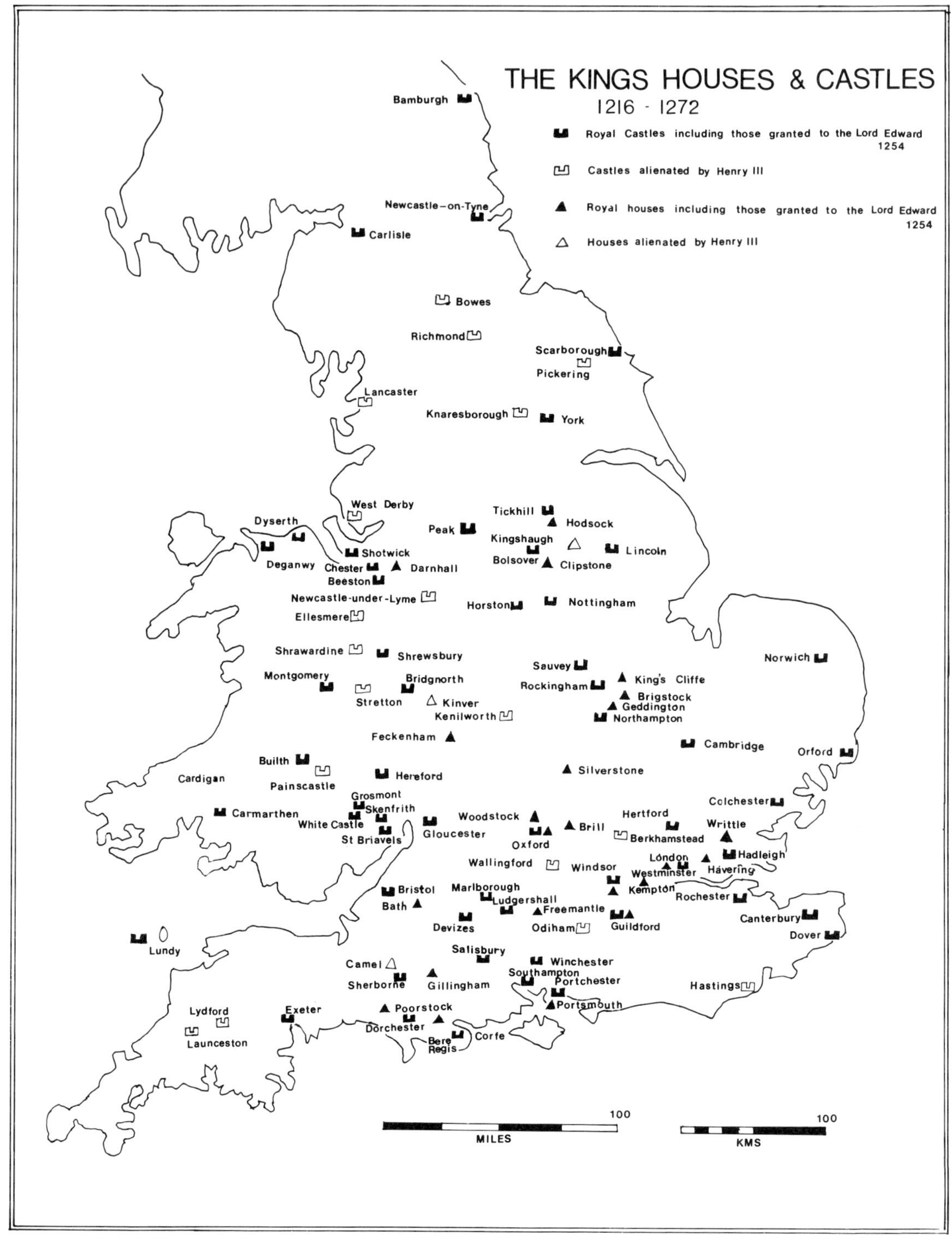

London), Kings Langley (Hertfordshire) and Sheen (Surrey). There was a gradual reduction of the total number of royal houses (Fig. 38). In Edward II's reign and early in Edward III's the total rose to 25, but during Richard II's reign the king had 16 or 17 houses. This was further reduced by the Lancastrians to 12 and by the Yorkists to 9 or 10.

38 Distribution map of the king's houses and castles 1216–72. (After Brown, Colvin and Taylor.)

The explanation offered by Colvin for this progressive reduction is that it reflects a decline in royal resources (Brown, Colvin, Taylor 1963, 243). Owing to shifts in the distribution of the nation's wealth, including the growth of towns, the population explosion of the twelfth and thirteenth centuries, the alienation of royal demesne and the increasing reliance by the Crown on running the country by revenue-derived taxation instead of from the direct exploitation of territorial estates, the kings of the fourteenth and fifteenth centuries were relatively less wealthy than their Norman and Angevin predecessors. And this at a time when they had become habituated to a higher standard of living; an increase in the quality of accommodation could only be maintained by reducing the number of residences. Only complete restructuring could have brought old-fashioned hunting lodges like Brigstock and Feckenham up to the standard of elegance of Eltham, King's Langley and Sheen.

Not only was the total number reduced, but their geographical distribution changed markedly towards the end of the Middle Ages. Nearly all the houses retained were within a day's ride of London and by the reign of Richard II, Clipstone was the only royal house, north of the Chilterns. Even Burstwick and Cowick in Yorkshire, convenient royal residences on the way to Scotland during a period when the king was invading or living in the land of his northern neighbours, were granted away in 1355 and 1370 respectively. The Lancastrian kings did not halt this shift towards London despite the extent of their huge territorial interest in the north and north-west. They expended little on Belper and Ravensdale in Derbyshire. Most of their time was spent in the south of the country or in France.

This remarkable geographical location of royal houses reflects the increase of centralization of royal government around the king's palace at Westminster (Cooper, 1938). The transference of the Exchequer from Winchester to Westminster in the early years of Henry II had begun the process. The Exchequer clerks were followed by the Court of Common Pleas. Edward I ordered his Chancery and Exchequer to remain at Westminster during his last expedition to Scotland. The Hundred Years War confirmed this tendency. It was easier to wage war on the French from a permanent centre in the south of the country. Tout reckons that the development of a capital city, wherein resided the chief departments of the central administration, took place in the second part of the fourteenth century (Tout 1934, 249–75).

Edward II made a notable series of acquisitions of royal houses in the south of the kingdom around London. His father had given him King's Langley when he was Prince of Wales. Byfleet (Surrey) had also been acquired before the beginning of the reign. Then in 1311 Bishop Anthony Bek bequeathed Eltham (Greater London) to the king; Edward II also took over Sheen (Surrey), held by Edward I's counsellor, Otto de Grandisson.

Edward III continued this concentration of royal residences in the south-eastern parts of the kingdom. He acquired Foliejohn, Hampstead Marshall and Wychmere (Berkshire), East Worldham (Hampshire) and Rotherhithe (Surrey). Much of his building work was lavished on Sheen, Havering, Hadleigh (Essex), Leeds (Kent) and Queenborough (Kent), all within one day's riding distance of the capital. Moreover, he maintained a ring of satellite houses and hunting lodges in Berkshire around the rebuilt castle of Windsor, at Easthampstead, Foliejohn, Henley on the Heath, Wychmere and a manor house in Windsor Great Park. His long decline in health in his later years resulted in a concentration of royal interest in the environs of Windsor.

Richard II, a king of great artistic sensitivity, had a strong personal liking for both Kennington (Greater London), a manor house he acquired from his father the Black Prince, and Sheen, where on an island in the Thames he built what Colvin has described as the first summer house known in English history. It was here at Sheen in 1394 that Queen Anne died and in a paroxysm of grief Richard ordered the palace where he and his queen had been so happy to be levelled. Henry V, however, decided to rebuild it and it remained a major royal house until 1499 when Henry VII built his new palace called Richmond (after his dukedom) on the same site after a disastrous fire. Henry VII and Henry VIII continued the tendency to concentrate on maintaining or acquiring houses near the Thames or within easy riding distance of the capital. Henry VIII showed the same predilection as John for acquiring the houses of his subjects. His passion for building was partly in emulation of his French royal contemporary, Francis I (Starkey 1991).

Location of royal houses

If it is hard to trace the tortuous reasons behind the changing distribution pattern of royal residences, it is similarly difficult to generalize about the choice of locations for royal houses in the Middle Ages. Clearly, in an age which produced Beaumaris, Beaumanoir, Beauregard and Belvoir such aesthetic considerations as a fine view were occasionally a factor but other reasons often predominated. It may help to look at the location of houses and palaces which continued for a long period in royal hands or which are known to have been favourite residences. William the Conqueror recognized the historic importance of Winchester to the late Saxon monarchs. He continued to site his treasury here and built a palace next to the cathedral with its mausoleum of Saxon kings and saints (Biddle 1976, 291). He also acknowledged and respected the capital significance and strength of London. When choosing locations near the capital the Norman kings were concerned to place their palaces of the Tower and Westminster *outside* and removed from the turbulent inhabitants of the city. The site of the Tower was deliberately chosen for strategic reasons: it dominated the city from the east but was also in command of the Thames, a key waterway in the kingdom (Brooke 1989, 33). The Saxon palace of Westminster a mile to the west of the city was in a curiously unimpressive site, as we have seen, wedged into 274m (900ft) between the abbey church and the river (Vince 1990, 32, 57). The King's house at Lincoln, if that is what it is, is sited in the extramural suburb of Wigford, a setting similar to the royal houses at Gloucester and Oxford (Stocker, 1991, 40).

At Westminster, proximity to the church of St Peter and its associations with Edward the Confessor, and access by the river, seem to have outweighed the natural disadvantages of a narrow and ill-drained site. So ill-drained was it that in the thirteenth century judges had occasionally to take boats across the flooded Westminster Hall to their courts. The attraction of the Thames as a highway and a waterside site grew stronger in the later Middle Ages. The king's houses at Rotherhithe, Sheen, Windsor, Greenwich and Gravesend were all on or near the river Thames. The Tudors added to these riverside amenities by reconstructing Richmond and acquiring Hampton Court and York House (to become Whitehall Palace) ready-made from Wolsey.

Other houses which were in the king's hands for hundreds of years occupied more obviously desirable sites. Clarendon (Fig. 39) lies within two hours' ride of Winchester along the edge of a wooded scarp 5.6km (3½ miles) east of the successful new town of Salisbury (James and Robinson 1985, 2–3). Its attraction to the Angevin kings was undoubtedly connected with its proximity to good hunting country. The royal house of Woodstock is similarly situated in formerly wooded tracts centred in the king's demesne forests of Woodstock, Cornbury and Wychwood (Bond and Tiller 1987). It stood 11.3km (7 miles) north-west of Oxford on a small hill rising above the banks of the river Glyme, close to where Vanbrugh's great bridge now spans the valley converted by Capability Brown into a lake. It was particularly beloved of Henry I for whom, according to the author of *Gesta Stephani*, it was 'the favourite seat of his retirement and privacy'. In the valley below were the royal fishponds. Spanning the valley are two causeways: one connecting the palace to Old Woodstock, one to New Woodstock. Here, about 0.8km (½ mile) to the north-east of his house, Henry II founded a new borough to provide lodgings for his courtiers. Nearby he built a bower for his chosen mistress, Fair Rosamund Clifford.

Despite the fact that the palace of Woodstock was totally destroyed in the eighteenth century by order of the Duchess of Malborough, the environs are easy to imagine (Fig. 40). The site of King's Langley, a favourite palace of Edward II and Edward III, however, is more difficult to reconstruct because it has been enveloped by suburban housing and school buildings (Neal, 1973). It stands on the top of the hill to the west of the present main road through the village and 0.8km (½ mile) west of the parish church. There were evidently three courts as well as barns and mills set close to the

39 Clarendon Palace (Wiltshire). The rambling layout of the palace is apparent amidst woodland along a ridge of high ground 5.6km (3½ miles) from Salisbury. In the centre is the aisled hall.
(Photograph: Cambridge University Committee for Aerial Photography, 1954.)

Great and Little Parks (Fig. 41). Adjoining the royal house to the north was the Dominican Priory where the body of the king's *mignon*, Piers Gaveston, was brought for burial after his judicial murder. Here, happy childhood memories allied to an attractive topography may well have influenced Edward II in his choice. The sepulture of the love of his life confirmed it.

Some houses were located for military reasons. Since they held territories on both sides of the Channel, English Kings needed houses on the way to Dover, the jumping off place for the shortest sea crossing to France. This accounts for the siting of the royal *camera* in the hospital at Ospringe (Kent), on Watling Street. Constant visits by the Plantagenets to France to conduct diplomacy, or simply to raid and invade, required war bases; Calais became the obvious

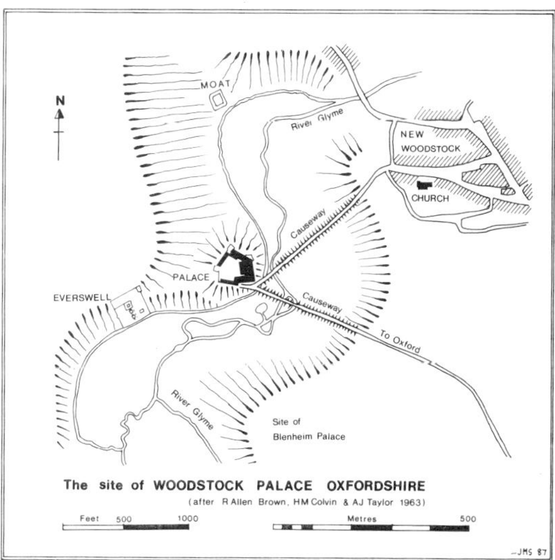

40 Site of Woodstock Palace (Oxfordshire). The valley of the river Glyme was flooded by Capability Brown in the eighteenth century and the southern of the two causeways converted into an island. The site of the palace had been levelled by order of Sarah, Duchess of Marlborough. (After Brown, Colvin and Taylor.)

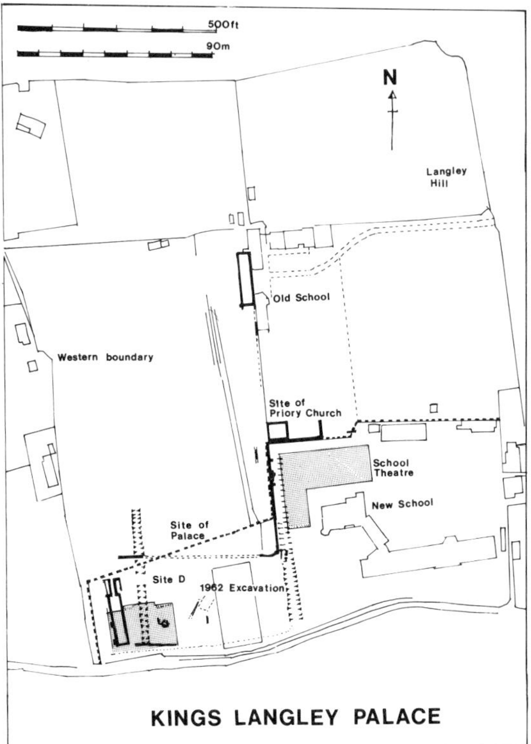

41 *King's Langley Palace (Hertfordshire). This was laid out round several courtyards. The wine cellar is the long building on site D. Some remains of the priory church can still be seen north of the palace.* (After Neal.)

fortified bridgehead for Edward III's wars after 1347. Henry V ran the administration of his freshly conquered duchy of Normandy from an embattled palace at Rouen. Like the Tower is was formidable enough to keep the urban inhabitants under subjection. An engraving in Vol. VII of *Archaeologia* gives a plan and elevation of this palace but unfortunately it was destroyed at the Revolution and its remains have been covered by a car-park.

Force was backed by religious sanctions. Each power, king and bishop, needed the buttress of the other if the hierarchial feudal society was to be maintained. This certainly led to conflict during the period of the Investiture Contest *c*.1080–1110 as each jostled for advantage. In archaeological terms the interdependence of the two powers is symbolized by the juxtaposition in close proximity of royal castle and episcopal palace in a number of English towns. Old Sarum and Lincoln are prime examples. The Normans built a royal castle within the Iron Age hillfort of Old Sarum; they also laid out a new cathedral within the defences of the newly formed urban place. Subsequently, Bishop Roger appropriated the castle and built a second palace within its walls. At Lincoln, whither the cathedral for central/midland England was moved from Dorchester-on-Thames by William I, the king built a castle within a Roman fortress on the spectacular hill-top ridge of Lincolnshire limestone. The symbolism of seeing both lay and ecclesiastical rulers lording it in concert from the tops of hills, cannot have escaped the shrinking subjects of Wiltshire and Lincolnshire.

The Scottish kings tended to fortify their palaces heavily. Both Edinburgh and Stirling are on volcanic rocks rising out of the lowland plain at key points in the communications system in the centre of the kingdom (Fawcett 1990). Defence considerations were also paramount at Linlithgow, where the palace is on a hillock above the town, which extends on a promontory into the loch to the north. Edward I relished it as a military base and it continued to be strongly fortified by the later Scottish kings, a contrast to the undefended nature of English royal houses (Pringle 1989).

Planning of royal houses and palaces

It is disappointing for the tourist to realize that most royal residences of the Middle Ages have disappeared without trace. The rich documentary record frequently mentions the different architectural components of royal houses such as hall, kitchens, garderobes and so on. Rarely, however, are the relationships between the different elements described, so that we often lack knowledge about the planning. One thing does stand out and that is the undefended nature of many of the king's dwelling places. It says much for the powerful personalities of the Norman and Angevin kings that they created a royal authority so great that they and their families were able to live a large part of their lives in undefended residences. The success of their adoption of primogeniture by the end of the thirteenth century allowed the centralized monarchy to survive civil wars and minorities (Schramm 1937). Admittedly the smaller hunting lodges like Writtle and Kinver had moats and palisades but these features were designed to deter outlaws from entering and plundering during the long absences of the king; they were not serious military obstacles. The largest complexes such as Westminster, Clarendon and Woodstock, lacked credibly defensive walls and towers although gatehouses are found. Even castles were places of imposing royal residences for most of the time rather than military bolt-holes.

Another characteristic is that these buildings are incoherently and irregularly laid out even if, as at Clarendon and Westminster, they have a prevailing linear alignment. An interesting indication of their rambling nature is given in the expression 'king's houses' (*domus regis*) by which they were known; only one, Westminster, the king's house a mile to the west of the capital, was referred to by contemporaries as a 'palace'. The latter term was derived from the nexus of grand town houses with gardens covering the Palatine Hill in Rome, where the main and typical imperial residence was sited (Millar 1977, 19, 22). English medieval royal houses were in fact constructed in a similarly piecemeal fashion, strung together with pentices or open-sided corridors, with no attempt to lay them out in an impressive or systematic way. This is surprising in view of the capacity for organized planning shown by cathedral or monastic builders. One reason is that royal palaces and houses were often built of flimsy and inflammable materials such as timber, thatch and shingles which frequently required refurbishing. Disastrous fires are recorded in the thirteenth century at both Westminster and Windsor. Whitehall burned down in 1512. Another reason is that they were not all kept in good order at the same time. Repairs were executed hurriedly in preparation for the coming of the monarch, who might stay for a few days and then depart leaving the house to become damp and untenanted and soon again in need of reconstruction.

Contemporary surveys call attention to the fact that each major function of a royal residence required a separate structure. At the hunting lodge built in Richard I's reign at Kinver (Staffordshire) (Brown, Colvin, Taylor

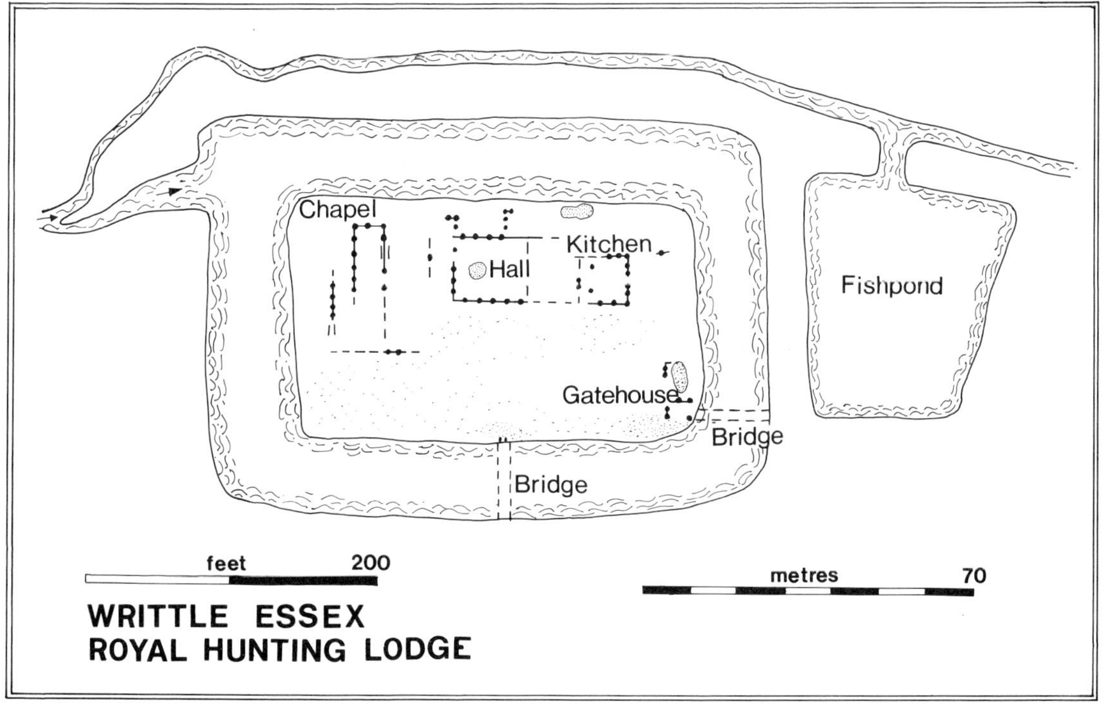

42 *Writtle (Essex) – a royal hunting lodge. The plan shows the dispersed nature of the various units making up this largely timber structure.* (After Rahtz.)

1963, 978) for instance, there was a hall with adjacent offices (buttery and pantry presumably), a kitchen, a chamber and a gaol (for forest offenders) within an enclosure fortified by a palisade 3.3m (10ft 10in) high and entered through a gateway defended with a brattice. A further adjunct was a fishpond. The layout of the hunting lodge at Writtle (Essex), built by King John in 1211, has been recovered by excavation (Rahtz 1969, Figs 7, 8, 9) (Fig. 42). The main building was really one range of chapel, hall and kitchen, occupying just under half of the enclosure. The next was apparently a large courtyard approached from two lodges, that in the middle of the south moat and that at the south-east corner. There was also a gatehouse.

The palace of Clarendon, the subject of intensive study of excavations carried out fifty years ago, grew in a sprawling fashion (James and Robinson 1988). The nucleus was a great hall which was surrounded by kitchens and other offices and stood on the edge of a steep northerly slope with a large courtyard to the south (Fig. 63). The great hall was entered by a porch, and three doorways in the screen led to butteries and a cloister around which were two kitchens. Further to the east were large suites of rooms, often independent structures but joined together by long pentices, open-sided covered walks. They were planned round gardens or grass plots. Here were the king's and queen's separate accommodation. In the larger houses, in fact, one aspect of planning which reflected the increasingly hierarchical state of the monarchy is the way in which separate arrangements were made for the households of the different parts of the royal family. The king had his set of rooms and kitchen, the queen and the king's eldest son had theirs. This is particularly true of a fully developed Edwardian castle like Beaumaris on Anglesey (Taylor 1985), which has a series of what might be described as self-contained royal accommodation units each serving one household. This probably also helps to account for the multiple chapels found in medieval royal palaces and the larger royal houses.

Parallel with this provision of separate accommodation for different households within the royal family was the development of a new English royal family estate. The principal function of the crown estate was seen as providing adequate endowment for all members of the royal family (Wolffe 1971, 52–8), this was in turn made necessary by the shrinking of that much wider continental 'family estate of the Plantagenets', the Angevin Empire.

Large-scale seignorial units were created for the upkeep of members of the royal family, the first being the county of Cornwall (1227) later to become an earldom and then duchy. There followed the county palatine and earldom of Chester (1246) augmented by Flintshire (1284), belonging inalienably to the king's eldest son from 1333. The royal county and honour of Lancaster were increased by the forfeited de Montfort lands in 1265 and by the forfeited Ferrers lands in 1266. This vast inheritance of the dukes of Lancaster was held with other gifts by Edward III's son, John of Gaunt. In this way the leading members of the royal family were set up as virtually independent economic units within the kingdom.

Towards the end of the Middle Ages there are signs of a move towards greater regularity of planning. This takes two forms, which are found in different places concurrently. The first is round great courtyards. King's Langley was built around three such courts: the inner, middle and outer courts were described as being cleansed in 1305–6 (Neal 1973, 34). One of these was known as the great court and contained the principal royal apartments including the hall, chapel and the prince's chamber (referring to the Prince of Wales who became Edward II). Separate provision for the queen was made in other apartments: her wardrobe was next to her chamber and her larder beneath it. Along the west side of the westernmost court excavation has unearthed a long wine cellar with buildings over. Down the other side of the court were kitchens, ovens and bakehouses. There were also a gatehouse, whose position is unspecified, a well-house, the prince's stable and the chancellor's stable. On the north side of the palace was the Dominicans' priory church crowned by a belfry with a clock added later by Edward III. In the fifteenth century the Scottish kings achieved a regular courtyard plan at Linlithgow, the wings of which were gradually joined together to present an externally unified design. It is multi-storey, perhaps owing something to French influence, and strongly defensive, presenting the appearance from the outside of a gigantic tower keep

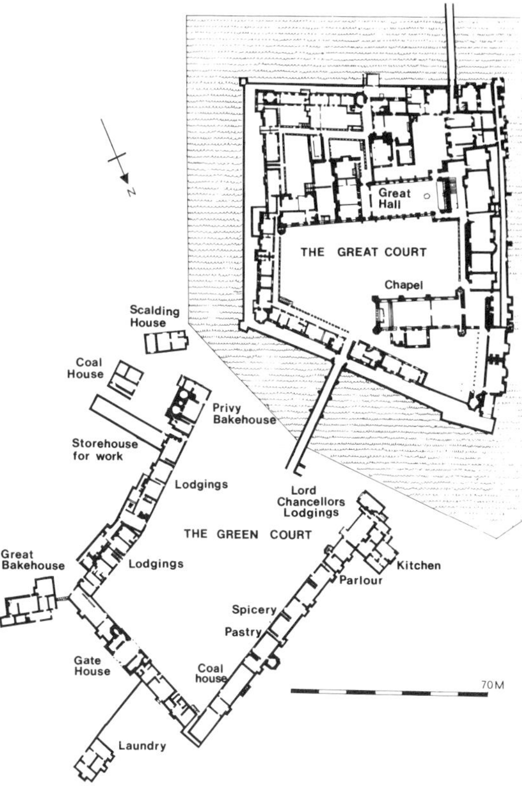

43 (Above) *Eltham Palace (Greater London) as surveyed by John Thorpe c.1603, with additional information derived from modern excavations.* (After Colvin *et al.*, 1982.)

(Pringle 1989). The south range is extremely English in appearance, not surprising in view of James IV's marriage in 1503 to Margaret Tudor, the daughter of Henry VII.

An entirely different plan involving the building of a number of separate units in series has been found by excavation at the Black Prince's palace of Kennington (Surrey) (Dawson 1976, Figs 2, 4). The hall was in the centre. To the north-west and adjoining it was the great chamber with the privy chamber over it. Separated from, but on the same alignment, was the queen's chamber surrounded by the privy garden. To the south of the hall and also in different buildings were the larder/saucery and the kitchen. At the south-eastern end of the site and at right angles to the line of the hall was a long stable block.

Eltham Palace (Greater London) in its early sixteenth-century state represents the apogée of late medieval planning (Fig. 43) and provides a prototype for the regular symmetry of a Tudor

44 *Eltham Palace (Greater London). The palace is approached by a stone bridge over the moat which divides it from the former outer courtyards. There was originally a gatehouse with a drawbridge but now it consists of four centred arches, stone ribs and pointed cut waters, dating from Edward IV's improvements.* (Photograph: J. M. Steane.)

45 Eltham Palace (Greater London). The excavated remains of the royal apartments, west side. The photograph is taken within the inner moat of Bishop Bek's palace, looking across the Tudor additions to the medieval buildings. (Photograph: J. M. Steane.)

Palace like Nonsuch (Strong 1978, 14–19). The quadrangular plan of the inner court was determined by the existence of Bishop Bek's retaining wall and moat (Fig. 44). The surviving remains of the medieval house include a long and extended retaining wall on the east side outside Bishop Bek's which is attributed to Queen Isabella, (1315–20). Within this moated *enceinte* were halls (in the plural), the king's and queen's chapel, a great bridge, a 'long chamber next to the king's great chamber', 'the bath house' and 'the princes tower'. Edward IV rebuilt the great hall in 1475–83, which survives, and the chapel which does not. We first hear of the outer court being entered by a gatehouse. A new bridge took the visitor or courtier over the moat into the great or inner court. The hall straddles the centre of the complex but around three sides were further rows of lodgings (Fig. 45). These are characteristic of domestic planning at the top end of society. Further small and enclosed courts were behind, housing the royal apartments, kitchen and other offices.

The apparently regular planning at Eltham was largely dictated by the site. The inner courtyard, 29.8 × 57.9m (98 × 190ft), with its ranges of surrounding buildings was the result of building round the pre-existing moated episcopal house. A sense of grandeur and symmetry crept in with the majestic scale of the outer court, 45.72 × 85.34m (150 × 280ft) lined with buildings, largely sixteenth century in date. Regular planning from the start, however, came in earnest with Bridewell and Nonsuch. The young Henry VIII early displayed his love of architectural ostentation in the building of Bridewell Palace between 1515 and 1523 (Gadd and Dyson 1981, Dyson 1989, 5–9) (Fig. 46). It provided him with a new London home after the burning of the old palace of Whitehall in 1512. Excavation in 1978, combined with documentary studies, has reconstructed the plan of the palace as consisting of a principal courtyard, the south wing of which terminated with a gallery along the Thames waterfront, and an outer courtyard to the east, close to the river Fleet (Fig. 47). To begin with, access to the palace was possible only by water. Even Henry VIII was not all-powerful when it came to building on or next to other people's property. Bridewell Palace was hemmed in by the Bishop of Salisbury's house and garden on the west and by St Bride's rectory and the town house of the abbots of Faversham on the north. The king had to wait until 1521 before he could accomplish the take-over of the latter property. He could then

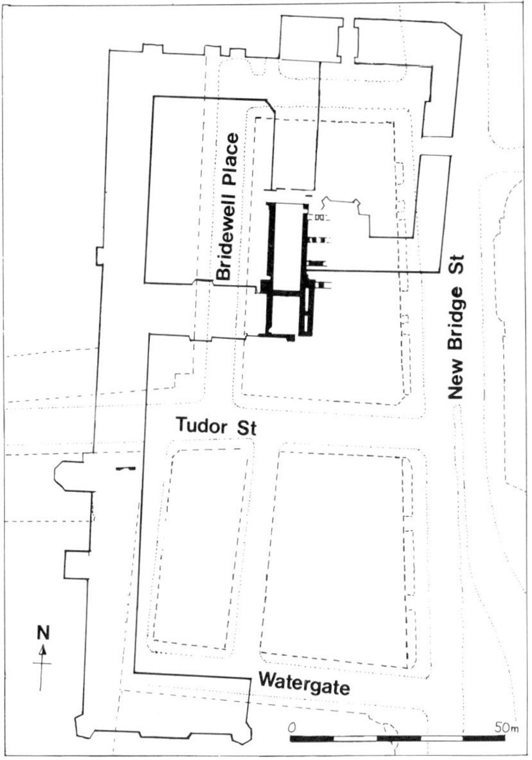

46 Bridewell Palace, City of London. A reconstruction of the plan of Henry VIII's palace (shown in solid lines) superimposed upon the modern street plan (shown in dotted lines) with the structures excavated in 1978 (shown in solid black). (After Dyson.)

extend a new outer courtyard to the east which provided him with his landward entry. Thus the regular plan was accomplished in two campaigns.

The fully-fledged, ordered planning of a royal palace is reached with Nonsuch (Surrey). Nonsuch Palace was built during the last nine years of Henry VIII's reign. The inner court was laid out over the foundations of Cuddington church; it was begun on 22 April 1538 and was rapidly brought to completion by 1544; the outer court was not entirely finished when the king died in 1547, having spent £24,500 on the buildings. The whole site was excavated in the two summers of 1959 and 1960 (Biddle 1961, 1–20) (Fig. 48). Interim reports tell us that the overall size of the palace was 114.9 × 61.6m (377 × 202ft) laid out in two equal-sized courts, 40.2 × 35m (132 × 115ft) with a smaller kitchen court lying to the east. The regularity of the planned layout was more apparent than real. It could be studied from the parchmarks revealed in the dry summers of 1989–90. The outer court was entered on the north by a broad four-turreted gatehouse. Within were suites of rooms, two storeys high, arranged on the 'college staircase' principle, opening off from the centre of both sides of the court. Entrances led west to a stable-yard and east into the kitchen court. The court itself was paved with flint, cobbling and paths of squared flagstones. The inner court was approached by a flight of eight steps through the inner gatehouse (cf. Hampton Court and the outer gatehouse of St John's College, Cambridge) and was similar in plan to the outer but had bay windows, facing inwards (two on each side), and an extraordinary south front which showed French influence in plan, form and execution. It had elaborate octagonal angle-towers as well as an off-centre subsidiary tower. It was built on lighter foundations (of chalk and stone rubble) than the outer court and was ashlar up to the first-floor level, above this the building was half-timbered. The decoration of the inner court building was remarkable and earned for the whole palace the name 'Nonsuch'. It covered all the inward-facing walls of the inner court, the whole of the south front, much of the corner towers, as well as the east and possibly the west faces of the court, which were 274.3m (900ft) in length and between 3 and 7m (10 and 20ft) in height. It consisted of large plaster panels, ornamented in high-relief with human and animal figures and studded with fruit and floral motifs. These plaster panels were held in position by timber framing covered with slate hangings, carved and gilded (Biddle, 1961, 1008). This somewhat overpowering decorative scheme greeted the courtier at Nonsuch.

While the basic plan of the palace is straightforward and largely symmetrical the actual functions of the rooms is more debatable. We await the full report of the excavations for guidance. In the meantime, it seems undoubted that the royal apartments were on the first floor, the 'kings side' being on the west and the 'queen's side' on the east; they were connected through the privy gallery in the southern wing. The ground floor was taken up with rooms housing the queen's servants. On the 'king's

side' a magnificent wide winding staircase led from the ground-floor guard chamber to a waiting room adjoining the presence chamber. This was a large room, where in 1599 Thomas Platter, waiting for Queen Elizabeth I to appear, noted the contrast between tapestried walls and the straw covering the floor, and the carpeted path leading to the queen's red-damask chair under a canopy fixed to the ceiling. Renaissance monarchs used this impressive symbol of sovereignty rarely but effectively (Baillie 1967, 169). Farther on, the preserve of the royal household servants and penetrated otherwise only by the great and powerful, were the privy closet and privy chamber. The closet was a small room used for private interviews; the privy chamber was where the king would normally take his meals. The king's bed chamber and other rooms were in the front of the south wing and the gallery was at the rear overlooking the courtyard. Garderobes were accommodated in the thick spine wall running down the centre of the south wing. The queen's rooms occupied the first-floor space over the wine cellar, the east and part of the south wings and included a back staircase, bed chamber, chapel and other rooms.

The archaeology of the building confirms what we know from other sources. It was not the first serious attempt to build in a purely Renaissance manner in England and was a curious mélange of traditional English (and Gothic) and Renaissance styles derived from France and Italy. Nonsuch sums up a number of aspects of the last few years of Henry VIII's reign. It was ruthlessly sited over a demolished church and was built using materials derived from the dissolved Merton Priory. Its scale, rapid execution and showiness illustrate the ambition, demonic energy and lack of architectural taste of its founder. Despite its relatively small size, compared with Hampton Court, it was hardly a simple rural retreat. The planning shows a decisive move in the direction of a more rigid hierarchical ordering of monarchical life. Simply by the fact of withdrawing from the more populous centres of court life, Henry was contributing to the mystique of the Tudor monarchy. The £24,000 he spent on the project was an act of reckless and ostentatious consumption which his government could ill afford. Despite the total demolition of the building only 130 years after its construction, the larger-than-life reputation of Nonsuch has survived.

That the Scottish kings were not far behind in sophisticated palace planning is demonstrated by the extraordinarily lavishly decorated royal apartments at Stirling, built by James V *c.*1540. It seems likely that the classical forms used, echoing work on the Continent, were the result of an influx of French masons encouraged by the king's two successive marriages to French princesses (Fawcett 1990).

47 Bridewell Palace, City of London. The excavations of 1978, showing the east range of the principal courtyard in the centre, the courtyard itself on the left, and the outer, entrance courtyard on the right. (Photograph: Museum of London.)

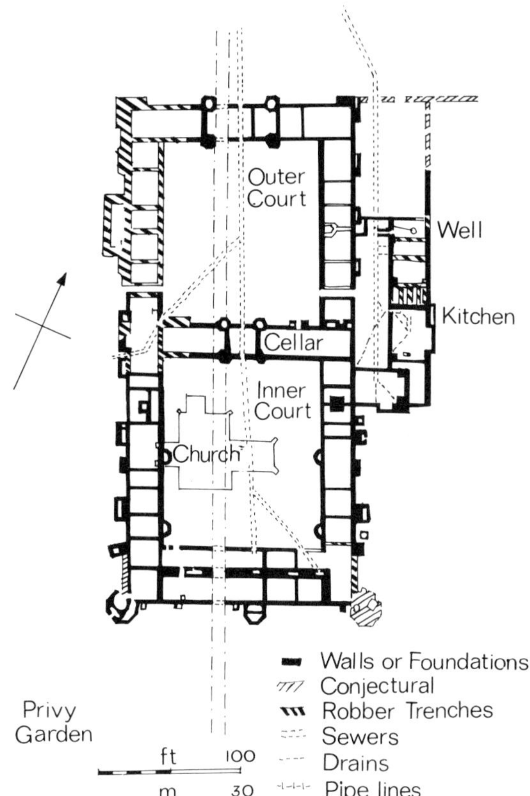

48 Nonsuch Palace (Surrey). The plan of Henry VIII's palace as excavated. Its symmetry, compared with the palace at Clarendon, is remarkable. (After Biddle.)

Halls

Far more is known about the defences of royal castles than about the buildings inside they protected. Few indeed of the medieval halls and other ancillary buildings of castles, palaces and houses have come down relatively intact. There are, however, three ways to gain an understanding of these medieval royal domestic buildings: through the physical remains which often take the exiguous form of post-holes, slots, footings or simply robber trenches, wall scars and weathering lines; secondly, by means of similar buildings which have survived relatively intact, such as the halls of castles built by nobles, bishops or barons; and lastly, with the help of such documentation as building instructions, accounts and surveys, which is profuse, at any rate for the thirteenth century. Despite the difficulties of reconstructing their appearance, all the documentary and archaeological evidence points to great halls remaining the centre of palaces and royal houses, the scene of great councils, lavish banquets and all the traditional ceremony of the court, until the end of the Middle Ages and well into the early modern period.

The positioning of halls inside castles or within the groups of buildings comprising the 'king's houses' is illuminating. At times residence preceded defence: the hall was there before the curtain wall itself, as at Pickering (North Yorkshire) (Fig. 49) and Corfe (Dorset). These, however, were both on the edge of the early fortified *enceintes*. When the curtain wall was built at Pickering in the second half of the twelfth century the west wall of the old hall was pulled down and the hall enlarged to the width of the new curtain (Thompson 1985, 14, 15, 18). At Corfe the eleventh-century 'old hall' in the west bailey shored up the curtain wall of 1202–4 which was built up against it, thus blocking its range of semicircular windows (RCHM 1970, 69, RCHM 1960, 30–6). In other castles the hall was placed in the centre of the defended area as in the surviving roofed baronial castle of Oakham (Rutland). At Windsor, Henry II's two-storeyed block of buildings known as *domus regis* certainly extended between and into two towers of the north wall of the fortified area, but the hall itself was at right angles to the wall. Later its site was built on by Edward III for a great chamber, and a new great hall arose occupying part of the south range and abutting on to the king's chapel. In other castles the hall was

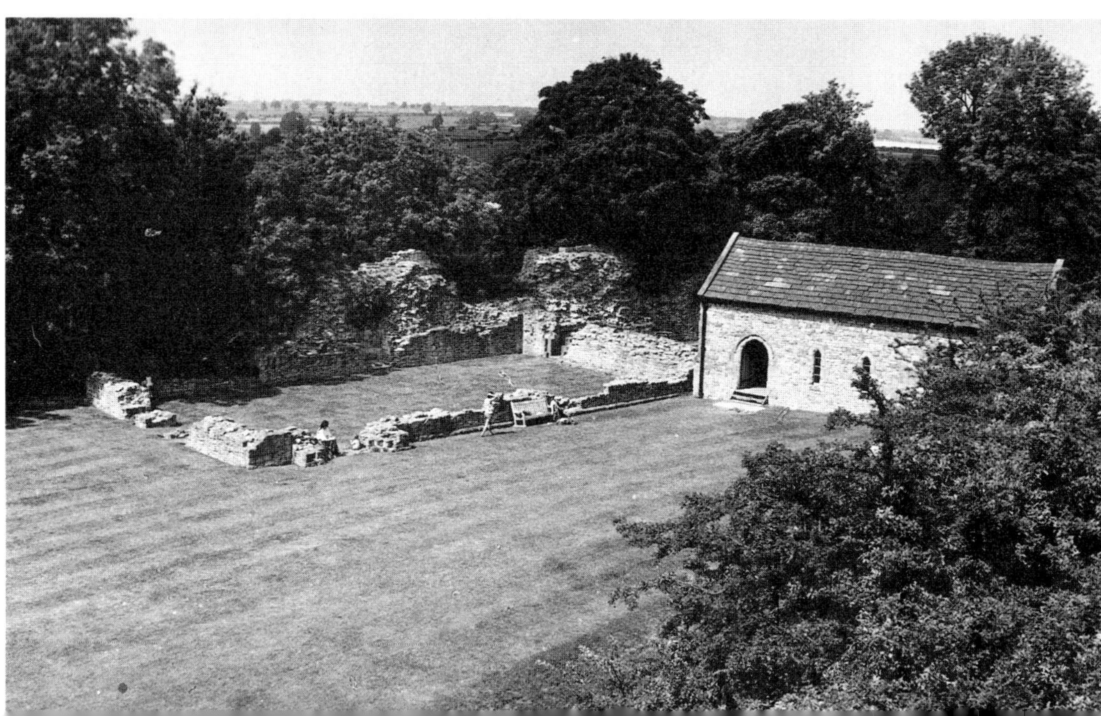

49 Pickering Castle (North Yorkshire). The building in ruins on the left is the New Hall, rebuilt in 1314 for the Countess Alice, wife of Earl Thomas of Lancaster. It had two storeys and a stone roof; it was used later as a court house and called the King's Hall or Motte Hall. To the right is the single-storeyed chapel in existence in 1227, which became known as the chapel of St Nicholas and was used for saying masses for the souls of the Dukes of Lancaster. (Photograph: J. M. Steane.)

deliberately built up against the curtain from the beginning. This had three advantages. It saved space, was economical with materials, and the curtain provided a firm base for lateral chimneys. At Conway (Gwynedd), for instance, the well-preserved great hall of the late thirteenth century occupies the whole of the south curtain (RCHM 1956, Caernarvonshire, Fig. 60). At Caernarfon (Gwynedd) also, although the evidence is much more fragmentary, the ruins of the hall abut the curtain wall, extending from the queen's tower to the chamberlain's tower (RCHM 1960, 135). Its west wall is in part common to the rear of the queen's tower to a height of not less than 11m (36ft) judging from the toothing in the masonry on the rear face: it bonds with the curtain wall up to half height. As castles became more compact in the later Middle Ages the hall might be found inserted as one storey in a gatehouse, as at Beaumaris (Anglesey). Here the south part of the first floor of the northern gatehouse served as a great hall. It was entered from stair turrets and communicated with the upper rooms of the bastions.

It is likely that most of the first few generations of royal halls built after the Norman Conquest were of timber earthfast construction. The so-called East Hall I at the royal palace at Cheddar was a major aisled hall with an arcade of ten bays and an entrance in the west end (Rahtz 1979, 170–7) (Fig. 50). It was

50 *Cheddar (Somerset), view looking westward. In the background to the right are ruins of the eleventh-century chapel. In the foreground concrete posts mark out positions of major timbers of the twelfth- and early thirteenth-century aisled halls of the royal palace. Beyond (under the school) are the remains of the tenth-century west halls.* (Photograph: J. M. Steane.)

dated to the twelfth century and was probably used by Henry I on his visits of 1121 and 1130. West Hall IV is an unaisled structure on the same alignment, and is a good deal smaller than East Hall I. It may have been built a little earlier but seems to have overlapped in use with it. The hall at King John's hunting lodge at Writtle (Essex) was also wholly of timber and was unusual in being almost square in plan (see Fig. 42); it was dated between 1211 and 1306 (Rahtz 1969, 51–6).

Entrance to the hall was usually by a doorway in a lateral wall. These early halls were seldom provided with porches, and despite the partial protection from draughts provided by a wooden screen at the lower end, a great hall must have been a miserably windy place. Blue smoke from the logs burning on the central hearth was inadequately conveyed out by the louvre in the roof. The floor was rank with rushes. In 1158 when Henry II and Louise VII were both at Bec in Normandy the Angevin

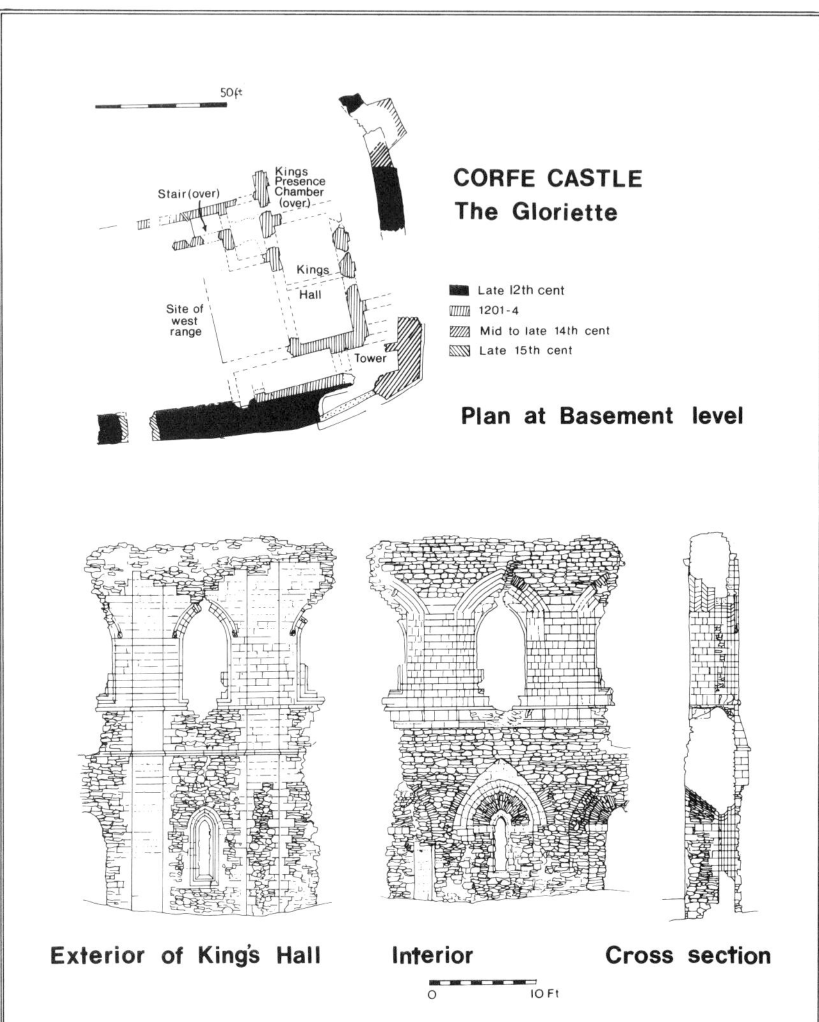

51 *Corfe Castle (Dorset). The Gloriette, a magnificent first-floor hall, was added by King John in the first years of the thirteenth century in one corner of the inner ward.* (After RCHM Dorset, 1970.)

53 St Mary's Guildhall, Lincoln. The west elevation built between 1150 and 1170 of a domestic complex which may have been the hospicium *or town-house of Henry II.* (Photograph: City of Lincoln Archaeological Unit.)

king insisted that Louis should sleep in the larger hall – as a place of greater honour – a rather dubious argument given the likely state of the draughts! The hall entrance itself might well be of some architectural pretension. The entrance to John's Gloriette at Corfe (Fig. 51) not only has a three-storeyed porch but also a fine doorway with crisp mouldings flowing right round the arch (RCHM 1970, 75). Henry III had porches added in the 1240s to Clarendon, Havering, Woodstock, Oxford, Ludgershall, Guildford and Gillingham.

Royal halls are of three main types. Some are constructed directly on the ground floor, some are built with cellars under them and some are on the first floor with an undercroft beneath. The successive timber halls at Cheddar were examples of the first type but three magnificent stone and timber survivals of royal ground-floor halls may be seen at Westminster, Winchester and Eltham (Greater London) (Fig. 52). The Guildhall at Lincoln (Fig. 53), which has recently been claimed as Henry II's *hospicium* in the city, has a large hall at first-floor level in the west range which would have been intended for important feasts and ceremonies, such as the crown-wearing itself (Stocker, 1991, 39). A vaulted basement dictated by the uneven exigencies of the site lies under James IV's hall at Stirling (Fawcett 1990, 20). An example of a *cellared* hall is found at Conwy Castle (RCHM 1956, 49–50). The Palace of the Black Prince at Kennington has produced an excavated example of an undercroft which presumably had a hall on top (Dawson 1976, 47). The base was about 0.75m (2½ft) below the ground level and there was a vaulted ceiling supported on two rows of

52 (Left) Eltham Palace (Greater London). The great hall of Edward IV begun in 1475, measuring about 30m (100ft) by 10m (30ft), has six bays divided by stepped buttresses. In each bay a pair of windows are set high up to accommodate tapestries. It was used as a barn in the nineteenth century but repaired in 1911–14. (Photograph: J. M. Steane.)

pillars. The excavator calculated that the first floor was about 1.8m (6ft) above the ground.

The larger halls were provided with nave and aisles and must have resembled contemporary ecclesiastical buildings. The aisles could easily have been subdivided into sleeping quarters for servants, guests and visitors. The very large-scale Norman Westminster Hall had a series of clerestory windows and wall passages enriched with historiated capitals, a few of which have survived and are to be seen in the Jewel Tower; their original location is uncertain (RCHM 1925, 122, pl. 177).

The great hall of Clarendon Palace was investigated and exposed in the excavations of 1933–4 (James and Robinson 1985, 90–6). It was the largest building on the site and substantial portions of medieval masonry can still be seen among the trees on this wooded ridge. It was a rectangular building dating from the twelfth century and measuring internally 25 × 16m (82 × 52ft). Five major entrances were identified: three doorways led west into the service area and there were also entrances in the east and south walls with a porch leading off into the courtyard. Within, the hall was partitioned by six piers forming two arcades of four bays and a central aisle 6.11m (20ft) wide. The floor was of chalk 7.6 to 12.7cm (3 to 5in) thick and at the east end of the hall there was a dais, the kerbing of which measured 3.35 × 10m (11 × 33ft). No doubt the king's seat, referred to in the documents, was placed on this dais.

Nothing is known of the roof structure except that the roof was clad in shingles, as were other buildings at Clarendon. From 1238–52 no less than 130,000 of these small wooden tiles were ordered for roof works in the palace in five consignments from the forests of Downton (Wiltshire), Gillingham (Dorset) and from the New Forest. Unfortunately, not a single one from Clarendon has survived in the archaeological record. Lead was used for gutters, ridges and flashings; some of this was mined in Derbyshire. The roof ridges were decorated with two lead balls (*pomellos*) and louvres were also possibly made of lead but more likely to have been fashioned of pottery.

Whereas it is possible to appreciate the scale of a medieval royal hall by looking at the flinty walls and pier bases of the great hall at Clarendon, this roofless ruin still leaves much to

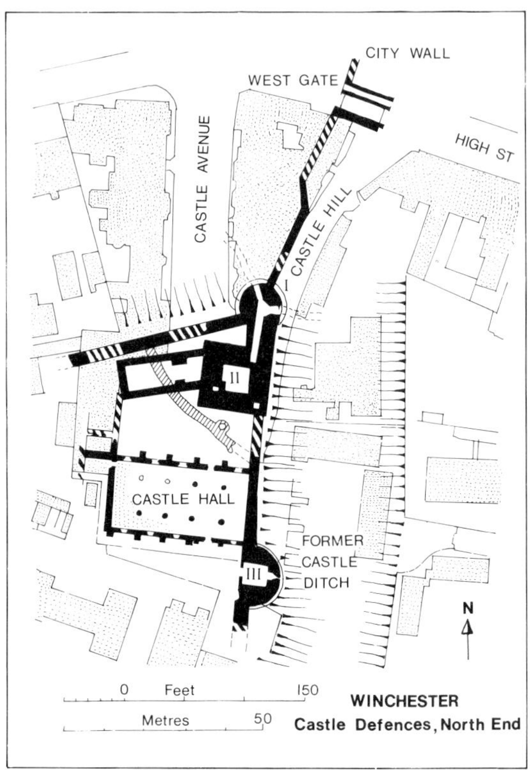

54 Winchester Castle (Hampshire) defences, north end, showing the immediate context of the hall. (After Biddle, 1965.)

conjecture. Another very good example is the archiepiscopal hall that survives in fragments at Canterbury (Rady, Tatton Brown, Bowen, 1991, 1–61). It was probably the prototype of the royal Winchester Castle Hall which is so much better preserved and has rightly been called 'the finest surviving aisled hall of the thirteenth century' (Portal 1899). The hall at Winchester (Fig. 54) was built between 1222 and 1235 at a cost of over £500. Standing in a commanding position above the town, it is 33.8m (111ft) long from east to west 16.7m (55ft) wide, and consists of a nave divided into two aisles of five bays by two rows of Purbeck marble columns composed of clusters of four slender shafts. Study of the outer stonework of the south wall (Fig. 55) reveals that the roofing in the thirteenth century consisted of a series of separate gables each containing one two-light window with transom, a quatrefoil in the head

55 Winchester Castle (Hampshire). The south wall of the castle hall. The former appearance of the gable windows of the thirteenth-century roof with their circular openings over the plate tracery of the double lights can be seen, together with the fourteenth-century blocking and raising of the walls. (Photograph: J. M. Steane.)

and a circular light above. When the roofs of the aisles were raised in the fourteenth century, the circular lights were removed but their stone frames were left blocked in the now heightened walls between the windows. It is likely that the steeply pitched roof covering at this time consisted of oak shingles.

The use of circular windows placed in the gable ends is a repeated feature of thirteenth-century great halls. Instructions were given by Henry III for their insertion at Woodstock and the castle at Marlborough; they were also seen in the gable of the hall in Chester Castle. In other instances, windows described as *fenestrae estantivae* were specified. *Estantivae* means upright and because there are references to roof, crests and gutters of such windows, it is likely that they were tall openings with independent gables and roofs set at right angles to the main roof, as described above at Winchester Castle Hall. By the end of Henry III's reign there was glass in most of the windows of his halls and chambers. Sometimes, however, there was only glass in the upper part, the lower lights still being closed by a shutter. Two types of lead came (the grooved metal frame) were in use: one with pronounced flashing and the other with the profile trimmed flat (James and Robinson 1988, 224–5). Attempts were made to regulate the passage of air into halls and chambers by the use of delicate gothic-traceried lead ventilators, found at both Winchester and Clarendon. Another category of window furniture from Clarendon and elsewhere is iron bars. 'And in the queen's hall let there be made a window toward the garden, well barred with iron.' Both window grills and individual bars have turned up in excavations. Henry III had a bad fright when a madman climbed through an unbarred window at Woodstock with intent to murder him as he lay in bed. The affronted king ordered iron bars to be placed in the windows of all his chambers – even across the vent of his privy which discharged into the Thames at Westminster!

Two royal halls of the later Middle Ages are at Eltham and Stirling. Edward IV's hall at Eltham seems to have influenced the design of the outsize structure at Stirling, now thought to be the work of James IV, *c.*1500. With its five great lateral fireplaces and hammer beam roof it was clearly intended primarily as a setting for major ceremonial occasions, not for daily usage. The irregularities of the castle rock on which it stands account for the vaulted basement underneath it (Fawcett 1990).

56 Hampton Court (Greater London). The great hall was built by Henry VIII in 1532–4 on the site of Wolsey's hall but on a larger scale. At ground-floor level are cellars lit by small two-light windows. Above is a great expanse of brickwork with five four-light windows with four-centred heads divided by buttresses rising on three steps. In the east bay is a large oriel window. The hall itself is built on the first floor with a central fireplace. (Photograph: J. M. Steane.)

How were these great buildings heated and lit (Gee 1987, 88–105)? The timber halls of the late Saxon and Norman periods had been warmed by central hearths set on round, octagonal or rectangular platforms paved with end-set stones or tiles. Clarendon great hall is likely to have been heated centrally because there were no signs of chimneys in the lateral or gable end walls (nor, incidentally, did the excavators find any evidence of a hearth). A central hearth was found at neighbouring Ludgershall, dating to the twelfth century. Despite the disadvantage of smoke and the encumbrance of a centrally-placed feature, this method of heating a great space continued to be used right up to the end of the Middle Ages. The heating of first-floor halls presented a greater engineering problem. Henry III ordered the Keeper of Woodstock Palace to make

> *a hearth of freestone, high and good in the chamber above the wine cellar in the great court, and a great louvre above the said hearth.*

The hall at Hampton Court, 1535, had a central hearth raised on an octagonal pier of the undercroft which had four brick ribs branching out on either side to support the hearth (Fig. 56). In the roof was a similarly ambitious smoke-vent, louvre or 'femerell' which has now been removed but is known to have been of three storeys, hexagonal, with a domed top (Salzman 1952, 219). In castles, on the other hand, fireplaces and chimneys placed laterally in thick walls seem to have been favoured from the twelfth century onwards. The hall at Edward I's Conwy Castle, for instance, has three fireplaces, one in each of the north, west and south walls. These were of impressive magnificence, as befitted the King's accommodation in a conquered land (RCHM 1956, 52, Fig. 61). Five lateral fireplaces of generous proportions were inserted into the walls of the vast hall of James IV at Stirling. Although of robust Renaissance design, the general impression is still medieval (Fawcett 1990). The floors of such wall fireplaces were again frequently of end-set tiles. A third solution was the back-to-back fireplace. Among the earliest known are three double fireplaces (*camini duplici*) provided in 1394–6 for a new gatehouse at

Windsor Manor (Bedfordshire). This system, economical of space and chimney construction, was also found in royal kitchens. Fireplaces in lateral and end walls were built more frequently in the later Middle Ages. The kings of Scotland presided over the ceremonial hall in Stirling Castle with a massive fireplace at their backs as well as four others heating the rest of the great space.

One aspect of great open fires which is often forgotten is that they provided a source of artificial light. This was supplemented in royal castles and houses by lanterns, torches, lamps and candles (Goodall 1980, 161–4). To find the way about the courtyards, stairways and pentices, lanterns were provided. Dark corridors were illuminated by torches and flares set in wall-mounted iron rings. Internal lighting problems were inadequately met by lamps and candlesticks. Cresset lamps, with oil and a floating wick set in a bowl or a funnel-shaped vessel designed for suspension are likely to have smoked and given a wavering light. Candles in the quantity required for adequate lighting of large spaces would have been costly.

Pricket type, socketed or composite candlesticks were commissioned from blacksmiths (Fig. 57). Single pricket spikes would be set on wooden bases, multiple spikes could be attached to a beam. Socketed candlesticks could be set on straight, angled or cranked stems. These might be jammed between stones in a

57 *Artificial lighting.* 1 *A pricket-type candlestick in which the end of the candle was impaled on an upright spike.* 2 *Candlestick containing a loop which gripped the body of the candle. Fifteenth century.* 3 *Pricket-type iron candlestick with elaborate tripod base.* 4 *Candlesticks of this type were usually reserved for the houses of the wealthy or for ecclesiastical use.* 5 *Multiple cresset lamp with small perforations for wicks.* 6 *Glass lamp found with thirteenth-century pottery. It would have contained oil with a floating wick and have been suspended from the ceiling.* 7 *Small pottery cresset lamp. Twelfth century.* 8 *Stone cresset lamp with handle.* (1, 4, 5–8 Winchester Museum, 2, 3, Museum of London.)

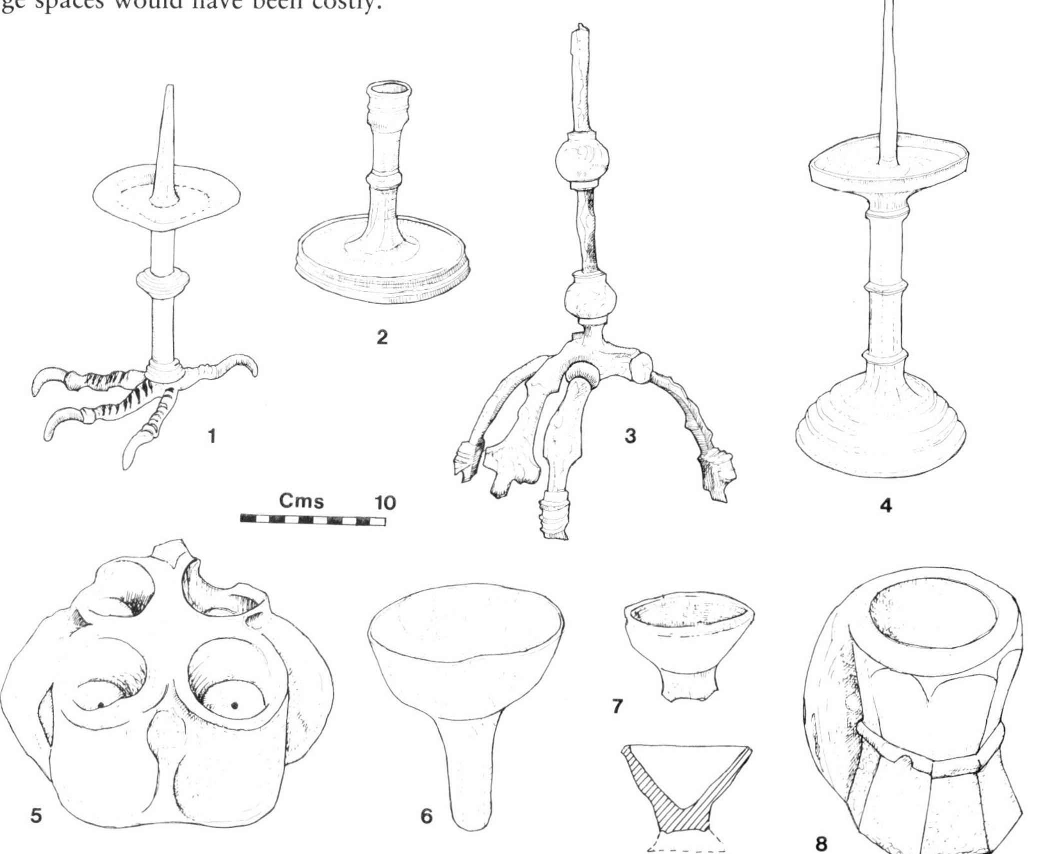

wall or attached to a pan which would catch the wax and serve as a base. Three-armed candlesticks have been found in ecclesiastical contexts such as Rievaulx and were doubtless part of the furnishing of royal chapels. A superb folding bronze and enamelled travelling candlestick has been found at the royal and monastic site at Grove (Berkshire). It is decorated with heraldic plaques and is thought to be late thirteenth or early fourteenth century (Baker 1981, 336–8).

Kitchens

One of the principal uses of the great hall was as a communal dining place. In monastic layouts the kitchen is nearly always placed in close proximity to the refectory, and when studying what is known of the layouts of royal palaces, it is certainly worth seeking the kitchen near the great hall. At Clarendon in the later Middle Ages the kitchens and their ancillary buildings were sited round an open quadrangle or cloister immediately to the west of the hall, surrounded by alleys or walkways 1.98m (6½ft) wide (James and Robinson 1988, 82–90). The earlier of the two kitchens, the so-called king's kitchen, may have started life as a detached building lying due west of the great hall. Kitchens were detached because of their fire risk to the surrounding buildings. At Clarendon there was a central chimney block with two large fireplaces of herringbone-set tile laid back to back. Further cooking facilities were provided by a fireplace/oven built against the north wall. This was 3.9m (13ft) wide, capacious enough to roast the proverbial ox, and built of herringbone tiles, but it had been altered to contain a circular oven. The date of the west kitchen was twelfth century but there had been extensive rebuilding in the fourteenth century.

On the north side of the kitchen cloister was another building identified as the kitchen of the household, or as the Edwardian survey calls it, the kitchen of the family (Philips 1833, 151–8). The survey suggests that by 1273 the original kitchen was continuing in use for the king, while the new kitchen, less than thirty years old, was devoted to preparing food for the household. It is not an unusual feature for a kitchen, preparing food for the king's mouth only, to figure in medieval royal documents. It is symptomatic of the increase in formalized etiquette found in later medieval palace life. Curiously, no reference is made in the latest report to the presence of fireplaces or ovens.

Set between the angle of the west and the north kitchens at Clarendon was a room identified as the *herlebecheria*: a scullery or slaughterhouse. The salsary, saucery or salting house, has been located to the south of the kitchen cloister. Running north–south was a water channel with stone arches. Such a drain may have been a 'blood and guts' drain for the salsary or it may have been used to sluice away the accumulation of surface water from the great courtyard.

When we turn to consider the culinary arrangements of a rural hunting-lodge such as King John's hunting-lodge, Writtle, some of the same characteristics are apparent (Rahtz 1969, 38–51). Rahtz found that the kitchen at Writtle was in one range with the chapel and hall. The kitchen and hall were probably separated in the earliest phase (*c.*1211–*c.*1306). It was rebuilt on a slightly larger scale during period II (*c.*1306–*c.*1425) and during this time there was a buttery and pantry of two storeys to the west. It was only in period III (*c.*1425–1521) that the close physical association between hall and kitchen was severed and the main rooms of the hunting-lodge were shifted to the western end of the moated enclosure.

The cooking at Writtle was done on a series of fireplaces and external or internal ovens. The presence of open-air ovens is of course a commonplace in medieval peasant farmsteads. It was the perpetual fire risks attendant on their hot and greasy trade which drove the medieval cooks out of doors. As in the north kitchen of Clarendon there were four pillar bases in the period II kitchen at Writtle. The excavator suggested that they may have supported a central chimney or vent.

The finest surviving royal kitchens of late medieval date are found at Hampton Court (Chettle, Charlton and Allan 1982, 25–8). The eastern section, entered first by visitors, is the oldest and was almost certainly built by Wolsey. At one end are the hatches with moulded oak frames and shutters, communicating with the serving place. There is a large fireplace in the north wall which was reduced in width shortly after it was built; subsequently alterations in the eighteenth century introduced a smaller fireplace and a row of brick ovens

inside it. Doors led to small annexes, probably store rooms. Henry VIII greatly enlarged Wolsey's kitchen to cater for his own even larger entourage (Fig. 58). Two narrow doorways and a wide brick arch lead into the new kitchen constructed for the king in 1529. It is now divided into two by a half-height partition wall. Following normal later medieval practice all the cooking was done over open fires in the huge four-centred arched fireplaces in the lateral walls. The massive brick chimney breasts and stacks are a noteworthy feature outside. The great height of the kitchens was another characteristic, doubtless an attempt to reduce the smoke, heat and smell generated by spit-roasting over open fires. Unfortunately, most of the original roofs have gone but the two end-trusses remain, together with stone corbels originally supporting the rest. There were also timber lofts serving as storage space for food equipment or as sleeping quarters for the scullion boys who worked the spits. The joist holes indicate these subdivisions of the upper parts of the kitchen.

The buildings and layout of Hampton Court are so complete that we can with confidence reconstruct how the whole Tudor culinary complex worked (Thurley 1990, 1–28). Recent displays bring the kitchen vividly to life. Larders sited around Fish Court stored fish and uncooked meat which were prepared and taken to the great kitchen for cooking. Bread and beer, staples in late medieval diet, were brought up from the buttery and cellars situated below the hall. The new kitchen of Henry VIII was designed to serve the common tables in the lower and main body of the great hall. Two large stone hatches in its south wall opened into a second serving place. From here the cooked food was checked out and carried across the north cloister and up the stairs leading into the screens passage across the lower end of the hall. At the other end, in Wolsey's kitchen, there was a serving place with hatches, as already noted. Here the cooked food was carried to the high table on the dais end of the great hall and to the watching chamber. This was a very large room

58 Hampton Court (Greater London). The great kitchen of Henry VIII, south side. The lateral chimneys with spit mechanisms are large enough to roast oxen. (Photograph: RCHM England.)

with a magnificent coffered ceiling where the household officials and some of the nobility dined. It is likely that the king ate privately much of the time in his own room served from his own private kitchen. Here, no doubt, only the finest food was cooked.

Water supply

Given the efficient arrangements made by monastic houses from the twelfth century to provide their communities with supplies of pure drinking water, it is not surprising that elaborate systems are found in the royal palace of Westminster. There are references to a water supply in connection with the palace in 1169–70. Five years later ten shillings was spend on a conduit. A fountain or a washplace is mentioned in 1183–5 when reference is made to a 'lavatory in the King's hall'. Fragments of a highly decorated Purbeck marble basin were found in excavation at Palace Yard, Westminster (Horsman and Davison 1989, 293). This was supplemented in 1287–8 by a new lavatory made within the lesser hall incorporating marble columns, five heads of gilded copper from which the water issued, and tin cups for drinking. Further overhauling of the palace's water supply took place in 1347–8 and a mighty octagonal conduit which lasted from 1441 until the last years of the Commonwealth rose in all its glory in Palace Yard, reflecting prestige on the later medieval kings of England. Its base was found in the salvage excavation of 1973 (Horsman and Davison 1989, 294).

Wine and beer cellars

Wine needs to be stored in cool, damp, dark conditions and in various palaces, castles and houses specialized buildings were constructed to create the correct environment (Fig. 59). Excavations at King's Langley and Clarendon have produced ample evidence of what these royal wine cellars were like. At King's Langley in 1291–2 Martin of Ray, mason, was paid £66 13s 4d for making a cellar for keeping the king's wine (Neal 1973, 31–72) (Fig. 60). The cellar found on the western side of the west court measured 22.5m (74ft) by 4.8m (16ft) internally. It was constructed in blocks of chalk with piers and jambs of Totternhoe stone. It was vaulted by being divided into six quadripartite bays, separated and supported by piers. The floor was of earth and had never been paved. Post-holes and a sleeper beam were interpreted as being connected with a bench for coopering tuns of wine. The height of the vault was about 3m (10ft) and the cellar was entered from the north side by a staircase 1.52m (5ft) wide, the steps of which were in Totternhoe stone. The door jamb was pierced by holes originally containing iron hinges for a wooden door or an iron grill. The excavators found blocked doors or light wells in the east, west and south walls of bay 1 (Fig. 61).

Wines for the royal palace at Clarendon were brought by the cartload from Southampton (James and Robinson 1988, 27). The quantities can be calculated from the Liberate rolls. On New Year's Day 1227 two tuns of wine were earmarked in the port for transport to Clarendon. Another two were despatched in January 1228 and thereafter two in April and five more in November. When the king planned to spend the period leading up to the Christmas feast at Clarendon before going on to Winchester the quantities were even higher. In December 1236 orders were issued from Marlborough for four casks of wine to be sent to Clarendon from Southampton. Ten tuns were required to supplement this, to be delivered 'with speed'. After Henry had arrived on 18 December he sent for four more. The quantities of wine in fact provide a barometer for royal use of the palace.

The principal wine cellar at Clarendon was known as 'La Roche'. It is still one of the most remarkable structures on the site with its well preserved entrance staircase, ashlar-lined walls, and even the fragment of a barrel vault. It is situated in a natural declivity and runs north-south with a northern stairway leading from a square paved area and aligned with the cellar entrance. The paved area is likely to have been the place where the wine carts were unloaded and where they turned but it is a mystery as to how the wine carts penetrated the palace precincts. The structure itself consisted of a stairway giving access to two cellars, one leading off the other and both aligned north-south. The walls of both cellars were constructed of 'Hurdcote stone' and 'local white

59 Hampton Court (Greater London). Cellar under the Great Watching Chamber. The raised platforms carried racking for wine or beer barrels. (Photograph: RCHM England.)

limestone resembling clunch'. The side walls to the staircase were lined with carefully dressed, diagonally-tooled limestone ashlar blocks. At the foot of the stairs were large post-holes which were thought to have supported heavy double doors. The north cellar was barrel-vaulted and there were two round-headed recesses in the north wall, interpreted as lamp holders. The excavators reckoned that the north cellar and staircase dated from the twelfth century and that in the thirteenth century the south cellar was added. This certainly fits in with the documentary evidence for the increasingly large supplies of wine required at the Wiltshire palace.

The royal chambers of Clarendon

To the east of the great hall at Clarendon is a rectangular block excavated in the 1930s and interpreted then and now as the king's living accommodation (James and Robinson 1988, 99–114; Eames 1965, 57–85) (Fig. 62). Its position is central to the north range and its eastern wall helps to form a small courtyard, on the north side of which is the so-called Antioch chamber, and to the east are the queen's apartments. The walls of the royal apartments were of large flints set in a matrix of medium-hard brownish mortar with traces of wall-plaster adhering to the outer walls. Evidently the principal chamber was on the first floor and consisted of a richly decorated upper hall. Scenes from the life of St Margaret, the Virgin and the four Evangelists, together with a series of heads of men and women, were ordered in 1246 to be carried out in 'exquisite colours'. The interior decoration included a green painted wainscot sprinkled with golden stars. Fragments of dark green and light apple-green painted wall plaster were found on the site. More fascinating were five eight-pointed lead stars and two lead crescents picked up in the area of the king's apartments and the Antioch chamber. It was observed that they had been gilded. The lead had been first whitewashed, then sized, and gold leaf was applied above the

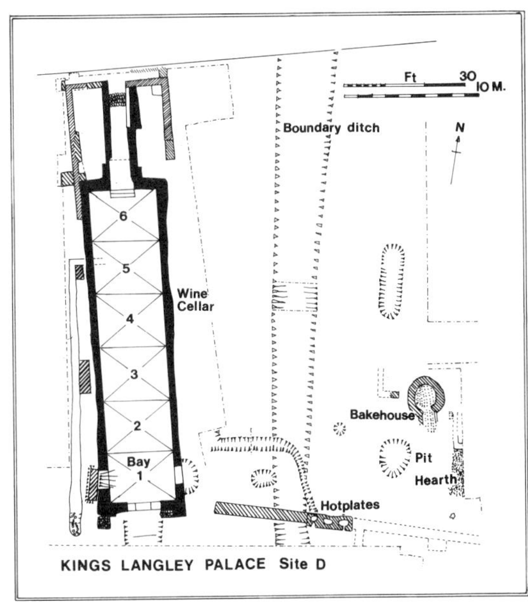

60 King's Langley Palace (Hertfordshire). Plan of excavations at site D, including the royal wine cellar and other buildings probably connected with the kitchens. (After Neal.)

size. They had central nail holes and flat backs and doubtless were nailed to flat surfaces forming an element in wall or ceiling decoration. Borenius pointed out that in 1251 the Sheriff of Wiltshire was commanded 'to paint the wainscot of [the Antioch chamber] of a green colour with golden stars'. He also cited a parallel – stars of the same type occurring on mouldings which ran across the mid-fourteenth-century wall paintings once to be seen in St Stephen's chapel, Westminster (Borenius 1943, 45–6).

Such lavish painted wall decorations were characteristic of Henry III's palaces and castles. There was already a tradition of such painting which went back to the twelfth century. Giraldus Cambrensis describes how Henry II (Henry III's grandfather) ordered an empty space of wall in a room in Winchester Castle to be filled with a painting of an eagle attacked by its four young, a rueful piece of symbolism referring to the rebellious behaviour of the king's four sons. Religious imagery usually held pride of place in decorative schemes; at Ludgershall, Northampton and Guildford the king caused paintings to be made of the parable of Dives and Lazarus, doubtless an exhortation to royal charity. Types and anti-types from the Old Testament and New Testament were set out in the 'chamber' at Winchester. In 1250 orders were given that in Winchester Castle 'the table of the king's bed' was to be painted 'with images of the guardians of Solomon's bed' (the scene described in the Song of Solomon, iii, 7–8). The Tree of Jesse and the Wheel of Fortune were painted on the mantel of the fireplace in the king's chamber at Clarendon. The king's personal taste accounts for the

61 King's Langley Palace (Hertfordshire). Excavations have revealed the nature and extent of the royal wine cellar in this house, beloved by Edward II. (After Neal.)

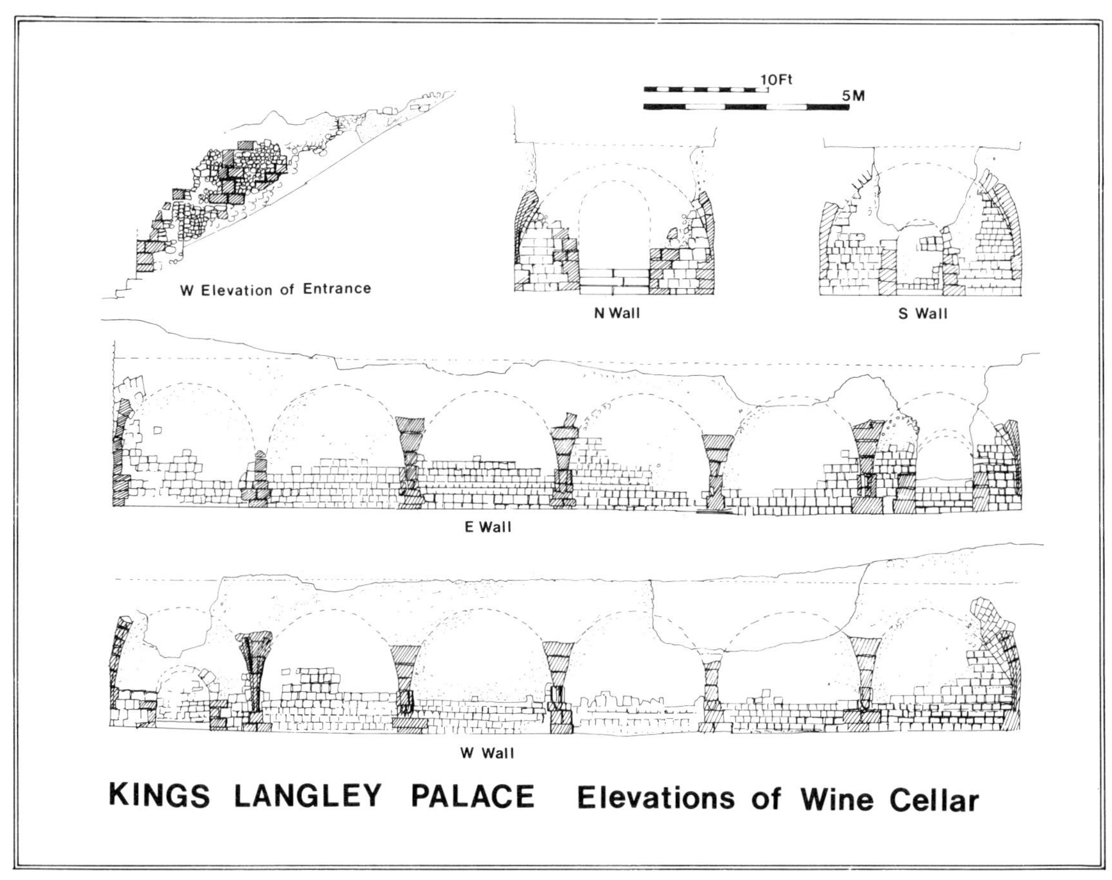

frequent presence of images of St Edward the Confessor and also the fact that the history of Joseph, an unusual subject, was painted twice, at the back of the king's seat in the small chapel of Westminster and in the new chapel of Winchester.

Non-religious subjects included the paintings of the Twelve Months which in 1265 were ordered to be painted 'on every side' of the chimney of the king's chamber at Kennington. Stone reliefs of the same subject decorated the hood of the fireplace in the queen's chamber at Clarendon. The story of Alexander was the subject which gave its name to one of the rooms at Clarendon. Another non-ecclesiastical subject was 'the story of Antioch and duel of King Richard', which really meant the third crusade and gave its name to the Antioch chamber at Clarendon in 1251. A similar subject was depicted on the walls of a room in the palace of Westminster and of one in the Tower. None of these figure paintings has been found intact but the lower part of the west wall of the Antioch chamber at Clarendon showed fragments of red masonry patterning on a white ground. It was very common practice in thirteenth-century buildings to prepare the wall in this way before painting figure subjects on top of the masonry patterns.

Henry III also made use of subject matter directly extolling the majesty of the monarchy. Kings and queens were depicted in considerable numbers in wall paintings and stained glass throughout his palaces and castles. In 1243 for instance Henry ordered 'a King and Queen sitting with the Baronage' to be painted over the dais to be erected in the hall of Dublin Castle. A strange subject with sinister portent was painted by Master William of Winchester:

> *A certain picture at Westminster, in the wardrobe where the king is wont*

62 *Clarendon Palace.* (Plan after James and Robinson.)

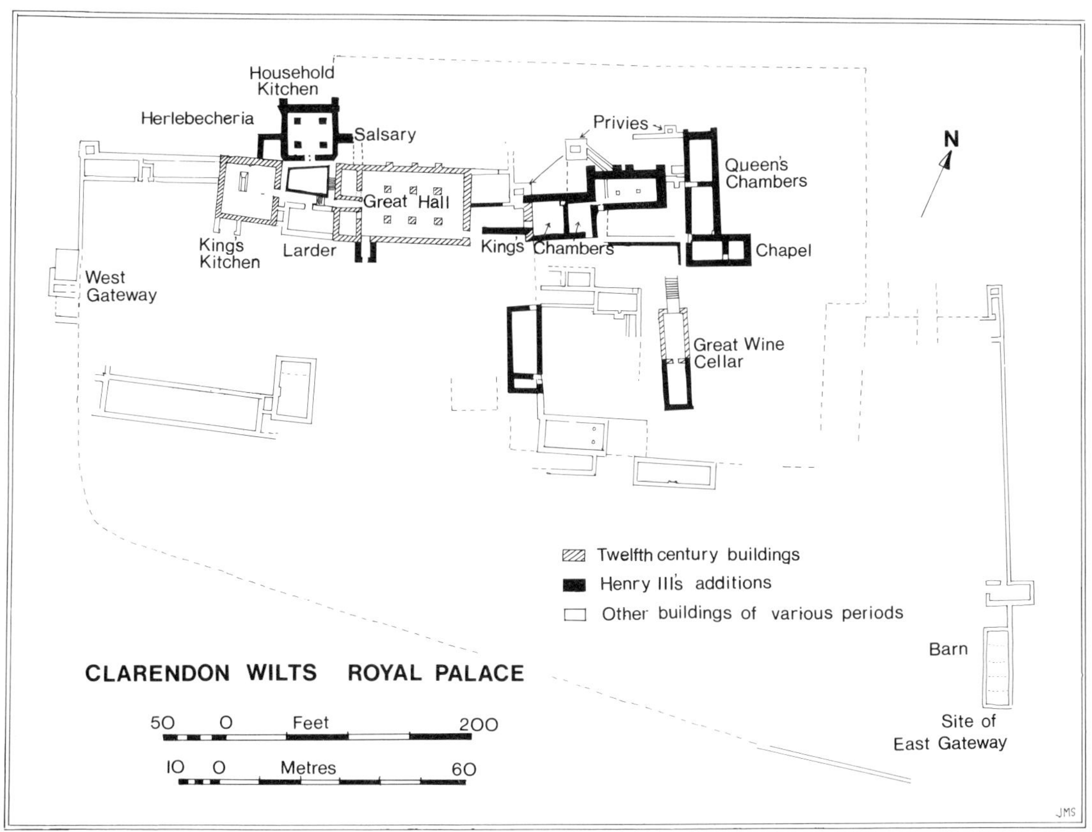

to wash his head, of the king who was rescued by his dogs from the sedition plotted against the same king by his subjects.

Several paintings with geographical subjects are known, though none have survived. 'A city' was in 1246 ordered to be painted over the door of the queen's chamber at Winchester. A map of the world was commissioned in 1239 to be painted in the hall of the same castle; a painting of the same theme, devised by Matthew Paris, was to be seen in the Painted Chamber at Westminster.

Heraldry, which figures so largely in early sixteenth-century buildings like Henry VIII's chapel, Westminster, begins to make an appearance in the repertoire of decorative motifs in royal residences in the thirteenth century. It was particularly effective in stained glass where small roundels of coloured shields were inserted in larger areas of plain or grisaille glass; one such roundel in the Burrell collection at Glasgow shows a shield bearing the royal arms, three golden leopards on a red ground differenced by a label of three points azure, which indicates an eldest son of the king. They were probably the arms of Edward of Caernarfon, Prince of Wales, and Earl of Chester 1300/1, or his son Edward, created Earl of Chester, Duke of Aquitaine and Count of Ponthieu in 1325. It is not known, however, from which building it came (Alexander and Binski 1987, 199).

63 *Windsor Castle (Berkshire) and Eton College (Buckinghamshire). The multi-towered skyline of Windsor seen from the Thames valley reminds us how Edward III refashioned the castle, at appalling cost, in the 1350s and 1360s as a centre of chivalry and to rival the Valois fortress at Vincennes. From Windsor Henry VI could watch the great chapel of his college at Eton, seen in the middle distance rising in the 1440s.*

In emulation Edward IV began to rebuild St George's chapel on a vast scale; the Tudors completed it as a dynastic monument and mausoleum. (Photograph: Cambridge University Committee for Aerial Photography.)

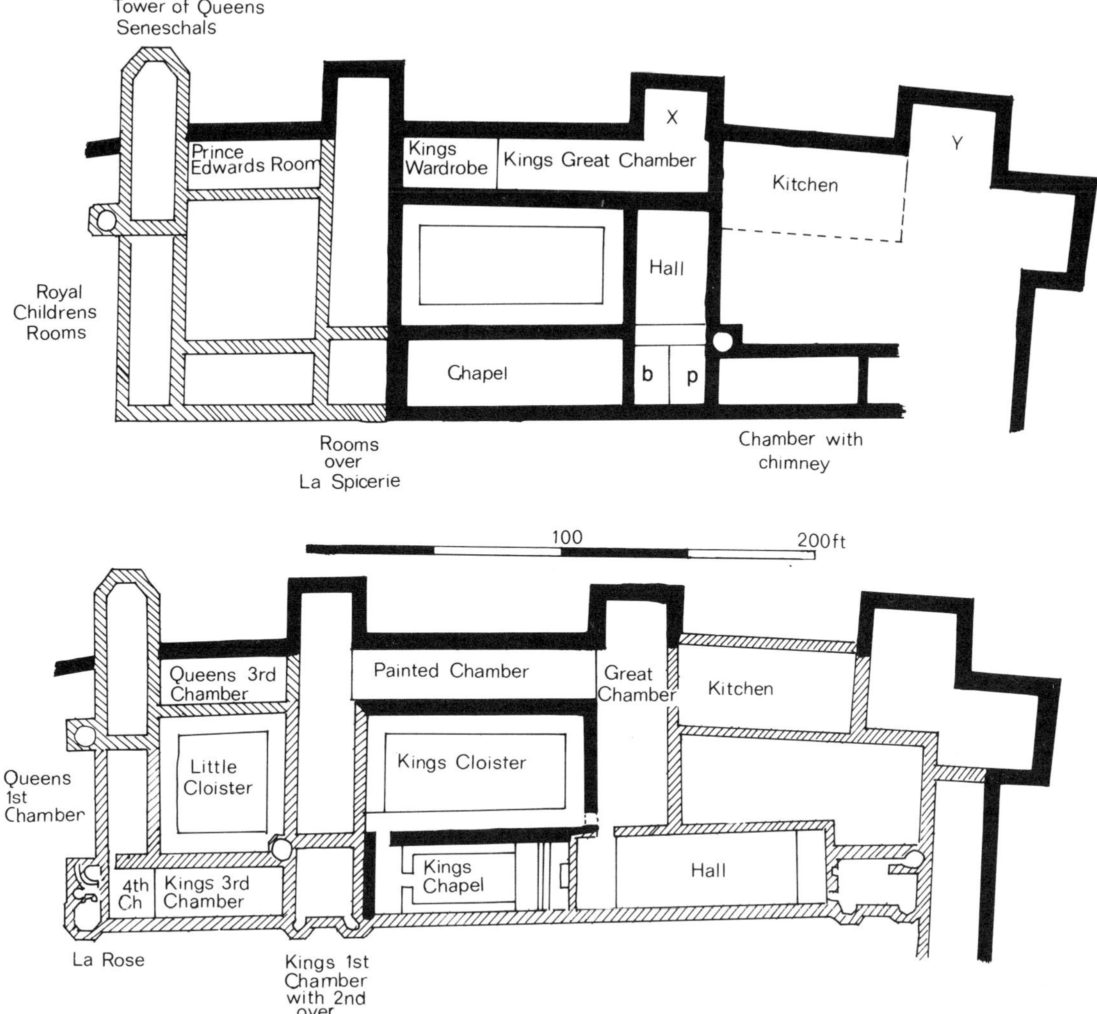

Royal apartments at Windsor in the fourteenth century

64 Windsor Castle. The development of the royal apartments. (Above) *Block plan of the first floor of the* Domus Regis *of Henry II with early alterations. The central feature is the king's cloister of 1195–6 with herb garden. To the right is the kitchen court. The hall has a buttery (b) and pantry (p). (x) and (y) are Norman towers raised 1240–41. The tower of the queen's seneschals was built 1244–5.* (Below) *The royal lodging in 1377, with alterations made by Edward III (hatched areas).* (After St John Hope, 1913.)

The first references to buildings at Windsor Castle (Fig. 63) occur in Henry I's reign; at Whitsuntide in 1110 he held his court at 'New Windsor which he himself had built', and this is thought to refer to the completion of a royal lodging in the upper bailey. By the end of the twelfth century there were other buildings rising from the lower bailey, including a *camera* or lodging of the king, a chapel, kitchens enclosed by hedges, a larder, an almonry and a great hall. Henry III was responsible for considerable restructuring of the royal accommodation at Windsor during his long reign (1216–72) (Brown, Colvin, Taylor 1963, 867). A new lodging was built for his queen, Eleanor of Provence, along the western range. It may have been in timber but she disliked it and in 1237 it was rebuilt according to her wishes. She gave birth to both a son and a daughter, and half-timbered chambers and nurseries were built for their use, arranged around a further court to the west of her lodgings. The king's great chamber in the outer bailey was destroyed by fire in 1295–6 but this was not immediately restored. It was left to Edward III to carry out between 1350 and 1377 an elaborate and expensive remodelling of the royal apartments at Windsor which cost the astronomical total of £50,772 (St John Hope 1913, 107–219).

Edward III had been born at Windsor on 13 November 1312 and was undoubtedly fond of the place, the chronicler Ranulf Higden relates how

> *our Lord the King, at the instance of William Wickham, clerk, caused many excellent buildings in the Castle of Windsor to be thrown down, and others more fair and sumptuous to be set up.*

These great works fall into three divisions. Edward's first scheme involved the construction of a hall or house for a proposed Order of the Round Table. The actual circumstances of the inauguration of the order are confused. This is perhaps understandable in the circumstances described by Adam de Murimuth, quoted below (p. 157).

In February 1343–4 the king began a hall or house for the proposed order and the work, involving hundreds of men, continued for 40 weeks. The building was 61m (200ft) in diameter and probably stood in the upper ward. It was abandoned before completion and the work was never resumed (see also p. 157). The second phase was undertaken between 1350 and 1356 when the chapel of Henry III, which stood in the lower bailey, was remodelled and refurbished to make it a fitting ecclesiastical focus for the king's new Chivalrous Order of the Garter – a project which replaced the original idea of the Order of the Round Table. To serve it a college of resident canons was founded with elaborate buildings. This chapel was almost totally replaced by an even finer one, Edward IV's chapel of St George, a century later, but the third part of Edward's work endured (Fig. 64). This involved the demolition of most of the old royal apartments in the upper bailey, including the half-timbered buildings of the western block built by Henry III for his children. Also, the unfinished Round Table of 1344 was taken down. The replacements began at the north-west corner and proceeded chronologically in a clockwise direction. They included a two-storeyed range with a set of five chambers at first-floor level beginning with a gatehouse named 'La Spicerie' and ending with a tower called 'La Rose'. The queen had a set of four chambers only, with a chapel, disposed about the lesser cloister. The first chamber was to the west of the cloister. The second extended up to and included the old Prince's tower. The third chamber was distinguished by being decorated with mirrors and probably extended along the castle wall. The fourth was known as the 'daunsyng chambre' and included the Queen's Tower. To the east of these a new hall was built in the same range as the chapel and the old hall was converted into a great chamber. At the far eastern end a new kitchen and gatehouse were built round a court. Temporary lodgings were provided while all this was under construction; timber-framed lodgings were crammed into the round tower for the use of the king and these have recently been excavated and surveyed (Kerr 1992). He could no doubt review the progress of his palatial new accommodation ranged round the upper bailey below. Further lodgings were built, round the east and south sides of the courtyard (St John Hope 1913, 194–5).

The plan of Edward II's operations at Windsor had a notable effect on two of England's most famous educational institutions. William of Wykeham was surveyor (*supervisor*) of the king's works in the castle and park of Windsor from 1356 till 1361. He went on to found New College, Oxford and Winchester College, and it has been plausibly claimed that the layouts of these two foundations have many similarities with the royal works at Windsor which were reconstructed during Wykeham's period of office (Wickham-Legg 1938, 83) (Figs 65–66). In particular both Windsor and New College are located within the towered *enceinte* of a fortification, a castle and the town walls of Oxford respectively.

The planning of the chapel and hall in all three complexes is on a continuous axis. Against a wall of partition between chapel and hall an elaborate reredos rose up above the altar at both Windsor and New College. An arrange-

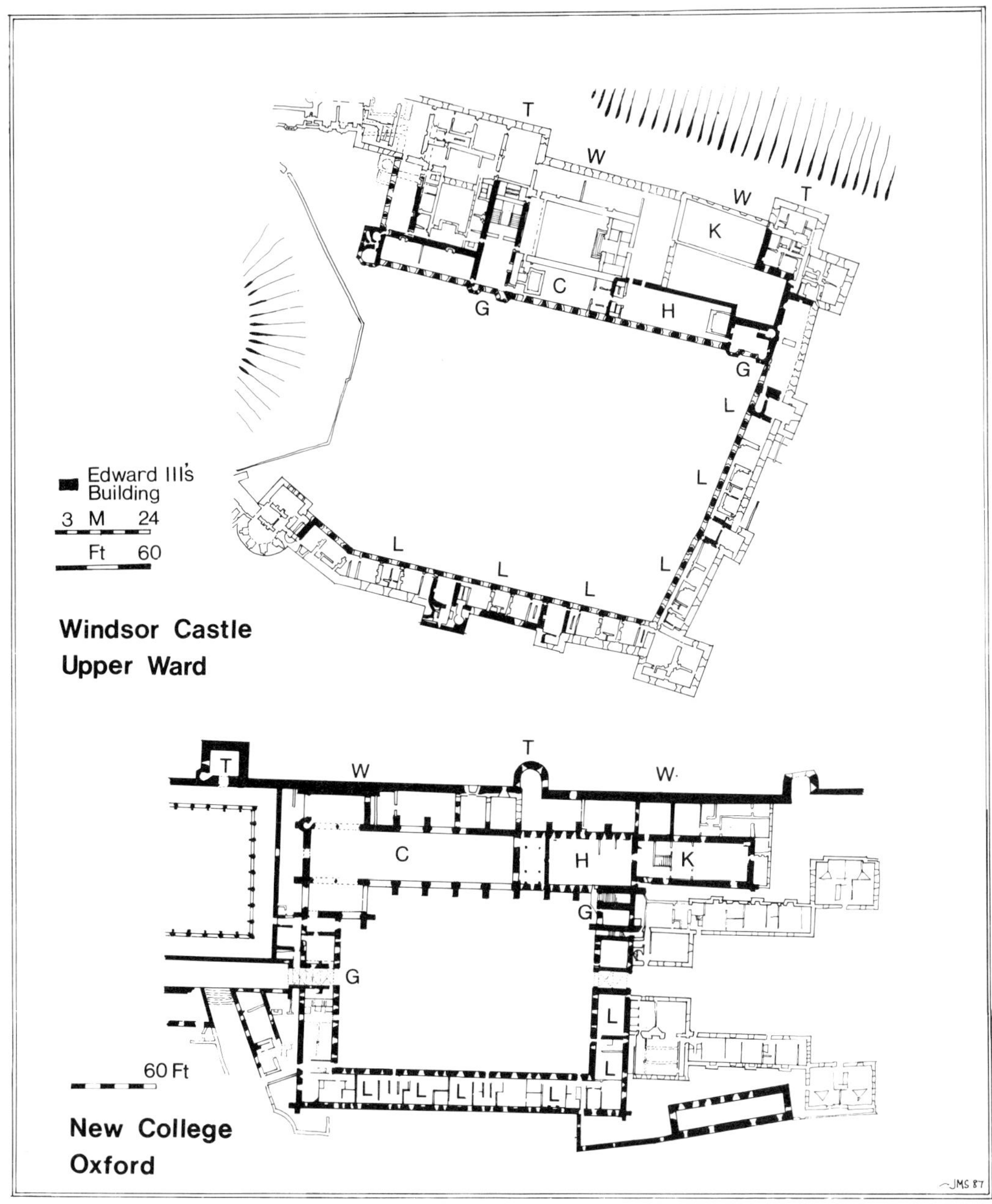

65–66 *Windsor Castle, Upper Ward, and New College, Oxford. William of Wykeham was responsible for the restructuring of the royal apartments at Windsor; he also founded New College, Oxford.*
Key: *H = Hall; C = Chapel; L = Lodgings; W = Wall; T = Tower; G = Gateway. The similarities between the two plans are striking.* (For Windsor, St John Hope, 1913. For New College, RCHM Oxford, 1939.)

ment to economize on space, found at both Windsor and New College, is the placing of the hall above an undercroft for offices and rooms for chaplains. The grouping of the royal apartments at Windsor (Fig. 67) is similar to the disposition of the warden's lodgings at Winchester and New Colleges; they all involve the use of chambers over towers. Moreover, the building of lodgings round the south and east sides of the upper bailey at Windsor produced a

67 Windsor Castle. Although heavily restored by Wyatt, who was responsible for the projecting tower on the right, the range on the left and the tower called La Rose were originally built by William of Wykeham for Edward III, and constituted one of the most grandiose sets of royal apartments in Western Europe. (Photograph: J. M. Steane.)

regular court lined on three sides with buildings. It may well have inspired William of Wykeham to plan his colleges round four sides of a quadrangle. Even the design of the windows of the hall seen in Hollar's drawings in Ashmole's *Order of the Garter* is the same as that of the halls of New College and Winchester. Edward III was consciously transforming Windsor from a fortress into a palace. To carry out his order, according to Higden,

> *almost all the masons and carpenters throughout the whole of England were brought to that building, so that hardly anyone could have any good mason or carpenter, except in secret, on account of the king's prohibition.*

Evidently the royal right of impressment was liberally used, while materials were brought together by using the royal prerogative of purveyance. The craftsmen were among the leading masons and carpenters of the day. Master Robert of Gloucester, John Sponle and William of Winford were included among the masons. William of Hurley was involved with the stalls in the chapel. William of Wintringham was in charge of the framing of the great hall roof at Windsor which can be seen in Hollar's engraving. William Herland also worked at Windsor (his son Hugh as we have seen was to create the finest roof of medieval England, that spanning Westminster Hall). Supporting these was a small army of freemasons, rough masons working on the Oxfordshire stone from Taynton and Wheatley, the Yorkshire stone from Stapleton and Roche Abbey, and greensand from Reigate (Surrey) (Brown, Colvin, Taylor 1963, 881). In 1360 the sheriffs of 13 counties were ordered to send 568 masons to Windsor. Many stayed only a few weeks and many more died. The local inhabitants sometimes suffered from the activity on such a lofty site. John Kasse was paid 20s for damage when a piece of castle wall fell on his house. John of Wingham was paid 5 marks for damage when rubbish was thrown on his property from the castle walls. The prioress of Little Marlow had to be compensated for injury to her crops by the royal carts carrying stone.

Carpenters and sawyers also made up the army of workers at Windsor. Whole woods were brought up *in grosso*. In 1351–2 £66 13s 4d was paid for 'wood in bulk at Cagham for the king's works at Windsor and Westminster'. 260 loads were brought from Cagham to Windsor costing £13 3s 11d. Wykeham bought whole woods at Farnham (for £166 13s 4d) and Combe (for £33 6s 8d) (St John Hope, 1913,

183). There were in addition the plasterers and daubers, glaziers and paviers, coopers and tilers, carters and smiths. All in all Edward III's efforts at Windsor represented a more effective scouring throughout the country for men and materials than anything done since his grandfather Edward I's works in Wales.

The result was a sumptuous palace which impressed contemporaries enormously. There were two bath houses; the queen had at least one of her rooms supplied with mirrors, and another is pleasingly referred to as her 'daunsyng chambre'. The interior decoration of the painted room is not known but the colouring of the fifth chamber of the king called 'La Rose' included azure and gold, green and vermilion. Bosses with carvings of roses are still in place in the vaulting (St John 1913, 191). A splendid reredos of carved alabaster for the chapel was brought ready made in ten carts from Nottingham in 1367. There were special mews for the king's falcons. Despite all this magnificence the comforts in Edwardian Windsor Castle would to us seem pretty basic. Good fires there were, as the list of rooms described as furnished with andirons and fire forks implies chimneys. The various items of furniture, on the other hand, do not suggest either luxury or even comfort. The seats were either benches or stools and the tables were boards laid on trestles. The arrangement in the hall was similar to that of a college at Oxford. At its upper end were three tables placed apparently end to end, on four trestles, and in the body five tables down each side. There was an eleventh table, presumably for carving at. The general air of temporary 'camping out' was suggested by the fact that the altar in the queen's chapel was provided also with trestles and was not a permanent structure of stone (St John Hope 1913, 195).

Royal apartments in the Wakefield Tower and Conwy Castle

The Tower of London is a fortress and a prison *par excellence* in the popular imagination, but during most of the Middle Ages it was also a major residence of the kings of England. The Wakefield Tower, built by Henry III in the 1220s and 1230s, reflects this dual function of military strength and residential splendour (Charlton 1978, 45–6; Hammond 1978, 15) (Fig. 68). When it was built it 'rose sheer from the River Thames on the outer curtain as an angle tower of the crucial inner palace ward' (Charlton 1978, 43). It performed a double military function in that it guarded the Bloody Gateway on one side and the king's privy postern, whereby the monarch could approach the Tower by river, on the other. Over the centuries it lost some of its stature because the ground mass was raised all round it, thus covering its base and plinth course. Archaeological excavation has now revealed these and a great deal more inside the tower. The postern gate, unblocked in 1957–8, leads directly into the ground-floor room and up a spacious newel staircase to the royal apartments above. The ground floor, when cleared of much rubbish, was revealed to be octagonal with a lofty recess in each face. The three southern recesses contain arrow loops originally covering the approaches by river; the north and north-west recesses contain rectangular windows. Most remarkable was the timbered ceiling which formed the floor of the room above. The joists are socketed into the walls and were originally anchored to a ring-beam embedded in the structure (Fig. 69). The chamber above has been interpreted as the privy chamber of Henry III. This upper room is also octagonal but the present windows and the vault are late nineteenth century in date. The original vault is likely to have been of timber. There are several indications that identify it as the king's privy chamber. In the south-east recess is an oratory, once separated by a timber screen provided in 1238. The fireplace has been restored from the surviving evidence of the outline and joist holes of its hood. The north-west recess between the fireplace and the original entrance is blank and this is thought to have been where the king sat in his chair of estate.

The Wakefield Tower is the only relatively complete fragment surviving of Henry III's residence in the Tower. Archaeological excavation has also recovered the footings of the west wall of the great hall. It is assumed that this would have been aisled with stone columns and would have had a steeply pitched roof with tall windows. At the west end was the king's great chamber at first-floor level through which he could communicate with the privy chamber in

68 (Above) The Tower of London. The Wakefield Tower, a great cylindrical flanking tower. When built by Henry III in the 1220s and 1230s, it rose sheer from the river as an angle tower of the inner ward. The construction of the wharf in front has deprived it of stature. In the upper chamber was the privy chamber of the king. A bridge was built connecting it to Edward I's apartments on the right. The windows are a nineteenth-century pastiche. (Photograph: J. M. Steane.)

the Wakefield Tower. The queen's lodgings were to the south-east of the White Tower; it seems from studying the bird's-eye-view of William Haywood and J. Gascoyne, 1597, that they were connected to the king's along the wall walk as well as through the hall.

The Wakefield Tower, in its excavated and restored state, sheds a vivid light on the residential accommodation which Henry III built in the Tower of London. It is, however, only a fragment. Clarendon provides a virtually complete ground plan, but of the excavated royal apart-

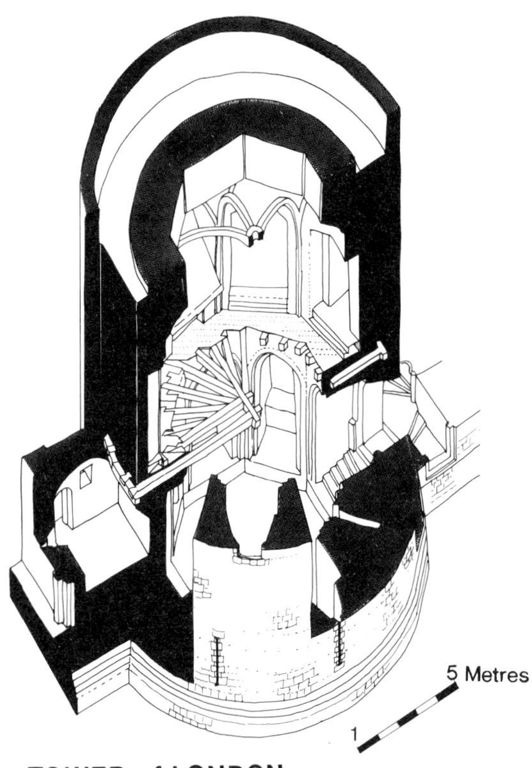

69 (Left) The Wakefield Tower, Tower of London. The royal apartments were in the upper room where there was a fireplace, an oratory and a recess for the chair of estate. Below the complex floor is a chamber with three arrow loops. (After Hammond.)

ments there are only wall tops and inevitably they give an imperfect view. If, however, we travel to Conwy Castle in North Wales it is possible to approach more closely to the physical surroundings which a thirteenth-century English king provided for himself (RCHM 1956, 46–55) (Fig. 70). The east ward was in effect a castle within a castle, designed to provide the sovereign personage with a safe lodging in the heart of hostile Wales. Access was not through the castle but by a special entrance from the water and thence by steep steps leading up through the barbican. Here in 1283 Master James of St George built a royal suite of apartments for King Edward I and Queen Eleanor. The contract cost £320 with another £100 for woodwork fashioned by Master Henry of Oxford. The apartments were all on the first floor. They were designed for a series of courtly functions, providing for royal business but at the same time protecting royal privacy. The king's hall was a public room with a pair of square-headed windows of great beauty looking on to the courtyard. The upper room on the east side was the king's presence chamber, designed as the stateroom in which councils would be held and distinguished visitors received in audience. Interconnecting with hall and presence chamber was the king's chamber or office. A window looks over the river giving a splendid (and tactically important) view. A convenient garderobe is at hand in the thickness of the wall while doors communicate with the royal bedchambers situated in the south-west tower. These are distinguished by fireplaces with complete hoods. Above the four circular towers of the castle are four turrets manned by the watchmen; from these turrets fluttered the royal standards.

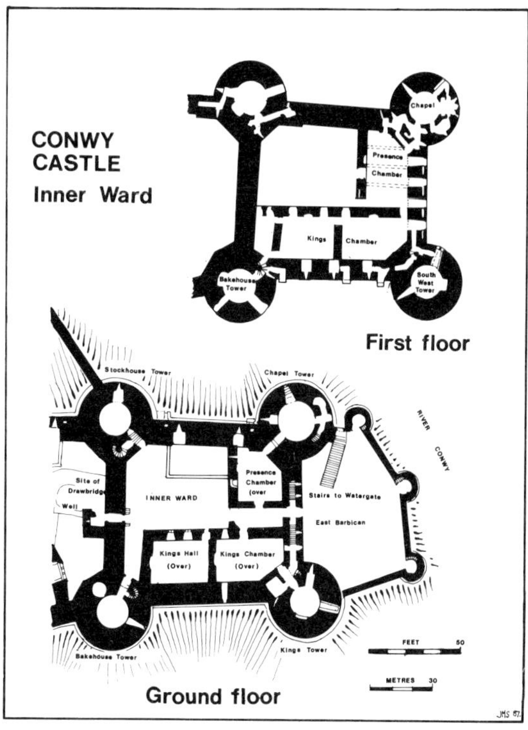

70 Conwy Castle. Inner Ward. The royal apartments neatly fit into the confined space of the eastern one third of the castle. (After RCHM Caenarvonshire.)

Privy chambers

It is noteworthy that one of the essential facilities enjoyed by royalty from the late eleventh century onwards was the provision of privy chambers. Salzman points out that even in these crude times modesty or shyness shows itself in the variety of euphemisms employed for the building itself (Salzman 1952, 281). It seems that the term 'privy chamber' *(camera privata)* nearly always refers to a private sitting room or a latrine. The commonest term was 'garderobe' but here the original meaning of the word, which was the place where clothes were kept, is ambiguous. The modern English 'cloakroom' is a close parallel because it often has a latrine attached. The two, wardrobe and privy chamber, are linked quite often in royal instructions. In 1248, for example, Henry III ordered a wardrobe, and a privy chamber to the same wardrobe, to be made in the royal hunting lodge at Brill. He wrote to the sheriff of Wiltshire ordering repairs to be made at the king's wardrobe at Clarendon

> *and to cause the privy chamber of the same . . . to be renamed and enlarged and to cause a wardrobe of the length of 30ft to be made before the said privy chamber.*

Again, the queen had a good wardrobe built next to the chapel of St Nicholas in Marlborough Castle (Wiltshire), which was equipped with a fireplace and a privy chamber. The sheriff of Hertford was ordered to lengthen the queen's chamber in the castle there by 20ft and to 'make a suitable fireplace and a wardrobe 20ft by 18ft and a privy chamber, corresponding to the chamber'.

Privies were often sited next to or leading straight off the royal chambers. At Guildford, for instance the sheriff of Surrey was ordered to make a door in the king's great chamber on the ground floor and by the door of a penthouse; and to cause a privy chamber to the said chamber to be made towards the ditch of the castle. The sheriff of Nottingham was instructed 'to make a privy chamber by the queen's chamber where the privy chamber of the long chamber by the hall is now' (*Cal. Lib. R. 1226–40*, 301, 320–1). Privies were provided with windows. At Clarendon, for example, orders were given to block up the door of the queen's privy chamber, leading to the grass plot, to roof the said chamber and to bar the windows with iron. Occasionally the form of the roof is mentioned. At Clarendon again 'a fair privy chamber was made thereto, well vaulted both to the upper and the lower storey'.

The siting and construction of privy chambers clearly exercised the ingenuity of medieval minds. They were often contrived in the thickness of the wall, with access from the chamber by way of a right-angled turn. This was probably on the principle of 'out of sight, out of mind' because medieval smells were not deterred by turning corners! There is a note of desperation in King Henry III's words to Edward Fitzotho, his Master of the Works:

> *Since the privy chamber of our wardrobe at London is situated in an unsuitable place, wherefore it smells badly, we command you . . . that you in no wise omit to cause another privy chamber to be made in the same wardrobe in such more fitting and proper place as you may select there even though it should cost a hundred pounds. So that it may be made before the feast of the translation of St Edward before we come thither.*

Henry III, in fact, showed a practical interest in sanitary engineering. In 1238 he ordered the Constable of the Tower 'to cause the drain of our privy chamber to be made in the fashion of a hollow column, as John of Ely shall more fully tell thee'. He had all the privies of Woodstock fitted with double doors in 1241.

The basic problem of medieval sanitation was that of keeping the system sweet and clean. Here the interminable progresses of the Norman and Plantagenet kings must have helped. After a period of intensive use the great houses and castles were abandoned temporarily by all but a skeleton staff. The place was left to air and to be spring-cleaned. Foetid garderobes could be cleaned to be made ready for the next visit of the royal master with his family and large train of attendants.

The methods used for cleaning out medieval garderobes varied according to the type and site of the privy chambers. In monastic buildings communal latrines or reredorters were frequently placed over drains which were flushed by rainwater or by streams. Most garderobes in castles debouched into stone-lined cesspits which had to be dug out from time to time. At Collyweston (Northamptonshire), the manor house of Margaret Duchess of Richmond, there were payments in 1500 'to the gong fermor for the feyng of XII draughtes'. Gong is another word for a latrine; 'gongfermor' was a man who had to 'fey' or cleanse cesspits.

Another method was to build the latrine jutting out from the wall of the building so that its contents were discharged down the wall or outside it into the moat or ditch. Edward I's Savoyard engineer and architect, Master James of St George, corbelled out the turrets containing the latrines from the walls of Harlech Castle which then shot their content clear. This was the principle used in the construction of twelve privies for the use of the royal clerks stationed in the town on Conwy, North Wales. A whole battery of them is still to be seen projecting from the town wall west of the Mill Gate. They cost £15. An alternative technique was simply to shoot the content out of an aperture in the wall. In 1313 Sir William de Norwice ordered a stone wall to be made to hide the filth issuing from the shoots from the garderobes in the Keep of the Tower. Stains from such shoots, and phosphate-rich patches below them, are worth searching for in the remains of castles. At Southampton Castle (Hampshire), a well-preserved garderobe was flushed out daily by the double tides which flow up Southampton Water (Oxley 1986, 29–31).

CHAPTER FOUR
Palace and castle gardens

Location of gardens

Unequivocal evidence is rare for the physical location of gardens in medieval royal palaces, castles and houses. As archaeological techniques improve, the slight remains of tree holes, bedding trenches, fence- and stake-holes and garden soil are likely to be recorded but in the meantime we have to rely on references in the public records. These were in the main addressed to people who clearly were familiar with the layout of the complexes of buildings and open spaces and therefore only needed to rely on the most laconic topographical directions.

Royal castles often had small gardens known as *herbaria* located within the walls. The *herbarium* has been variously translated as 'garden', 'herb garden', 'lawn', or 'arbour'. It seems clear that the word need not imply more than a patch of grass or cultivated ground, but if it was enclosed by a wall or fence, or hedge, it might then be taken as a garden within a garden. We are told that the sheriff was ordered to repair the *herbarium* within Gloucester Castle (*Cal. Lib. R. 1260–7*, 82). The Constable of Windsor Castle had instructions to repair and amend the king's gardens (*herbaria*) in the castle when necessary (*Cal. Lib. R. 1260–7*, 175). The garden appears on Norden's plan of 1607 and measured 2.2ha (5.5 acres). It was next to an orchard and together they amounted to 5.3ha (13 acres). There was a similar situation at the Tower of London with gardens both inside and outside the fortifications. In other places the garden was situated next to or below the royal apartments and was evidently part of the special amenities afforded to royal persons. At Arundel Castle, for instance, there was a *herbarium* in front of the king's chamber. At Feckenham a privy chamber was ordered to be made in the king's chamber on the north side towards the garden (*Cal. Lib. R. 1251–60*, 7). Similarly, at Marlborough there was a great lawn below the king's chamber (*Cal. Lib. R. 1251–60*, 280). At Woodstock there were two gardens (*herbaria*), one on each side of the king's chamber (*Cal. Lib. R. 1245–51*, 186) and at Clarendon, a herb garden was made under the king's chamber (*Cal. Lib R. 1245–51*, 239). Harvey has suggested that a reason for this may have been that pleasure was taken in viewing complex patterns of plants (later knots) from above (Harvey 1981, 80). This is hinted at in the royal palace at Clarendon; here there were rooms which seemed specially sited for the views they afforded of the gardens. When the garden was outside the walls it was of course vulnerable in wartime. That at Caernarfon suffered damage at the hands of the Welsh and 24s was spent in 1295 on repairs, in digging and hedging it. A garden might even be a threat to security of the fortifications. Gardens outside the walls of one of the castles guarding English territory around Calais in northern France had to be removed to protect the sentries guarding the walls at night.

Enclosure

A sense of enclosure seems to have been inseparable from the idea of the garden in the Middle Ages. Gardens were surrounded with walls and hedges to keep thieves and unwanted animals out. Privacy was also at a premium since life in the royal baronial and ecclesiastical households was lived in public and the garden provided a refuge from unwelcome intruders. This is made explicit in the instructions given to the bailiff of Woodstock: 'to make two good high walls round the queen's garden so that no one can get in, with a suitable and pleasant herb garden by the King's stew [fishpond], in which she can walk, and with a gate to the garden from the herb garden which adjoins the chapel of Edward the King's son' (*Cal. Lib. R. 1245–51*, 292). The garden at Windsor had a wall of earth but we also hear of thorns and great switches of alder being carried from the forest of Windsor to enclose the king's garden there (*Cal. Lib. R. 1251–60*, 155). The garden at Everswell in Woodstock Park had doors which required five locks (*Cal. Lib. R. 1251–60*, 3). The Constable of Wallingford (Oxfordshire) was in charge of what were virtually fortified gardens at the castle. They were ditched and hedged and at least one was entered through an outer door and an inner wicket gate for which he bought hinges, screws, hasps, latches, locks and keys. At Odiham (Hampshire) an enclosed garden was made in the park for the queen's use. It was surrounded by an outer hedge 610m (2000ft) long, had an inner enclosure of a boarded fence with five doors and contained seats protected by a turfed roof and a garderobe screened by a hedge (Brown, Colvin and Taylor 1963, 767–8). This garden seems to have been detached and at a later date such a detached garden would have been known as a pleasance.

Plants

It is difficult to recreate the appearance of medieval gardens. There is a singular shortage of recognizable plants in manuscript illuminations of them. One reason for this is that a large proportion of medieval gardens were laid down to grass. This was more in the nature of herbage than lawn and of course had to be mown by scythes, thus producing hay. Grass and hay in fact figure prominently in the few horticultural accounts which survive. In these, plants bought outside are occasionally mentioned but most seeds seem to have been home grown. Judging from the large quantities of fruit trees bought there must have been nurseries in places like London and Oxford. The bailiff of Woodstock, for example, was ordered to buy 100 pear saplings and plant them in the king's garden at Everswell (*Cal. Lib. R. 1260–7*, 154). Again, the sheriff of Wiltshire was ordered to have saplings (*entas*) bought and planted in the garden at Clarendon (*Cal. Lib. R. 1267–73*, 148). Edward I's first queen, Eleanor of Castile, seems to have been a zealous gardener; she obtained the lease of King's Langley from the Earl of Cornwall in 1279 and spent two years making a new garden and stocking it with vines and fruit trees. By 1280 she was buying grafts of the 'Blandural' apple. Edward I also took a great interest in gardening (his experience on the crusades when he must have seen Muslim gardens probably explains this). Near mills to the west of the Tower of London 9000 turves were laid; grafts of pear trees called 'Kaylarell' were bought which cost the prodigious sum of 3s 6d each; others were bought for 1s, while 2s 6d was spent on rose trees and 1s on a quart of lily bulbs. Other plants mentioned in accounts for royal gardens at the Tower and Westminster in Edward I's reign include quinces, peach trees, gooseberry bushes, peony roots, cherry trees, willows, white roses, sage and fennel. At Chester 200 apple and pear trees were bought in 1287 and the gardener's obligation was to find worts (caules) from Michaelmas to Lent and leeks throughout Lent. This is a comparatively rare reference to vegetables, which were regarded with suspicion by most medieval upper-class palates (Harvey 1981, 81–2).

The frequency with which vines are mentioned in accounts of medieval royal gardens reminds us that the climate in the twelfth and thirteenth centuries was generally milder in the summer months than it became in the later Middle Ages (Steane 1984, 174–6). Vines were evidently grown as far north as the royal manor of Burswick in the East Riding of Yorkshire in the fourteenth century. There were terraces for vines outside the Tower of London. Gardens with vines and pear trees, grass plots and paved walks embellished the royal palace at Westminster (Brown, Colvin and Taylor 1963, 547). Here the trellises supporting the vines are mentioned. Master Maurice, the gardener, obtained 700 willow plants for this purpose and to make covered walks (*alaturae*) in the queen's *herbarium*. Similar frameworks called 'vynerodds' were bought for the vines of the great garden outside the moat and the smaller garden within it at Eltham Palace. Here Jean Froissart, the chronicler, walked round the garden with his English friend Sir Richard Stury, and found it 'very pleasant and shady for these walks [*allées*] were then covered with vines'. There had been a vineyard at Windsor Castle since 1156–7. Considerable sums were spent on this in Edward III's reign in 1361–2. Included were the cost of plants from La Rochelle and the wages of the master vintner, a Frenchman called John Roche, which amounted to £157 13s 1d. How far the grapes grown in English vineyards were edible is questionable. In the 1360s panniers were brought to convey the grapes and other garden produce from Rotherhithe Manor (Surrey) to the king wherever he might be. The wine at Windsor was of a sufficient quality for the king to make gifts of it both to his queen and his mistress, Alice Perrers (Brown, Colvin and Taylor 1963, 881). More frequently, however, it is likely that the produce was classed as 'verjuice', an acid vinegary liquor suitable only for cooking (McLean 1981, 256–7).

Garden features

Already by the thirteenth century gardens were fitted up with various furnishings to provide open-air diversion for the court. At Guildford, one of Henry III's favourite houses, the king built a cloister with Purbeck marble columns to adorn the garden (Brown, Colvin and Taylor 1963, 124). At Windsor there was a court with covered alleys and a herb garden in the centre. An iron trellis (*trellicum*) was commissioned at Woodstock. In 1444–7 a cloister, probably of timber, was built at Sheen with an octagonal lead cistern in the middle fed by an underground conduit. There was an aviary at Winchester Castle in the twelfth century and another in the next century at the palace of Westminster.

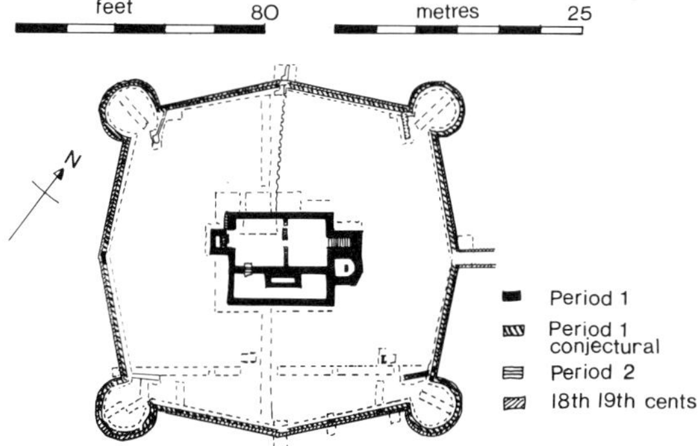

71 Nonsuch Palace (Surrey). Plan of the Banqueting House. (After Biddle.)

The potential of water as a garden feature was increasingly being realized. It is difficult to assess how far fishponds were constructed in or near *herbaria* for practical or ornamental purposes. At Hampstead Marshall (Berkshire) there was an east and west garden and the former contained a fishpond. The Jewel Tower at Westminster was built 'on the edge of the King's garden' and was surrounded on three sides by a moat which acted as fishponds. At Winchester £2 3s 9d was spent on a turfed enclosure, with water running through the middle. Here a plausible attempt was made in the 1980s to reconstruct a medieval royal garden to the south of Winchester Castle Hall (Queen Eleanor's Garden). There are turf seats, water running in an open channel down the middle, a fountain, an arbour with a camomile lawn and a pleached alley. Planting was restricted to those species known to have been in use in the thirteenth century.

One of the most fanciful and long-lived garden conceits to be invented in the Middle Ages was the summer house or gazebo. The first seems to have been built by Richard II in the 1380s at Sheen. Here on an island in the river Thames was raised a small timber-framed building equipped with benches and trestle tables. It is not known whether this was destroyed with the rest of the palace, when in anguish at the death of his queen the king ordered the site to be razed. In the 1440s there is another and similar structure mentioned in the Sheen accounts known at the 'Erberhouse'. In the same category of insubstantial garden buildings was the 'hauntepace' or 'spyhouse' built in the great garden of the mews at Charing Cross. It had plastered walls painted green.

Such medieval gazebos were the forebears of Tudor banqueting houses. Nonsuch Palace had a banqueting house situated to the south-west (Biddle 1961) (Fig. 71). Excavation in 1960 established that it was built on top of a mound revetted with walls and bastions of a ground plan resembling the Henrician coastal fort at Camber. The cellars of brick and stone underlay a building measuring 13.4 × 11.6m (44 × 38ft). It was of two storeys and timber framed. Here light refreshments were consumed while entertainments were in progress on the surrounding platform. From the roof Henry's courtiers and guests would have been able to follow the progress of hunting within the encircling park.

The idea of building a room with a view had occurred at least two centuries earlier. In 1354 a balcony was constructed at the king's manor house of Woodstock outside one of the king's daughters' windows to give her a view of the park. The view could also be turned inwards by means of erecting galleries in the covered walks surrounding and overlooking the garden itself. The palace of Richmond, virtually rebuilt on the site of the earlier palace of Sheen and renamed by Henry VII, was equipped in this way. Antonius van den Wyngaerde's pen-and-ink sketches show such timber-framed, two-storeyed structures, open below and enclosed above, providing perfect dry and wet weather facilities for walking (Colvin, Summerson, Biddle, *et al.* 1982, 227–8). Galleries providing through communication to rooms at an upper level were a commonplace in medieval courtyard inns, but the evidence as to whether the idea was applied to royal gardens is as yet inconclusive.

The gardens at Everswell, Woodstock

Amongst the most remarkable gardens created by a medieval English king was that at Everswell in Woodstock Park (Oxfordshire). Here, early in the twelfth century, Henry I had enclosed a large park. Within the stone wall he kept his menagerie, which is said to have included lions, leopards, lynxes, camels and a favourite porcupine sent to him by William of Montpellier. Here, a few hundred yards from the important royal manor house and hunting-lodge, Henry II is reputed to have built a bower or pleasance in which, according to popular tradition, he installed his beloved mistress, Rosamund Clifford (Bond and Tiller 1987, 46–7).

Everswell is a curious tangle of legend and fact. Legend from the fourteenth century reported that the king's mistress lived at the centre of a maze, a labyrinth or secret chamber of Daedalian workmanship. The royal records are less exotic and more prosaic. In 1166 a payment of £26 9s 4d was made 'for the works at the well or spring after which Everswell was named'. There were 'larger' and 'smaller' pools, the former surrounded by a 'great cloister' and the latter by benches. A herb garden was made there in about 1240 and the 'cloisters round the pools' were ordered to be paved and wainscoted in 1244. Another herbarium was made in 1251–2 and in 1264 Henry ordered 100 pear trees to be planted in it. Colvin has suggested that there may well have been an attempt to recreate in pools, cloisters and orchards the scene described in the twelfth-century romance of Tristan and Isolde (Brown, Colvin and Taylor 1963, 1015). Another source of inspiration may have been the rural pavilions and water gardens built by the Norman kings of Sicily, imitating Arab garden designs. Henry II had diplomatic contacts with the Norman Sicilian Court, and indeed his daughter Joanna married King William V of Sicily. There were considerable remains of Everswell as late as the seventeenth century and John Aubrey the antiquary made a sketch plan of the ruins. From his notes it seems that there were 'ruins of a noble gatehouse or Tower of entrance', 'Three baths in trayne', 'A pond in the court', also a seat and 'two niches . . . very much ruined'. The site is much changed today because the lake created by Lancelot 'Capability' Brown's improvements in the landscape of Blenheim Palace has largely covered the site of Everswell, but the uneven ground along the lakeside around the spring conceals the foundations of the complex of medieval buildings. There is also one pool remaining below the spring. Apart from this the only indications that Fair Rosamund's Bower once existed here are a few scraps of medieval pottery on the surface and some limestone paving which disappears beneath the waters of the lake.

The pleasance in the marsh at Kenilworth

To the west of the castle at Kenilworth (Warwickshire) are pleasant grassy meadows which were once covered by the waters of an artificial lake. This was formed by damming at the eastern end; it contributed to the defences of the castle and was drained when the castle was slighted in 1649. This mere was also a breeding ground for fish and was the scene for

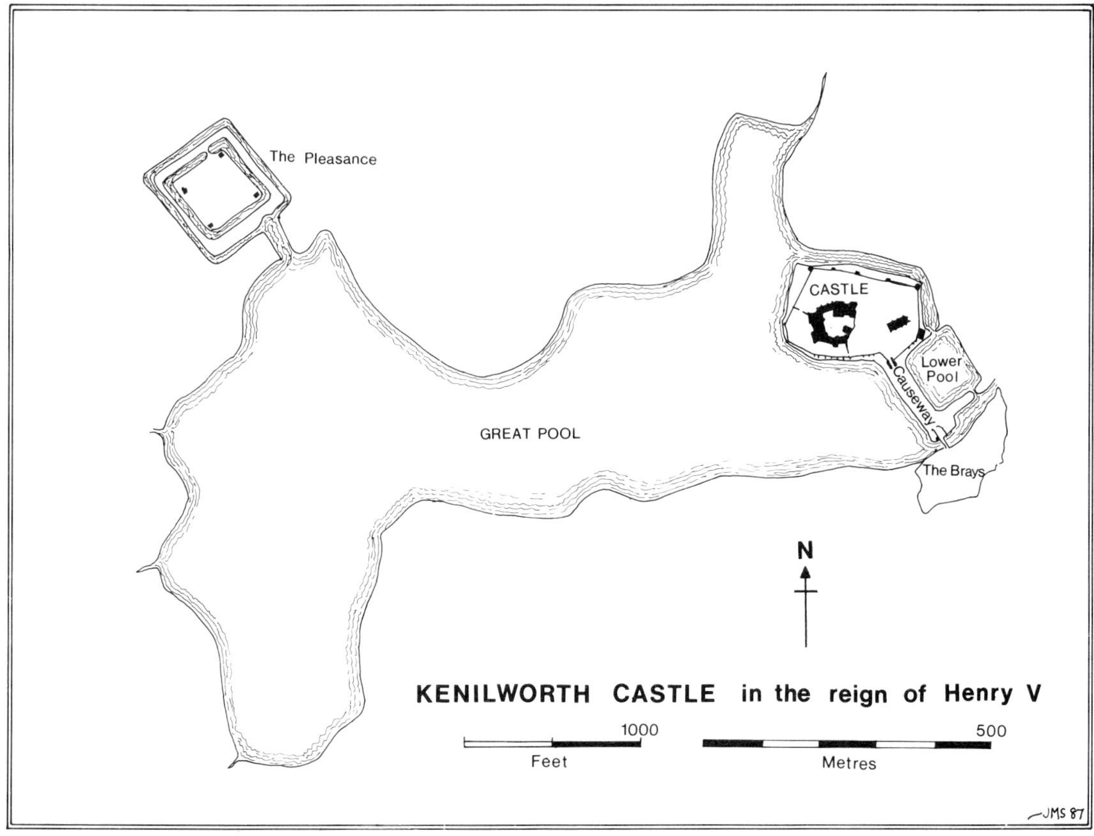

72 *Kenilworth Castle (Warwickshire) in the reign of Henry V, showing the location of the Pleasance.* (After Brown, Colvin, Taylor.)

Henry V's reclamation of part of the marsh and construction of a pleasance in the north-west corner half a mile from the castle (Thompson 1964, 222–3) (Fig. 72). Here, according to Elmham's metrical life of Henry V, 'there was a fox-ridden place overgrown with briars and thorns'. The king caused two concentric rhomboidal moats about 12m (40ft) apart to be dug; the inner one encloses an island about 113m (370ft) long each side. A dock was dug connecting the pleasance to the lake. Within the moated area were four corner towers. The garden was in the centre and surrounding it were timber-framed buildings, including a 'pretty banqueting house of timber [which] bore the name of pleasance'. This was taken down in Henry VIII's reign and re-erected in the base court of the castle. The site is now grassed over but the earthworks are well preserved and from the air present a dramatic view of an early fifteenth-century piece of horticulture (Fig. 73).

Gardeners

Since the monarchy moved around the country with the court from one house or castle to another, only a few residences were occupied for long periods. Windsor Castle and the Palace of Westminster certainly were almost continuously lived in, Clarendon and Woodstock similarly, in the twelfth and thirteenth centuries. Eltham, Sheen and King's Langley were also occupied for long periods during the fourteenth and fifteenth centuries. Consequently, gardeners are only found regularly at these few places; they were not paid great sums – two and a half or three pence a day, considerably less than master masons or master carpenters. Pay was often in arrears: Alan the Smith and William the Gardener who dwelt in the Tower were paid 40s for the year past. A number of the royal queens brought in foreign gardeners from the continent. There was a Provençal gardener in

73 Kenilworth Castle (Warwickshire). The Pleasance. Henry V reclaimed part of the marsh and constructed a moated garden here. The dock can be seen in the upper part of the photograph leading into the site of the lake. (Photograph: Cambridge University Committee for Aerial Photography.)

charge of the royal garden at Windsor when Eleanor of Provence, Henry III's wife, was Queen of England. Fulk le Provincial continued working in the garden until his death in 1277 (*Cal. Lib. R. 1267–72*, 217). Queen Eleanor of Castile had Aragonese gardeners working for her at her manor of King's Langley in the next reign.

During the fifteenth century, as well as gardeners there were (in a number of houses) minor royal posts involving the keepership of parks and gardens. Richard III during his brief and shaky tenure of the crown attempted to build up his power-base by a judicious display of patronage. Among the grants recorded in his first year were the keepership of the gardens at Greenwich (to John Fulthrope), the Mare (to Edward Gower), the Tower (to Symond Dowsying), Woodstock (to Richard Croft and Thomas Croft), Kennington (Sir Robert Percy) and Eltham (to James Pemberton); also, 'we have yevern and graunted unto him [John Piers] the office of maistere of oure vynyaede or vynes nigh oure castelle of Wyndesore otherwise called the office or keper of oure gardyne called the vyneyarde nigh unto oure said castelle for vid a day.' The places mentioned here are of some significance, and the linking of the gardens with the park in a number of instances is a useful reminder that the park in the future was to be found among the embellishments of great Tudor establishments, creating a setting for both houses and gardens (Steane 1989, 218–21).

CHAPTER FIVE
The peaceful activities of court life

An itinerant court: travel

The early medieval English kings were forced into an itinerant mode of life by a number of circumstances as has been noted already. Their territorial dominions were on both sides of the English Channel and, at their widest extent, in Henry II's reign, stretched from the Cheviots to the Pyrenees. The scattered nature of the royal estates required incessant travelling by a hungry mobile court. What economics dictated politics confirmed. The ruler needed to stamp his will on turbulent and potentially disaffected subjects from time to time by actually putting in an appearance. The king was also under an obligation to lead in war, to sit in judgment and to supervise in administration. All these tasks had preferably to be undertaken in person. This implied travel on a truly massive scale. A medieval English king, consequently, had to have a robust constitution, able to stand up to the rigours of the appallingly strenuous travelling schedule imposed by the job.

What emerges from study of the itineraries is a pattern of constant movement, with the transport of men, goods and animals of the court as a major undertaking (Hindle 1976, Hindle 1978). Of the first ten years of the reign of John more than four were spent abroad by the king, and during the space of one year we find that he changed his residence upwards of 150 times (Hardy 1829, 125). The court regularly travelled between 56km (35 miles) and 64km (40 miles) a day and on occasions 80km (50 miles). Matthew Paris, writing a generation later, remarked that John travelled '*citius quam credi fas est*' (more speedily than one could possibly believe). A particularly graphic example of this was the court's journey from Marlborough, departing on 19 November 1200, to Lincoln covering 241km (150 miles) to arrive on 23 November; the motive for this excessive speed was that the king of Scotland was due to do fealty to John on 22 November (so even at that the king was a day late).

The average number of moves per year by Henry III through a long reign (1216–72) was about 80, though after 1250, as the king grew older, his movements declined rapidly. He made 26 moves in 1263 and only 22 in 1271. Edward I, like King John, was able on occasions to show an astonishing turn of speed, even in winter. On his return from campaigning in Scotland in January 1300 he covered the 579km (360 miles) from Bamborough (Northumberland) to Windsor in 25 days (and this included six days when he rested) (Gough 1900, II, 185). On average Edward made 107 moves a year.

Edward II, commonly considered to be a less energetic and effective monarch than most, nevertheless undertook a punishing series of progresses (Hallam 1984, 4–6). Obviously some of his visits were one-night or two-night stops on the way to more extensive stays at such places as Winchester, Windsor and Westminster where presumably court and king recuperated. How far royal itineraries were deliberately designed for the king to visit all areas of his kingdom is worth asking. Edward's speed of travel could also be relatively gentle. In 1307 he, his court and household left Carlisle on 4 September; he was through Penrith on the following day and reached Brough on 5 September, Ripon on the 8th, Knaresborough on the 9th, York on the 12th and Doncaster on the 13th. He tarried at the royal hunting lodge of Clipstone in Sherwood from 18 to 26 September before pushing on to Newstead on the 28th and Lenton on the 29th, reaching Nottingham on 4 October; thence to Leicester (9 October) and afterwards via Northampton, Hanslope, Leighton Buzzard, King's Langley, St Albans, Hatfield and the Tower of London to reach Westminster on 27 October. Within two months the king had travelled the length of his land from Carlisle to Westminster.

One of the fastest journeys accomplished in the fourteenth century was that undertaken by Edward III who in 1360 left his army leaders and legal experts to settle the terms of the treaty of Brétigny and returned to England. He landed at Rye 'towards evening' on Monday 18 May, and 'riding thence forthwith [he] repaired to the Palace of Westminster on the morrow afternoon' ('*quasi bassa hora nona*'). The route has been reconstructed as follows: Rye, Beckley, Northiam, Tonbridge, Sevenoaks, Farnborough, Bromley, Lewisham, New Cross, Cornhill, London, Westminster. The total distance is 103km (64–5 miles) – a remarkable feat of break-neck riding, equally testing for men and horses. (Hewitt 1983, 39).

The practical problems of providing the royal court with large numbers of horses to meet their needs at all times has recently attracted historians interested to know how medieval knights supplied themselves with warhorses (Davis 1989). During the period 1250–1350 the best military warhorses (or *destriers*) would cost £50–100 or even more. The horse ridden by the non-knightly man-at-arms was a rouncy (*runcinus*) costing £5–10. The best horse for hunting was known as a courser (*cursarius* or *fugator*) and might cost from £10–50. The most expensive riding horse was the palfrey (*palfridus*) also costing £10–50. There were also pacing horses (*gradatii*), amblers (*ambulatorii*) and trotters (*trottarii*) which gave an easier ride because they moved both their left feet forward together and then both their right feet. Packhorses could be had quite cheaply, at about 7s or 8s; they were used by the army, by royal and noble householders and by market folk. At the bottom of the scale was a peasant workhorse known as a *stottus* or an *affer*; this could be bought for as little as 2s 6d (Davis 1989, 67).

By the end of the thirteenth century the Marshalsea was the department of government in charge of the provision of royal horses. It not only organized those which were stabled with the household but also ran the various studs and farms over the length and breadth of the kingdom. The marshals were, to begin with, smiths and horse doctors. Such men as Richard the king's marshal *c*.1232–41 and Ellis of Rochester *c*.1257–69 were in charge of the king's horses generally, supervising their maintenance, selling those that were not required and buying new bloodstock, often from abroad. Prize horses were shipped in from La Rochelle or Bordeaux and also may well have come from Spain. In 1242 the king sent Bernard, son of William de Banares, to Castile to buy horses there. Lombard horses were also beginning to make an appearance in London in Henry III's reign (Davis 1989, 85). The two favourite stables in the southern Midlands were at Woodstock and Hertford. Odiham (Hampshire), Henley Park (Surrey), Tonbridge and Knole (Kent), Rayleigh and Writtle (Essex), Hadenham (Cambridge), Cornbury and (North) Oseney (Oxfordshire), Hampstead Marshal and Stratfield Mortimer (Berkshire), Cippenham (in Burnham, Buckinghamshire) and Yardley Hastings (Northamptonshire) all had parks where the king's horses were kept. In the north, royal horses were housed at Macclesfield and the Peak. A stable was built for 200 horses at Clipstone (Nottinghamshire) in 1282–3 but in size this was quite exceptional.

A good deal is known about one royal stud in operation in southern England during the fourteenth century. John and Henry III were responsible for building the castle of Odiham (Hampshire) beside old water meadows. Its polygonal flint keep is surrounded by earthworks which formerly housed stabling for 200 horses. In the fields around was pasture for the king's horses. When Simon de Montfort, the king's brother-in-law, visited Odiham, he brought with him more than 300 horses causing a serious depletion of oats in the castle barns. There are frequent mentions of farriers' work: 120 horseshoes and 1000 nails were purchased on 24 April in the year of his visit. Eleanor de Montfort also kept colts in the park in the care of her *colterius* and five saddles were purchased for them (Macgregor 1983, 64, 68–9, 71). John St John's account shows there were no receipts from pasture and herbage as the king occupied 'the whole pasturage in the park and outside with his foals and other livestock'. The king's stud was kept in a 3.6-ha (9-acre) meadow called 'Closmed' and of the 345 perches of paling remade at this time, 145 were used to enclose this meadow. Hay, straw, oats and bran were fed to the king's colts here in 1312. The seven grooms were paid 2d a day. A survey of the king's stud in the park at Odiham was carried out by Master William Mareschal, keeper of the king's great horses and in 1339 William Trussel, constable of Odiham Castle was ordered to repair defects both in the granges and in the colts' stables in the park at Odiham and to repair a place called 'Pinfauld' – perhaps an enclosure for breeding. In 1361 a general sale of 'all horses, mares and studs' in the king's park at Odiham and eight other parks was ordered 'except for ten of the best mares to be kept safe for the king's use' (Macgregor 1983, 96–7, 101, 104).

When a fourteenth-century king and his household crossed the channel about 1000 horses might be transported with them. They required a little army of grooms and stable boys under the supervision of the marshals of the stable to control them. These accompanied the horses and supplied the horseshoes, bridles, hobbles, ropes and other pieces of harness. The great horses had their keepers who conducted them to various places along the itinerary of the progress making purchases of hay, oats, litter and brushwood for them and arranging their stabling (Byerly and Byerly 1977, xxxv). It is not surprising that such valuable animals were given names. John Brocas bought a number for the king in Ireland in 1340 including Grissel de Borton (£24), Lyard de Burgh (20 marks), Ferrant Mackgibbyn (20 marks) and Ferrant Moyn (12 marks) (Hewitt 1983, 26).

It is unusual to find physical evidence of the horses themselves but Hewitt is over-pessimistic when he says 'We have no skeletons, no photographs, no accurate measurements' (Hewitt 1983, 9). The bodies of medieval horses were seldom buried intact. At Odiham, however, exceptional siege conditions probably account for the burial of two horses, weighed down by mangonel shot (Barton and Allen 1985, 2). Horse bones are rarely found with other animal bones in pits containing food refuse. At Bedford, however, a single square pit was found to contain 3000 horse bones. The main limb bones were present but heads and feet were absent. Walter of Henley (Oschinsky 1974) wrote that the only value of a horse once dead is its skin so it is reasonable to suppose that the heads and feet had been sent with the skins to the tannery (Grant 1984, 182). Horses were present, presumably for traction or for riding, at the high status site at Sandal (West Yorkshire) (Griffiths 1983, 345). None of the horse bones found at the royal castle of Portchester showed evidence of butchering and there was a general assumption in the medieval period that horse flesh was not fit for human consumption: the ox 'was mannes meat when dead while the horse is carrion' (Grant 1984, 181). Attempts to reconstruct medieval horse size have admittedly so far proved elusive although a range of sizes can be demonstrated, a fact that the horseshoes witness. Some were small enough to have been classed as donkeys or mules; a few reached the height of 1.6m (63in) and an average for the period is reckoned to have been rather less, around 1.4m (55in) (Grant 1988, 160, 177–8).

While the skeletal remains of horses are often disappointingly inadequate, fragments of harness and horse furniture do survive which provide hard information instead of the vague pictures painted in illuminated manuscripts or engraved on seals (Saunders and Saunders 1991, 17–28). They also give authentic glimpses of chivalric splendour. The distinctive heraldic insignia of elaborate pendant fittings attached to leather harness enable us to link owners, their horses and the places where they lost such items. A tiny gold shield-shaped escutcheon with the arms of John, Duke of Bedford (1389–1435), brother of Henry V, Regent of France from 1422 until his death, was recently found by a metal detector on the foreshore at Greenwich (Campbell 1988, 312–4). A four-lobed pendant of copper with champlevé enamel in two colours was found at Rievaulx Abbey (Yorkshire) (Dunning 1965, 53). The ground is blue with fleurs-de-lis and in the centre is a shield with three leopards on a field of red enamel. It is most likely to belong to the reign of Edward II; the fleur-de-lis is probably a compliment to his wife, Isabella of France.

Horses were only one element in the complex chain of getting the royal party on the road. The provision of carts was the second (Willard, 1926, 363). The household ordinance of 1279 laid down that the wardrobe should have three long carts; and the pantry, buttery and kitchen one long and one short each. An account of 1285–6 indicates that other departments within the household such as the scullery, larder and pitcher house were also equipped with single short carts. The total at that time numbered seven long and five short carts. Each was looked after by one carter and one fore-rider. In addition, there were 41 packhorses to convey the furniture of the royal chapel, the cross of Neath (a war trophy captured from the Welsh), the silver of the kitchen, the bench of the hall, the king's robes and his bed. They were all transported in this circus-like manner (Byerly and Byerly 1977, xxxv).

The carters were often engaged in purchasing spare parts and carrying out running repairs. The accounts are full of items of expenditure on replacement horse collars, girths, saddles, clouts to patch woodwork, grease, harness bands, strips of metal, and wood for supporting floorboards (Byerly and Byerly 1977, 13). The royal itineraries could in fact be traced on the ground by a trail of broken and discarded wheels, axles and pieces of worn-out vehicles and equipment.

When the royal household moved between manors, large quantities of clothing and chamber textiles were regularly transported; with them went plate and personal jewels, baggage of all kinds packed in a variety of ways. These included oaken chests complete with ironwork and locks which might be footed to protect them from the damp, and with domed lids to throw off water. Such equipment is mentioned in the Liberate Rolls of Henry III, 1229:

> *Pay Thomas Spigurnel, sergeant of the king's chapel, 17s 3d to pay for the new equipment bought for the chapel, to wit a saddle for the sumpter-horse, 6s, and for a chest, 6s, and for a housing 22d . . .*

Other containers mentioned in the Liberate roll were waxed canvas, for trussing and packing and coffers, which were leather-covered boxes with domed lids and handles. Saddle bags were attached to the saddles of sumpter horses (Eames 1977, 112–13).

A remarkable series of medieval chests and coffers is preserved in the Public Record Office, Chancery Lane, London (Fig. 74a–d). Dating from *c.*1360 are two connected with historical events: the ransoming of David Bruce, King of Scots (Fig. 74b); and the Treaty of Brétigny. A third was a travelling chest or 'standard', believed to have belonged to Henry VII's mother, Lady Margaret Beaufort, who died on a visit to Westminster Abbey in 1509. It was of oak, painted red, and the lid was covered in *cuir bouilli* (leather soaked in oil and spirits to make it waterproof), the lid shaped so that rain would drain away easily. The chest, which is now lost, was bound with iron straps while for easy transporting there were handles on the back and front. Clothes and linen would have been carried in this, and it would have been locked securely; the hasps of two locks were enclosed on three sides by iron strips attached to the lock-plates, to prevent the hasps being prised open. A fourth chest or coffer, dated by tree-ring analysis to *c.*1255 (Fig. 74d), was quite small, 32 × 121 × 30.5cm (12½ × 47½ × 12in), constructed of good quality quarter-sawn oak and divided into four completely separate compartments, each with its own lid and lock. It has highly decorated ironwork fittings (Jenning 1974).

Before passing on to consider the question of more permanent accommodation, it is worth pausing for a glimpse of the peripatetic court moving across the country, and the perpetual problem of temporarily housing its motley entourage. In 1306, Edward I was nearing the end of a long and vigorous life. He was worn out with campaigning against the Welsh, Scots and French. He reached Newcastle on Tyne in August, *en route* for a last invasion of Scotland, and moved thence to Lanercost Priory by Michaelmas. Ahead of the royal party went an officer whose job it was to see that the houses in which the king was to sleep were properly cleaned. There was a large party: the king and queen; the other members of the royal family who habitually accompanied the king on campaign; the various officers of the household; John de Drakensford, keeper of the wardrobe; the king's chaplain; his two surgeons; two messengers; two porters; two trumpeters; seven valets of the king's chamber; three *garciones* (grooms); 23 sumpters, whose task it was to pack and transport the household material; two servants responsible for looking after the books, vestments and ornaments of the chapel; four servants of the wardrobe; 55 other servants connected with the kitchen, buttery, almonry and other departments; 45 sumpters

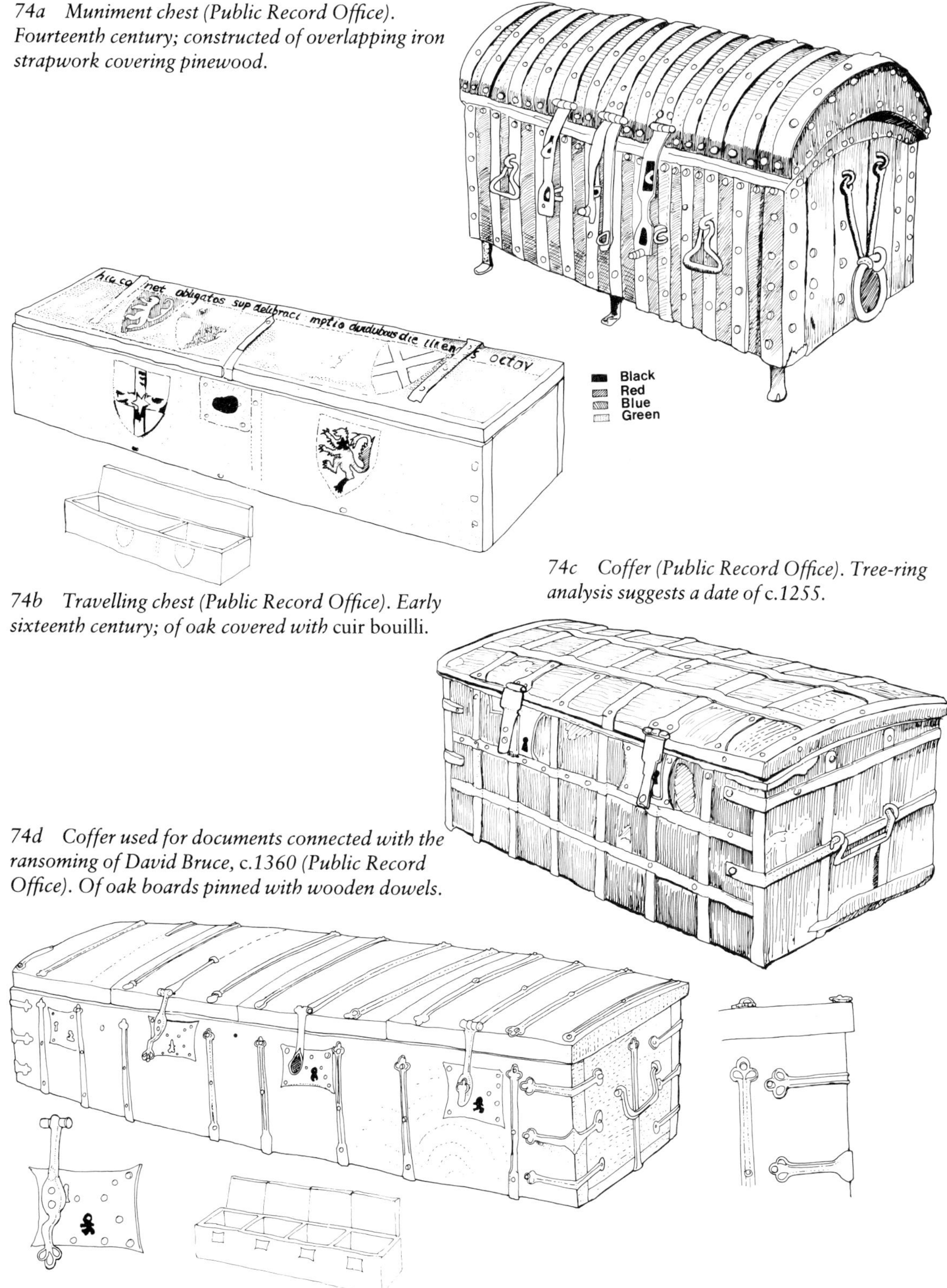

74a Muniment chest (Public Record Office). Fourteenth century; constructed of overlapping iron strapwork covering pinewood.

74b Travelling chest (Public Record Office). Early sixteenth century; of oak covered with cuir bouilli.

74c Coffer (Public Record Office). Tree-ring analysis suggests a date of c.1255.

74d Coffer used for documents connected with the ransoming of David Bruce, c.1360 (Public Record Office). Of oak boards pinned with wooden dowels.

looking after the robes and bed of the king; 22 grooms and huntsmen. Altogether a total of 200 had to be accommodated in the priory. Clearly the monks of Lanercost would remember the king's stay for a long time to come!

The king and queen were installed in the guest house. The more important members of the court were probably accommodated in the priory house and claustral west range. Wooden huts were erected for the rest and a tent put up for Thomas Brown the poulterer (Moorman 1952). Such temporary arrangements were necessary while the court was peregrinatory. Once it started to become more fixed in location, its members made more permanent arrangements for their accommodation in or near Westminster.

The size of the court and its accommodation

As long as the court was perpetually on the move its numbers remained small. In Henry I's time (1100–35) the household servants numbered about 150. Between the thirteenth and fifteenth centuries the court became a fixed institution; it steadily grew in size and cost. Naturally, the size of the royal household fluctuated with the personality of the ruler, the political situation and the state of the nation's finances. In the later part of Edward III's reign the number was between 350 and 450. Henry V's reign saw a reduction to about 200

75 Silver-gilt casket with heraldic decoration (British Museum). This may have been used as a chrismatory, a receptacle for holy oils, or as a jewel case; the heraldic arms are in quatrefoils on each side and are those of Margaret, half-sister of Philip IV of France who married Edward I in 1299, and Isabella, daughter of Philip IV of France who was betrothed to Prince Edward, son of Edward I, in 1303.

(Rosser 1989, 40). By 1450, the household under Henry VI had expanded to about 800 servants (Given-Wilson 1986, 259). Under Edward IV the numbers in the Yorkist court settled down to about 400. These officers, servants and hangers-on were the outward and visible symbol of royal power but they must have constituted a busy and at all times costly and potentially chaotic element in life at Westminster, or Eltham, Windsor, Sheen or wherever the king happened to be. The chronicler John Hardyng brings this out:

Ten thousand folke by his messis
tould
And in the kechin three hundred
servitours
And in eche office many occupiours;
And ladies faire with their
gentilwomen,
Chamberers also lavenders
[launderers]
Three hundred of theim were
occupied then.

Already by 1300 the embryonic town of Westminster, which was growing up at the gates of the abbey and the palace, had been colonized by a body of ministerial property owners. Along the roads and lanes in the precinct of the royal palace was a huddle of houses belonging to families holding royal office. The households of subsidiary members of the royal family also demanded accommodation within the town. On the north section of the palace precinct, for instance, there evolved in the thirteenth century the great house (*mansio*) of Almayne recalling the builder and first occupant, Richard, Earl of Cornwall, King of the Germans, 1257–72. It was here that in 1243 Richard's marriage to Sanchia of Provence was celebrated with a feast, according to Matthew Paris, of thirty thousand dishes (Rosser 1989, 25).

In the later Middle Ages, magnates, archbishops, bishops and some of the other great churchmen of the land acquired or built town houses in or near London. It was convenient to be near parliament, which was increasingly centring its activities on Westminster, the law courts and the royal court itself. Favoured areas were just outside the city walls: Southwark and along the main road linking the City and Westminster. Considerable space was required to house the retinues which accompanied magnates and ecclesiastical potentates on their travels. The normal size of a noble household was between 80 and 100. The royal household as has been noted, was five or six times that number (Given-Wilson 1986).

Access by river seems to have been a key determinant in the location of three great metropolitan houses whose plans have been recently recovered by excavation. In the midst of wharves, warehouses, and brutal modern office blocks in the London suburb of Southwark are the remains of the Bishop of Winchester's town house (Carlin 1985, 33–57). To visualize its layout one must recall the still surviving Lambeth Palace up river. Winchester Square was the courtyard, on the north side of which was a first floor hall, 24.4 × 11m (80 × 36ft) over an undercroft. Three doorways leading to the offices survive and above these a magnificent rose window of clunch (a hard chalk) gleams in Gothic splendour (Cherry and Pevsner 1984, 583).

76 A royalist badge – the letter 'R' crowned with some added tracery. 25mm (1in) high × 23mm (7/8in) wide. From Billingsgate, London. (After Mitchiner.)

Further upstream on the north bank was Baynard's Castle (Fig. 77), its principal frontages to Thames Street on the north and the river to the south. Excavations along the waterfront in 1973 (Marsden 1973, Schofield 1984) showed that the great house was built largely on reclaimed land. It was rebuilt after a fire in 1428 by the Duke of Gloucester, uncle of Henry IV. It subsequently became the London residence of the House of York and consequently the scene of several crucial national events. In 1461 it was at Baynard's Castle that the crown was offered to Edward IV, and again in 1483 to Richard III.

77 Baynard's Castle, City of London. The excavations viewed from the south, showing the late fifteenth- or early sixteenth-century turreted frontage. (Photograph: Museum of London.)

Tudor drawings depicted a many-towered front facing the Thames. The excavators showed that the great house consisted of a quadrangle with two octagonal towers at the corners and a western extension round a second court. Stretching between the towers in the east court was a range with five projecting bays, characteristic of Henry VII's riverside palaces of Richmond and Greenwich (Dyson 1989, 9). Stow states that 'about the yeare 1501' Henry VII

> *repayred or rather new builded this house, not imbattled, or so strongly fortified Castle like, but farre more beautifull and commodious for the entertainment of any Prince of greate Estate. (Quoted in Brown, Colvin and Taylor 1982, 50.)*

Baynard's thus developed from the residence of one of the greatest families of magnates in the kingdom into a royal palace. Henry VIII, soon after his accession, gave it to Queen Catherine of Aragon and subsequently it was bestowed on the succession of royal wives.

A similar fate befell York Place, the London residence of the Archbishops of York. It was situated outside the precinct of the palace of Westminster, again lapped by the waters of the Thames, and had been in the hands of the archbishops since the early thirteenth century (Rosser 1989, 21). From time to time, kings preferred to live there. Edward I, for instance, after Queen Eleanor's death, seems to have developed a distaste for his own palace, and decided to stay at the archbishop's palace a few hundred yards down river (Brown, Colvin and Taylor 1963, 505). York Place was largely rebuilt, on a palatial scale, by Cardinal Wolsey who held the see of York from 1514. It then was handed over by the doomed minister to the king to become the royal palace of Whitehall.

Three hundred years of confused building schemes have produced a maze of conflicting archaeological evidence at Whitehall; added to this are a delay of 25 years in publishing reports and a cloak of official security which makes it almost impossible to penetrate the buildings and inspect the physical remains. The resulting difficulties in interpreting the earlier phases of the buildings on the site have proved well-nigh insuperable (Colvin 1982, 300–15, Green and Thurley 1987).

The documents make clear that the cardinal-archbishop took advantage of the site's accessibility to waterborne transport. He shipped in Reigate stone from the wharves at

> *Fauxhalle; chalk from Greenhithe; stone was imported from Bernay in France by water from 'the blakewall' and Sainct Kateryn poole' at 4d a ton. Burford Stone was also bought from Mr Verthe, the King's Mason.* (Harvey 1943, 51.)

It is not known how far the site was already cluttered with buildings when Henry Redman laid out the archbishop's palace with great hall and chapel aligned north-south, close together and across a small court. The great kitchen was probably to the north of the hall but has not so far been excavated (Colvin 1982, 305). The wine cellar built under the great (watching) chamber survived into the nineteenth century when it was recorded (Smirke 1834, 116–8). It has recently been removed from its original position, and jacked up at inordinate expense. Wolsey was not content with the normal archiepiscopal appurtenances; he soon had in hand the building of an armoury, a gallery, a dining chamber and a cloister. By 1519, the Venetian ambassador was able to report that the Cardinal had 'a very fine palace where one traverses eight rooms before reaching his audience chamber'. Such state was more appropriate to a baroque royal palace than to the town house of the archbishops of the northern diocese (Baillie 1967, 169–200).

York Place was surrendered by Wolsey to his royal master in 1529. Henry's major restructuring at Whitehall (as it came to be popularly called) began in 1531. In this year the area west of the street now known as Whitehall was cleared of buildings to provide recreational facilities for Henry VIII. Extensive standing remains, mostly in brick, of tennis courts, bowling alleys, lodgings, and the park wall were uncovered (Green and Thurley 1987). Together with the tiltyard, pheasant yard and the cockpit, they provided Henry VIII and his court with an imposing sports' complex. In addition the context of formal gardens, orchards and the royal hunting park of St James has been elucidated. The series of buildings shows the remarkable symmetry and order of Henry VIII's master plan. Within seven years the new acquisition was officially renamed 'the King's Palace of Westminster'.

The changing nature of the court: liveried retinues

As the court grew in size it became steadily more formal, and far grander, providing for the king's needs and glorifying his majesty.

> *There was a growing feeling that the royal household must provide a* permanent *spectacle of majesty, that splendour and luxury should be the constant accompaniments of the great. (Given-Wilson 1986, 258.)*

During the fourteenth and fifteenth centuries the English court grew more showy, politically more challenging, and more conscious of its rivals on the continent of Europe, particularly the French and Burgundian courts. The result was an enormous rise in its cost. Between 1360 and 1413 the kings of England spent over one million pounds on the wardrobe alone at an average of almost £20,000 a year. If one includes the great wardrobe, the privy wardrobe, and the chamber, the total cost to the Exchequer of the household departments was half as much again – say over £1,500,000

78 The badge of lion passant guardant, *with tail raised and wearing an open form of crown. The guardant head shows a large protruding tongue. A traditional royal badge throughout the fourteenth century. Under Richard II the crowned lion guardant had been granted as a crest to Mowbray, Duke of Norfolk. Henry VI used the lion as one of the supporters of his arms.* (After Mitchiner.)

or an annual average of about £30,000 a year. This amounted to about a third of the total national revenue (Given-Wilson 1986, 259)

One of the most expensive recurring items in these household accounts is the maintenance of the king's knights and esquires who provided the heart of the royal 'affinity' or power-base. Both Richard II and Henry IV, for instance, 'retained' large groups of between 250 and 300 followers; these numbers were between four and eight times greater than those retained by most dukes and earls (with the sole exception of John of Gaunt, Duke of Lancaster, King of Leon, who presumably was considered to be in a class by himself and retained about 220 men). These retinues were distinguished by differing liveries which were granted them by their lords.

Livery was of three types: livery of hats or hoods (*chaperons*); livery of cloth (suits either half-length or full length); and livery of signs or badges (*signes* or *signa*). These little leaden or copper alloy badges have survived in the archaeological record in their hundreds wherever there were centres of political activity (Fig. 79). The Thames foreshore, London, has been particularly productive; it is likely that here they were discarded in a hurry, their owners wishing to escape the consequences of being on the losing side in some political downturn.

Perhaps the most dazzling find of the Thames mudlarks was an SS collar in silver, now in the Museum of London (Spencer 1985, 449) (Fig. 80). This was a livery collar worn by the supporters of the Lancastrian party. It originated with John of Gaunt, Duke of Lancaster, father of Henry Bolingbroke; a window in Old

79 A royalist, openwork pewter pin badge; the sun with broad and narrow rays alternating. An early form of the 'sun in splendour' badge dating from period of Edward I to Edward II; 29mm (1¼in) diameter. From Billingsgate, London. (After Mitchiner.)

80 A silver collar of 'SS' found at Kennet Wharf, midway between Queenhithe Dock and Southwark Bridge. It was found submerged below 1.5m (4ft 11in) of late medieval deposits of mud, and broken in two. It is likely that its owner had got rid of it after 1461 when the Lancastrian livery had fallen out of favour. (After Spencer.)

St Paul's Cathedral contained his arms within a collar of SS. He is known to have given a collar of SS to his nephew, King Richard II, who wore it in compliment to him (Fletcher 1924). The meaning of SS is cryptic; it has variously been interpreted as referring to 'seneschallus', 'seigneur' and 'soverayne' (of Castile). What is undoubted is that it appealed to Henry IV, who used it before 1399 and adopted it as an official Lancastrian livery insignia, giving swords and collars bearing its mark to his supporters (Alexander and Binski 1987, 526). Their alabaster effigies lie up and down the land proudly displaying this evidence of their Lancastrian affinities (Fletcher 1924, 82, Gardner 1940, 27–31).

A second royal livery badge, equally celebrated, was the white hart, devised by Richard II from his mother's white hind badge and a punning allusion to *Rich-hart*. He is said to have first used the device at the Smithfield tournament in October 1390 (Fig. 81). It is found in association with the sun-in-splendour on his standard and was peppered over the internal string-course below the great windows of his restructured Westminster Hall. Richard II distributed this device of a white hart, couching (lying down) with a crown, collar and chain attached, to his servants and adherents (Pinches

81 Hart badge, one of the chief badges adopted by Richard II, probably promoted as a pun on his name ('Rich-hart'). 62mm (2½in) high × 60mm (2⅜in). From Billingsgate, London. (After Mitchiner.)

82 A royalist livery badge. The star in crescent (sun and moon) was a traditional Plantagenet emblem whose major period of popularity was from the time of Richard I to that of Edward I. As a metallic retainer's badge it enjoyed a phase of popularity c.1400. From Steelyard, London. (After Mitchiner.)

1974, 62). When a well was being deepened at the pilgrimage centre of Walsingham (Norfolk), in 1971, a half-mould for making badges of a hart was found. The Countess of Oxford, seeking to overthrow Henry IV, had many such devices made of silver and gilt. The issue of livery badges was commonly thought to threaten public order and was legislated against frequently in the parliaments of the 1380s and 1390s. The white hart, however, caught the popular imagination; inn signs still commemorate it in many places.

The whole matter became one of public dispute again in Edward IV's reign, the middle of the fifteenth century, and the famous Dunstable Swan Jewel may well date from this time (Fig. 83). This exquisite object (now in the British Museum) modelled in gold decorated in white enamel is tiny, only 32mm (1¼in) high and 25mm (1in) long; the chain is 83mm (3½in) long. Objects using this technique occur in the collections of the Duke of Berry and it is likely to have been made by Parisian goldsmiths (Cherry 1969, 41). The swan badge had been used by the great house of Bohun, earls of Hereford and Essex. Mary de Bohun, who married the earl of Derby, later Henry IV, and thus brought half the Bohun inheritance to join the Lancastrian lands, bore it (Fig. 84). It was

83 The swan brooch from Dunstable (British Museum). The jewel is made of gold, the swan's feathers being formed of white enamel. Round its neck is a coronet to which is attached a miniature chain (not illustrated). Probably French work, it may have been given by the king to one of his supporters.

84 A badge of a chained swan, from Bull Wharf. The swan badge had been used by the house of Bohun, earls of Hereford and Essex. It became a badge of Henry IV and V through the marriage of Mary Bohun and Henry IV. (After Mitchiner.)

found carved in the frieze on the chantry tomb of Henry V, their son, in Westminster Abbey. It descended to Henry VI and was used in the seal of Edward, the son of Henry VI and Margaret of Anjou (Wagner 1959, 127). In 1459 Margaret rallied Lancastrian supporters by issuing 'a lyvery of Swannys to all the gentlemenne of the countre and to many other thorought the lande; trustyng thorough thayre streyngthe to make her sone Kyng' (Cherry 1969, 50). So it is possible that the Dunstable Swan Jewel may have been given away as an elaborate royal gift to a political supporter.

To distribute rich and elaborate gifts was expected of kings. King Alfred, who disposed of a fortune equal to some £2000 in silver, about 813kg (4/5 of a ton) in weight, was described by his friend Bishop Wulfsige as 'his ring giver . . . the greatest treasure – giver of all the kings' (Maddicott 1989, 5). Rings continued to be traditional royal gifts into the medieval period. From the reign of Edward II, special rings were made known as cramp rings; such talismans were reckoned to relieve muscular pains or spasms, and more especially epilepsy (Bloch 1973, 93). Henry III paid William de Gloverina £64 7s 4d for 3 gold buckles, 141 precious rings of gold and 3 girdles; also Richard Abell £88 0s 1d for 11 precious rings of gold, 45 buckles, 21 massive rings worth £7 3s 1d and 6 girdles, and £76 18s 4d for 22 buckles and 24 precious rings of gold. (*Cal. Lib. R. 1251–60*, 145). The king frequently donated such objects as oblations to shrines, as

> *10 marks for a buckle, bought and offered in the king's name at the shrine of St. Thomas the Martyr at Canterbury*

and

> *8½ marks for a buckle taken from the sacrist of Westminster to make the king's oblation at St Edward's shrine on Palm Sunday.* (Cal. Lib. R. 1267–72, *1256, 1467.)*

Henry III had heraldic belts of tablet woven braid with metal and silk brocading made as diplomatic gifts. One such present for Thibaut, Count Champagne, was found in the grave of Infante Fernando de la Cerba, eldest son of Alfonso X of Castile at the monastery of Las Huelgas, Burgos, Spain. A similar belt was found in a garderobe pit in Old Sarum Castle (Saunders and Saunders 1991, 53).

Since the king converted such a large proportion of his moveable wealth into jewellery he frequently had to pledge it in order to secure loans. Hence a mandate to Philip Lovel, treasurer, and Edward de Westminster

> *if they have not the money at hand, to obtain it by any means from merchants; Jews or goldsmiths, pledging the king's jewels therefore if necessary.* (Cal. Lib. R. 1251–60, *309.)*

The royal jewels followed the king on his journeys up and down the land and required special arrangements to be made for their security: the sheriff of Middlesex was ordered to provide Andrew Poynant, the king's clerk,

> *whom the king has sent to London for his utensils and jewels to have transport and a sure escort to bring them to Woodstock against the coming feast of the annunciation.*

Banquets and their organization

Preparations for banquets also led to high expenditure on goldsmiths' work. Henry III was lavish in spending (often money which he had to borrow) in advance of feasts at the great Christian festivals. Abel the goldsmith was paid £10 and William of Gloucester £55 18s 4d for jewels bought by them and delivered to the keeper of the wardrobe at York at Christmas (*Cal. Lib. R. 1251–60*, 55). The occasion was the marriage of Margaret the king's daughter to the king of Scotland.

Only rarely do examples of royal plate survive. During excavations in October 1986 on the site of Shrewsbury Abbey, a silver bowl was found in a medieval rubbish pit dated to *c.*1350 (Campbell 1988). It was 92.4 per cent silver with a mark enclosing a leopard's head stamped on the rim indicating that it was up to the sterling standard. Its function was probably that of a 'saucer', used to contain mustard, milk, custard and sauces. Edward II owned 279 such saucers in plain silver at Caerphilly in 1326–7. The Shrewsbury bowl may have been lost by a royal visitor to the abbey, perhaps by Edward III himself.

The sole surviving representative of medieval secular plate at its most sumptuous is the royal gold cup of the kings of France and England now in the British Museum (Dalton 1924). It is of solid gold, weighs 2.04kg (68¼oz) and is 235mm (9¼in) high. It consists of a cover and bowl of two plates, the outer of which is covered with enamelled ornament. The cover, bowl and stem are magnificently decorated with subjects associated with the life and miracles of St Agnes, executed in brilliant and translucent enamels: crimson, sapphire-blue, a bluish-neutral tint, a brownish-black and a golden yellow. For the faces and hands a transparent colourless enamel was used which enhances the rich underlying gold. The cup was made in Paris for Charles V, who possessed some 25 gold cups. It came into the possession of the Duke of Bedford, the brother of Henry V, the Regent of England and France, possibly as a result of his supplying Charles V's financial needs.

It is difficult to assess how far such gorgeous plate was actually used for conveying food and drink at royal banquets. We can be certain that

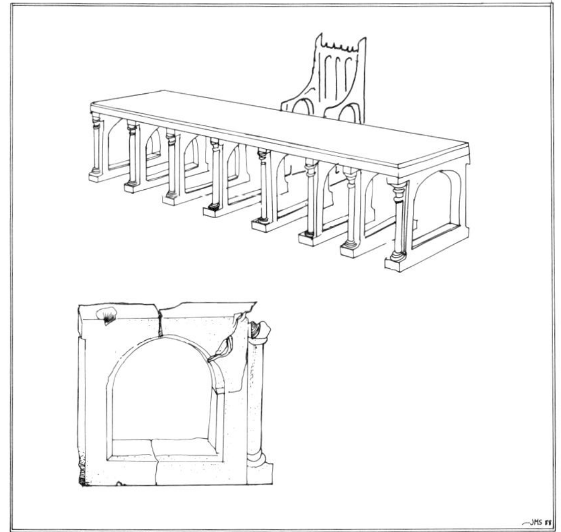

85 Westminster Hall. Fragments of a medieval marble table found under the floor of the hall and now to be seen in the Jewel Tower. The table is estimated to have been roughly 6m (19ft) long by 1m (3ft) wide.

it was displayed (Fig. 85). Special items of furniture were designed to show off lordly collections of plate, their size and complexity varied according to the status of their owners; they were described variously as buffets, dressoirs and cupboards (Eames 1977, 55–72). The courts of England, France and Burgundy all used the stepped buffet as a barometer of power. Henry VII had a stepped buffet of nine or ten stages to show off his plate at a banquet at Richmond Palace. They must have been very much like the dressers used in seventeenth- and eighteenth-century farmhouses. One buffet with royal associations has survived from the fifteenth century. This belonged to the household of Marguerite of York (sister to Edward IV who married Charles the Bold of Burgundy) as the heraldry carved on the doors indicates (Eames 1977, pl. 32). It has been cut down but its original form can be reconstructed from a buffet in the Vleehuis Museum, Antwerp; despite its mutilation it is of interest as a documented artefact – the only medieval banquet furniture with English royal connection to come down to us. Gold and silver vessels on the tables of royal banquets were supplemented by vessels in bronze and pottery. Metal vessels of any kind rarely survive; their remains were subject to corrosion and they were in demand for recycling. Hence it was with considerable surprise that Her Majesty's troops, storming thc palace of the Ashanti King Prempeh at Kumasi, in 1895, came across a mighty copper alloy jug, 40.2cm (15¾in) high, with the royal arms of England as used in the period 1340–1405 on the front (Fig. 86). Even morc rcmarkable, the seven-sided lid, with further heraldry dating it to Richard II's reign, is intact. It is likely to be the work of a London bell founder. The inscription reads:

HE THAT WYL NOT
SPARE WHEN HE MAY
HE SHALL NOT SPEND WHEN HE
WOULD
DEME THE BEST IN EVEY DOWT
TIL THE TROWTHE BE TRYID OWTE

A second jug, now in the Victoria and Albert Museum, cast in the same workshop as that found in Ashanti, is of the same general design but in addition has crowns cast on the spout and sides. The English inscription means,

86 A jug dating from reign of Richard II (British Museum). On the front are the royal arms of England as used during the period 1340 to 1405, with the crown above and two lion supporters. On each side of the neck are three roundels with a falcon spreading its wings. The badges on the lid with stags couchant indicate the reign of Richard II. The jug was possibly the work of a London bell founder. (Photograph: J. M. Steane.)

'God's grace be in this place, amen. Stand away from the fire and let just one come near'. Analyses of the metal have shown a close similarity between both jugs. The British Museum (Ashanti) jug has 70 per cent copper and 12 per cent lead; the Victoria and Albert Museum jug has 77 per cent copper and 12 per cent lead (Cherry 1987, 525).

Other bronze vessels known as 'lavers' or 'ewers' and used for washing, specifically for hand-washing at meals, were also to be found on royal banquet tables. In contemporary manuscript illustrations and in paintings of the fifteenth-century Flemish school such ewers are shown paired with basins, but these being of thinner, beaten metal were more subject to corrosion and have rarely survived. One elegant ewer, with a pear-shaped profile, a curved handle springing from the neck, a simple pouring lip and tripod feet, comes from Gower near Swansea (Lewis 1987, 80). It has been suggested that this was associated with the presence of Edward II and his court in the town in 1327. It certainly has an elegant inscription in French in Lombardic capitals round the body which translates, 'I am the Laver Gilbert, who carries me off may he obtain evil from it'. This has a courtly flavour.

Such precious or base metal containers must always have been limited to the top ranks of courtly society. The very large numbers of people who were fed at court would have used ceramic and wooden wares. Large consignments of pottery were ordered for the royal household against Christmas, Easter and the other major feast days and were obtained direct from potters working on the estates of the local magnates concerned (Le Patourel 1968, 120). A number of orders between 1260 and 1265, varying in size between 500 and 1000 pitchers, were booked at Kingston-on-Thames (Surrey) for transportation to Westminster. The potters who stoked the rival kilns at Laverstock near Salisbury received similarly massive orders to serve the royal court between 1267 and 1270, the price and cost of transporting 1000 pitchers to Winchester was 25s. Two years previously a similar number cost 20s and the freight charges were 5s 10d, for a distance of some 32km (20 miles). These Laverstock pitchers were distinctive articles with a certain robust if ungainly charm; it must be admitted that they were not particularly refined vessels for royal tables (Musty, Algar and Ewence 1969). The royal household was habitually at Clarendon from late November until mid-December and at Winchester for Christmas for three of these years, when large purchases of Laverstock pots were made. Kings, bishops, and nobility took their pottery in carts with them when on the move. Bishop Swinfield lost a cart-load of kitchen gear in 1289 and at least 3000 Laverstock pitchers must be lying in pieces somewhere in Winchester (Le Patourel 1968, 120). The royal army, when campaigning, similarly took its pottery with it; material from the Edwardian castles of Wales includes vessels from various parts of England; a Brill (Buckinghamshire) type of pot has come from Rhuddlan; a jug from the Bristol region has been found at Beaumaris on Anglesey; Conwy has produced pottery from the central and northern Marches and south Staffordshire (Moorhouse 1983, 77).

Only a few scraps of medieval secular furnishings have come down to us. Most medieval tables were 'boards' of timber planking set up on trestles; they could be removed and stacked against the wall when not in use. Stationary tables were less often used and a special Middle English word 'table dormant' was used to describe them. 'King Arthur's Round Table' 5.5m (18ft) in diameter and weighing 1219kg (1 ton 4 cwt), which hangs on the wall of Winchester Castle hall is an untypical if not a unique object (Fig. 87). Dendrochronology has established that the construction date is *c.*1250–65. The timber work is of considerable interest (Biddle, forthcoming) and it is likely that the carpenter had studied the construction of large wooden wheels used for mangonels, windlasses for raising building materials, or the wheels of windmills and watermills. After drawing his design he framed a heavy square with a void central area, of oak baulks measuring 255 × 102mm (10 × 4in) laid flatly in place, its corners jointed by haunchless tenons. Four clasp arms were fitted within the square, cross-halved together and chase-tenoned into the interior edges of the square. The central pedestal and circular stretcher were then assembled. The circular table-top was formed by fixing twelve radial timbers or 'compass arms' resembling the spokes of a wheel. The rim and the frame were fitted with ledges for the support of the 51 oak planks, plus four for the centre sawn or split to a thickness of 25mm (1in). It seems that four and possibly up to seven or eight trees were used to produce these boards; they were of high quality and well seasoned and must have been set aside for several years in preparation for the job. It is likely that the table was covered with fabric, even leather, during the Middle Ages. The present painted surface is clearly of Tudor date. The wood was prepared with a ground composed of chalk and animal glue. Over this was painted a figure of King Arthur, a double rose of the house of Tudor and an inscription identifying the king and the names of 24 knights round the table. It seem most likely that the table was decorated to prepare for the visit to the city of Henry VIII in 1516.

The table's original function is more elusive but the superior materials accumulated and stored over a long period of time, and the craftsmanship employed in its construction, imply that this was a unique table dedicated to a high purpose. It might have been made as part of the original furnishings of Henry III's Winchester Castle Hall. More likely it was made by Edward I to accommodate the guests at a tournament in Winchester.

The organization which lay behind the provisioning of these great royal feasts attests to the efficiency of thirteenth-century English government. Preparations would need to be started months in advance. In 1244 for example, 300 pigs were sent from the manors of the bishop of Winchester to be fattened in Clarendon Forest, together with 300 others which were taken to Chute Forest, to be fed on acorns and mast in anticipation of the king's Christmas feast. The pigs were despatched on 2 September. Ten weeks later orders were sent for all the pigs to be driven to Westminster without delay. If you had been invited to share the king's Christmas dinner that year, you could have met the bacon for it walking along the rutted tracks from Hampshire towards Westminster. The meat courses for Christmas 1240 required 5 bulls, 80 porkers, 58 boars, 40 roe deer, 1500 lambs, 200 kids, 1000 hares, 500 rabbits; in addition, orders went out for 7000 hens, 1100 partridges, 312 pheasants, 100 peacocks and 20 swans from Cambridgeshire and Huntingdonshire, 10 from Buckinghamshire and Bedfordshire and as many as possible from the lands of the bishop of Winchester and of the late earl of Warenne, together with 20 herons or bitterns, and if possible, in excess of 50 cranes (James and Robinson 1988, 30–1). The sheriffs of counties all over southern and central England were ordered to have bucks taken in the king's

87 *Winchester Castle (Hampshire). The back of 'King Arthur's Round Table' showing the massive central clasp-arm assembly and the matrices in the radiating spokes into which the legs of the table were originally fitted. The study of the timbers of the table suggests it was made in the middle of the thirteenth century by a millwright skilled in the building of great wheels for wind and water power.* (Photograph: Hampshire County Council.)

forests and the carcasses well salted and carried to the king at Westminster without delay. Such depredations damaged the thirteenth-century environment. The wild boar was hunted to extinction in most parts of the country and disappears from the forest records after about 1260 (Rackham 1980, 181, 183).

When we come to analyse the contents of kitchen refuse deposits in royal palaces, it should be possible to decide how untypical these gargantuan meals were when matched against the more run-of-the-mill daily diet of the royal court. The difficulty is that these deposits are inconveniently sparse. At Clarendon, one of the most extensively excavated medieval royal palaces, very little of the kitchen refuse was systematically preserved for study in the 1930s by the excavators, who were more interested in following wall lines and collecting artifacts (James and Robinson 1988, 260). For what it is worth, ox, sheep, pig, horse and dog were all found with most of the bones split and broken – in addition there was red deer (in greater numbers than fallow deer) roe, rabbit as well as goose, domesticated fowl and heron. Perhaps the most surprising item of diet at this inland palace site is the presence of shellfish; oyster shells were greatly outnumbered by whelk shells.

At Portchester (Hampshire) the food remains were treated by the excavators with the importance they deserved (Cunliffe and Munby 1985, 300). Here there had been occasional royal visits. In 1273, the castle was granted by Edward I to his mother, Queen Eleanor, who held it until her death in 1290. Subsequently, it was held by Queen Margaret from 1299–1317 and Queen Isabella from 1327–30. The court and its entourage ate beef, mutton and pork predominantly, the meat arriving as joints or butchered carcasses. Boars' heads and sucking pig were present; game such as venison, rabbits and hares added a welcome variety. The estuarine environment of Portchester provided a wide range of birds and fish, doubtless decoyed or netted, including teal, wigeon, partridge, curlew, pigeon, rock dove and others. Among the fish conger eel, cod, long, bass and plaice (or flounder) were predominant. A number of the fish could be caught from small boats in the sheltered waters of the harbour or from the shore line, but conger eel, large cod, ling, herring and hake required deepwater fishing. It is likely that these were salted down. During the fourteenth century, when Richard II carried out large-scale additions to the royal apartments in the castle, swan and a feast of game birds of all kinds make their appearance. Evidently, the residents of the castle now had a strong interest in wildfowling and in enriching their already sumptuous diet (Cunliffe and Munby 1986, 266).

The complicated arrangements for ensuring a ready supply of freshwater fish for the royal table at great feasts and during Lent have recently been studied in some detail (Steane 1988). The king had his own ponds attached to a great many royal houses up and down the land; to these were sent his itinerant specialist fishermen with orders to catch, store and transport fish. Sometimes the fish were salted, sometimes put in pastry cases (*in pane*); at times they might be cooked in jelly. On other occasions fish such as pike might be transported live, wrapped in grass. Ten places in the twelfth century are mentioned as having fishponds belonging to the king. This had increased to 33 in the thirteenth century, but of these only a very few were spasmodically used by the court for its supply of fish; these were Brigstock (3 times), Feckenham (3), Fosse (1), Havering (1), Kingscliffe (4), Marlborough (14), Newport (1), Silverstone (5), Stafford (3). When the court was at Westminster it used the produce of the Northamptonshire ponds. When it was at Windsor, Winchester, Woodstock or Clarendon, it drew on Marlborough. An intriguing addendum is the royal exploitation of episcopal fishponds during the vacancies of fat sees such as Winchester (Roberts 1984, 125–138).

When Edward I's family were staying at the manor of Langley, near Colnbrook (Buckinghamshire) in 1290, it is again interesting to note that despite the difficulties of transport to this inland site, marine fish and shellfish were available.

> *For 300 Herrings [bought] of Roger de Freincourt 23d. For haberdines [species of salt cod called such from city of Aberdeen] 9d. For 3 congers of the same 6s. For 3 gallons of oisters from same 3s 3d. For welkes from same 13d.* (Lysons 1806, 353.)

The Sunday tabloid newspapers regale us occasionally with details of the banquets consumed by royalty at Buckingham Palace or the Guildhall, presumably to point the contrast with a nation fed on fishfingers and mushy peas. Archaeology provides similar evidence of a stark distinction between the quality of diet enjoyed by the nobles (and the occupants) of Baynard's Castle, City of London, and the common people outside. Baynard's was once owned by the mother of Richard III and later came into the hands of Henry VII who converted it into a palace. Measurement of the metacarpal bones of cattle found in the refuse pits dug within the castle grounds dated *c.*1520 showed they were much larger and more robust animals, bearing more flesh, than those recovered from the municipal rubbish dump outside dating from *c*.1450 and eaten, presumably, by less affluent citizens (Keeley 1987, 280). Further evidence from bird bones showed that the castle household were consuming peafowl (*Pavo cristatus*), crane (*Grus grus*) and great Bustard (*Otis tarda*); among fish were cod (*Gadus morhua*), conger eel (*Conger conger*), ling (*Molva molva*) and turbot (*Scophalalmus maximus*), with some sturgeon (*Acipenser sturio*), roach (*Rutilus rutilus*) and salmon (*Salmo salar*) consumed in lesser numbers (Keeley 1987, 280).

When invited to dine at the royal table in the twelfth or thirteenth century, the courtier or guest would have come equipped with his knife. It is probable, in fact, that both men and women carried knives with them; and before the fourteenth century only the host or favoured guests would expect to find a knife set before them at meal times. Manuscript illuminations showing feasting scenes indicate that on average there were two knives per seven diners. Sharing a knife, like sharing a cup, was a mark of confidence and trust. Different tasks in the kitchen or at table required different types of knife. The carver, for instance, needed long, broad-bladed, parallel-sided knives. The etiquette of knife usage at table was carefully controlled by a series of treatises on courtesy and carving: 'Bring no foule knyfe unto ye table', stated one of the fifteenth-century courtesy books for the young, while another urged , '[Do not] foule ye borde clothe with ye knyfe'. The pantler, the guardian of the royal bread, would have had four designs of knives: the chaffer, for large loaves; the parer; the trencher knife for smoothing edges; and the mensal knife reserved for removing the choice upper crust for its presentation to the lord. Presentation reminds us of the degree of custom and ceremony with which meals of the great were taken. All these different kinds of blade figure in the remarkable record of knives published from recent excavations in London (Cowgill, de Neergard and Griffiths 1987).

As the fourteenth century progressed there was an increase in the number of longer, more elegant knife-blades in London, coupled with extensively decorated scale-tang handles (a type of knife design with plates riveted on to a central tang). This was accompanied by a decline in the number of carrying knives and their scabbards. It is plausibly suggested that we have here evidence for the emergence of the table knife, supplying, as one of its characteristics, a decorative element to laying the table.

Richard II, as we have seen a king of undoubted artistic sensibility, made further contributions to civilized life: he was the first monarch to use the handkerchief and he is also credited with the introduction of the fork. Until then it was considered proper to cut up food with the knife and transfer it to the mouth by way of the fingers. To spear it with the knife was regarded as a mark of low breeding. The consequence was greasy fingers and the need for finger bowls and acquamaniles bringing rose-water to the table. These latter were of copper alloy and took the form of horsemen, frequently mailed knights; down-market versions might be produced in ceramic. Potters also produced puzzle jugs which soaked the unwary (McCarthy and Brooks 1988, 56, 57, 114, 130).

Richard was also quite unusual in the personal interest he took in fine cooking and the zest he had in experimenting with new combinations of contrasting flavours. His court cookery book *The Forme of Cury* was compiled by his master cook and states in the prologue that Richard is accounted 'the best and ryallest vyander of all Christian kings'; it consists of 196 recipes. Spices figure largely in its pages; a distinction is made between *whyte powder* (ginger or a combination of ginger or mace with confectioner's sugar), *powder fort* (ginger or a blend of cinnamon and mace) and *powder douce* (one or more of the sweet spices – anise, fennel and nutmeg). Pepper was one of the most highly prized spices, perhaps because of the strong belief in its digestive qualities. Kings carried quantities of these supplies around with them on their travels. An order went out to the sheriff of London to cause 40lbs (18kg) of dates, 6 frails of figs, 4 boxes of pressed grapes, 4 dozen towels, 4 pieces of leyre cloth, 5 or 6 packets of good ginger to be delivered at Marlborough (*Cal. Lib. R. 1226–40*, 247). One inventory dating from Edward I's reign lists almonds, rice, ginger, galingale (an East Indian spice), pepper, saffron, caraway, cumin, sugar and other luxuries (Prestwich 1988, 159). With such ingredients available *The Forme of Cury* was able to promote highly exotic dishes such as oysters in Greek wine, rabbits in syrup, spices, Brie and egg tart, tripe in gingered broth (known as 'Noumbles'), elderflower cheesecake and golden spicy pork balls (Sass 1976).

We have already noted that the wealthier elite – royal, great noble and religious households – regarded wine as a necessity and purchased it in bulk; for the poor it was a luxury, bought a little at a time, invariably through a retailer or a taverner. The king had two main methods of acquiring wine. He could buy it overseas, thus importing it directly himself, with the responsibility for the transit from Bordeaux or Anjou to the royal residences being the concern of the royal butler or the royal officials in Gascony. The great bulk of purchases, however, took place in English rather than Gascon ports, with the port of London dominating the royal share of the English medieval wine trade. The fourteenth century saw the increasing centralization of government at Westminster; the king's household was more frequently to be found either in London or at one of the suburban manors with easy access to the capital. The royal butler therefore bought great quantities of wine from importers and stored it in the cavernous cellars under Westminster Palace each year, whence he sent it east to Eltham and Canterbury, south to Banstead, Byfleet, Farnham, Sheen, Guildford and west, up river to the royal houses at Staines, Windsor, Henley, and over land to Wallingford and Woodstock (James 1971, 180).

Wine was an expensive and perishable commodity demanding careful handling, expert knowledge and skill in selecting, blending, tasting, casking, coopering and storing. It required damp, cool underground conditions such as stone-vaulted cellars; darkness, however, might encourage the vintner to dupe the unwary into purchasing bad wines adulterated with the dregs of good wines or mixed with white of egg, honey and other sweetening matter. At the port of Southampton, 29 medieval town houses have survived in part or in whole; a number have undercrofts with masonry barrel vaults. Some of these were doubtless used as wine cellars for storing and, possibly, retailing wine and other goods (Faulkner 1975, 81).

All this transporting of wine implies decanting it in smaller containers than the great casks used in the ships. Parts of an actual medieval wine barrel were found in a Norman pit at Pevensey Castle (Sussex). The capacity was 37.6 litres or 8.27 gallons (Dunning 1958, 214). A cask of this capacity and its contents would have weighed about 41–45kg (90lbs); it would not have been beyond the capacity of one man to carry one on his shoulder. The Bayeux Tapestry illustrates a similar-shaped barrel being loaded in this way by a man engaged in provisioning William's fleet.

Furnishing and clothing the court

Even the most cursory glance at accounts and inventories of late medieval aristocratic households highlights the important role of the manufacture and sale of cloth; it accounted for about a tenth of aristocratic consumption (Dyer 1989, 78). In common with the other great aristocratic *ménages* the royal family bought clothing for themselves and their dependants and they purchased liveries for the servants. Clothing was so highly valued that the top civil servants did not despise receiving as part of their remuneration a free annual issue of robes. Crown officials also laid out large sums in buying fabrics for beds, hangings and other soft furnishings. The one aspect in which royal clothing and furnishings differed markedly from other, similar aristocratic material was the costliness of its display. Embroidery workshops were set up in London providing a luxury service to art-loving kings like Henry III and Edward III. The so-called *opus anglicanum*, embroidery in gold and silver thread, was famous throughout Europe, and was in such demand that the papal court had a collection of over one hundred vestments decorated with English embroidery.

The physical traces of royal medieval textiles are fragmentary, as relatively little fabric has survived through six or seven centuries. In practice only religious embroideries have come down to us in anything approaching their original condition and in reasonably large numbers. They benefited from the more protective environment of the church and from being taken abroad. In two or three cases, however, there are surviving textiles which can be linked unequivocally with the royal family and which therefore are of extreme value in reconstructing what has been lost.

One such piece of heraldic embroidery, of the second quarter of the fourteenth century, was displayed at the 'Age of Chivalry' Exhibition. It ended up as part of a chasuble but is thought to have begun life as a royal horse-trapping, and it shows leopards of England embroidered in silver and silver-gilt thread, with pearls and cabochon crystals on red velvet – altogether a work of stunning richness. It has been linked with Edward III's visit to his brother-in-law, the Emperor Ludwig, at Coblenz in September 1338 (Alexander and Binski 1987, 202). Embroidery to service the needs of chivalry and war was much in demand in the 1330s and 1340s, the early years of Edward III's reign. His official embroidery workshop, significantly, operated on a war footing in the Tower of London under the direction of the Royal Armourer, John of Cologne (Alexander and Binski 1987, 159).

Great courtly occasions such as victory in war, or the birth of a royal child followed by the rite of churching – the act of thanksgiving for the woman's survival of the dangers of childbirth – were attended by religious ceremonies and jousts. All these required suitably rich backgrounds to be provided by the needles of the embroiderers. In 1332, for instance, the churching of Queen Philippa, the baptism of the king's daughter, Isabella, and a tournament were all held in succession at Woodstock. Purple silk for different altar frontals had been purchased, worked with various birds, beasts, babewins (grotesque monkeys) and serpents in different colours, and bed hangings decorated with the arms of England and Hainault. Similar elaborate arrangements were made for the queen's churching after the birth of William of Windsor in 1348. The queen's tailor completely redecorated her suite; ceremonially arraying her chamber with red sindon (linen) patterned all over with the letter 'S' in gold leaf. This, incidentally is an indication that the origin of the Lancastrian SS collar may be some thirty years earlier than is generally assumed (Egan and Pritchard 1991, 42). Moreover, two beds of estate were re-covered – one with scarlet covers for the queen, the other with green taffeta for the young prince, embroidered with red roses and figures (Vale 1982, 64, 139).

The royal bed had been given a place of considerable symbolic significance by both the early French and English monarchies. The Capetian kings held *lits de justice*, when they made solemn legal pronouncements. When their Valois successors died their bodies and funeral effigies were placed on *lits de parade*, *lits d'honneur* or *lits de parement* (Giesey 1960, 3). The first English royal state bed of which we have any record was the elaborate one Henry III had made for himself for the Painted Chamber at Westminster. Round it were posts painted green with gold stars powdered all over and Master William was paid 20 marks for decorating the 'tabernacle' (Brown, Colvin and Taylor 1963, 497). Lethaby may not have been far wrong when he compared its likely appearance to the canopied tombs of the Abbey, such as that of Aymer de Valence. The box-like tomb resembles the bed, the soaring, pinnacled, painted upper works reminding one of the tabernacle. The exact position of the bed in the Painted Chamber is known because there was a mural painting representing the coronation of St Edward the Confessor at the head of Henry III's bed (Alexander and Binski 1987, 341–2). Whether the king actually went to sleep in this particular bed is debatable. Ceremonial 'beds of estate' were, in fact, more like canopied thrones than modern beds and they dominated the rooms in which they were placed. They were used by kings and queens to receive important guests such as foreign diplomats in audience. Consequently, they were fitted out to reflect in the magnificence of their decoration the wealth and social prestige of their owners. When Edward III's son Lionel, then aged three, was betrothed at Dunstable to Elizabeth de Burgh, an eight-year-old heiress, in February 1342, the festivities included a tournament. Lavishly embroidered beds of state were provided. Lionel's was red with knots and leaves, roses and quatrefoils enclosing a shield with his arms. The king's was green, with quatrefoils made of dragons enclosing a shield with the arms of England and France (Vale 1982, 64). A good impression may be gained of how one of these medieval royal apartments would have appeared furnished by visiting Leeds Castle (Kent); here in the Gloriette, surrounded by the waters of the moat, a plausible modern reconstruction has been made of the rich hangings and the canopied beds of state and other furnishings with which a fourteenth-century English queen would have been supplied.

The king's bed in the thirteenth century was a relatively simple piece of furniture. The fact that it could be packed up and carried on campaign in Edward I's reign suggests that it was a pretty spartan affair. A considerable degree of formality attended the royal bed-making in the Renaissance palaces of Henry VIII. First, a groom or a page was told to take a torch and

> *to goo to the warderobe of the kynges bedd and bryng theym of the warderobe with the kynges stuff unto the chamber for makying of the same bedde.*

A search was then instituted:

> *a yoman with a dagger to searche the strawe of the kynges bedde that there be none untreuth therein.*

From the rest of the description it appears that the bed-making involved a 'bedde of donne' which had to be beaten and 'tufted', a bolster, pillows,

> *then ii yomen next to the feete to make the seers as the vssher shall teche theym. And so then every of them sticke up the aungel about the hedde, and to lette downe the corteynes of the sayd bedde or sparver.*

Once the bed was made, a squire was set to guard it and take good heed

> *that noo man wipe or rubbe their handes uppon none arras of the kynges, whereby they myght bee hurted, in the chambre where the kynge ys specially, and in all other.* (Brooke 1786, 311–14.)

When it came to the provision of clothing for members of the royal family different kinds of cloth were purchased in bulk and made up in the household. By the mid-fourteenth century it is clear that there were quite high standards of cleanliness and hygiene, at any rate in the top echelons of society. Here, the rules of hospitality demanded that a traveller should be offered fresh clothes and washing facilities as well as food and a bed. There is ample evidence from the wardrobe accounts of 1344–5 that Edward III and his family were well supplied with underclothing (Staniland 1978, 223–34). It was made up by a member of the household from lengths of linen supplied to the king's tailor. The under breeches for men looked like pyjama trousers with long straight legs attached to a belt or breech clout. Hose, cut on the cross so they would fit smoothly, and seamed down the back of the leg, were fashioned of fine woollen cloth and tied by ribbons to the breech clout. A final undergarment for the king was the *camesia*, an undershirt, lined throughout, buttoned down the front to the knee, with long lined sleeves buttoned to the elbow. The underwear worn by queens and princesses was more basic than this, and consisted only of two garments – a linen under-tunic (*camisia*), a long, simple, round necked affair, with straight sleeves, and stockings (*caligas*) of cloth, worn to above the knee and held in place by ties or garters. The garter in use in the 1340s however, was in the nature of a ribbon and bore no relation to the heraldic garter which became the insignia of the chivalric order.

For upper and outer wear the principal garment for both sexes in the middle of the fourteenth century was the tunic, over which a further garment, the 'super tunic', was sometimes worn. Additional descriptive terms such as 'buttoned', 'open', 'closed', 'long', 'short', 'flounced', are added with great regularity and there are other terms – some Latin, some French – which are not fully understood, such as 'cotehardie', 'ghita', 'cloca', 'mantellum', 'jupon'. What is clear is that the upper and outer garments could be ordered in sets termed *unam robam*, or separately. The king, for instance, had one robe consisting of six garments – one cloak, two open super tunics, one closed super tunic, and two tunics, plus three hoods. Similarly, the queen had a robe of five garments numbering two super tunics, one cape, one mantle and one tunic. The seasonal temperatures produced different requirements which were met in three ways: addition or subtraction of layers of clothing; thicker or thinner cloth; the use of furs for increased warmth in the winter. The most extensively used fur in the Edwardian court was miniver, the pale winter bellies of red squirrels.

Whereas most of the textiles composing medieval clothes have rotted beyond recall many of the metal accessories of costume have

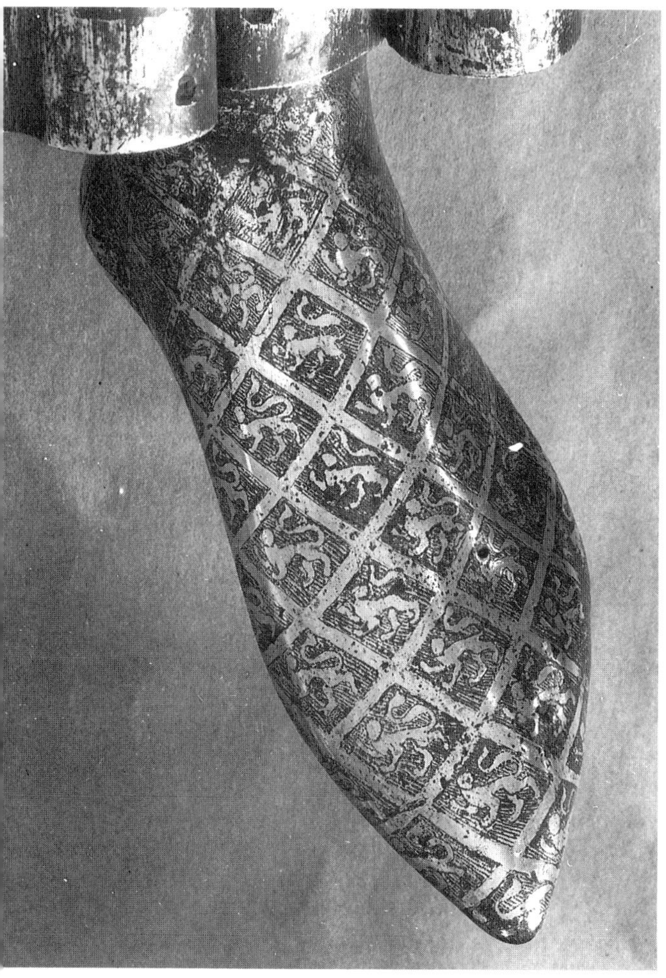

88 The tomb of Henry III in Westminster Abbey. Detail of a shoe. The decoration, of lions framed by lozenges, was probably embroidered on the original article. (Photograph: Warburg Institute.)

survived. The hundreds of finds from medieval London have recently been usefully described (Egar and Pritchard 1991). Tapering tubes of copper alloy protected the ends of laces and facilitated threading them through eyelets. These 'points' as they were called, were used to supplement buttons in lacing the upper garments of both men's and women's dress. Figurative mounts of the Lombardic letter 'H' decorated belts (the 'H' may well refer to Henry). The girdle worn by Anne of Bohemia (d. 1394) on her effigy is shown stamped with flowers against a background of hatching. Richard II's clothes were sometimes finished with small bells and this fashion, borrowed by the king from continental courts, was aped by his courtiers (Egan and Pritchard, 336).

The senior officials of the royal household and the chief officers of the departments of government throughout the land received robes as an important part of the rewards of office. As they rose in rank the quality of the material improved. The Justices of the King's Bench and Barons of the Exchequer, for example, received robes at the feasts of All Saints, Christmas and Pentecost. Their winter robes were of coloured cloth with fur and a hood of lamb skin. At Christmas, the robes were again of coloured cloth but were supplemented by a hood and fur of miniver and a deerskin. The summer robes given out at Pentecost were of coloured cloth lined with silk. The robes of royal officers were not just warm and serviceable; they were meant to be seen at a distance, to be instantly recognizable out in the forest or in a court room. Their quality displayed rank. The details of their garments may have been coarse – there was no fine work – but the meaning was unmistakable. Authority was written into these ritualized robes. They set their wearer apart from ordinary men.

One starting point for an understanding of medieval royal footwear might be the feet of the Plantagenet effigies in Westminster Abbey (Fig. 88). The tomb of Henry III shows shoes decorated with lions framed by lozenges, presumably indicating embroidery. Such elaborately decorated shoes are very rare in the archaeological record from the thirteenth century (Grew and de Neergaard 1988, 79–80, 114). The effigy of Edward III shows shoes decorated with panels of leaves separated by the arms of a stylized cross. Drawings by Smirke of a wall painting once in St Stephen's Chapel at Westminster (Fig. 89) and now in the Society of Antiquaries show one figure wearing shoes decorated with an architectural design reminiscent of the rose window of a Gothic cathedral. Such openwork decoration has been found on recently excavated shoes in the City (Grew and de Neergaard 1988, 82, 84).

89 The mural formerly at the east end of St Stephen's chapel, Westminster in a copy made by Richard Smirke, just prior to its destruction c.1800, *showing the rich oil-based colouration and gilt surface texturing of the murals formerly in the chapel (originally executed between 1350 and 1355). In the upper register is the Adoration of the Magi. The young king on the left is most fashionably dressed, having slippers with a rose window design. In the lower register, beneath an elaborate arcade, kneel the male members of the royal family, led towards the high altar by St George. Behind the saint are King Edward III; Edward, Prince of Wales; Lionel, Duke of Clarence; John of Gaunt, Earl of Lancaster; Edmund, Duke of York; and Thomas of Woodstock.* (Photograph: Society of Antiquaries, London.)

CHAPTER SIX
Formalized violence: hunting, hawking and jousting

Hunting

Hunting was a highly regarded pastime in the Middle Ages; indeed while warfare was undoubtedly the most prestigious physical activity, the chase came a close second. There were intimate connections between hunting and fighting. From hunting the young male royalty and nobility learned horsemanship and management of weapons, and gained an insight into woodcraft, terrain and strategy, all techniques used in war. We are told by the author of the twelfth-century *Dialogue of the Exchequer* that

> *the forests are also the sanctuaries of Kings and their chief delight. Thither they repair to hunt, their cares laid aside the while, in order to refresh themselves by a short respite. There, renouncing the arduous but natural turmoil of the court, they breathe the pure air of freedom for a little space*... (Quoted in Johnson 1950, 60.)

Hunting made huge demands on the robust constitutions of its devotees; it was a valuable way of channelling the extraordinary energies of the Norman and Angevin kings. Rackham has recently questioned whether there is any truth in 'one of the common factoids that we learnt at school... that English kings were passionately fond of the chase' and that forests were 'reserved to the king for hunting' (Rackham 1989, 51). It is true that we have to rely on the generalizations of chroniclers, who rarely thought it necessary to record in detail the king's presence or otherwise on the hunting field; but the evidence for the overwhelming importance of hunting in the lives of a number of kings seems to be conclusive. Royal reputations were made or unmade on the hunting field. The Anglo-Saxons could hardly credit William the Conqueror's fanatical ardour for the chase.

> *He made many deer parks; and he established laws therewith; so that whosoever slew a hart or a hind should be deprived of his eyesight. As he forbade men to kill the harts, so also the boars; and he loved the tall deer as if he were their father. Likewise he decreed by the hares that they should go free. His rich men bemoaned it and the poor men shuddered at it.*

It brought about the violent end of William Rufus, who was struck by an arrow while hunting near Brockenhurst in the New Forest; whether this was an accident or the result of a conspiracy is unclear. It brought to the throne, however, Rufus's brother, Henry I, whose love of pet animals was well known. He fenced in the park at Woodstock for his menagerie which included lions, leopards, lynxes, camels and a porcupine.

Master Wace describes William of Warenne, Earl of Surrey, ridiculing Henry some years before his accession for having studied hunting so thoroughly that he could tell the number of tips in a stag's antlers simply by examining his footprint. Earl William mockingly referred to Henry as 'stagfoot' for having turned a joyous mindlessly athletic pastime into a science (Mayr-Harting and Moore 1985, 30–1).

Henry II, according to Walter Map, 'was most knowledgeable about dogs and birds and a very keen follower of hounds' (James 1983, 477). He is described by Gerald of Wales

90 The Savernake horn (British Museum). Detail of the fourteenth-century horn which may have been in the possession of the Sturmy family, hereditary wardens of Savernake forest. Three of the panels round the rim show a king, a bishop and a huntsman, the rest are the animals of the chase. (Photograph: British Museum.)

as 'addicted to the chase beyond measure ... at crack of dawn he was off on horseback, traversing the wilderness, plunging into woods and climbing the mountain tops.' It is possible that nearly a third of England was forest in the twelfth century. The king's favourite residences were hunting lodges at Clarendon and Woodstock but the reason for his interest in forest areas of the far north, rarely if ever visited, such as Amounderness in Lancashire or Pickering in Yorkshire, was economic not sporting.

His youngest son John shared this passionate interest in hunting: 'He haunted woods and streams and greatly delighted in the pleasure of them.' He sometimes hunted on holy days and salved his conscience by generous almsgiving to the poor. A hundred paupers were fed at Newcastle in 1209, 'because the king went into the woods on the feast of St Mary Magdalen' (Harting 1883, 48). On the eve of losing the duchy of Normandy the over-sanguine king made arrangements for wild animals to be trapped in the New Forest and sent over the Channel with horses, dogs and falcons so that he could be sure of having plenty of game and hunting gear when he arrived. Henry III's interest in the royal forests centred around them as sources of royal patronage in the form of donations of deer and timber. Edward I was said by the chronicler Nicholas Trivet to have been mainly interested in stag hunting and that he preferred to go to the kill with his sword rather than relying on a hunting spear. His real love, however, was falconry (Prestwich 1988, 115). Edward II spent long sojourns at his Buckinghamshire manor of Langley but while he developed a taste for country pursuits these involved peasant tasks such as digging and ditching, much to the disgust of his courtiers and the scorn of the magnates. During his long reign, the interests of Edward III shifted from war and chivalry to hunting; in his later years he maintained a ring of satellite houses and hunting lodges round the rebuilt castle of Windsor, so that in whatever part of the Forest he chose to hunt there was a house which he could use for food and shelter. Hunting continued to be a favourite sport of royal princes throughout the later Middle Ages. Richard II paid £25 to a London goldsmith in 1386 when he was 19, for a knife to be used in the woods and a hunting horn of gold, embellished with green silk tassels. The famous *Master of Game*, a translation (by Edward Duke of York) of Gaston Count of Foix's *Le Livre de Chasse* was dedicated to the Prince of Wales who became Henry V in 1413. Even Henry VI, a king not renowned for physical prowess, went hunting hares and foxes when he was 12, staying at Bury St Edmunds in the winter of 1433–4. Edward IV is reputed to have met his future wife Elizabeth Woodville under a still surviving oak tree in Whittlebury Forest (Northamptonshire); presumably he was hunting at the time. He took care to entertain the leading citizens of London at his hunting palace of Havering. Little Edward V during his short life of 12 years is said to have been devoted to horses and dogs while he lived at Ludlow Castle, before he fell into the clutches of his uncle, Richard.

Most of these statements about the prowess of medieval kings in the hunting field are unsatisfactorily imprecise. Actual records of the king's hunting in person are surprisingly few. One reason may be that the king possibly hunted as a guest in other people's parks and forests more often then he did in his own. Also, it may be that to attribute to a king skill and courage in hunting was more a declaration of what was expected of him than a record of what he performed.

There is no doubt, however, that deer were eaten in quantities on the greater feasts of the church, at court festivities such as weddings, knightings, pregnancies and consecrations. Henry III exploited the animal resources of his forests to the full when preparing for Christmas at York or the feast of St Edward at Westminster.

Rackham has calculated that in an average year up to 1260 Henry III took 607 fallow deer, 159 red deer and 45 roe deer, together with 86 wild swine. Of the fallow he ate half at his own table, gave a third away for the use of his friends and one sixth away (live) for stocking parks. Of these 607 fallow deer (325 bucks and 282 does) 526 came from forests and the rest from royal parks or vacant episcopal parks (Rackham 1980, 181). It has been suggested that venison was a food highly favoured for ceremonies. More questionable is whether the love of hunting had a serious economic motivation.

It might be thought that by the early Middle Ages the hunting and gathering element in the economy at large was no longer of great consequence. This is borne out in household accounts but archaeological excavations of castles and other noble residential sites tell a different story. Accounts indicate that only about seven per cent of the meat supplies of the higher nobility was consumed in the form of game (Dyer 1989, 60). At Okehampton Castle (Devon) red deer appears as an element in the pre-1300 levels (Grant 1988, 165). From the fourteenth century fallow deer actually contributed over half the bone material of the main mammalian species, outnumbering cattle, sheep and pig. The bones of the hind limb were much better preserved than those of the fore limb. Clearly haunches, which provided substantially more meat, were brought to the castle by preference. Similar evidence was noted at Sandal Castle (West Yorkshire) (Griffith *et al.* 1983, 341). Here fallow deer reached nearly 40 per cent of all bones in the period 1100–1400 but after 1450 they declined, a fact which coincided with the passing of Sandal to the Crown and may indicate that there was less hunting under the new absentee landlords. Much smaller proportions of deer bones were present in the royal castle of Portchester but here again fallow deer predominated (Cunliffe and Munby 1985, 255–6).

Field archaeology during the last thirty years has provided a plethora of new evidence for the physical changes wrought in the landscape to adapt it for the hunt. *Forests* were large tracts of country belonging to the Crown and subject to Forest Law (Cantor 1982, 56–85). *Chases* were, in effect, private forests which a few great nobles and ecclesiastical lords were permitted to create on their estates. *Parks* were securely enclosed areas, relatively small in extent and part of the demesne land of the lord of the manor. *Warrens* were essentially game parks filled with animals, principally hares and rabbits.

Within the forests, and at times outside their bounds, were parks, distinguished from them by being fairly small in size, usually between 40.5 and 81 ha (100 and 200 acres), and by the fact that they were enclosed (Steane 1975, 211). To retain the deer and other animals within the park it had to be completely and securely enclosed. This was done by an internal ditch with a substantial earthen bank or linear mound topped by a wooden pale, quickset hedge or more rarely by a stone wall. Some idea of the cost of the works necessary to keep a park enclosed may be gleaned from the occasion when Edward III granted license to Queen Philippa to make a park in the bailiwick of Brigstock within Rockingham Forest (Northamptonshire). He appointed Walter de Wyght, king's yeoman, keeper of the park

> *to have the enclosure finished, make dykes there, and deer leaps* [saltus] *and lodges* [lugeas], *to have the palings of the park repaired with the timber of the park and to make trenches* [clearings] *in the park,*

taking care that the wood cut down in such trenches be sold or made into charcoal as shall be most to the queen's profit; also to hire carpenters and other workmen required for the works and take carriage for the timber and other necessary things as was ordained. (Cal. Pat. R. 1348–50, *552.)*

The king's park at Moulton, 3km (2 miles) north of Northampton, was enclosed as early as the reign of Henry II and here, evidently, the task of enclosing the park was shared from an early date by surrounding townships. By the sixteenth century stones inscribed with the names of townships were built into stretches of the walls, and some of these survive today (Steane 1975, 228–9).

The deer leap was a gap in the earthen bank matched by a pit or hollow inside the park boundary. It was designed to allow the deer to run up the ramp and jump into the park, but to prevent them doing the reverse trip. Only a few royal licenses to impark were endorsed with the right of constructing deer leaps since such contrivances were a steady one-way drain on deer from the royal forest. This is made clear by a grant such as that to Ingram de Fednes at Gayton 'provided that it is so enclosed that the king's deer cannot enter therein' (*Cal. Charter R. 1257–1300*, 14).

In addition to being hunting preserves, parks were used for the pasturing of cattle and sheep (agistment), for the production of timber and underwood, and for turbary (peat). Stone quarrying, pannage for pigs, fishing and rabbits were other sources of income contributed by parks. It is noteworthy that most of the early medieval parks in Northamptonshire were situated on the edge of cultivated land, their boundaries often coinciding with those of the parish. They are well away from main centres of settlement and are thus sharply distinguished from Tudor and Stuart parks which were often designed to act as the foil for a large house (as at Holdenby and Burghley). There are four such parks carved out of the forest on the edge of the cultivated areas surrounding the villages of Brigstock, Sudborough and Grafton Underwood.

Ecologically these ancient parks are important because they conserve rich fauna and flora.

91 Tollard Royal (Wiltshire), King John's House. The hunting lodge of c.1240 *had a medieval north-western addition remodelled in the later sixteenth century, and a medieval south-western addition of which only the foundations remain. The lodge, which was in the middle of Cranborne Chase, had a first-floor hall and undercroft. It was recorded by the owner, Lt. Gen. Pitt Rivers.* (Photograph: J. M. Steane.)

The ancient pollard oaks of Windsor Great Park and Blenheim Park (formerly the park of the royal manor of Woodstock) are among the oldest living things in England. The huge crevassed shells of their trunks and the antlered skeletons of their few remaining branches belie the fact that there is plenty of life in these dotards yet.

Once the park was enclosed it could be stocked. Kings used their forests and parks as reservoirs of deer, which they distributed to friends, favourites and servants. The Close Rolls of the thirteenth century in particular are littered with references to this practice. In Northamptonshire, for instance, William de Ferrers, Earl of Derby was granted 15 does and 5 bucks to stock his park at Higham by gift of the king. William de Cantilupe was given 8 does and 2 bucks from Rockingham Forest to stock his park at Harringworth, and Gilbert de Millers, when starting his park at Overston in 1255, was given 10 live does (*decem damas vivas*) from the forest of Salcey. The roads of medieval England must have been creaking with wagons loaded with bound deer (Steane 1975, 214).

Much is known from documentary sources about the techniques used in medieval hunting, and archaeology occasionally supplements this information. Since the hunt was regarded as basic training for war and an essential part of the upbringing and education of the aristocracy, from the age of seven to eight boys learnt the arts of handling a horse, using weapons and moving across the countryside in a company. The animals of the chase – red deer, fallow deer, roe deer (up to 1338, after which it was no longer protected because it was thought it drove out the other species) and wild boar – were put up by their hunting dogs and pursued by small groups of knightly or noble gentry. From numerous illustrations such as those in the *Queen Mary Psalter* it seems that they also shot at running prey from horseback by means of bow and arrows but it was difficult to inflict a fatal wound in this way. In fact by the fifteenth century organized royal and aristocratic hunting had developed into two main forms. There was the following on horseback across country of a pack of hounds which pursued the quarry to the death; and the shooting of driven game with the bow and arrow.

Clearly hounds played a major role in hunting. Edward, Duke of York, in his book *The Master of Game* describes 'a hound as the most reasonable beast and the best knowing of any beast that ever God made'. In all medieval hunts a mixed pack was used. First there were liemers, the scenting dogs who were used before the hunt to track the game to its lair and then move it when the hunt was in position. Secondly, there were running dogs in the charge of servants called kerners. These hounds were called harriers, brackets or raches. Thirdly, there were greyhounds in the charge of fewterers. These were of miscellaneous breeds (dogs like Irish wolfhounds, Scots deerhounds and smooth-coated Italian greyhounds) and hunted by sight.

The day's sport had to be carefully mapped out beforehand so that everyone had a clear idea of the country to be hunted over and the game within it. Once the terrain and the direction the hunt was to take were known, the fewterers or greyhound-holders, each with two or three greyhounds on leash, proceeded to their appointed stations or trysters. Each tryster held a bowman or two and a *chasse-chien* with a brace of raches or scenting hounds. The harriers were sometimes, but by no means always, released in a single pack. As the stag flashed by so the fresh groups of hounds were uncoupled and those that were run out dropped behind. Nightfall might come before the hounds finally fell upon their exhausted quarry.

The physical attributes of the medieval hunting dog can be reconstructed from manuscript illuminations, from effigies and brasses and from the bones of the animals themselves (Fig. 92). Iconographic evidence suggests that dogs varied greatly in size, and there were many different types. The measurements of bones bear this out. The dog bones found at Portchester came from a small number of individuals buried together and were probably hunting dogs, pets or guard dogs kept at the castle. A few had cut marks on them and were presumably eaten. The excavations in the outer bailey in the medieval levels showed an increase in dog bones compared with the Saxon period (Cunliffe 1977, 231). The measurements indicated a wide range of sizes but one very large animal represented by several bones (found in Pit 30) may have been a wolf.

The bones of red deer, roe deer and fallow

92 Higham Ferrers (Northamptonshire). Memorial brass of William Chichele, brother of the Archbishop of Canterbury, and Beatrice his wife, 1425. Increasingly in the later Middle Ages brass effigies are shown with their feet resting on dogs rather than lions. (Photograph: J. M. Steane.)

deer were all found at the site, with a marked increase recorded in the later periods of medieval occupation, notably of fallow deer. The area to the north of Portchester was a royal forest, known as the Forest of Bere. It is tempting to connect the evidence of dog and deer bones with hunters and hunted. Not all dog bones came from hunting dogs, however. At Upton (Gloucestershire) where no deer remains were found, there was a powerful heavily-boned animal unlikely to be swift enough for herding or the chase, doubtless it was a guard dog.

The question arises, where were these hunting dogs kept? Also, who trained them and provided for their needs? One *ad hoc* solution adopted by the king was to make individual officers responsible for maintaining hounds. The Sheriff of Northampton for instance saw to the keeping of the king's greyhounds at the royal hunting lodge of Geddington, paying ½d each for their upkeep (*Cal. Lib. R. 1251–60*, 270, 322). In the early thirteenth century kennels were established in the Royal Park at Odiham (Hampshire) for 120 hunting dogs. It is likely they were treated better than poor folk: on 5 May 1265, during the visit of Eleanor of Montfort to Odiham, half a quarter of grain was distributed for the poor over eight days, while castle dogs received three quarters of grain over a ten day period.

The other main method of royal hunting as it developed in the fifteenth century was what became known as the 'stable' – the shooting of driven deer from butts. It is to this practice that Edward, Duke of York, devotes most attention and by his time elaborate ceremonies had developed with it. In most royal forests there were specially constructed enclosures called in English deer hedges, or hayes, into which deer were driven. Some were natural features such as amphitheatres or glades; others had more or less permanent hedges and were similar to deer parks. The fewterers and their leashes of greyhounds went with the beaters to stations on hill tops to drive down and keep the deer in position. As they were driven past the 'trysts' in glades along the rivers, royalty and nobility shot with their bows and arrows. Greyhounds were unleashed to pursue wounded animals into 'receiving stations' where they were finished off, cleaned skinned and butchered with complex ritual (described in *Sir Gawain and the Green Knight*). The hounds were fed offal soaked in blood and the flesh was taken back to the castle. This goes far to explain the observed fact that bones from the more desirable haunches of venison are likely to be found in greater numbers at castle and residential sites. The butchering was clearly done at the place of kill.

Hawking

The other great field sport keenly followed by medieval royalty and nobility was hawking. This was given the stamp of extreme respectability by the Emperor Frederick II who wrote a remarkably detailed and scientific treatise, still in use today, entitled *De Arte Venandi cum Avibus* ('Concerning the Art of Hunting with Birds') (Wood and Fyfe 1943). He claims in the first chapter that falconry is more noble than other forms of hunting because of the difficulties encountered in acquiring the necessary skills. This has the result that 'many nobles and few of the lower rank learn and carefully pursue this, and one may properly conclude that it is intrinsically an aristocratic sport'.

The sport of hawking was enjoyed by the late Anglo-Saxon monarchy. William of Malmesbury records of Edward the Confessor: 'there was one earthy enjoyment in which he chiefly delighted which was hunting with fleet hounds whose opening in the woods he used with pleasure to encourage; and again with the pouncing of birds, whose nature it is to prey on their kindred species'. His successor Harold is shown on the Bayeux Tapestry carrying a hawk on no less than four occasions, and on two panels his captor, Guy, Comte de Ponthieu, is also shown carrying a hawk.

At least two medieval English kings seem to have shared the Emperor Frederick II's enthusiasm for hawking. Some of John's more remarkable acts of almsgiving are attributable to the king's refusal to stop hawking on important feast days (Harting 1883, 78). In 1212–13 on Wednesday, the Feast of the Innocents (28 December) at Ashwell (Cambridgeshire), alms were contributed by the king to 350 paupers; he had taken seven cranes with his hawks, for each of which he feasted 50 paupers, each being given a penny. At Lincoln on the Wednesday following the Feast of Purification the king went with his gerfalcons to capture cranes and commanded that 100 paupers be fed with bread, meat and ale to the amount of 13s 4d. King John, moreover, commanded that his favourite gerfalcon, Gibbon, should have plump goats and good hens to eat, with hare once a week. Edward I, despite a reputation for enjoying stag hunting, seems to have had a real love for falconry (Prestwich 1988, 115). There is a considerable surviving correspondence dealing with his falcons and hawks. He did not adopt the same careful scientific approach as the Emperor Frederick II, but when choosing stock went for the biggest birds, imagining that they were therefore the best. Frederick, on the other hand, spent a number of pages painstakingly describing the precise coloration and build to look for in a prize bird. Edward

93a A badge of an eagle crowned and gorged with closed wings, found at Swan Lane, London; 50mm (2in) high × 58mm (2¼in) wide. The crowned eagle was an emblem favoured by Henry IV (After Mitchiner.)

93b Badge of Edward III: a griffin standing right with wings displayed and tail raised; 34mm (1⅜in) high × 38mm (1½in) wide. From Billingsgate, London. (After Mitchiner.)

also employed somewhat primitive methods to cure his birds when they were ill, including having a wax image made of an ailing bird which he then presented before the altar of St Thomas Becket at Canterbury.

Hawks could be acquired straight from the wild, they could be bought or they could be obtained by gift. Frederick II was clear in his advice that falcon eggs hatched under the hens produce birds of little value to hunters. He was of the opinion that the young birds should be left in the nest as long as possible because the parent birds were always the best trainers of young falcons. As soon as they were fledged it was up to the falconer to capture them. In 1250 the bailiff of Woodstock had the custody of an eyrie of falcons. Bishop Swinfield's fowler watched the falcon's eyries in June in order to capture the young birds. Another method of acquiring falcons was by purchase. They were imported from Norway and bought for the king at Boston and Lynn during the twelfth and thirteenth centuries. In Lincolnshire payments to the Crown were sometimes made in falcons instead of currency; in this way two gerfalcons were exchanged for a licence to take corn to Norway. The prestige of falconry is well illustrated by the fact that birds frequently figure as gifts between royalty. A special messenger came from Henry III to Lynn in 1245 to collect six gentle falcons, a gift from King Hakon. Edward in 1276 received eight grey and three white gerfalcons from the King of Norway, some of which he forwarded to the King of Castile: 'We send you 4 grey gerfalcons, two of which are trained to fly at the crane and heron; as to the other two you can use them as you think best.'

The training and the care of the king's hawks was a long and difficult process which required detailed administrative arrangements. A number of sergeanties were held by some form of hawk service (Kimball 1936, 103–6). An outstanding falconry sergeanty belonged to the Hauville family and was connected with the manors of Hacconby (Lincolnshire) and Dunton-cum-Doughton and Kettleston (Norfolk). The tenants had to act as keepers, purchase falcons, deliver those the king sent as gifts and receive the birds presented to the king. Another method was to employ professional falconers who spent their whole time training and keeping the falcons or hawks in readiness for the king's sport. Hugh de Erlham was one of these officers in Henry III's reign; he had six of the king's falcons mewed at Geddington hunting lodge (Northamptonshire) and was given ½d a day for the maintenance of each of them.

Each hawk required constant and intense supervision from the falconer on a one-to-one basis. During the training and manning period they had to be well fed with freshly killed meat; otherwise their feathers would show 'hunger traces'. The fully grown birds were taken by candlelight to have the needle points of their talons clipped, their jesses (short leather leashes) and bells attached and their eyes sealed. In his treatise Frederick claims to have introduced the hood to the West (Fig. 94a) and describes the other devices used by the falconer: the leash, jesses, bell and swivel. He discusses the proper way of carrying hawks on a fist, by holding the jesses or short leash, and states that a recently caught falcon should be carried around without being fed for 24 hours. 'Then the bird, fatigued by this exhausting treatment and more or less tamed by it' is given a cold ration. The bells have several uses. The falconer knows from their ringing that the falcon has flown down or fallen from the perch and he can go to her assistance. They can also be heard from a long distance when the bird is lost or out of sight. The glove is also a vital piece of falconer's equipment (Fig. 94b). Other devices include the drawer, the creance and the lure, all used in training the falcon. The falconer's bag was employed to carry the lure and the hawk's food. It was attached to the belt.

The housing of hawks could involve the construction of mews. Frederick erected 20 large castles in his favourite province of Apulia including one, Castel de Monte, which was especially designed to house the emperor's falcons. The tops of several towers were fitted up for housing falcons, while other rooms were pigeon houses. The Emperor's treatise describes how a mews could be built. It might be

> *a tower somewhere in the country, or an isolated high building with no forest or trees near by, for young birds should be fed and raised in surroundings similar to those the parent birds would have selected.*

An artificial nest was built of materials like those of the wild eyrie. This small place was to be open on three sides and exposed to the morning and evening sunshine.

> *Nearby in the mews there should be placed water in a basin or tub about half a foot in height, making it possible for the birds to bathe whenever they wish.*

The mews were also provided with proper perches, upon which the birds could rest and to which they would readily return.

English kings also built mews for their falcons, albeit not on so magnificent a scale. Henry II, in 1181 or 1182, bought a messuage in Winchester which he converted into mews for his birds (Biddle 1976, 52). Besides the mews it contained rooms for the falconers, a chapel, a dovecot, an oriel and a stable. Edward I built a more impressive establishment at Charing Cross, featuring a turfed garden and a lead bath for the birds, supplied with running water from a ground foundation with four outlet spouts shaped like leopard heads and a statuette of a falcon in the centre. There were other mews at Bere, Brigstock and Nottingham.

Increasingly, as bones are carefully collected from archaeological contexts, it will be possible to study the remains of the birds themselves. At the royal castle of Portchester those of a goshawk and a sparrowhawk have been found (Cunliffe and Munby 1985, 269). Goshawk and peregrine falcon remains have turned up at Lincoln. At Deddington, a baronial castle in Oxfordshire, an extraordinary collection of bones of raptors came from a late twelfth- or early thirteenth-century latrine pit and from a late thirteenth- or fourteenth-century cesspit (Ivens 1984, 130–7). The species represented included a peregrine falcon, a kite, a montague's harrier, a kestrel, several hen harriers and three buzzards. Of these, only two, the peregrine and kestrel, are known to have been used as hunting birds by medieval falconers. What were the other raptors' bones doing in the castle? A plausible suggestion is that Deddington Castle was being used for raising falcons over a long period of about 75 years; hawk nestlings could have been raised with the kites and buzzards serving as foster mothers, thus saving on the services of valuable hunting birds.

If hawk bones are rare in the medieval period,

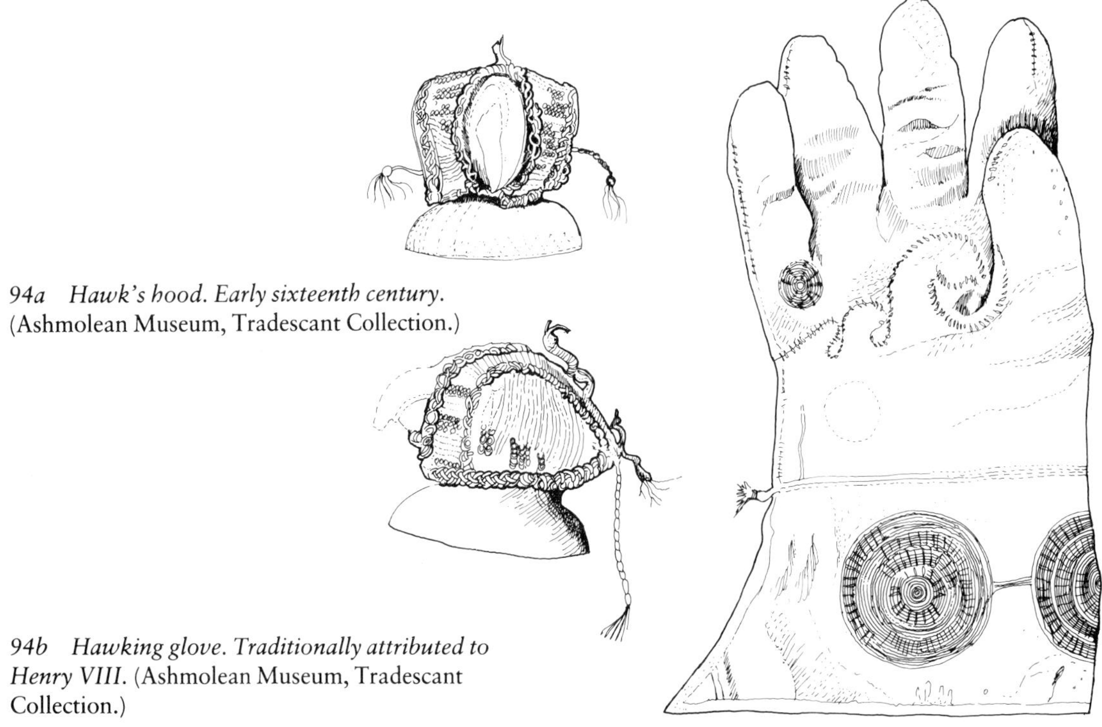

94a Hawk's hood. Early sixteenth century. (Ashmolean Museum, Tradescant Collection.)

94b Hawking glove. Traditionally attributed to Henry VIII. (Ashmolean Museum, Tradescant Collection.)

hawk trappings are exceedingly scarce. Only two examples of medieval hawk rings are known. One from Hedingham Castle was inscribed 'Ox-en-for-de' (Hedingham was owned by the de Vere Earls of Oxford). A second ring, now in the British Museum, is made of gold and was found near Biggleswade. It is inscribed 'Sum regis Anglie' on one side and 'Et comitis Herefordie' on the other and presumably belonged to Henry IV (*Gentlemans Magazine* 1795, 65, 474). In addition there is a hawk's hood in the Ashmolean Museum (Fig. 94a) which apparently is the one referred to in the 1656 catalogue as belonging to Henry VIII (Macgregor 1983, 226–8). Certainly Henry VIII's passion for the sport is well documented; his interest in hawking increased as he grew older and was less able to indulge in the more strenuous forms of the chase (Starkey 1991, 163–5). On 8 June 1547 Marke Myllener delivered to the King '11 doz. hawk's hoods at 8d' and '1 doz. of large hawk's hoods 6s'. This makes it possible that the Ashmolean hawk's hood is one of those made for the king in his later years. It is made of leather to which is sewn a cover of red fabric, probably originally velvet. At the front of the hood is an opening for the beak. At the rear the hood is split to enable close fitting, while drawstrings attach it to the hawk's head. It is decorated with gold wire embroidery. The Ashmolean also has a hawking glove which may similarly have belonged to Henry VIII (Fig. 94b). It is made of red-brown doeskin with an overlaid panel of grey-white kid, and embroidered with rows of silver-gilt thread arranged in circular motifs on the gauntlet.

Tournaments and the archaeology of chivalry

Tournaments were first introduced in France during the eleventh and twelfth centuries. At this period French knights were pioneering a new form of shock combat. Armoured riders holding heavy lances under their right arms trained themselves to charge, putting their full weight behind their weapons, aiming to unhorse their opponents. They teamed up with other knights and sought excitement, danger, prestige and profit by taking part in so-called *mêlées*, aiming at overwhelming the opposition by sheer weight and momentum. Such fighting was highly relevant to real combat and might involve as many as two hundred active participants on each side. It was barely distinguishable from war. The sole difference, it has been said, between war and the early tournament was one of intention: the death of an opponent, a prime aim in war, was a matter for regret in a tournament (Bowker 1986).

Tourneying quickly became an established habit among the knightly class of Western Europe but changed markedly in form in the later Middle Ages. Instead of massed fighting involving large bodies of men it became more common to hold jousts in which each knight could fight for himself in a restricted space marked out by fences. Actions were more open to observation and became subject to a gradual accumulation of customary rules of conduct; jousts were attended by spectators, with ladies awarding prizes, and were controlled by specially appointed judges and heralds. The development of specialized armour reduced the number of dangerous wounds but also incurred heavy costs, so that the sport grew more elitist and relied more on patronage.

The English monarch was deeply involved in the practice. Politics usually dictated whether the Crown favoured or frowned on tournaments. William of Newbury, writing in 1198, declared that tournaments had been forbidden in the reigns of Henry I and II and that if knights wished to take part they had to go abroad. This prohibition broke down during Stephen's reign and it is noteworthy that the tournament flourished in the reigns of Henry III and Edward II, both kings who failed to keep on good terms with their baronage and were faced with civil war.

Henry II allowed his knights to tourney abroad and indeed his sons were noted tourneyers. Henry, the Young King, and Geoffrey of Brittany were both permitted to lead large groups of adventurous young men out of the country to take part in tournaments. Richard I encouraged the practice and was himself a distinguished tourneyer, but he was also conscious of the potential for tournaments to be perverted for political purposes. He addressed a writ to his justiciar announcing that tournaments were to be allowed only at five named sites in England: between Salisbury and Wilton (Wiltshire); Warwick and Kenilworth (Warwickshire); Stamford (Lincolnshire) and

Warinford (Suffolk); Brackley and Mixbury (Northamptonshire), and Blyth and Tickhill (Nottinghamshire). The fact that quite large areas were named, points to the practice in these early mêlées of ranging over a wide stretch of countryside. Of these five places only one, Salisbury/Wilton, was in a river valley; all the rest were set among hills, providing a greater opportunity for a wide variety of fighting including the ambush. Such regulation of tourneys enabled the king to keep a watchful eye on them (Bowker 1986, 11). The sites straddled the major routes to London, making them accessible not only to knights travelling from other counties but also to government control. It is significant that the north and west were left without a site; these areas were, politically and militarily, notoriously unstable areas.

The monarchy at other times attempted to control tournaments by issuing prohibitions. These mostly came from Henry III and Edward II; neither king showed much aptitude for military leadership, and they could not successfully participate in tournaments to win their subjects' respect. Piety may well have explained Henry III's abstinence from tourneying but the political instability of these reigns was a potent enough reason for prohibition. *Hastiludes* 'spear games' literally, were politically dangerous as gatherings where malcontents could meet to discuss and plan opposition to the Crown. They might also be used as a cover for pursuing private feuds. A plot was uncovered to kill Gaveston, the king's favourite, at the Stepney tournament held to celebrate Edward II's coronation. Further assassination attempts were planned, in Richard II's reign to murder John of Gaunt at a *hastilude* in Westminster Hall in 1386, and to wipe out Henry IV and his sons at *hastiludes* in Oxford in 1400.

Edward I, on the other hand, encouraged tournaments; he was a warrior who built up a European reputation and acquired considerable expertise in the lists. While still heir to the throne he took a party of newly-made knights including John of Brittany, Henry of Alman (Richard of Cornwall's son and the king's cousin), two sons of Simon de Montfort, Roger Clifford and others on a tourneying tour of Europe which lasted two years. Such adventures could be hazardous. During a tournament mêlée against the duke of Burgundy's force known as the Little Battle of Chalons, the duke seized the king round the neck and tried to drag him off his horse.

Edward not only patronized the sport and participated in it with success but used it to buttress his regime and promote his policies. He was sufficiently conversant with romance literature to exploit to the full the Arthurian origins and overtones of the Round Table (Loomis 1953, 114–27). After forcing Llewelyn to do homage following his successful campaign in North Wales, Edward and his wife visited Glastonbury and on 19 April 1278 ordered the opening of Arthur's tomb 'to link', in Powicke's words, 'the English royal house with the great patron of Glastonbury and to confirm the truth of his burial'. He may also have been concerned that Arthur, whom legend credited with an intention to return to defeat the enemies of the Britons, should be seen to be well and truly dead. It is one of the first instances of archaeology being used for purposes of government propaganda. Leland describes the tomb in his visits of 1534 and 1539 as being of black marble with two tiers at each end and an effigy of the king at the foot. In 1279 Edward was 40 years old and a guest of Roger Mortimer at Kenilworth Castle. Mortimer invited 100 knights and 100 ladies to a 'Round Table' (a gathering of knights) at which he celebrated his farewell to arms. Edward knighted Mortimer's three sons and Mortimer received a present of barrels of gold from the king's sister-in-law, the Queen of Navarre. In 1283 the Arthurian connection was pursued further. Llewelyn had been slain at the end of the second Welsh campaign and the king retained as a token of submission certain relics treasured by the Welsh. The 'crown of Arthur' was presented to Westminster Abbey, an offering similar in symbolism to the handing over of the Stone of Scone by the defeated Scots. A Round Table was held to celebrate the victory at Nevyn (Caernarfonshire) on 27–29 July 1284.

Further Round Tables were held by Edward at Canterbury (1299), Falkirk (1302) and Westminster (1306). At the latter the feast ended with a very Arthurian flavour. The king had knighted his son Edward of Caernarfon, and invested him with the Duchy of Aquitaine, and the young prince had knighted 300 of his companions in Westminster Abbey. Then the party adjourned to Westminster Hall where two servitors bore in a large tray with two swans covered in a network of gold. The king swore on the swans and before God that he would avenge the wrong Robert Bruce had done to God and the Church and that thereafter they would go on crusade (Loomis 1953). Such an Arthurian action exemplifies his desire to associate himself and his knights with all the virtues of romance heroes, including their invincibility. For a time, wars and tournaments merged imperceptibly. This is demonstrated vividly by the showpiece siege of Stirling of 1304 which Edward I ran in much the same way as a tournament. He constructed a viewing gallery from which the ladies of the court could watch the trials of a new siege engine called the 'Warwolf' (Bowker 1986, 41). This procession of campaigns mingled with *hastiludes*, spectacles and banquets, and the invitation to women to take part, all contribute to a picture of Edward liking to think of himself in the role of *Arthurius redivivus*.

It was not until the reign of Edward III that the crown developed the potential of the tournament to the full. Edward III was a keen tourneyer himself and his subjects were able to identify with their king's chivalric interests. Instead of suppressing *hastiludes* by royal prohibition he judiciously patronized them. To celebrate the end of campaigns in Scotland in 1333–4 and again in 1342 he organized a series of *hastiludes*. No less than 250 knights took part in the latter year, including six earls and the king himself. Edward fought as a simple knight-batchelor, a way of proving himself, as well of following the popular custom of bearing the arms of another knight or fighting completely incognito (Bowker 1986, 86). The victory at Crécy was followed by another series of *hastiludes*. They increased the king's prestige abroad and demonstrated English military superiority to the whole of the continent of Europe.

Edward III went much further than these transitory events in his attempts to institutionalize chivalry and link it with the fortunes of the English monarchy. Windsor Castle became the natural centre of operations. Not only was it the king's favourite residence, it was also the legendary locale of Arthur's Round Table. Here Edward held *hastiludes* in 1344. Adam de Murimuth describes the occasion in detail:

> *the feasts that were expensive and abounding in the most alluring of drink they were sustained to the satiety of everyone. Among the lords and ladies dances were not lacking, embraces and kissings alternately commingling. Among the knights continued joustings were being practised for three days.*

The king, however, had further intentions. He summoned the participating knights to meet in the royal chapel to witness his oath 'to begin a Round Table in the same manner and condition as lord Arthur, formerly King of England, appointed it, namely to the number of 300 knights'. To house this prestigious order of chivalry he commanded a hall or house for the Round Table to be built at Windsor Castle, circular in shape, 200ft (61m) in diameter, and with 40,000 tiles covering the walls. This proved over-ambitious and the imminent French war soon diverted resources away from it. The scheme was abandoned and even the site is uncertain. W. H. St John Hope thought that it was in the great courtyard of the upper bailey.

A second a more successful attempt was made after the Crécy campaign and led to Edward III's foundation of the Order of the Garter. Its purpose was, in Keen's words, 'to glamorize the standing of the war which he was waging against the king of France, to present the war effort in the light of a great adventure pursued by a noble and valiant company of knights against an adversary who was unjustly withholding from their sovereign his rightful inheritance' (Keen 1984, 184). One of the strangest features is that the order took its symbol from an item of ladies' underwear. The story of how Edward III, at a ball in Calais, retrieved the garter of the Countess of Salisbury (allegedly his *amoureuse*) and bound it on his own knee saying 'Honi soit qui mal y pense' is apocryphal. It began, however, to circulate from an early date.

The foundation of the Order of the Garter was shot through with the religious, martial and social aspirations of the day. The religious connotations of the order, the cult of St George and St Edward, the endowment of their chapel, the lavish provision of masses for departed members, were there from the first. The organization was strongly military if not militaristic.

The division of the members into two groups according to their seating in St George's Chapel, one headed by the king himself, the other by the Black Prince, is significant. It has been plausibly suggested that Edward III had in mind two potential tourneying teams when he founded the order. What is certain is that Garter knights were regarded as prime targets for jousting challenges by foreign knights. Chivalry was an elitist lay creed and the Order of the Garter was quintessentially aristocratic. This is borne out by the crests and arms of heraldic achievements of the companions, which were fixed to their stalls in the Garter Chapel at Windsor, a continuing reminder of the social exclusiveness of the membership.

The chapel had originally been started by Henry III in 1260 in honour of St Edward the Confessor. Edward III now partially rebuilt it, and fitted it up as the chapel of the new fraternity in honour of Almighty God, the Blessed Virgin Mary, St George and Martyr and St Edward the Confessor. New stalls were made for the knights and canons; above the seats were suspended each knight's helm, crest and sword. As soon as a founder member died the statutes enjoined that a shield of his arms made of metal and his helm were to be fixed to the back of his stall. Henry VIII made two changes: that the plate of a knight should be put up within a year of his installation, instead of at his death, and that foreign knights might set up plates of any size or fashion they pleased (St John Hope, 1901).

The result is a late medieval heraldic display second to none in Europe. No less than 46 stall plates of knights of the Garter that are anterior to 1421 have survived. Over 80 have come down from the period 1348–1485. These magnificent insignia of helms, crests and mantlings, shields and scrolls are blazoned in shining coloured enamels on gilt copper plates. The dimensions of the plates vary from 102mm (4in) to 280mm (11in) in length, while several foreign examples exceed 381mm (15in). A particularly fine one is that of Ralph Lord Bassett, elected to the order about 1368, who died in 1390. It consists of three separate elements, all beautifully enamelled and in an excellent state of preservation. The shield of the knight's arms is in red, gold, black and silver; this is surmounted by the helm, mantling and crest, a great boar's head issuing from a coronet with jewelled circlet. The third plate is a large roundel, probably intended for a target with a part-coloured field in red and blue, charged with a gold escarbuncle having a bleeding heart in its centre. Before 1421 most of the plates were cut to the shape of the design; from 1421 to 1475 nearly all were quadrangular. Those from the period 1475 to 1500 closely resemble the armorial designs found on monumental brasses of the same period and were probably engraved by the same artists. The shape of the shields is nearly always that of the plain 'heater'; the helms drawn in profile are depicted in silver, garnished with gold, most of the early ones are shown as tilting helms with the front rounded or pointed. It is evident that a number of the plates have been reversed to face a different way and have been engraved, palimpsest fashion, on the other side, presumably when they were moved from one side of the chapel to the other. The helms and crests were then recut to ensure that they still faced the altar.

The tournament was a political, military and social event. It also developed into a vehicle for lavish spectacles and, in some senses, empty ritual towards the end of the Middle Ages. The preparation of appropriate embellishments for tournaments, banquets and masquerades, such as the emblazoning of arms and devices on banners and the provision of elaborate costumes and masks, occupied painters and embroiderers attached to the Great Wardrobe of the royal court. A number of techniques were employed by the craftsmen. We know for example that in 1345–9 a jousting tunic (*cotamura*) for Edward required one and a quarter ells each of red and blue cloth to form the fields of the quarterings of his arms. The *leopards passant guardant* and fleurs-de-lis were formed from one and a half ells of yellow cloth also provided. The fortuitous survival of the jupon of the Black Prince which was hung above his tomb in Canterbury Cathedral shows an even more sumptuous technique (Mann 1950, 19–20). This must have been a splendid garment cut so as to fit closely to the body, laced up behind through eye-holes and worn over tourneying or war armour. The royal arms of France and England quarterly front and back were formed of four squares of velvet, two red and two blue laid on linen with a layer of wool padding between and the whole quilted together by vertical stitching. The fleurs-de-lis and leopards or lions of the charges are embroidered in gold thread on separate pieces of velvet applied to the rest. This same *appliqué* technique was used for enriching tents and pavilions for the royal household. John de Zakerly made tents in 1350–2; a large blue linen tent was powdered outside with stars and inside with crowns, both made of yellow worsted. Another of green linen was lined with red buckram (a cotton material) studded with yellow eagles. A less tedious way of producing a brightly decorative effect was painting in colours directly on the cloth. This was used for painting flags and streamers used to decorate ships of war. Wax was applied as a sealing agent which protected the painted textile from salt sea spray. A showy effect could be gained by stamping or painting of gold and less often silver on such fine materials as cendal, a silk, or sindon, probably a fine cotton. In 1348 for her churching celebrations after the birth of William of Windsor, Queen Philippa was equipped with a set of room hangings of red sindon stamped with the letter 'S' in gold leaf. The Victoria and Albert Museum in its textile collection has a small fragment of such a hanging. It measures 135 × 210mm (5½ × 8½in) and has a gold fleur-de-lis stamped on it. A dark stain appears to be the adhesive.

At the other end of the scale of elaboration is the heraldic embroidery, possibly from a horse trapper, now in the Musée National des Thermes et de l'Hôtel de Cluny, Paris. It is likely to date from before 1340 since it shows the leopards of England, not the new arms, quarterly France and England, which were adopted in this year. The skill of the embroiderers is spectacular. On a ground of red velvet, silver and silver-gilt thread and coloured silks act as a foil to a mesh of pearls and cabochon crystals. Such rich textiles make it easier to recreate in the mind's eye the splendour of the processions which came to be held on the first day of jousts and marked the opening of festivities. The route from the Tower of London to one of the most popular tournament sites at Smithfield in fact acquired the name of Knightriders Street. Chroniclers tended, as time went on, to describe the processions at greater length than the tournaments themselves. Edward III took a leading part in providing masks and costumes for knights and ladies entering cities where jousts were to be held. In 1348 these costumes numbered 288 for Lichfield, 44 for Canterbury and 12 for Bury. At Lichfield the King issued blue tunics with white hoods to 11 of his chamber knights and 20 other knights, while 28 ladies were given blue gowns with white hoods. Richard II, though not famed for his military prowess, satisfied the London citizens' appetite for rich pageantry to the full. In 1390 he led 20 knights, all bearing the same device of the white hart ('Rich-hart' = Richard), chained and gorged with a golden crown. This was displayed on the clothes, armour, shields and horses' trappings during the company's parade through the streets from the Tower to the tournament at Smithfield. The Wilton Diptych displays this imagery of the white hart; badges of the white hart in bronze alloy and the base metal, lead, show that the heraldic emblems of the king's affinity were distributed to the people (Fig. 81).

Weapons and armour used in tournaments

The list of socially important men who were killed tourneying is impressive and hundreds of simple knights were also among the casualties. Even the royal family was not immune. Geoffrey, the fourth son of Henry II, was killed tourneying near Paris in 1186. In the great mêlée the armour worn was the same as that used in war. The joust however was a different matter because here a knight had to be able to receive and withstand a single blow with the full weight of horse and rider behind it. A revolution in armour occurred to meet its needs.

Little more than a few scraps of mail, a helmet or two, and some swords have survived from the military equipment of the twelfth and thirteenth centuries. This has mainly to be reconstructed from effigies, monumental brasses and manuscripts. The lightest defences were made of quilted fabric worn beneath other armour; this served to deaden the weight of blows received and helped to minimize bruising. Linen studded with metal was also used to deflect sword blows and served as a lightweight addition to tourneying armour. Mail, in which steel rings and chains were interwoven or riveted, was flexible and comparatively light. It was worn over the quilted defences and was particularly valuable in protecting joints such as necks and armpits. It had two disadvantages however: its matted surface did not encourage

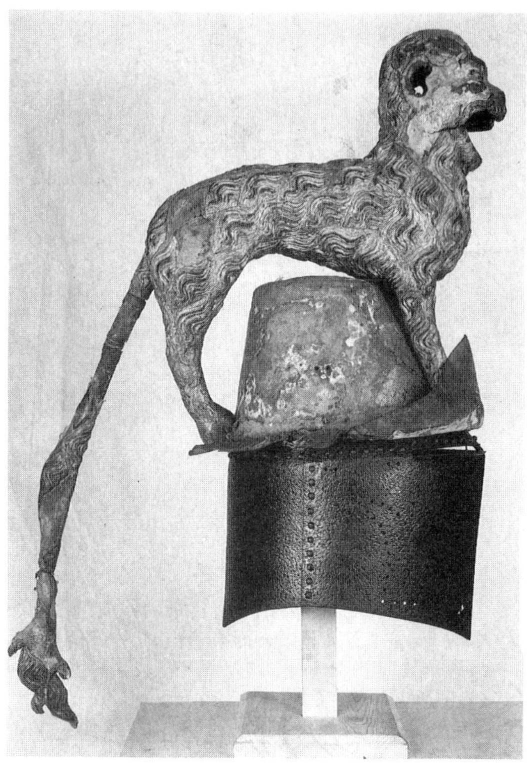

95 Canterbury Cathedral (Kent). The Black Prince's funeral achievements. Helm and crest. The helm (31cm (12in) high), was designed to wear over the visorless bascinet and was becoming less used in battle but still continued for many years in the tournament. It is made of three parts riveted together and has two horizontal vision slits with a series of small circular ventilation holes – arranged as a three-pointed coronet. The crest is 74cm (29in) high and is in the form of a lion statant guardant, *made of moulded leather and canvas, covered with gesso on linen and painted.* (Photograph: HM Royal Armouries.)

a blow to glance off, so that blows in battle could lead to severe bruising; and if the blow penetrated the mail the broken links tended to become embedded in the wound. Great advances in metalwork skills, pioneered on the Continent in the fourteenth century, produced plate-metal armour which was closely fitting, flexible , resisted blows and was still fairly light.

The huge iron helm remained a distinctive and unchanging feature of tournament armour from the twelfth to the mid-fourteenth century. In the twelfth century it was cylindrical in shape with a flat top; vision was provided by two eye slits and ventilation by a number of holes. It rested on the shoulders and was fastened by the buckles to the body armour. A fine example and rare survival of a fourteenth-century tourneying helm is among the Black Prince's funeral achievements in Canterbury Cathedral (Mann 1951, 24–6, Mann 1954, 12–14). It is made of iron sheets skilfully constructed of three parts riveted together: a front and back plate, and an upper in the form of a pointed dome (Fig. 95). There are two horizontal slits in front with the edges turned down for protection, while – a princely touch – breathing holes forming a pattern of a crown of three fleurons are pierced on the right side. An iron chain attached the helm to the breastplate, allowing it when not worn to be carried slung behind the shoulder. The weight of the helmet is 3.2kg (7lb 2oz) – this makes it likely that it was the real thing, not a piece of state armour fashioned for funerary purposes. The crest is that of a lion standing upon a cap of maintenance or cap of estate. Both are made of leather with canvas glued over the joints and moulded with great artistry. The lion's hair is suggested by lozenges of plaster, each stamped with a patterned die and glued to the leather. The high crown of the cap of maintenance is coated with crimson-painted plaster, diapered with small gilt roses. The turned up brim was originally painted white and studded with black ermine tails. One small detail is that the inside of the hat is lined with red velvet. Such great helms with crests are found sculptured on hundreds of the alabaster tombs and engraved brasses of lords of the fifteenth century; they act as pillows for the heads of the knightly effigies.

The only piece of body armour in the Black Prince's achievement is a pair of gauntlets (Mann 1942, 113–22) (Fig. 98). They illustrate the technical achievements of fourteenth-century armours and also give a glimpse of the splendour of equipment which tournaments inspired. They are made in hour-glass form, the

98 Canterbury Cathedral (Kent). The Black Prince's funeral achievements. A pair of gauntlets. Gilt copper or copper alloy and leather. Riveted inside are leather finger-strips to which are riveted in turn small overlapping plates (Photograph: HM Royal Armouries.)

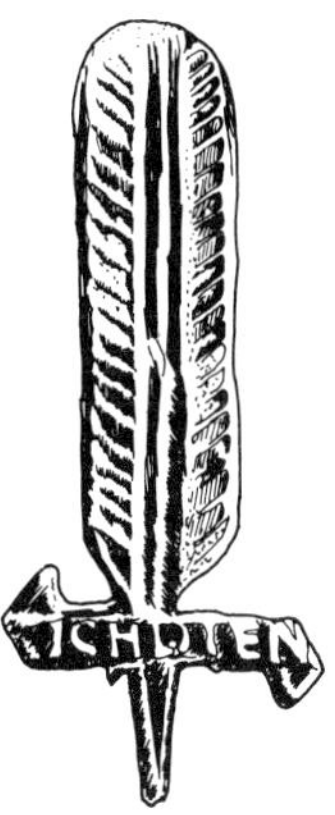

96 *An ostrich feather badge with label across the base of the quill reading* ICH DIEN *(I serve) (52mm (2in) high), from Vintry, London. The ostrich feather was introduced as a Plantagenet badge by Edward III, it first received the inscription* ICH DIEN *when used by his son, the Black Prince. This particular one may have been made for distribution at the funeral of the Black Prince in 1376. He died at Westminster and his body went in procession to burial at Canterbury.* (After Mitchiner.)

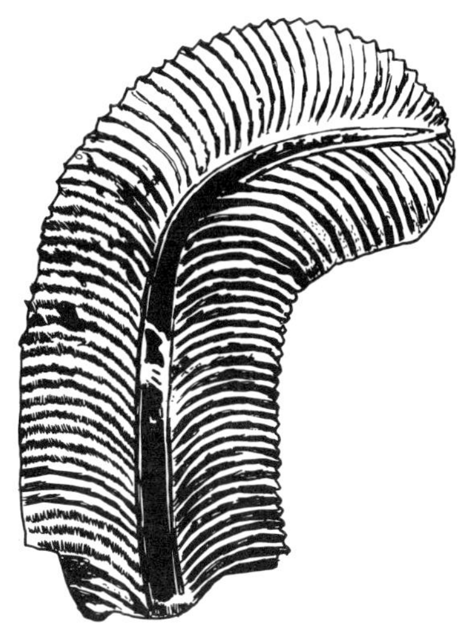

97 *A large ostrich feather with the top bent over to right, a badge of the Black Prince and thereafter of the Prince of Wales. (63mm (2½in) high by 55mm (2in) wide).* (After Mitchiner.)

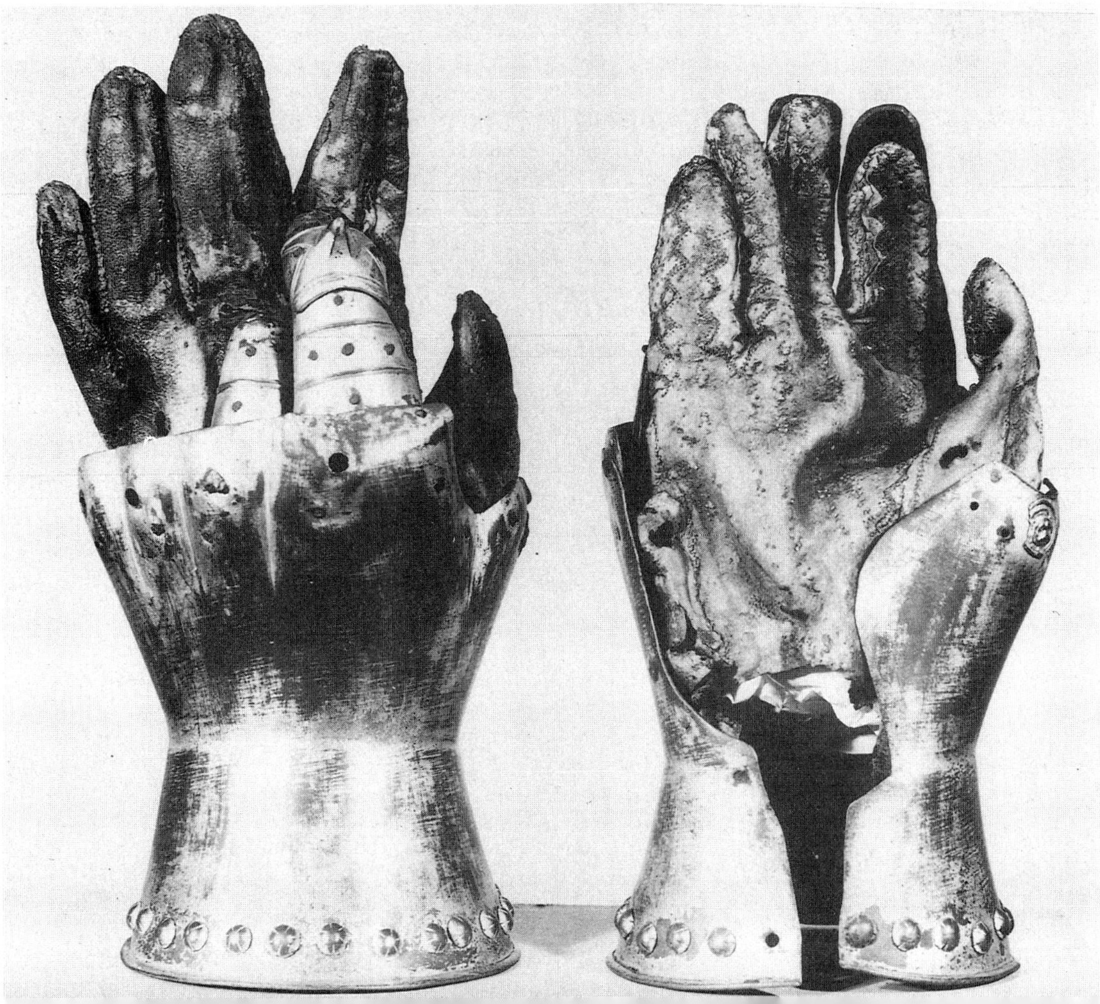

99 *Canterbury Cathedral (Kent). The Black Prince's funeral achievements. The shield. Made of poplar wood (73cm (29in) high) covered with canvas and faced with paper covered by leather; the heraldic charges were applied in moulded leather. The shield bears the full arms, for war. Apart from the Henry V shield, it is the only one known to survive in Britain dating from the Middle Ages.* (Photograph: HM Royal Armouries.)

main part being fashioned from a single plate wrapped round the hand behind the fingers and embossed slightly over the knuckles and metacarpal bones. The leather fingerstrips have riveted small overlapping plates. At the base of each thumb is a circular stud cast with a leopard's head in relief, while the knuckles are set with gadlings, small cast figures of leopards. The lining gauntlets of buff leather are embroidered in silk with zigzag patterns.

The Black Prince's shield is heater-shaped, slightly concave towards the body, and made of poplar wood, glued on both sides with layers of linen, on the front with paper finished with gesso (Fig. 99). The applied heraldic charges are made of boiled leather shaped in high relief fixed by small tacks. It is painted and gilded; the fields are punched over with numerous small crosses. The back is painted green and contains various holes indicating where the brases for the arms and the guige for hanging it round the back were attached. There is no trace of a cadency label (to indicate the arms of the eldest son of the king) but a drawing *c.*1600 in the library of the Society of Antiquaries (MS62) shows one. The shield is an example of a standard thirteenth- or fourteenth-century type; but apart from Henry V's shield in Westminster Abbey is the only one to survive in Britain.

The sword which accompanied these other funeral achievements has vanished but parts of the scabbard and belt have survived. For a complete sword with royal associations we have to turn to Ireland where a sword supplied from the personal armoury of Henry IV was given to the Mayor of Dublin and his successors. It is a 'hand-and-a-half' sword of steel with a tapering, straight, double-edged blade of flattened hollow-diamond section, cruciform in structure with a plummet shaped pommel and straight cross. It is inscribed on the original scabbard mount *sovereyne sovereyne* together with forget-me-not (Germander speedwell) flowers and ostrich feathers – all indications that the sword belonged to Henry, Earl of Derby and Duke of Hereford before he became king of England.

CHAPTER SEVEN
The monarchy, religion and education

The foundation of monasteries

In the early Middle Ages the patronage of religious houses was one of the preserves of the great and powerful. Kings and feudal lords, lay and ecclesiastical, founded monasteries for various reasons. Traditionally, Battle Abbey (Sussex) was said to have been founded after a vow made by Duke William before the Battle of Hastings, as stated in a forged charter of 1154, but in fact the monastery is more likely to have resulted from an arrangement made between the papacy and the king in *c*.1070. William was formally recrowned by papal legates, and heavy penalties were imposed on the Normans for the bloodshed of the invasion and the subsequent pacification of England. The name 'Battle Abbey' demonstrates well the arrogance and self-confidence of the conquerors. William insisted that the high altar was to be on the spot where Harold was killed. The site, a narrow ridge on open heathland, appalled the monks and involved them in extensive terracing and the construction of massive undercrofts. The plan of the east end of Battle Abbey as it was built in the thirteenth century was derived from Henry III's rebuilding of Westminster Abbey 1246–59; it was a *chevet* of five radiating chapels. During the fourteenth century the abbots were the main organizers of the defence of the coast between Romney Marsh and Pevensey Levels. They built the remarkable gatehouse which dominates the place, like a miniature keep, capable of resisting the French raids which plagued the coastal areas of eastern Sussex.

Rufus, allegedly a homosexual and on bad terms with the clergy, was uninterested in church building but his younger brother, Henry I, founded the great Benedictine house of Reading in honour of the Virgin Mary and St John the Evangelist. The location of the monastery on the navigable Thames and at the division of the great western road along which flowed the traffic from London to Oxford, Worcester, Gloucester, Hereford, Bath and Bristol was likely to give the house significance. There seems little doubt that Henry I planned Reading as a mausoleum for his family. It was endowed with an important relic, the hand of St James. His body was brought from Normandy and laid to rest in the presence of Queen Adeliza and King Stephen. In 1156, Henry II's eldest son William was buried at Reading at the feet of his great-grandfather. The political interests of the Angevin monarchy, however, were now drawn across the Channel and Fontévrault became for a time the burial place of the dynasty.

Henry II promoted his royal reputation as a *fundator* of abbeys to absolve himself from guilt connected to the murder of Archbishop Thomas Becket. He had been condemned by the Pope to personal participation in a crusade but this was commuted to the foundation or refoundation of three religious houses (Hallam 1977, 113–32). Archaeology has demonstrated that Henry did not receive his absolution on the cheap. The Augustinian house at Waltham was rebuilt on an immense scale. Excavations revealed that the total length of the new church was 122m (400ft) and that it was in the form of a double cross, with two axial towers and two pairs of transepts connected by a nave 39.6m (130ft) long. The rebuilding of Amesbury nunnery is recorded on the Pipe Rolls as costing £881. Henry III and his queen both favoured the house and Eleanor of Provence was buried here on her death in 1291. The new Carthusian foundation at Witham was the least expensive of the three absolution churches. It cost £466 and recent excavations have shown that the buildings included a church laid out along the north side of a great cloister. Around this were the cells of the inmates (information: Ian Burrow).

Regard for the memory of his beloved mistress, Rosamund Clifford, motivated Henry II to favour the Benedictine nunnery at Godstow (Oxfordshire). 'For love of her', says Roger of Hovedon, 'the king conferred many benefits on the convent'. Money, timber, shingles and lathes were donated by the king. Bishop Grosseteste in the next century was shocked by the cult growing up around the burial place of Fair Rosamund and ordered that her remains be taken out of the church and buried in the churchyard. Little now remains of the site except a large walled enclosure in water meadows by the Thames, a two-storeyed late medieval building, some earthworks interpreted as fishponds and a few tiles picked out of the river.

John's reasons for founding a Cistercian monastery at Beaulieu (Hampshire) were twofold. He had quarrelled with the Cistercians and Hubert Walter induced him to found an abbey of their order in England by way of a penance. He was also planning to found a church where his body would ultimately find a resting place. This never happened because, as already described (p. 44), John was taken from Newark where he died to be buried in Worcester Cathedral. His great abbey, however, came to fruition. The church was one of the largest Cistercian buildings in England, 102.4m (336ft) in length and 56.6m (186ft) across the transepts. Beaulieu was munificently endowed with a collection of estates in west Oxfordshire and Gloucestershire. The grange at Great Coxwell acted as the estate centre and a great barn of the thirteenth century still survives, its roof-carpentry manifesting the skills of the Cistercians which are found in other houses of their order in the Low Countries (Horn and Born 1965).

Henry III's works at Westminster Abbey were on such a large scale that they will be separately described. His charitable works included gifts of building materials to many new houses of Franciscan and Dominican friars. He also made himself responsible for a *domus conversorum* in London – a home for converted Jews – and a hospital dedicated to St John at Oxford. Henry's brother, Richard of Cornwall, also founded an important monastery at Hailes (Gloucestershire) which was famous for possessing a relic of the Holy Blood (see p. 190).

Edward I began the construction of a great monastery at Vale Royal in Cheshire in 1277 in fulfilment of a vow made during a perilous sea crossing in the winter of 1263–4. His intention was that it should be more magnificent than his grandfather John's foundation at Beaulieu and larger than his uncle's church at Hailes. For the first few years the work was carried forward with great energy; then unfortunately war broke out in Wales and the money was diverted for the construction of castles and the payment of troops. Moreover, the king formally withdrew his support by stopping payments in 1290 – 'because the king has ceased to concern himself with the works of that church and henceforth will have nothing more to do with them' (Brown, Colvin, Taylor 1963, 252). The result was that the work proceeded very slowly and the church remained unfinished, its walls and vaults exposed to the wind and weather. In a great gale on 19 October 1360, the nave collapsed, its columns falling 'like trees uprooted in the wind'. The excavations of 1911–12 determined the plan of the nave and transepts. The 1958 excavations recovered the plan of the 1359 additions to the original structure, built with money supplied by the Black Prince. The east end was apparently in the form of a *chevet* consisting of seven radiating polygonal chapels and 6 three-sided interspaces, a total of 13 chapels (*Med. Arch.*, III, 1959, 302–3). The length of the church was at least 128m (420ft), or more than 3m (10ft) longer than Fountains Abbey.

Edward II's Dominican priory in his manor of King's Langley was sited next door to one of his favourite houses; it gained added importance in the king's eyes when the body of his murdered favourite Piers Gaveston was interred there in 1315. The surviving fragments of the conventual buildings are constructed of flint rubble with stone dressings and are in the grounds of a school (*V.C.H. Herts*, ii, 238–9). Edward III seems to have accepted responsibility for continuing the building of the church, whose overall length was greater than that of any English Dominican church with the exception of the London Blackfriars (Brown, Colvin,

Taylor 1963, 263). He also founded a house for Dominican nuns at Dartford (Kent), following a vow of Edward II.

Henry IV was exonerated by the Pope from responsibility for the 'martyrdom' of Archbishop Scrope by an undertaking to found three religious houses. It was left to his son, Henry V, to carry this out by establishing the three monasteries near his favourite manor house at Sheen (Surrey). The Charterhouse was sited in what is now the Old Deer Park at Richmond. Houses for the Celestines and Bridgettines, two strict orders, were to be built on the other side of the Thames in the royal manor of Isleworth. The courtyard at Syon House probably perpetuates the plan of the Bridgettines' cloister, and five bays of a fifteenth-century vaulted undercroft remain below the west range. The Carthusian house was on a great scale with a cloister quadrangle roughly 106m (350ft) square. Although some of the buildings lasted into George III's reign only the site and a fragment of window tracery seem to have survived to the present day. The Celestines' house never really got off the ground, because of hostility between England and France, and despite royal resources being expended on building, the monastery remained an expression of hope rather than actuality.

Westminster Abbey

Little is known of Edward the Confessor's abbey church of St Peter at Westminster, begun *c.*1045–50 and consecrated in 1065, except the plan of the eastern arm and the west end (Clapham 1934, 20). Excavations under the present church have uncovered the lower part of the north wall of the choir and part of the main apse. The choir consisted of two bays with solid side walls ending in a semicircular east end. The surviving remains of early monastic buildings indicate that the crossing and the transepts occupied the same position as those features in the later building. Further archaeological work in 1930 laid bare the western part of the south arcade of the nave and the south-west tower. The nave would seem to have consisted of six double bays with alternate cruciform and square piers. This building, despite its large size, doubtless seemed dark and crude to people in the thirteenth century aware of the exciting new developments in Gothic architecture taking place in England and northern France. The resources for the great undertaking to rebuild would need to be equally great but fortunately for the monks of Westminster the Crown was preparing to involve itself.

100 A badge of the royal crown; either a royal livery badge or a pilgrim badge from shrine of St Edward the Confessor, Westminster. (After Mitchiner.)

Henry III had strong personal reasons for wishing to rebuild Westminster Abbey. It afforded him an opportunity to give concrete expression to his devotion to St Edward (Fig. 100). Also, it provided him with the chance to fulfil his architectural ambitions. There seems no doubt that he was not only a religious *dévot* but a well-informed and artistically sensitive ruler. Up until now he had confined his building talents to castle towers and palace chapels. From 1245 he was able to lavish expenditure on rebuilding the coronation church of his ancestors and bringing it up to date to accommodate the fashionable cult of the Virgin. He also had in mind the concept of Westminster becoming the burial place of himself and his predecessors. Anjou had been lost by his father. Fontévrault, the mausoleum of the Angevin kings, was now in the heartland of the French. From 1246 it seems that Henry III had already decided that he wished to be buried at Westminster (*Cal. Charter R.* 1, 306) and this was affirmed in the will he made in 1253.

The money for rebuilding the abbey on a scale commensurate with Henry's ambitions flowed from many sources. The core was provided by the treasury which had orders to pay 3000 marks (i.e. £2000) a year to the keepers of the works. This sum was supplemented from time to time by money from the issues of the great seal, which produced between £300 and £400 a year, and contributions from the mints at London and Canterbury. The wardrobe also gave sums occasionally, and the sacrist was called on to hand over offerings from the altar of St Edward. The monks were even forced to contribute to their own building fund when the headship of their house fell vacant. Fines, debts and amercements made up the rest. Despite these measures, virtually the whole cost was borne by the king; the progress of the works was tied closely to the political history of his reign. When the king was in difficulty with the baronial opposition, resources dwindled and the works almost came to a standstill. The cost of this, Henry's greatest building enterprise, amounted to well over £40,000, a sum representing the best part of two years' income. Colvin reckoned in 1963 that the modern equivalent was not less than four million pounds (Brown, Colvin, Taylor 1963, 130–57), but Wilson computed a much larger sum in 1986, commenting that, if one allowed for the smallness of the thirteenth-century economy relative to ours, the figure would have to be reckoned in 'billions' (Wilson *et al.* 1986, 30).

The king entrusted the keepership of the works of the new abbey church (Fig. 101) to Edward of Westminster, one of his most experienced and responsible servants, who had worked for him in the palace. A special 'exchequer' was set up, complete with chequered cloth and tallies. It has even been suggested that some of the tallies have survived (Noppen 1949, 22–5). Of the keeper's records nothing remains earlier than 1264 except some 'particulars' of payments to workmen and a confused statement of receipts for 1249–53. The documentary situation improves after 1266 when the accounts were regularly enrolled on the Pipe Roll. The works at Westminster were under the control of a series of master masons. Master Henry may have been a Frenchman who

101 Westminster Abbey; portions built by Henry III, 1245–1272. (After Colvin.)

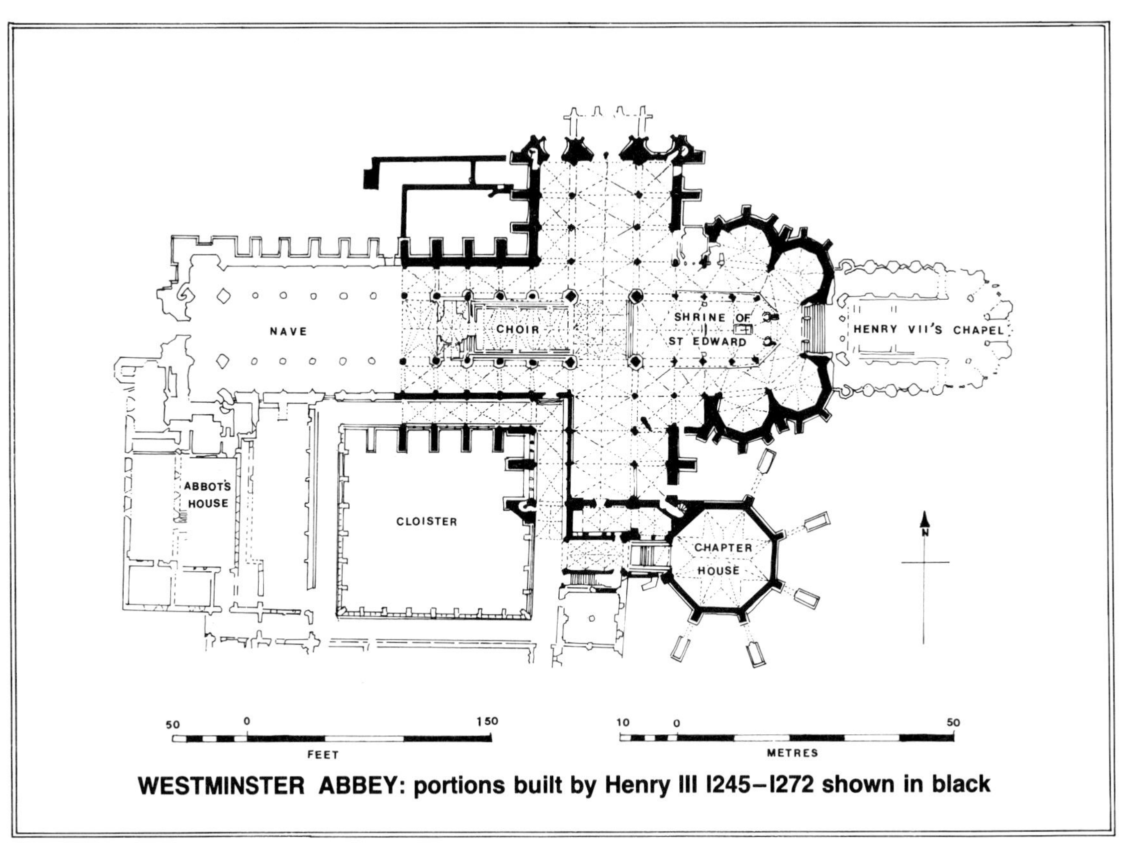

came from Rheims, or an Englishman who had worked at Rheims and who was therefore *au fait* with the new developments in French Gothic. He was succeeded by Master John of Gloucester who from 1255 had two other master masons working under him, Master William de Wauz and Master Richard of Eltham. In 1260 Master John died and his place was taken by Master Robert of Beverley. From a close study of the standing buildings it is possible to detect slight changes in the design of the fabric which can be related to the change-over of master masons.

The most remarkable feature of Westminster Abbey is the degree to which it reflects French influence (Webb 1956, 109–15). The plan of the church included an eastern chevet with radiating chapels, a return to the apse and ambulatory plan. This had almost ceased to be used in England since the early twelfth century but one example from the early thirteenth century, also a royal foundation, was the Cistercian abbey of Beaulieu (Hampshire) founded by King John. The plan of the new building at Westminster was constrained by two factors. First, the position of the dormitory on the east side of the cloister buildings fixed the placing of the south transept. The new Lady chapel begun in the 1220s was well to the east of the apse of the eleventh-century presbytery, suggesting that the scheme for rebuilding had been foreseen and perhaps begun some years before 1245. The setting out of the new structure was performed with extreme accuracy, which implies that the former building had been levelled, allowing the surveyors a free hand.

A second and even more obvious example of French influence at Westminster is the design of the north front (Lethaby 1906, 123–4). This has been completely encased in modern restoration several time since its construction, but the main lines are known from Lethaby's patient reconstruction from drawings and from the accounts of different architects who have worked on it (Wilson 1986, 44–5). The north transept front was developed as a state entrance for the king (Perkins 1952, 22–3). It was near the palace and would save the long walk to the west entrance with the subsequent difficulty of access through the nave, which remained under construction for another 300 years (Rackham 1909, 35–81). The west front of Amiens cathedral provided the prototype for the design. We find there three similar steeply gabled porches standing out flush with the lower parts of the dividing buttresses. Above the lateral porches at Amiens the west windows of the aisles are deeply set in recesses, a curious feature which is also seen at Westminster. In both buildings an external wall arcade of coupled lights runs right across the front below the rose window.

The proportions of the building at Westminster are also attributable to French Gothic. Its great height in proportion to its breadth strikes the visitor immediately. Most of the greater English churches were planned on a ratio of 1 : 2 which resulted in comparatively low vaults. The great Gothic cathedrals of France with double aisles were based on a ratio of 1 : 3. Westminster was an attempt to achieve the soaring grandeur of a French church on an English plan. While the height from ground level to the keystone of the vault is 31.4m (103ft), 11.3m (37ft) less than Amiens and 16.4m (54ft) less than Beauvais, the effect of extreme verticality is comparable. The stability of such a tall structure is assured by highly developed flying buttresses. These are particularly impressive on the south side where they have to pass across the cloister, and the distance from the outside face of the buttress in the cloister-green to the plane of the clerestory is, measured horizontally, 15.2m (50ft). Each buttress has three fliers over the cloister and two fliers above each aisle making a total of five in all to each 'archiboutant'.

The main building materials used in the construction of the abbey were stone, timber and lead. Kentish ragstone was brought in for the foundations and the rough walling. It came by water from quarries near Maidstone. Freestone for mouldings and carvings was brought by land from Reigate and Chaldon (Surrey), and many shiploads came across the Channel from the quarries at Caen. What most strikes one about the interior is the profuse use of gleaming blue-brown marble from the Purbeck quarries at Corfe (Dorset). The cost of freight varied from £4 to £5 according to the size of the vessel. Caen stone cost from £5 to £12 a shipload. Structural timber for the roof was carried to Westminster from royal woods in Essex and the Weald in Kent. Other recorded supplies came from Roger de Mortimer's park at Stratfield (Berkshire), and from the woods of the

Crevecoeur family at Bockingfold (Kent); Roger of Leybourne made a present of 40 oaks from woods near Maidstone in 1266. Lead for the roof came from Derbyshire by way of Leicester and Northampton. Much was bought at the summer fair of Boston whence it was carried by water to Westminster.

There was considerable specialization of function within the workforce employed on building Westminster Abbey (Colvin 1971, 249). Seven principal types of workmen were taken on. These were masons, carpenters, marblers, polishers, smiths, plumbers and glaziers. From the accounts it is possible to enumerate the total work force. From 28 April to 6 December 1253, for instance,

> *For wages of 39 white cutters [freestone masons] 14 marblers, 20 layers, 32 carpenters, together with John of St Albans, 3 painters, 13 polishers, 19 smiths, 14 glaziers and 4 plumbers, £14 12s. For the wages of 150 labourers with Keepers, clerks and the charges of two carts daily £6 16s.*

By far the greatest number were 'white-stone' cutters followed by marblers and layers. The total labour force averaged 300, exceeding 400 only for a few weeks in June and July. As the winter approached workers were laid off and reduced to 100. The number fluctuated both according to the seasons and also as a result of financial crises which caused stoppages from time to time. The only men being paid a regular stipend were the masters of the works such as Master Henry and Master John of Gloucester. They were paid double when they went travelling in search of materials and labour. The rest were paid by the week or for specific tasks which they undertook at fixed rates. An example of this can be taken from the 1253 accounts. Here Master Aubrey, who was the sub-contractor of some consequence, was paid in the second week after Easter

> *for the arrears owed for tracery and . . . 66s., for 53 feet of parpent [stone occupying the full thickness of a wall, with two worked faces] stone at 4d. a foot, 59 feet of voussoirs with fillets at 3½d, a foot., 221½ft. at 3d. a foot, 50 assizes [shaped stones possibly forming a segment of a column] at 5d. each, 42 jambs, 22 feet of mullions, 243 feet of cerches [stones cut to form a segment of a circle] 9 feet of bosseus [a rounded moulding], and seven steps cut by task, £7 13s 1d.* (Colvin 1971, 251.)

One problem the masters in charge of the works had to contend with was absenteeism. Among the workers whose names indicate that they came from France several appear to have gone away. Matthew and Henry de Rems undoubtedly came from Rheims, Richard Norman and Richard of Caen were of Norman origin. None of them was reckoned to be a master. They were bracketed together as masons who had failed, for whatever reason, to complete their tasks.

Another obstacle was the extraordinary number of saints' festivals or holidays which interrupted the normal six-day working week. A compromise solution was worked out by which alternate holidays were provided with pay 'the king always has one feast day, beginning with the first (in the month) and the workmen the other' (Colvin 1971, 10).

The evolution of the abbey can be inferred from the documents which have survived and, more importantly, from a study of the structures themselves. Here the records of G. C. Scott and W. R. Lethaby are of surpassing value. Both architects knew the abbey intimately. Lethaby reckoned that he had made a thousand visits. It seems that the transepts, the crossing and the whole of the eastern arm, with the Chapter House and its vestibule were built in one sustained effort in the years 1246–59. It is commonplace in medieval church construction for the eastern end to be built before the rest and it is likely that the ambulatory and its radiating chapels were completed before the transepts. The lower part of the north transept was built later than the corresponding portion of its fellow in the south. The windows of the south transept are later than those of the north, and the bosses with naturalistic sculpture in the high vault confirm this later date.

Once again the characteristics of the bay design reflect French inspiration. The design of the interior elevation of the eastern end of the church consists of a tall acutely-pointed arcade, a tribune or triforium with its own external windows, a clerestory and a vault. In the choir the vaulting is quadripartite and has a longitudinal ridge rib and also wall ribs. Lethaby pointed out that the Westminster vaults resembled those of France in their height, but the filling 'instead of being, as in French work shaped so that as they rise they work out parallel to the ridge, are set across the web of the vault' (Lethaby 1906, 128–9). The springing of the vault is in large blocks of carefully wrought stone, on a system known as *tas de charge*. This, says Webb, is a constructional trait which is extremely French (Webb 1956, 109–15).

Very French too, is the design of the windows; both in the aisles and the clerestory they consist of two-foiled lights of lancet proportions surmounted by a circular foiled figure. The stonework is what is known as bar tracery and is made by filling the head with a skeleton construction of arches or curved members, parts of arches or parts of circles. The design is very close to that of Rheims which figures in Villard d'Honnecourt's notebooks (Hahnloser 1972, 60–1).

Another constructional feature which links Westminster with French churches is the use of wooden and iron ties (Wilcox 1981, 104). Across the springings of the arches and across the aisles of the eastern end and the three northern bays of the apse and connecting them are wooden ties. Throughout the rest of the work iron ties occupy similar positions. As the building progressed, more efficient methods were used to attach these. To begin with they pass through the caps of the piers. Later it was found to be better to insert only hooks, to which the bars of iron, which curve up in the middle, were attached afterwards. As Lethaby says 'the whole construction is laced up with iron ties to an extent which is without parallel' (Lethaby 1906, 139). The value roll of 1253 mentions a large quantity of iron 'For 59 hundred weight of tough Gloucester iron with iron parts and other ironwork £20' (Colvin 1971, 237). Wilson has recently suggested that many of the iron ties may be replacements from the time of Wren's surveyorship of the fabric (Wilson 1986, 63).

The interior of Westminster Abbey is remarkable for the complexity and elaboration of its decorative treatment. This must be connected with Henry's consciousness that Westminster was a coronation church as well as destined to become a royal mausoleum (Tudor Craig *et al.* 1986, 106). The main arches of the arcade are elaborately moulded, a typically English characteristic of the thirteenth century, and the spandrels are covered with diaper, small in pattern towards the east end but on a rather larger scale as one moves west. It was covered in red and gold paint in the thirteenth century (Wilson 1986, 67). In addition the spandrels of the transepts are enriched with sculptured angels. The arches of the tribune storey have two sub-arches and traceried heads and are built double with two complete planes of arches. These carry the very thick wall of the clerestory level.

One decorative theme which recurs again and again throughout the part of the abbey built by Henry III is a pattern based on the rose. One of the spandrels of the eastern wall arcade is carved with a trellis of roses. The eastern jambs of the door from the church to the cloister are studded with roses. The ground arches of the end wall of the south transept have the same feature. Roses are carved on the centre of some portions of the square diaper on the walls. Some of the ambulatory vault bosses are carved in the form of roses. There is also the design of the great circular rose windows at the north and south ends of the transepts. The north rose at Rouen dating from *c.*1280 is very similar to the Westminster rose window, the open spandrels, number of rays and foiling being features shared. There is a four-piece tile design in the Westminster chapter house floor representing a rose window. *Rosa alba* became an English garden favourite in the Middle Ages (McLean 1981, 165–6). It was incorporated into the great seal of state by Edward I in honour of his mother, Eleanor of Provence, whose emblem it was. The red *rosa gallica* was adopted by Edward's brother, Edmund, the first Earl of Lancaster, in honour of his second wife, Blanche, who also used it as a badge. The rose, therefore, not surprisingly appears scores of times as a decoration painted on the mouldings of Edmund's tomb. One of the little shields on the south side hangs on an exquisitely carved rose tree. Henry III used the rose in other buildings. In 1240 he ordered 'the Chamber of our Queen' at the Tower to be whitened 'and newly painted with roses'. The flower had a resurgence of heraldic interest in the war-torn fifteenth century.

The most splendid piece of decoration in the abbey is the presbytery pavement. As Perkins describes it,

> *in front, spread out like a great sea, lay the glorious pavement of Abbot Richard de Ware; like the forest of pillars which shoot upwards all round, its wealth of marble, bronze and mosaic was richly polished. Before its original lustre had been dulled with ill usage it is said to have reflected surrounding objects with an almost mirror like effect.* (Perkins 1938, 11.)

Abbot Ware, who was elected in 1258, went to Rome to get his election confirmed by the Pope. Despite being short of funds he brought back materials and workmen for the construction of two mosaic stone pavements (Scott 1863, 97–103; Lethaby 1906, 309–28; Lethaby 1925, 217–33; Perkins 1938, 24; Crowther 1987, 50–5).

Strictly speaking the Westminster pavement is not mosaic but *opus sectile*, a term which denotes 'cut work'; this technique involves each stone being cut to the size and shape dictated by the pattern, similar to the pieces in a jigsaw puzzle. The most common shapes found are triangles, squares, rectangles and lozenges shaped like diamonds or curved like petals. The workmen involved, the so-called *marmorani* or the Cosmati school, included two who left their names embedded in their work: Odericus was the artist of the presbytery pavement and Petrus Civis Romanus of the pavement around St Edward's shrine (Fig. 102).

The materials these Italian craftsmen used have recently been examined, with exciting results (Foster 1990, 1–8; Foster 1991). The Cosmati favoured three stones: purple porphyry, green porphyry and *giallo antico* or 'antique yellow'. Purple porphyry with its characteristically speckled appearance was highly prized and extremely rare; it came from

102 *The shrine of St Edward the Confessor in Westminster Abbey. It consists of a rectangular structure with trefoil-headed recesses on each side for insertion of diseased limbs by pilgrims. The whole of the panelling, shafts, reredos and cornice was formerly enriched with marble and glass mosaics, now lost, gradually picked out by generations of visitors. The shrine was finished in 1268 by Peter, a Roman of the Cosmati family. See also Figs 19–20.* (Photograph: RCHM England.)

only one source – mines in the mountains of the eastern desert of Egypt which had closed down in the fifth century BC. Medieval craftsmen had to acquire it second-hand from the ruins of classical buildings. The same was largely true of the green porphyry mined in Classical times from the Spartan quarries of Greece and known as *serpentino*. The smooth-textured limestone known as *giallo antico* provided a suitable contrast. There is a spectacular central roundel of onyx, a semi-precious chalcedony with bands of variegated colour, also small quantities of alabaster from Staffordshire. The presence of opaque red, blue, turquoise and white glass in the pavement encouraged analysis which led to the conclusion that the material had probably been made in western Europe, perhaps at Venice or Corinth, where traditional Islamic manufacturing techniques had been imported. The long and elaborate brass inscription in the pavement, transcribed in the fifteenth century by John Flete, a Westminster monk, and now reduced to a mere eleven letters, was shown on analysis to have been made of Continental latten. This was the same material as a series of steelyard weights, manufactured centrally under the authority of Richard, Earl of Cornwall on behalf of his brother, King Henry III (Fig. 103). The letters and the weights were thought to have emanated from the same royal workshop (Foster 1990, 7). The least satisfactory element in the pavement is the use of Purbeck marble in place of the harder and more desirable white Italian cippolino marble, and alabaster. Aesthetically, Purbeck's dark tone tends to play down rather than to heighten the colours of the designs; it is also notoriously susceptible to damp, suffering from surface decay which loosens the *opus sectile* patterns in a potentially disastrous way. Moreover, since part of the inscription has the letters inlaid in beeswax, instability seems to be built into the pavement.

The presbytery pavement is thought to be the largest area of mosaic of these craftsmen north of the Alps. Its iconography is complex and obscure but recent speculations have revived interest in its meaning (Foster 1991, 80–167). The design consists of two squares, a larger enclosing a smaller, and together they form a wide border. Within the smaller square is another lozenge-shaped square which encloses a central globe filled with a modern slab of pink marble 76cm (2ft 6in) in diameter. Two other bands diverge towards the cardinal points and become the extreme borders of four smaller circles. There are three inscriptions of brass letters let into the borders of Purbeck marble, but owing to the fact that this material is badly worn and the beeswax has disintegrated they have nearly disappeared. Enough, however, survives to be certain that the whole design is a kind of map of the universe. The inscription round the innermost circle declares that it is a microcosm of the macrocosm. From this emanate four lesser spheres and again four greater spheres beyond. Around the five circles is an inscription which calculates the appointed duration of the world. A hedge lasts three years, a dog lives nine years, a horse lasts 27 and so on, always trebling the last figure, through man, stag, raven, whale, till 19,683 years is reached

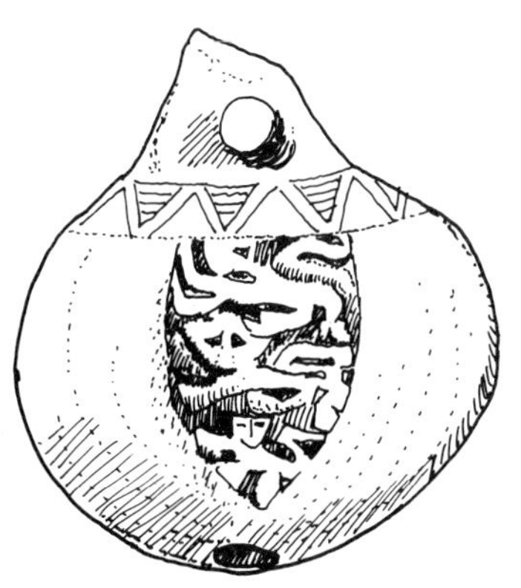
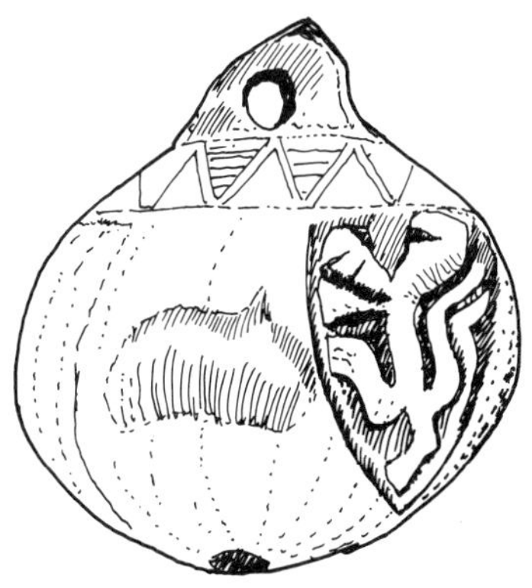
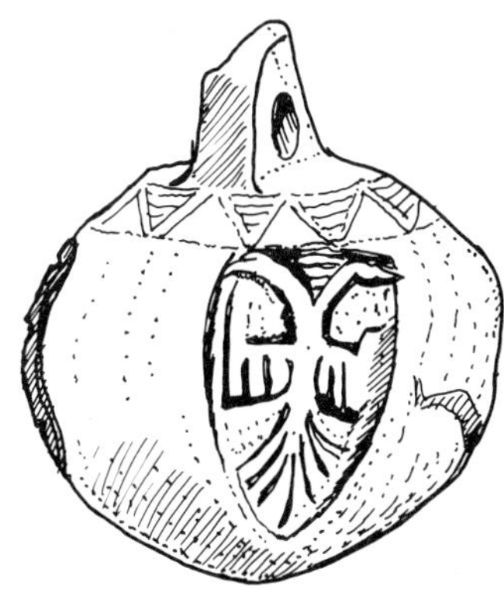

103 Steelyard weight, manufactured under the authority of Richard, Earl of Cornwall. From Drayton (Oxfordshire). (Ashmolean Museum.)

for the end of the world (Foster 1991, 80–110).

It is all very well to explain the iconography of the pavement, but its function still remains elusive. Pamela Tudor Craig, considers that 'its pattern of circles and squares can be read at the simplest level as a map for the liturgical rite of the sacral dimension of the coronation' (Crowther 1987, 54). She plausibly suggests that upon its central circle it was intended that each future king should receive the innermost sacrament of his crowning. Here the rite of anointing, in which both the king and the queen were bared to the waist, was witnessed by clergy alone. This part of the ceremony, performed almost secretly in the intimate heart of the building, was in contrast to the public throne set on a platform high under the crossing where the king received the recognition and homage of his people (Tudor Craig 1986, 98).

One other decorative scheme which has attracted attention from successive students of the abbey is the series of heraldic shields which enrich the spandrels between the arcading on the walls of the nave aisles (Williamson 1929–30, 46–53; Tudor Craig 1957, 104–5). These are cut in stone and stand out in high relief from the surface of the wall. They were suspended by straps hanging from two heads which served as supporters. The idea of this scheme may well have been initiated by the king himself, who paid a visit to France in 1254 and was entertained by Louis IX in a great hall which was decorated in this way: 'The French King dined with the English King and a number of his company . . . in the Palace of the Old Temple . . . this banquet was given in the Great Hall of the Temple in which were hung up according to continental custom, as many bucklers as the wall could hold.' At Westminster the shields of the Holy Roman Empire and St Edward the Confessor are followed by those of the kings of England and France, Provence and Scotland. Farther west were shields bearing the arms of the great English barons: Clare, Bigod, Montfort, Warenne, Bohun and Aumale on the north, and de Quency, de Lascy, Richard Earl of Cornwall and another unidentified one on the south side. It is not very likely that these shields were intended to commemorate benefactors who had contributed towards the cost of the building. It is more likely that the royal arms thus represented were the houses connected by marriage to the royal family of England. The others were simply those of the great barons of the realm. The fact that de Montfort's arms are represented suggests that the building had advanced as far as the third bay on the north by 1264, since it is not likely that the arms of Simon de Montfort (the king's brother-in-law) would have been set up at royal expense after his rebellion and death at Evesham in 1264–5.

The Chapter House

The Chapter House and its crypt must have been started concurrently with the church. Matthew Paris refers to it as 'the incomparable chapter house which the king had built'. References in the fabric account for 1253 show £20 being spent towards the task work of the entrance to the Chapter House and 'for 340 ells of canvas for the windows of the chapter house £4 6s 4½d'; they indicate that the work is almost finished (Colvin 1971, 215, 236).

The structure had a chequered career. Though primarily intended for daily meetings by the abbot and the monks it was often used by other bodies, and in the later Middle Ages was one of the meeting places of the knights and burgesses summoned to attend the king in Parliament. When the Commons were housed in St Stephens chapel from the reign of Edward III onwards the Chapter House was used, or abused, as a repository for the records of the Exchequer and other courts. The vaulted crypt underneath in the meantime was used in Edward I's reign as a treasury for the wardrobe.

Scott found it in an appalling condition (Scott 1863, 39–43). His illustrations show the tiled pavement buried under a secondary floor, the wall arcades and entrance underneath hidden beneath shelving, galleries and staircases. The vaulting had been taken down in 1740 but the central pillar of Purbeck marble still remained. Finally, the windows had been walled up with a considerable part of their slender Gothic tracery embedded. Scott studied the remains intensively and made interesting discoveries. He found, for instance, that the window over the doorway was blocked with stone, and these ashlar blocks to his surprise consisted 'entirely of the lengths of the moulded ribs of the lost vaulting, carefully packed like wine bottles in a bin, with their moulded sides inwards'. He also found a recess: 'my curiosity being excited I let down into it by a string a small bull's-eye lantern,

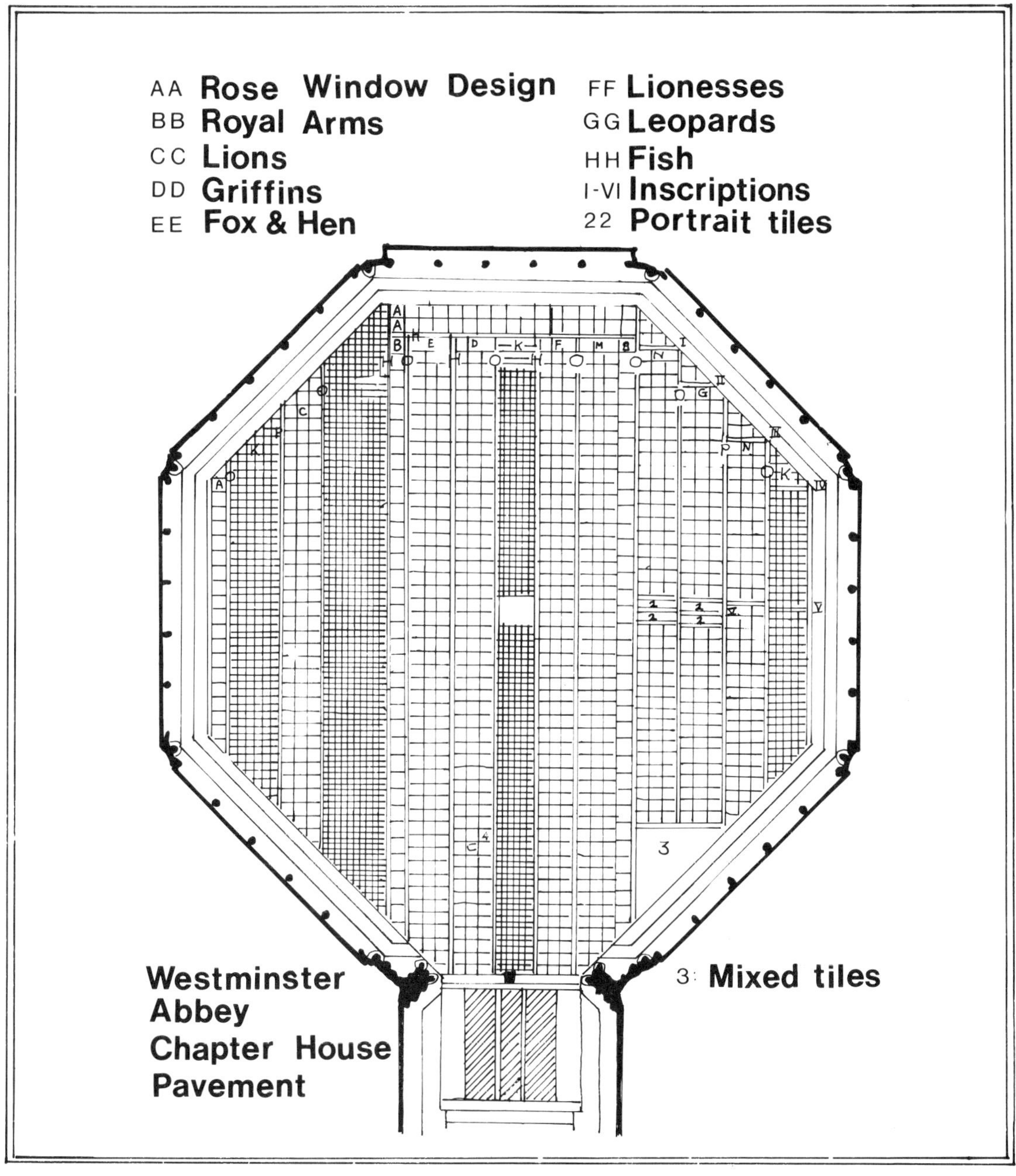

104 Westminster Abbey – the Chapter House pavement. (After Clayton.)

when to my extreme delight, I saw that the mysterious object was the head of a beautiful full-sized statue in a niche'. This proved to be a Virgin, part of an Annunciation scene which was one of the finest pieces on display in the 'Age of Chivalry' exhibition of 1988. To locate the details of the doorway, he

> *had to creep on a mass of parchments and dust ten feet deep, and, after taking out the boarding of the back of the cases, to examine and draw, by the help of the little bull's eye lantern . . . a most laborious operation, and giving one more the look of a master chimney sweeper than an architect.*

The Chapter House was of octagonal form, 17m (56ft) in diameter and in its original state used a daring mode of construction. The vault was supported by a slender central column of Purbeck marble. It was strengthened by iron ties, the hooks for which remain. Apart from this, the walls were largely traceried windows with slight buttresses between. After about a hundred years it was necessary to strengthen the vault supports and four flying buttresses were built. When Scott restored the Chapter House he did not put back the iron tie bars, but in the roof above the vault his engineer added an iron framework from which the vault hangs.

The tiled floor is the most splendid to survive in England from the Middle Ages (Fig. 104) (Clayton 1912, 36–75). It was discovered and published in 1842: 'on the removal of the boarded floor the pavement was found to be in a very perfect state, few tiles being broken, and the colours in many parts as brilliant as when first laid down' (Cottingham in vol. XXLX of *Archaeologia*, 1842). Each tile is an accomplished picture or design made by printing the pattern on to the darker clay and then inlaying lighter material; the tile is then glazed. This has the effect that even when the glaze has worn off the picture on the tile tends to wear through rather than wear away. The layout is simple while the pattern on the individual tiles is elaborate. The entire floor is covered with parallel strips of tiles with different patterns 'as though the building had been spread with rolls of carpet, east to west forming, as it were, a foot mat under the eastern side, but two narrow bands of the royal arms run right across the building' (Rigold 1976, 29). The shields bearing the arms of King Henry III show the leopards of England with wyverns and centaurs in the spandrels (see Fig. 12). They are among the earliest surviving representations of the royal arms of England. Towards the north is a design of a rose window; like many of the tiles in the Chapter House the complete pattern is made by combining four tiles. Further figured tiles show a seated king playing with a small dog; a queen with a falcon on her wrist, and a bishop or mitred abbot (Fig. 105). These may be complimentary references to the abbey's patrons. Also, there is a musician playing a harp with a plectrum and another playing a rebeck or primitive fiddle. There are three lively figures from the hunt – a horseman, an archer and a stag pursued by a dog (Fig. 106). Bands of tiles have a fish, which is taken to be a salmon although it looks more like a pike. This is a reference to the tithe of fish which the abbey claimed from the Thames fishermen, said to have been granted when St Peter arrived in person to consecrate the church. There is also a tile showing St Edward the Confessor and the pilgrim. In the south-eastern part of the pavement is a damaged inscription in separate lines of Lombardic letters. The whole can be translated, 'As the Rose is the flower of flowers, so this house is the house of houses, which King Henry, a lover of the Holy Trinity, dedicated to Christ, who loved . . .'

The abbey's reconstructed nave remained incomplete for a hundred years. No late medieval king dipped his hand in his pocket so generously as Henry III. Only £6056 was donated by royalty of a total of £21,000 spent before 1534. This included £1685 by Richard II, £3861 by Henry V and £519 from Edward IV and his family. The monks themselves had to bridge the gap (Wilson 1986, 31).

Henry VII's chapel

The last major royal structural addition to the abbey was the replacement of the thirteenth-century lady chapel by Henry VII's chapel. However, if Henry Tudor's plans had been fulfilled the chapel would not have been called after him at all but after his revered predecessor, the Lancastrian king, Henry VI. Henry VII had won the crown at Bosworth Field and strengthened his claim both in Parliament and through his marriage with the house of York. Personal piety and political necessity required that the king's uncle Henry VI be given posthumous honours. To begin with it was intended that both Henries would lie in a new chapel to the east of the Yorkist St George's chapel, Windsor. A number of witnesses, however, asserted that Henry VI had willed that his

105 The so-called portrait tiles in the Chapter House, Westminster Abbey: (left) *the king, crowned, full face, wears a beard and has a dog beside him;* (centre) *the queen, seated on a settle with a low back;* (right) *King Edward the Confessor and the pilgrim.* (After Clayton.)

body be buried in Westminster. The chapel was begun after the thirteenth-century chapel had been removed, and the foundation stone was laid on 24 January 1503; the canonization process was started *in tandem*. In the event this ultimately failed, 'the scandal being that Henry VII found it cost too much', but the building of the chapel made good progress and by the time of the king's death was almost complete.

Despite the fact that it is the most recent part of the abbey it is also the most inadequately documented major building in the history of the king's works. We do not even know for sure who designed it. In the king's will drawn up in 1509 there is mention of 'a plot made for the same chapel and signed with our hands'. This has disappeared. So have 70 sketches of segments of vaulting and other architectural details recognized by nineteenth-century antiquaries as contemporary with the building. It is likely, however, that Robert Vertue, Robert Janyns and John Lebons were associated with the design. Colvin considers Robert Vertue, who had been a junior mason at Westminster Abbey in May 1475 and who, with his brother William designed Bath Abbey, as the most likely. Wilson however picks Janyns as the strongest candidate, citing the closest parallel, Henry VII's tower at Windsor and pointing out that the main interior elevations are closely modelled on St George's chapel, begun by Janyns' father Henry and continued by the son between *c*.1495 and 1506.

The labourers took down the thirteenth-century lady chapel in 1502–3 and the adjoining chapel of St Erasmus built by Queen Elizabeth Woodville. Thereafter it is difficult

106 Thirteenth-century tiles from the Chapter House, Westminster Abbey showing hunting scenes. (After Clayton.)

to trace the progress of the works. Since the building accounts have so completely vanished we have to rely on various observers' opinions about the origin of the materials. John Stowe reckoned that the chapel was built of stone from Huddlestone in Yorkshire, from the same source as the stone used for King's College chapel, Cambridge. Wren, responsible for the fabric at the end of the seventeenth century, refers to the use of 'tender Caen Stone' from Normandy. The report to the parliamentary commission for the repair of the structure in the early nineteenth century refers to Kentish ragstone in the foundations, Kentish stone from Maidstone in the plinth, Huddlestone stone in the corbels and springing pieces to the flying buttresses, Caen stone in the superstructure and Reigate stone from Surrey in the screens to the north-east and south-east chapels. Judging from Cottingham's illustrations and descriptions the exterior was in shocking disrepair at the time. The windows were in decay and were propped up with timbers; the flying buttresses and octagonal turrets were in a shapeless and dangerous state of ruin. Various stones at roof level with dates from the eighteenth to the twentieth centuries are visible today, recalling the fact that the building has been completely refaced over that period, much Bath stone being used; but at least one flying buttress still has quantities of Caen stone in its flier. The result of this recasting is that the building has lost much of its subtle external detail. It has become simplified, rather as if a model of it had been magnified; it is now, in Lethaby's apt words, 'only a full-sized copy of itself'.

The design consists of a nave and chancel with side aisles. The nave is 16.8m (55ft 4in) long and 10.5m (34ft 6in) wide and 18.3m (60ft) high. It occupies four arches on each side which, previous to the putting up of the stalls, communicated to the side aisles. The five sides of the chancel form entrances into five small side chapels, each of which had an altar with niches and statues. The vault is a 'tour de force'; it appears to be a fan vault of extraordinary richness but is in fact a groined vault which depends on a series of great transverse arches. This is very apparent when one walks along boards between the roof and the top of the vault. Below are seen the solid bands of masonry arches, and curving down in a series of dished cones are the superbly masoned fan vaults, each with a great pendant hanging below them. The shell of the vault is of masonry only 89mm (3½in) thick. The weight of this roof is counterpointed by stout buttress fliers, which in turn are weighted down by pinnacled buttress piers, designed as a series of octagonal turrets rising from the ground and finished as ogee cupolas encrusted with crockets.

Perhaps the most memorable characteristic of the chapel is the richness of its decoration. This appears to have been as a direct result of the king's wishes:

> *the windowes of our said chapell be glased with stores [stories] ymagies, armes, bagies [badges] and cognoisaunts, as is by us redily divised and in picture deliv'ed to the Priour of Sainct Bartilmews besid Smythfeld, maister of the works of our said chapell; and that the walles, doores, windows, archies and vaults and ymagies of the same our chapell; within and w'out be painted, garnished and adorned with our armes, bagies, cognoisaunts and other convenient paiteng, in as goodly and riche maner as suche a work requireth, and as to a kings werk app'teigneth.*

The insistence on peppering the whole work with the royal heraldry reveals, presumably, one of the principal motives behind the work, that of dynastic aggrandizement. The exterior of the chapel is encrusted with badges, mainly the portcullis and the rose. The portcullis, frequently crowned, commemorated Henry's descent from his mother's family, the Beauforts. Because his title was strengthened thereby he added the motto 'Altera Securitas'. His other cognizance, the white and red rose, was a reference to the union of the two houses of Lancaster and York by his marriage with Elizabeth of York. The use of the fleur-de-lis recalled his descent from a daughter of the king of France. Scrambling down the edges of the flying buttresses are lions, dragons and greyhounds; all are heraldic fauna connected with the Tudor dynasty. The dragon was the ensign of Cadwallader, last King of the Britons, from whom Henry VII was said to derive his pedigree. A red dragon painted on white and green silk was his standard; the one used at Bosworth was offered up among the other trophies of victory at St Pauls. The greyhound was the left-hand supporter of the king which he bore in right of his wife, Queen Elizabeth of York, who was descended from the Nevilles. Finally, inside, over the baldachino of Torrigiano's altarpiece (unfortunately destroyed in 1643) angels acted as supporters for the royal arms.

This tedious insistence on the multiplication of royal badges, to the exclusion of all others, contrasts with Henry III's practice 250 years earlier. Here the royal arms were sparingly used to decorate the king's work in the abbey, and only in conjunction with the coats of arms of other royal and baronial families. In Henry VII's chapel it is as if Tudor absolutism allied to their basic insecurity has driven out all other ideas of decoration. It is echoed by similar work at King's College chapel, Cambridge.

Turning to the sculpture in the interior, there is another dimension of the same theme on a band all round the chapel. Below the cells of the clerestory windows and in other vacant spaces stood serried rows of apostles, saints and prophets – paralleled in the king's will where he declared his trust in the 'singular mediacions and praiers of all the hoie companie of heven; that is to saye, Aungels, patriarches, prophets, Apostels, Evangelists, martirs, confessours and virgyns'. It is as if the big battalions 'covering the whole gamut of later medieval religious hierarchy' (Stone's phrase) are being paraded in support of the Tudor dynasty. An additional indicator is the presence of one or two obscure Breton saints to whose intercession Henry had appealed during the years of exile before Bosworth.

St Stephen's chapel, Westminster

One of the most noteworthy losses in the history of English architecture was the destruction by fire in 1834 of St Stephen's chapel in the Palace of Westminster. Fortunately, however, it had become the object of antiquarian research in the eighteenth century, albeit of a primitive and ill-informed kind. By piecing together the descriptions made by such observers as Carter, Smith and Mackenzie, by removing the thick layers of conjecture and the webs of distorting theory, it is possible to recover a good deal of the original appearance of the building (Topham 1795; Smith 1807; Mackenzie 1844; Hastings 1955). Detailed building accounts of certain phases of the construction and decoration have fortunately survived (Brayley and Britton 1836).

St Stephen's chapel had a very chequered career before its destruction. It was built by the three Edwards to emulate and to out-do the private chapel of the French king the Sainte Chapelle in Paris. In its time it was the very latest in Gothic magnificence; the court School of Masons tried out here the most advanced techniques of structure and decoration, and architectural historians have seen in it the genesis of the Perpendicular style in England (Hastings 1955).

At the Reformation the chapel was relegated to the use of the House of Commons (Butt 1989, xxiii). The historic seating arrangements of the House of Commons derive from the medieval layout of the chapel. The lobby comprised the first two bays of the chapel. The Speaker's chair was in front of the altar stone; members still bow to the Speaker's chair. The members occupied the existing stalls of the canons which had been increased and lengthened towards the east end. They face one another as the canons used to do. The medieval work was almost completely hidden under wainscoting and ceilings but when the house was enlarged to provide space for the hundred additional Irish members at the end of the eighteenth century a number of discoveries were made.

The general external appearance of the chapel was recorded in a series of drawings and engravings by A. van den Wyngaerde, a little known artist of *c.*1600 and Wenceslaus Hollar. J. Carter (1748–1817) made an elaborate set of drawings of the chapel for the Society of Antiquaries in about 1791 (Topham 1795–1811). At the time of making these drawings, much of the structure of the chapel was still 'perfect or traceable'. Englefield (President of the Society of Antiquaries) stated that Carter was 'under extreme difficulty of access to the lower parts of the chapel which he could only draw by lanthorn light and nearly lying under the benches'. Carter was a fervent defender of ancient buildings and carried on a vitriolic campaign against the architect Wyatt, preventing his election to the Society of Antiquaries. Unfortunately, he could not resist attempting to reconstruct the broken parts of the building according to his own fancies 'to add honour to our antiquitia while others (such as Wyatt) are so ardent in their zeal to violate and destroy them'. Wyatt, in turn, excluded Carter from examining the medieval remains uncovered in the course of the so-called 'alterations'. Fortunately J. T. Smith was able to record them (Smith 1807). He also had his problems since he was not allowed to hold up the process of destruction. He went there as soon as it was light, worked on until 9 o'clock,

> *and the workmen very often followed him so close in their operations, so as to remove in the course of the same day on which he had made his drawings the painting which he had been employed in copying that very morning.*

He drew 200 topographical subjects of which, he remarked, 122 are no longer existing as they have been 'either pulled down, totally defaced or the stones entirely destroyed'.

Both Carter and Smith were voluntary recorders. The Commissioners of Works employed F. Mackenzie to carry out an official survey after the conflagration. The result was a series of magnificent architectural drawings (*The Architectural Antiquities of the Collegiate Chapel of St Stephen*, London, 1844) which were unfortunately marred by a considerable injection of fantasy. He had the work of his predecessors, as well as the smoking burned-out remains of the building, to go on, but it is difficult to be sure where his actual observation ends and guess-work begins. The result has been called 'an unsubstantial vision'!

A much firmer but less visual approach was made by E. W. Brayley and J. Britton in *The History of the Ancient Palace and Late Houses of Parliament at Westminster* (London, 1836) where they transcribed the building accounts and put them in chronological order.

Edward I's decision to rebuild St Stephen's chapel was part of his general refurbishing of the Palace of Westminster in anticipation of his remarriage after the death of Queen Eleanor of Castile. The parallels of this work with the 50-year-old Sainte Chapelle in the principal royal palace of France are striking (Dillange 1985). Their position, dimensions and extremely rich decoration are alike; moreover, both buildings are divided into an upper and lower chapel. At Westminster the lower is called St Mary-in-the-Vaults (Fig. 107). The upper is raised on this vaulted undercroft and is reserved for the use of the 'seigneur' while the lower was for the dependants. The Sainte Chapelle was designed so that the household in the lower chapel could hear Mass celebrated in the upper chapel. The cloister at St Stephen's was also of two storeys – an idea paralleled by the double cloister at St Pauls seen in Hollar's engraving – and both were designed by William de Ramsay.

The external appearance of St Stephen's was that of a tall, very high, narrow building, constructed at right angles to the great hall and to the river Thames. At the four corners there were battlemented octagonal stair turrets. There were pinnacled buttresses standing away from the walls and rising above the line of the parapet. It was of five bays and the upper chapel was lit with two ranges of four-light windows. The exterior was remarkable for a tracery grid which conceals the structural realities. There was no horizontal element marking the internal floor level and the mullions of the space which took the place of the triforium were continued across the deeply recessed windows of the lower chapel. There was a massive three-storeyed cornice behind which springs the clerestory. Mackenzie, imaginative though he is, convincingly argues the case for the existence of the clerestory, which was removed together with the timber vault by Wren in 1692.

The interior of the chapel was similarly remarkable for its innovations. The design was by Michael of Canterbury whose only previous royal commission was the Eleanor Cross in Cheapside. It is not surprising that the chapel incorporates elements of the so-called 'micro architecture' found in the Eleanor Crosses and derived ultimately from the portals of thirteenth-century French cathedrals. These include the series of narrow upright panels of tracery on the canopies of the wall arcading under the windows. Further, there were tall statue-sheltering canopies between the windows, and the spandrels were covered with a web of tracery, while the cornice is capped with pierced tracery. All this was possible

107 *The palace of Westminster: Chapel of St Mary. Designed by Michael of Canterbury and finished c.1320–7, it has five vaulted bays with large carved bosses. It is so much restored and covered internally with paint and gilding that it is difficult to tell how much is medieval work. Above it was the chapel of St Stephen.* (Photograph: J. M. Steane.)

because the wall surfaces had been freed by the omission of vaulting. The chapel was in fact roofed with timber: the carpenters are found in the rolls carving bosses for the roof and there are purchases of Estrich boards, nails and glue. The 'Vousura' was the responsibility of William Hurley in or about 1345.

It took another 20 years to complete the glazing and decoration of the chapel and the effect must have been incomparably sumptuous. The painted decoration, the most magnificent programme of the century, was rediscovered under the wainscoting of the Old House of Commons. The scheme can be reconstructed from accounts by J. T. Smith and Richard Smirke and some few fragments, now in the British Museum, were saved. It included infancy and patron subjects on the east wall. Smirke's copy of this in the Society of Antiquaries' Library gives a convincing impression of the richly oil-based colouring and lavish gilt surface of the murals (Alexander and Binski 1987, 499–500, Fig. 89). In the upper register is The Adoration of the Magi with a young king bearing a pyx and a sceptre; another king bears a magnificent incense boat before the Virgin who is seated on a throne placed obliquely to the line of vision. In the lower register are painted male members of the royal family. They are led by St George, who, like the Virgin, represents the religious sentiments of the Order of the Garter founded in the 1340s. Behind the saint are King Edward III and his five sons all kneeling and all in armour (see Fig. 89). The painting shows both Flemish and Italian influence. Italian sources are also apparent in the scene from the Book of Job, painted in tempera and oil with gilded gesso, removed from the chapel and preserved in the British Museum (Alexander and Binski 1987, 499). The handling of perspective, the use of Tuscan architectural motifs, directional lighting and facial types all are found in contemporary Italian mural painting.

The records are particularly informative about the names of artists and the materials they used. The whole operation was under the control of Hugh of St Albans; he had the unenviable task of impressing painters for the work from Kent, Middlesex, Essex, Surrey and Sussex. If they opposed or proved rebellious they were to be committed to prison. The materials included flagons of painters' oil, brushes made of squirrels' tails, hogs' bristles, peacocks' and swans' feathers, vermilion, verdigris, azure, white and red lead, as well as royal paper for the painters' *patrons* (patterns). The rich effort was above all due to the use of many thousand foils of gold and silver, for every available surface was painted, gilded, diapered or stencilled. Many of the ornaments were not of stone but of plaster stamped with what are called 'pryntes' in the records. The walls also contained canopied niches in which were suspended (by cramps of iron) carved images including one by John Le Wayte – 'three kings to stand in the tabernacles' – and images of 'two sergeants at arms'. Such elaboration was typical of the luxurious and ostentatious display favoured by the courtly Edward III.

The glazing of St Stephen's chapel at Westminster

One of the final tasks in building the chapel was the glazing of the windows. Here again the physical evidence is incomplete but Smith found and conscientiously recorded a large number of fragments (Smith 1807, 232):

> *the discovery of the painted glass in the windows of St Stephen's chapel is to be attributed to the indifference of the workmen who were employed to block up the original windows in the reign on Edward VI which was effected by covering the iron bars and the pieces of glass which remained in the plaster on either side.*

These fragments were discovered when the House of Commons was enlarged in 1800. Smith published three plates entitled 'Specimens of Painted Glass from St Stephen's Chapel'. In the first are fragments with painted representations of foliage on the surface of the glass. In the second are painted animals and pieces of borders. The third shows different parts of the human figure and the inscriptions that accompanied them. The windows as well as the walls were painted with the arms of England and France, lions and fleurs-de-lis being found among the pieces.

Much fuller details are given in the accounts, a long parchment roll recorded by Robert de Campsale, clerk of the works in the king's palace of Westminster 1352–5 (Salzman, April 1926, 14–17, Oct 31–6). It appears that the stonework of the windows was complete by *c.*1349 because canvas was bought to block up the windows to stop the weather from damaging the building. The first step in getting the glazing under way was to gather a workforce and accumulate tools and raw materials. On 30 July 1349 John de Brampton was ordered to buy glass in London, Staffordshire and Shropshire for the King's chapel. By the end of the year glass of various colours, silver filings, geet, gum arabic and other materials had been bought and stockpiled in Westminster. In the following year John de Lincoln, master of the glaziers, was appointed to select glaziers and other workmen throughout 27 counties. There would appear to have been four grades of workers. The chief of the master glaziers who designed the figures was John of Chester; he earned the considerable sum of 7s a week. Below him were master glaziers who received a shilling a day. Ordinary working glaziers were paid 7d or 6d a day, and their mates 4d or 4½d.

It is likely that the building was still scaffolded, but doubtless repairs had to be made. At any rate we hear of new material being paid for:'To Agness Disshere for 50 logs of alder [*log de alneto*] for the scaffolds of the painters and glaziers 10s. To the same for 50 hurdles for the same 12s 6d'. In the meantime in the body of the chapel below the scaffolding, tables were set up for the glaziers to work on. Frequently mentioned is ale for washing the drawing tables (*tabulas pictabules*) for the glaziers' work. The master glaziers drew out the coloured cartoons for the panels, full size, on the flat whitened surface of these tables. The working glaziers laid the pieces of different, coloured glass over the cartoons and proceeded to cut it to the required shape. This was done by heating a grozing iron and drawing the hot point over the glass. This caused a crack which was then enlarged to a break. The smiths provided the grozing irons: '4 July. To Simon Le Smyth for seven grozing irons [*croysonns*] bought for breaking and working glass at 1¼ each – 8¾d.'

Much of the glass was plain and uncoloured and was brought to Westminster from the Wealden glass furnaces around Chiddingfold (Surrey). Samples of such material weathered to a pale-green can be seen in Guildford Museum.

> *30 October. To John Alemyne for 303 weys of white glass: each hundred of 24 weys and each wey of 5lbs for glazing the said windows at 12s the hundred 37s 6d. To William Holmere, for carriage of the said glass from Chiddyngfold to Westminster 6s.*

Coloured glass is, however, also frequently mentioned: red, grey or green ('glaucy') 'azure coloured' or simply glass 'of various colours'. This is likely to have been imported from the Continent.

The next stage involved the painting of the glass to fill in details of faces, foliage, animals and so forth. For painting the chief materials were 'arnement', a black stain made from oxide of iron, silver filings (used to produce a yellow stain), and 'jet', a glass-maker's flux consisting of black glass containing a high proportion of lead. These materials were ground by using 'a bronze mortar with an iron pestle' and a 'plate of iron with an iron muller [*molour*] bought for the purpose'. The painting was fused on to the surface of the glass by heating in a furnace. From frequent references to cole (*charcoal*) and firewood it seems that this also was done on the spot.

The glass next needed to be fitted together and was held in position by closing nails, then leaded and soldered. Simon the Smith charged 6d for tallow (*cepo arietino*) which was mixed with filings (*lymail*) to make solder (*soldar*) for the glass windows. The final stage was to hoist the glass panels into place and fix them in the windows. A strong iron framework was required to support the considerable weight of the glass. This again was smith's work and we find Andrew the Smith charging 'for various crampons, barres and soudeletts for the glass windows weighting 51lbs at 2d a pound'.

It is possible to calculate the total area of glazing in St Stephen's chapel. Salzman worked out that 5244lbs or 2379kg of glass were bought and that 2½lbs (1.1kg) of glass were needed to make 1sq.ft of window. The total area of windows amounted to 21,000sq.ft or 1951sq.m. The cost was 2s 6d per square foot (.09sq.m). St Stephen's, like its prototype the Sainte Chapelle, was a veritable iconographical glasshouse.

The rebuilding of St George's chapel, Windsor

The Plantagenets had lavished attention and resources on their religious foundations at Westminster. The Yorkists switched the focus of their architectural ambitions to Windsor. Edward IV set in train the total reconstruction of the chapel of St George to replace that erected by Henry III and made into a collegiate establishment by Edward III. It is likely that he was fired to emulate the great chapel at Eton College, the foundation of his pious dynastic rival and predecessor Henry VI, which was now rising, slowly and uncertainly, in the flat Thames meadows below the castle rock of Windsor. A more decisive reason was to provide the somewhat shaky Yorkist line with an architectural expression of the glory of the dynasty, in a place already linked with the most distinguished medieval English kings. Thirdly, Edward was providing himself with a majestic last resting place which in the future would supplement Westminster Abbey as a royal mortuary chapel.

In 1473 Richard Beauchamp, Bishop of Salisbury, was appointed master and surveyor of the king's works at the chapel of St George. The chapel was planned to stand immediately to the west of the existing chapel, and Beauchamp was given permission to remove any walls or buildings in the way. The former great hall and vicar's lodgings were cleared and the master mason was appointed. He was Henry Janyns, probably the son of Robert Janyns who was warden of the masons at Eton college from February 1448/9. Henry had himself trained at Eton under John Clerk, and in February 1459 Clerk had left him in his will all his tools, 'pictures' and 'portraitures'.

The rebuilding of the chapel of St George was extremely costly. Up to £1000 per annum was put aside to pay for the works. The principal sources of income were the issues of the lands of the late Earls of Shrewsbury and Wiltshire, Sir William Lovell and Lord Morley, all in the king's hands during the minorities of their respective heirs. These moneys were topped up with grants from the Exchequer. The plan was grandiose in scale, with a total length of 72.2m (237ft) (Eton chapel was 63.7m (209ft) long), and consisted of a presbytery and choir of seven bays with aisles extending a bay further east and connected by an ambulatory. In addition there was a crossing (but no tower) and north and south transepts which ended in half octagonal chapels. Another polygonal chapel carried up as a three-storeyed tower stands at the south-east corner and is balanced on the plan by a rectangular vestry on the north. The southern external elevation is distinguished by its polygonal projections, a continuous range of large clerestory windows, flying buttresses with a pierced parapet punctuated by figured finials, and lofty domed stair turrets at the west end (Fig. 108).

The archaeology of the building provides a number of valuable insights into the political and religious preoccupations of its makers. In five places on the outside of the chapel, on the end wall of each transept and in the mid bays of the south choir aisle and the nave aisles, a large rose on a lozenge or square of sunbeams, with a crown over it, is carved in high relief. This is the well-known heraldic badge of Edward IV and emphasizes the element of dynastic display; but there is also a religious significance because on the seeded centre of each rose is a small crucifix. It would appear that the king's badges were also being utilized as consecration crosses. If so there should have been twelve, and it is a plausible suggestion that the incomplete number was due to the fact that the rest of the chapel had not been completed in King Edward's time.

A second feature which has political connotations is a piece of sculpture in the first bay of the south aisle which forms a vestibule to the chapel to the south of it. On the key of its fan vault are the figures of Edward IV and Bishop

108 Windsor Castle, St George's Chapel, south front, west end. The western stair turrets topped with cupolas have parallels in King's College Chapel, Cambridge. (Photograph: J. M. Steane.)

Beauchamp kneeling on either side of the Cross Neyt. This was the portion of the true cross which had belonged to the princes of Wales; it was part of the spoil handed over to Edward I in 1283 at the close of his successful campaign in Wales. 'He set such store by it that he carried it about the country with him and at great festivals such as the Epiphany or the feasts of the Holy Cross it was brought out and solemn offerings made to it on his behalf.' Edward III was also accustomed to take it on his travels, but on the foundation of the Order of the Garter in 1348, the Cross Neyt was given by the king to the chapel of St Edward and St George. Edward IV wished to emphasize his connections with the Plantagenets by thus representing his association with this, the most sacred relic of the order and the chapel.

Another indirect reference to the politics of the day is the polygonal chapel to the south built to contain the relics of Master John Schorne, the saintly rector of North Marston. Edward IV was anxious to have the relics at Windsor to provide a counter-attraction to the alleged miracles occurring in embarrassing numbers at the tomb of his saintly predecessor and political rival, Henry VI, buried at Chertsey. He prevailed on Pope Sixtus IV to license the removal of Master John's remains in 1478.

While Edward was king the remains of Henry VI were left in obscurity at Chertsey, whither they had been removed after his mysterious death in the Tower. The government had given out that Henry died from 'pure displeasure and melancholy', but popular belief was that he had been murdered, possibly by the Duke of Gloucester. Prominent political figures who died by violence were likely to earn a popular reputation for sanctity. In Henry VI's case, bouts of insanity and a reputation for other-worldliness in his own lifetime may have encouraged the formation of a saintly cult. Richard III took steps to supervise this phenomenon more closely when he authorized the removal of the body of Henry VI from Chertsey to Windsor. Although not canonized he was popularly regarded as a saint and pilgrims flocked to Windsor, contributing to a decline in the numbers wending their way to the shrine of St Thomas at Canterbury.

A rather unseemly wrangle followed: the abbeys of Chertsey and Westminster both put forward claims to the body. Chertsey's claim was on the grounds that Richard III had taken it by violence to Windsor. Westminster based its case on the fact that workmen and vergers at the abbey had clear recollections that Henry had marked out a place for himself in the abbey choir during his lifetime. The canons of Windsor joined in, strenuously arguing in favour of the saintly royal corpse remaining there. The upshot was that the new chapel prepared at Westminster was used for its founder, Henry VII, while Windsor kept Henry VI under the south aisle of St George's chapel. His arms are carved in the fan vaulting over the bay in which he had been reburied after his arrival from Chertsey.

Other royal chapels

In an administrative sense the royal chapel was an itinerant institution of clerks, chaplains, records, plate, vestments and draught animals which accompanied the king on his travels and used the buildings as and when the court arrived at different houses and castles. The king, as we have seen, combined in his person both lay and ecclesiastical roles. He ruled the church through his episcopal appointments. Hence the importance of controlling the election of bishops. The constitutions of Clarendon laid down that elections to vacant abbacies and bishoprics in the king's gift were to take place 'in the King's Chapel'. The chapel was also the power-house wherein the priest-king daily renewed his divine strength. Here was the seat of the representative of a higher and more than earthly justice, the stage where the king played out his ritual and sacral role.

Several royal chapels have survived in the immensely strong and enduring stone tower keeps of the eleventh and twelfth centuries. Such is the outstanding chapel dedicated to St John in the White Tower of London (RCHM 1930, 88–90). This is a complete aisled church fitted into a corner of the Tower, with its apsidal end projecting.

Keeps such as the Tower of London, as Brown notes, were designed by the twelfth-century engineers with great ingenuity: 'rather like the designers of modern submarines, they packed all the military and domestic needs into the self-sufficient confines of their keeps.' At Dover, for instance, there are two chapels in the keep, one above the other in the same building. The lower chapel is decorated by arcading, with round-headed moulded arches and chevron ornament, and by cylindrical columns with stiffly foliated capitals. As in parish churches there is the usual piscina or drain to the right of the altar for washing the sacred vessels. The upper chapel is the more important of the two and is approached through the residential accommodation for the king or important visitors, in the second-floor level of the keep. It has a sacristy, a nave and a chancel, and is richly decorated with wall arcades round moulded arches with chevron ornament; groined vaults spring from cylindrical shafts with foliated capitals. At Rochester (Kent), similarly, the chapel is situated in the top storey of the keep forebuilding, designed to be *en suite* with the second and principal residential stage of the keep.

Of all the medieval English kings, Henry III was the most assiduous builder of chapels. The question arises, what were his motives? What Powicke refers to as 'his moods of pious exaltation' were frequently 'seeking divine sanction for his rapid changes'. The chronicler put it as follows:

> *the less he was clever in his actions within this present world the more he indulged in a display of humility before God. On some days he heard mass three times, and as he longed to hear even more masses, he had them celebrated privately.*

The chapels multiplied. Colvin has calculated that in nearly all Henry's manor houses there were separate chapels for himself and his queen; altogether he maintained at least 50 chapels for the exclusive use of himself and his household. Forty of these were in his houses and ten more in the residential castles of Windsor, Winchester, Ludgershall, Marlborough, Nottingham and Northampton. In addition oratories were built in places like Westminster and the Tower. At Westminster there was a small quatrefoil opening about 1.2m (4ft) above the floor to enable the king to see the altar from his bed. Master Peter, the king's painter, had to repair this 'little chapel next to the king's bed' and to block the draughts coming from the window. There was also an oratory in the south-east recess of the Wakefield tower of the Tower of London. This was divided from the rest of the chamber by projecting spurs of masonry, fortified by a wooden screen in 1238. Within were the usual fittings of aumbry, piscina and opposed sedilia (Curnow 1977, 170–1).

If Henry III had built nothing else his record in the construction of new chapels would have been memorable. They amounted to 18 new ones, ten for his queen and eight for himself. When he was abroad he visited yet more chapels and churches. He saw the Sainte Chapelle in Paris, which St Louis was building, at the same time as he was reconstructing Westminster Abbey. A contemporary poem makes him declare that if he could he would have put it in a cart and brought it back to England with him just as it stood! Most of his new chapels were small simple rectangular buildings, frequently but not invariably described as being of two stages and raised on undercrofts. This was in order to separate the king from his household when worshipping. At Kempton a two-storeyed chapel was built 'in such wise that in the upper part a chapel shall be made for the queen's use so that she can enter the chapel from her chamber and in the lower part shall be made a chapel for the use of the king's household'. The same arrangement (on a much larger scale) prevailed in the fourteenth century, as we have seen, at St Stephen's chapel, Westminster and at Windsor. Hampton Court chapel, built by Wolsey but lavishly embellished by Henry VIII, was designed with two stages: the household occupied the floor below, the king and queen sat in two special pews or Holyday closets in the gallery (Chettle, Charlton, Allan 1982, 23). Chapel design, in fact, mirrored the hieratic and hierarchic roles of kingship.

One unusual characteristic which needs explanation is the multiplication of chapels in royal houses and castles. There were for instance, six chapels in Winchester Castle, though it is unlikely that they were all in concurrent use. When Henry III came to the throne there was one chapel at Woodstock; at the end of his reign there were no less than six! One reason for this was the growing practice of one castle or palace containing several suites of rooms occupied by different households, each carrying on a self-sufficient existence. The king's household was separate from that of the queen and the king's children had their own households. Little Prince Henry, Edward I's second son, had his own household with 80 knights as compared with his uncle Edmund's 100 knights. Edward of Caernarfon similarly had his own separate household on a larger scale. Such households had sufficient numbers and cohesiveness to require spiritual benefits in their own chapel. The other reason is linked with the sacral role of kingship already mentioned. Royal progresses were, at least in part, processions from one sacred spot to another. They could take place in miniature within the palace or castle precincts as well as in the kingdom at large.

These twelfth- and thirteenth-century chapels were not always built of very long-lasting materials and many quickly fell into decay. King John is recorded as having built a chapel at Sauvey Castle out of timber (Braun 1943, 85). The chapel at Kempton was thatched with straw and built of plaster, doubtless on a timber frame. The Constable of St Briavel's was ordered to build 'a chapel of wood with posts' before the door of the king's chamber in the castle (*Cal. Lib. R. 1226–40*, 250, 262). Rochester seems to have had a wooden chapel of two storeys in the thirteenth century; presumably this was in addition to the already mentioned chapel in the stone keep forebuilding (*Cal. Lib. R. 1245–50*, 211).

The canons of St Pauls had a chapel at Barnes (Surrey) made of plaster of paris! (Information: W. J. Blair.) A more common roofing material than thatch, but equally short-lived, was shingles. Robert de Aundely was ordered to make 70,000 of these wooden tiles in the forest of Gilllingham and deliver them to the sheriff of Wiltshire to roof the king's chapel in Salisbury castle.

Although the structural evidence is nearly always limited to foundations and the lower part of the walls (at best), in most instances a good deal is known about the decoration of royal chapels in all their painted and glazed splendour because the documents, in particular the Liberate Rolls, add detail, colour and life to the archaeological record. They were often wainscoted (for instance at Feckenham, Geddington and Woodstock) and the walls were plastered internally and painted. Woodstock old chapel had a painting which has been described as

> *of the story of the woman condemned for adultery and how the Lord wrote on the ground and how the Lord gave a stroke to St Paul . . . and in the upper part of the chapel the story of the Evangelists in like manner.* (Cal. Lib. R. 1251–60, *24.)*

At Geddington the king's and queen's chapels were richly decorated, being painted with green and spangled with gold, and the king's chapel was divided with a screen between the chancel and the body of the building, with a door in the centre and two seats on either side (*Cal. Lib. R. 1251–60*, 21). The chapel of the castle at Nottingham had a picture of St Katherine painted in front of the altar and another above it with her story. It was richly furnished with a silver chalice, a missal, an antiphonary, a breviary, a gradual, a troper, a psalter, a hymnary, all manner of bodily vestments, towels, a lamp, vials, a censor and a cross to place above the altar (*Cal. Lib. R. 1251–60*, 11).

At Clarendon the building which housed the king's chapel is thought to have been constructed under Elias de Dereham in 1234–7. It was on the first floor of a two-storeyed building immediately to the east of the wardrobe and buttressed with Chilmark stone on the north side. Sculpture decorated the chapel. By 1250 there were statues of St Mary, St Edward the Confessor and cherubim, while gilded angels glittered above. A single stone angel's wing with visible gilding and paint was excavated in 1938 (James and Robinson 1988, Fig. 94, No. 73, pl. LXVb). More exciting, on the ground floor below the chapel was found the tumbled heap of tiles which had originally made up a great concentric pavement in the upstairs chapel (Eames 1980, 34). A segment which has now been plausibly reconstructed after a good deal of trouble can be seen in the medieval tile room at the British Museum. It includes tiles of ten different sizes from ten circular bands each of which had been decorated with a different inlaid design. Plain green glazed tiles from ten narrow circular bands and a number of smaller segmental tiles, each decorated with a single letter of the alphabet or a single stop, were recovered. The tiles belonging to the outermost and innermost bands had no assembly marks but the rest had various nicks and Roman numerals incised on the undersides which guided the pavier when he laid the complex design. A plausible inscription was made up in the British Museum laboratory – PAVEIMENTUM HENRICI REGIS ANGLIE – but it may well have been longer. The kiln that produced the tiles for this pavement was also found by the excavators of Clarendon in 1937. This has been lifted and rebuilt in the British Museum (Eames 1980, 28–30).

Archaeology provides us with information about the architectural shell of these royal chapels. In their own times they were of course filled with music and chanting. We are almost totally ignorant about exactly what music was sung or what standard of performance was reached. At Windsor Castle, however, a graffito was recently noticed inscribed on the walls of the Treasaunt, a passage running parallel to the present Dean's cloister. This was, for more than two centuries from the time of its building in *c.*1240, at the very centre of the liturgical and ceremonial life of the royal chapel. The graffito is in musical notation and is based on a system of diamonds and rectangles; its position suggests that it is to be associated with the religious ritual of St George's chapel which was based on the Sarum usage, or with the Garter ceremonial. Its finder thinks that it may have been used as a faburden part for the harmonic embellishment of plainsong, in connection with Rogation Litanies, Office Hymns or the Magnificat (Jones-Baker 1984, 373–6).

The itinerant nature of royal life meant that the chapels as well as the houses often grew damp, their walls cracked, glass fell out and they quickly decayed. Hence the flurry of maintenance activity and efforts to get buildings ready when the king announced his programme of visits. The bailiff of Gillingham must have been plunged into disarray when he received orders

> *to finish the king's building and chapel without delay, to put glass windows* [vitrea] *in the chapel, and repair and mend all defects so that all may be well at the king's arrival, which as he hopes is within 15 days from Trinity.* (Cal. Lib. R. 1251–60, 202.)

It is appropriate to conclude by once again stressing the itinerant nature of medieval royal life. Restlessness, and a desire to be on the move, was endemic in the upper echelons of medieval society.

The Crown and pilgrimage

Walsingham

The power exerted by the relics of Our Lady at Walsingham sprang originally from a shrine erected as a place of private devotion by a great lady, Richelde of Ferraques (Fig. 109). A small chapel was constructed in imitation of the Holy House at Nazareth around 1130. Not long afterwards Walsingham Priory was founded alongside and a little to the south, and a statue of the Virgin Mary with infant child was placed inside the Holy House. Further shrines and relics were added during the later Middle Ages, including the Knights Gate, the relic of the holy milk of the Virgin enclosed in crystal, the finger of Saint Peter and the spring of holy water. What is undoubted is the reverence inspired by this place of pilgrimage, situated as it was in an out-of-the-way part of the Norfolk countryside. From the thirteenth century until the Dissolution travellers came in their thousands.

These pilgrims included a number of monarchs (Dickinson 1956, 17–19). Walsingham's rise to fame can be attributed more to Henry III than to anyone else. In 1226 he visited Norfolk and spent the two days, 3–4 April 1226, at Walsingham. On 4 April he granted the priory the right to hold a weekly market and a fair on the vigil and day of the Holy Cross. Thereafter he made frequent visits and also gifts, including timber for buildings, wax and tapers, and, in 1246, the generous donation of 20 marks to make a gold crown and place it on the image of St Mary of Walsingham. The king's deep devotion to the shrine passed on to his son, Edward I. Edward's zeal for the shrine arose from the occasion when he was playing chess in a vaulted room and happened to move away just before a large stone fell from the roof on to the spot where he had been sitting. He attributed his escape to St Mary of Walsingham, and visited the place no less than 12 times during his reign (List and Index Society, Itinerary of Edward I, Vol. 135).

Edward II made fewer visits to Walsingham and the scale of his offerings was much smaller.

When he was still the Lord Edward in 1300 he offered a shilling at the high altar and 7s at the altar in the chapel of Our Lady. It was not until 6–8 October 1315 that he visited the shrine as king. Edward III, on the other hand, was a frequent visitor in the early years of his reign; he came nine times between 1328 and 1343 but there are no signs that he visited Walsingham in the remaining 34 years of his reign. Richard II came with his queen in 1383 (Ormerod 1990, 850–8).

The shrine evidently continued to be of national importance in the fifteenth century. Henry V was there in 1421 during his last visit to England and in 1427 Queen Joan (Henry IV's widow) came. Henry VI made visits in 1447, 1448 and 1459. Edward IV licensed the priory to acquire in mortmain lands and rents to the value of £40 yearly 'that they may pray for the good estate of the king and Elizabeth his queen and for the king's soul after death'.

Walsingham continued to attract the devotions of the great right up to the Dissolution. We are told by Polydore Vergil how, in the crisis of 1487 when the Tudor throne was in great peril, Henry VII 'came to the place called Walsingham where he prayed devoutly before the image of the Blessed Virgin (who is worshipped with special devotion there) that he might be preserved from the wiles of his enemies'. After he had defeated Lambert Simnel he sent his standard 'to offer thanks for the victory in the shrine of the Blessed Virgin and to place the standard there as a memorial of the favour he had received from God'. As well as three further visits Henry remembered Our Lady in his will, leaving an 'ymage of silver and gilt'. Henry VIII shared a similar devotion, at any rate in the earlier part of his reign. He is said to have walked barefoot to the shrine and offered Our Lady a necklace of great value. He endowed a candle there and paid for the very expensive glazing of the Lady Chapel (by Bernard Flower, the royal glazier, who became famous for his work at King's College, Cambridge). This was in the nature of a thank offering for the birth of the young Prince Henry on New Year's Day 1511. Unfortunately, the Prince was soon dead and Henry's search for a male heir had to start all over again. It would lead ultimately to the greatest act of vandalism in English history – the Dissolution of the monasteries.

109 An openwork pilgrim pin badge in the shape of the Walsingham 'Holy House' with scenes of the Annunciation and an image of the Walsingham Madonna. It measures 80mm (3¼in) high by 55mm (2¼in) wide, from Queenhithe, London. (After Mitchiner.)

Archaeology has shed somewhat fitful new light on the nature of the shrine (Green and Whittingham 1961, 255–89). The original 'Holy House' was supposed to have been erected in AD 1061. It seems to have been a free-standing wooden structure, referred to by Erasmus when he visited Walsingham in 1514 as '*ligneo tabulato constructum*'. The form of this primitive shrine is depicted in some of the pilgrim badges: it had steep gables and possibly arcaded sides. In the fifteenth century a stone-built chapel was erected round the platform on which the shrine stood. From the foundations of this, uncovered to the north of the priory church in 1961, the excavators were able to establish that the building had three bays with doors in the middle of three walls. Pilgrims would enter the chapel from the church, pass into the house, and leave by the north door. Erasmus describes the statue of Our Lady as standing in the dark on the right, lighted only by candles.

The great popularity of Walsingham is borne out by the sheer number and multiplicity of pilgrim badges (Mitchiner 1986, 32–6, 97–104, 138–42). Among the designs were miniature horns with the words AVE MARIA stamped on the side, the horn supposedly representing that blown by the Angel Gabriel at the Annunciation. There were also openwork monograms reading MARIA with a suspensory ring above. The so-called Annunciation badges were rectangular pieces of base metal with the winged Angel Gabriel standing on the right facing Mary; between them is a lily pot symbolizing her purity. A more complex version of this is set in two storeys of the Holy House. The 'Madonna and Child' statue appears in the central doorway of the lower storey. This last motif also served as the sole subject of some badges. There are badges with the crowned initial 'M' and, finally, ampullae, little leaden flasks in the shape of a pouch or a scallop shell with a crowned letter 'W' on them, sold as containers for holy water. The Walsingham pilgrimage, although increasing in popularity during the fourteenth century, was still overshadowed by the very large numbers of pilgrims visiting Canterbury. This is mirrored by the relative recovery rates of pilgrim badges in London from Walsingham and Canterbury. In the fifteenth century, with the growth of the veneration of the Virgin, this evened out and in the years leading up to the Dissolution badges from Walsingham exceeded in number those from Canterbury.

Canterbury

As well as being responsible for his assassination, Henry II was personally involved in the beginning of the cult of St Thomas Becket. On 12 July 1174 he made his own pilgrimage to Canterbury, dismounting at Harbledown, two miles from the city, and walking barefoot for the rest of the way. The 'foot' badges may well allude to this part of his penance. The king was scourged by the monks as retribution for his part in the murder and afterwards received a phial of holy water. What is strange is that the martyr, Thomas Becket, despite being the archetypal turbulent priest, succeeded thereafter in attracting successive members of the royal family to his shrine. Henry II, after his dramatic act of penance, won a commanding victory over the Scots, and attributed this to the forgiveness of the saint (Warren 1973, 135). The ambitious marriages he arranged for his children resulted in the cult of St Thomas developing an international rather than insular character (Borenius 1970, 13, 48, 52). Henry's eldest daughter, Matilda, came to Canterbury in 1184 with her husband, Duke Henry the Lion of Saxony and Bavaria. The worship and representation of the saint followed her to Germany. The cathedral of Brunswick was consecrated in 1226 on 29 December, the day of St Thomas. The south choir wall is covered with painted scenes of the history of Becket. The cult was introduced into Spain by Eleanor, Henry's second daughter, who married Alfonso II of Castile. She founded a chapel of St Thomas in Toledo cathedral *c.*1174; another chapel in the cathedral of Siquenza has late twelfth-century wall paintings of St Thomas. The saint's martyrdom is vividly portrayed in paintings in the church of St Maria Tarrasa, 24km (15 miles) from Barcelona. When Henry's youngest daughter, Joan, married William the Good, King of Sicily in 1177, the murder of the archbishop and her father's remorse were fresh in her mind. In William's cathedral of Monreale is the first extant representation of Becket in mosaic, a stylized, named figure wearing the pallium.

The monarchy continued to reverence the shrine of St Thomas throughout the thirteenth century. John was sufficiently devout to go on a pilgrimage after his coronation to the shrines of St Thomas Becket, St Alban and St Edmund, even though his presence was urgently required in Normandy. Henry III was among the witnesses when on 7 July 1220, the remains of Becket were translated to the new shrine in the cathedral. The almonry accounts reveal a special interest felt by Edward I and his family in the cult of St Thomas (Taylor 1985, 291–7). In 1285 the royal family, consisting of Edward, the queen, the little Lord Edward (not yet 15 months old) and his five sisters travelled from Westminster to Canterbury by water and by road, reaching Canterbury on 6 July (a five-day journey). The customary offerings were made and Edward also made a major contribution to the refurbishment of the shrine by presenting four elaborate statuettes in gold set with emeralds, sapphires, garnets and pearls at a cost of £347. A revealing insight into the king's simple faith is recorded in 1286, when he sought St Thomas's intervention to cure the indisposition of one of his gerfalcons. This was extended to intercession for the royal offspring in 1300 when gold florins were placed on the altar at Canterbury in the name of 'the foetus then existing in the queen's belly'. Edward I visited Canterbury at least 37 times and his son Edward II 16 times. Doubtless one reason for such frequent visits was that it was a convenient stopping place *en route* to or from France, but in this the monarchy led the way in what became the most popular pilgrimage of medieval England.

The archaeological study of the 300 Canterbury pilgrim badges (more than for any other site in Europe) provides a tangible index of the phenomenal popularity of the cult of St Thomas (Mitchiner 1986, 51–75, 86, 155–66, 237). The peculiarly horrible violence of the crime was recalled on the early ampullae which are stamped with a picture of Becket falling to the soldiers' swords. In some badges the casket shrine is portrayed with his mitre on top while a monk stands in attendance. Others stress the quality of the offerings to the saint, with a small monk pointing to the great ruby donated by the French King Louis VII. Some show images of ships, alluding to the exile of the archbishop in France. A sole figure of St Thomas in the act of blessing is another design. The 'Becket on horseback' badges, particularly common in the fourteenth century, commemorated Thomas's return from exile in France; this was the subject of an annual festival known as '*Regressio Santi Thome*'. As the cult of relics developed, so emphasis was directed by the badge makers to the parts which represented the whole; Becket's vestments, gloves, girdles and the sword that killed him, were all singled out as subjects for the little leaden tokens. The Canterbury bell in miniature was also very popular. In the fifteenth century the high-relief 'bust of Becket' showing the mitred archbishop became fashionable. As the fortunes of the Canterbury shrine faded during the last few decades before the Reformation so these badges degenerated in design. They ended up as small flat objects with simple ornaments, a travesty of their former glory.

Royal visits were often linked with the perils of travel. Edward III, for example, returning to England from France, reached Weymouth after a frightful stormy journey lasting ten days. As soon as he had recovered sufficiently he went on pilgrimage to Our Lady of Walsingham, to Canterbury and to his father's shrine at Gloucester to give thanks for his deliverance from the waves (Packe 1983, 130). It has been suggested that his pilgrimage was in part a propaganda exercise aimed at fomenting nationalistic support against the French (Ormerod 1990, 859).

Henry V performed the Canterbury pilgrimage three times in his reign, for three different reasons. In 1413 he gave a funeral feast in honour of his dead father, the cost of which amounted to £127 7s 2½d. He paid another, purely devotional visit a month later to the shrine of St Thomas on the occasion of the great translation festival and to offer in person a golden head wrought with pearls and precious stones, ordered at a cost of £160. After the victory of Agincourt he called in at Canterbury on his way from Dover to London to celebrate his triumph. He was met by Archbishop Chichele and a long procession of clergy (Wylie 1914, 47–8). The monks of Christ Church were thus able to pump a continual stream of offerings into their rebuilding programme, which transformed the nave and central tower of the cathedral at Canterbury in the fifteenth century.

Bromholm and Hailes

The other shrines closely associated with the monarchy owed their reputations to relics rather than to events. Bromholm was formerly a little known priory on the remote Norfolk coast, 8km (5 miles) from North Walsham (Simpson 1874, 52–61). It became celebrated throughout Christendom because of a relic of the true cross brought to England from Constantinople in 1205–23 (Wormald 1937–8, 31–46). This was in the form of a patriarchal cross, a cross with two transverse pieces, the upper one being the shorter of the two. On 5 April Henry III paid his first visit to Bromholm. The relic, in fact, was already celebrated enough to attract the attention of the great. The king granted the priory an annual fair to be held for three days on the feast of the Exaltation of the Cross – 14 September. Gifts of silver-gilt images and wax to make tapers followed, and other visits were made in 1232, 1235, 1238, 1248 and 1251. After 1251, references to the Holy Cross of Bromholm become scanty. Like other centres of pilgrimage it had started with an enormous popularity boosted by visits from the monarchy and the nobility and then settled down to a more humdrum existence. Chaucer and Langland both mention the cross of Bromholm. Henry V, on 25 April 1416, gave the prior and monks four pipes of wine annually from the ports of Yarmouth and Kirkby. Veneration of the Holy Rood remained popular, but during the fifteenth century devotion to the Sacred Heart began to rival it (Fig. 110). This can be traced from a study of pilgrim badges; representations of the Sacred Heart amidst flowery clusters tended to replace depictions of the Holy Rood (Mitchiner 1986, 39–105, 142–4).

The priory of Bromholm, despite its success as a pilgrimage centre, never grew beyond a very modest size. The largest number of monks recorded was 25 in 1298. During the later Middle Ages the priory lands were much encroached upon by the sea and part of the house was burned down. Papal support in the form of appropriations of churches and indulgences continued but royal interest seems to have declined. The Cross disappeared, like the shrine and bones of St Thomas, in the orgy of destruction wrought by the dissolution of the monasteries.

The second shrine which owed its fame almost entirely to a relic was the Cistercian Abbey of Hailes (Gloucestershire) (Denholm-Young 1947, 74). This was a late foundation made in 1246 by Richard, Earl of Cornwall, brother to Henry III, with monks coming from John's abbey at Beaulieu. Richard was fulfilling a vow made when he was in peril at sea on his way home from Gascony in 1243. The abbey was consecrated in 1251, when the king and queen and all the notables of the land were present along with Grosseteste and 12 other bishops (Fig. 111). It only became a centre of pilgrimage when Edmund of Cornwall presented to the abbey a relic of the Precious Blood authenticated by the guarantee of the Patriarch of Jerusalem.

Excavations at the site of Hailes Abbey have revealed that a complete rebuilding of the east end of the church was undertaken to accommodate the shrine and the expected concourse of pilgrims (St Clair Baddeley 1905, 58; Knowles and St Joseph 1952, 124). A *chevet* or coronet of semi-circular chapels was built around the head of the presbytery (Fig. 112).

110 A pilgrim badge commemorating the Sacred Heart at Bromholm (Norfolk). It takes the form of an angel, winged and crowned, facing and holding a crowned Sacred Heart. From Billingsgate foreshore, London. (After Mitchiner.)

This included a semi-circular aisle or processional path passing between the shrine and the front of the chapels. The excavators also found the rectangular base of the shrine, 2.4m (8ft) in breadth, 3m (10ft) long and 61cm (24in) high. Judging from the seals of Hailes and from literary evidence the relic was contained in a crystal or glass bottle, through the sides of which it was viewed by pilgrims.

Pilgrim badges show Edmund bringing the relic to Hailes, or alternatively carrying it in procession. In the fifteenth-century badges the Earl appears wearing a tunic and cape, bareheaded, holding a sword in one hand and in the other holding aloft the reliquary containing the Holy Blood; it is circular in shape and surmounted by a cross (Fig. 113). The Holy Blood of Hailes came to an ignominious end, being dismissed as duck's blood by Henry VIII's crude chemical analysis before being cast away (Mitchiner 1986, 112, 190).

The politics of pilgrimage

Towards the end of the Middle Ages we find the Crown increasingly aware of the political gains sponsored pilgrimage could bring to the dynasty. The concept was not new. Edward III endowed a magnificent tomb to his murdered father at Gloucester (see Fig. 28). Miracles are said to have taken place and Gloucester became a centre of pilgrimage. For similar political purposes he promoted pilgrimage to Pontefract to commemorate a most unlikely candidate for sainthood, the brutal, treacherous and rebellious Thomas, Earl of Lancaster, who had been executed there in 1322. For Edward the point was that Plantagenet blood had been spilt. A fourteenth-century wall-painting in the Oxfordshire church of South Newington shows a popular conception of the martyrdom of this 'Blessed Thomas' (Tristram 1955, 228) next to a representation of the murder of Becket.

The most remarkable example of the Crown manipulating popular religion for its own purposes concerned the cult of Henry VI at Windsor (Spencer 1978, 235–64). The last member of the Lancastrian dynasty may have been put to death in the Tower within hours of Edward IV's victory at Tewkesbury. As mentioned above, the Yorkist king gave out that Henry had died from 'pure displeasure and melancholy' and arranged for his body to be taken to St Pauls and there briefly exposed to public view. To forestall the flowering of a popular religious cult he had the murdered king buried in the seclusion of Chertsey Abbey. Within a year, however, came the first manifestations of a cult in far off churches like Ripon and Durham. Edward attempted to control this unofficial pilgrimage as already noted (p. 183) in setting up a makeshift counter-attraction at Windsor by installing in his chapel of St George the remains of John Schorne. Schorne was an early fourteenth-century parish priest from North Marston in Buckinghamshire who became a saint by popular consent and whose

111 Tiles paving the eastern arm of the abbey church at Hailes (Gloucestershire). All the heraldry is associated with the founder, Richard of Cornwall, king of the Romans, his three wives and the families whose lands Edmund of Cornwall had acquired. (After Eames, 1980.)

112 Hailes Abbey (Gloucestershire). Founded in 1246 by Richard, Earl of Cornwall, younger brother of Henry III, and endowed with great liberality. In 1270 Richard's son, Edmund, brought to Hailes a relic of the Holy Blood which was accommodated in a shrine in the rebuilt east end of the presbytery. The rebuilding carried out in 1271–7 took the form of a chevet – an apse with encircling ambulatory crowned by five radiating chapels. (Photograph: Cambridge University Committee for Aerial Photography, 1957.)

greatest exploit had been conjuring the devil into a boot! Pilgrims were provided with badges illustrating John Schorne, bare-headed, wearing a long robe: in front of him was a long boot with the devil's head appearing at the top. Nevertheless people began to trek to Chertsey as the news of miracles connected with Henry VI spread. Richard III, unable to suppress this potentially anti-Yorkist cult, decided to put it under close supervision by having King Henry's body moved from Chertsey Abbey to St George's Chapel Windsor.

For Henry VII, relatively unknown to his subjects, this was a heaven-sent opportunity to win posthumous popular affection and esteem for his uncle, on behalf of the Tudor dynasty. King Henry's cult was stimulated by the production of hymns, books of hours, statues, panel paintings, stained glass windows and hundreds of pilgrim badges. These last portray the king robed in state, wearing a ponderous crown and holding an orb in one hand and a sceptre in the other (Mitchener 1986, 231–2). At his feet are the heraldic antelope or the lion. No one was bothered that the object of their devotions in real life had gone around dressed in shabby clothes, including an old hat, and eschewed royal sartorial splendour as much as he could. He is also shown on the badges riding a richly caparisoned ambling horse as in royal progresses, a similar pose to that on badges depicting Becket's return from exile. Over 90 badges of Henry VI have been found, illustrating the meteoric rise of this novel cult. This can be compared with the three hundred of St Thomas Becket, belonging to a period four times as long. Henry VII went on to start official proceedings to secure the formal

113 A pilgrim badge from Hailes Abbey (Gloucestershire). It shows the Earl of Cornwall on horseback holding up a phial of Christ's Holy Blood. (After Mitchiner.)

canonization of his 'martyred' ancestor. He also proposed to bury him beside himself in his new chapel at Westminster. Neither of these projects was ultimately successful. They were quietly dropped but the cult, because of its royal connections, was allowed to outlive the Reformation by a few years. A massive money box made of wrought iron and decorated with the initial 'H', with four keyholes and as many money slots, still stands, 1.22m (4ft) high, in St George's Chapel. It reminds us of the time when pilgrims sought relief from the troubles of this world by visiting the shrine of good King Henry of Windsor.

114 A pilgrim badge of King Edward II of Gloucester in the form of a crowned bust of Edward II, resembling the sterling bust on royal pennies. Circular openwork pin badge. From Brookes's Wharf, London. (After Mitchiner.)

The archaeology of royal charity

Charity was a central preoccupation of medieval society, as the extraordinary number of hospitals founded in the period demonstrates. In England alone at least 220 hospitals were started in the twelfth century and some 310 in the thirteenth century (Rubin 1987, 1). Kings involved themselves in charitable giving of many kinds – granting gifts, founding hospitals and almonries, bestowing food, money, clothes and spiritual care upon strangers, travellers, the sick and the infirm. Clearly there was an element of selfless denial in this but it has been noticed by Rubin that 'gift giving was also part of the symbolic articulation of social and personal relations'. Kings dispensed charity on a large scale because it was expected of them (Johnstone 1929, 149–67). Even John, not famed for his spiritual interests, did not lag behind in conspicuous display of almsgiving and entertainment of the poor. There was, however, an element of reciprocity and exchange. In return for the foundation of hospitals and colleges their members were bound in return to seek intercession for the souls of the founders. The hospital at Ospringe (Kent), founded by Henry III soon after 1230, was staffed by a master and brethren, among whose duties was the celebration of masses for the souls of their founder and of his royal predecessors and successors (Drake 1914, 37). Such prayers, with their rich display, buttressed the social status of the founders, as well as being valued for their spiritual efficacy in saving souls. Charity bound the poor and the rich together in medieval society. Henry III seems to have had this in mind when he ordered the images of *dives et pauper* to be displayed in his palaces. In 1246 he had them painted in the hall at Ludgershall 'on the end wall opposite the dais'. The same subject also figured in glass in the king's hall at Northampton and was painted 'opposite the king's seat' in the hall at Guildford.

The volume of royal almsgiving during the reign of Edward I has been calculated from detailed analysis based on the survival of a number of royal wardrobe books recording the activities of the royal almonry (Taylor 1985, 257–89). It shows that as the court in 1283–4 moved up the Marches of Wales and across England to Lincolnshire and Yorkshire, and thence back to Wales, it provided general poor relief to a large number of people. The units receiving benefit amounted to 34,858; on these people £1363 6s 1d was spent in that year. A second group were the sick or infirm made well by receiving the healing touch of the royal hand. Each was given 1d. The queen when on progress also distributed alms; 2s a day was assigned to her for this purpose. Sometimes there were more general distributions of royal largesse to mark particular occasions; these might include a deceased royalty, a celebration of a royal birthday or a thanksgiving for a safe crossing.

Both Henry III and Edward I made frequent subsistence grants to the newly founded orders of friars in the towns they visited. Even this did not exhaust the almsgiving proclivities of the king and queen. Whenever they visited a shrine or altar in churches, chapels, abbeys or cathedrals they offered oblations. Often these were, inexplicably, in multiples of 7d. The Royal Maundy in the 1280s involved the King, Queen, Princess Joan and Princess Elizabeth and disposed of various small sums. Other sums were expended on the maintenance of royal chapels and their furnishings, and grants were made towards the building works of abbeys and churches. Two young men studied at Oxford at the king's expense enjoying what in effect were king's scholarships. Edward also contributed towards the travelling expenses of various individuals; there is a poignant entry recording the cost of sending the daughters of the executed Prince Dafydd of Wales to their banishment in an assortment of English nunneries. The king also paid various funeral expenses, including oblations at masses celebrated in Bangor for the soul of his nephew, Henry of Brittany; the gravestone was paid for out of the king's alms.

Royal hospitals

Widespread though these eleemosynary transactions may have been, the most permanent form in which royal charitable impulses expressed themselves was the foundation of hospitals. Henry III, as befits the great benefactor of Westminster Abbey, led the way. Two good examples of hospitals which he assisted have recently been excavated. The hospital of St John the Baptist in Oxford was not originally a royal foundation but in 1231 Henry III gave it a new and better site outside the east gate of Oxford, the former Jewish burial ground (Salter 1914, 77). He also provided timber from the royal woods at Brill and Shotover which at the time extended up to the city (*Cal. Close R. 1231–4*, 35, 74). Gifts of fuel and venison were lavished on the house by the king (*Cal. Close R. 1231–4*, 62, 384).

The area covered by the buildings of the hospital is co-extensive with Bishop William of Waynflete's foundation of Magdalen College (Fig. 115) which absorbed the by-then decayed institution in 1456 (Gunther 1917, 393–434). Certain dimensions and orientations of the hospital buildings were perpetuated in the new college; parts of the chapel, infirmary hall and kitchen are embedded in the present buildings at Magdalen. The hospital cartulary supplies more evidence of the various elements of the complex. There were a refectory, capable of feeding about 18 persons, separate dormitories for the brethren and sisters (to hold about 10 and 8 respectively), a ward for the infirm (always between 1 and 10 in number), a chapel for the brethren, a chapel for the infirm, some small rooms to house 6–8 people who bought corrodies (a form of annuity or insurance for old age, buying a place in an institution such as a hospital of monastery), or who were sent by the king for life, a room for the master, a chapel house, and a chapter house. What seems to have happened is that the centre of the site was cleared for the great buildings of the college round the quadrangle while on the periphery the structures connected with the hospital were left as offices and dwellings for the first President, scholars and workmen. Subsequently most of these were taken down and doubtless their materials embedded in the collegiate buildings.

There was a long two-storey block on the north side whose layout was followed by Waynflete for orientation when he planned the great quadrangle of the college. Its east end was furnished with an elaborate system of isolated sanitary annexes which looked like, and

115 Magdalen College, Oxford. The foundations of the medieval hospital of St John the Baptist below the eastern range. An ashlar-lined channel is seen running down the centre. The infirmary hall was to the left and the river wall to the right. (Photograph: Oxford and County Newspapers.)

subsequently were, connected into five large buttresses. North of this building Agas, a Tudor cartographer, shows in his *Map of Oxford* a long two-storey building. This, Gunther suggests, was where the sisters of the hospital may have resided; it certainly had a secluded and pleasant position near the Cherwell with a garden behind; it was converted into a stable between 1674 and 1735.

Chapels were key buildings in medieval hospitals, since spiritual health was thought to be conducive to bodily well-being. St John the Baptist's hospital, Oxford, had two chapels, one of which has largely survived in the range bordering the High Street (Gunther 1917, 404–23).

The other major fragment of hospital buildings still standing is on the eastern edge of the site and consists of the old college kitchen block, 'a large and rather gloomy old room with a very high roof of strong timbers'. It may have been the refectory. An excavation carried out in 1986–7 in advance of building new college kitchens to the south showed a massive river wall continuing on the same alignment as the old kitchen range. Along the inside of this wall was an ashlar-lined culvert with evidence of ashlar arches at intervals of 2.9m (9ft 6½in). There was a flight of steps within the building for access to the river, which suggests that water may have had some part to play in the healing process. Four pier bases found *in situ* created a puzzling plan for this building. The excavator has, however, identified it as the eastern part of the a 18-m (59-ft) wide infirmary of the twin-halled type found also at St Nicholas, Salisbury and St Mary's, Ospringe (Kent) (Durham 1991, 17–77).

Such a hospital had a multi-purpose function. In its earliest phase it was used as a place to entertain strangers and was called 'the lodging of the hospital outside the east gate' ('*herebergeria hospitalis extra portam orientalem*'); its site outside the gate on a main road was convenient for this. Subsequently the main purpose of the hospital seems to have been to nurse the sick. As in monastic infirmaries there was no full-time medical man on the staff; sickness was treated with good food, rest and spiritual benefits. The hospital was also a place where royal servants were sent to end their days in comfort after a long employment with the Crown.

The second example of Henry III's charitable endowment was the Hospital of St Mary of Ospringe, commonly called the Maison Dieu, founded soon after 1230 (Drake 1914) (Fig. 116). Here the king may well have been influenced by the example of the Justiciar Hubert de Burgh, who had founded a Maison Dieu in Dover *c.*1221 for the maintenance of the poor and infirm and for the pilgrims passing through the port on their way to Canterbury or the Continent. Ospringe is on the Roman Watling Street, the main road between London and Dover; it was also on the direct route from London and the eastern counties to the shrine of St Thomas at Canterbury. The Masters and brethren had a four-fold function: to be hospitable to the poor and to needy pilgrims; to relieve lepers; to pray for the king, his predecessors and successors; and to maintain royal accommodation known as *camera regis*, a form of staging post conveniently situated on one of the main routes of royal travel.

Study of a survey of 1571 backed up by an excavation of 1977, prior to residential development, revealed the neatly laid-out hospital precinct (Smith 1979). A culverted stream ran north–south down the centre of the site, flowing under one side of the common hall (a feature paralleled in the hospital at Oxford). Adjoining the twin-aisled, single-storeyed infirmary hall was a *necessarium* (a communal lavatory). West of these lay the kitchen and 'service' yard with bakehouse, well and lay-servants' quarters. East of the stream was the 'precinct', around the chapel, camera, gatehouse and staff accommodation. To the north of this lay part of the hospital cemetery, a dovecot and a large pond. To the west of the hall was a small garden close with surrounding pentice. The whole was a self-sufficient community.

Most of the buildings at Ospringe have their counterparts at St John the Baptist's hospital, Oxford, except for the building devoted to royal accommodation (*camera regis*). It consisted of a four-bayed undercroft with three central pillars or posts. The substantial buttressing suggests there was a first floor or *camera* approached by an external staircase on the south side. This great room was probably heated by a lateral fireplace. A high level of interior finish was suggested by the thick layer of plaster, including pieces with dark fleck 'false

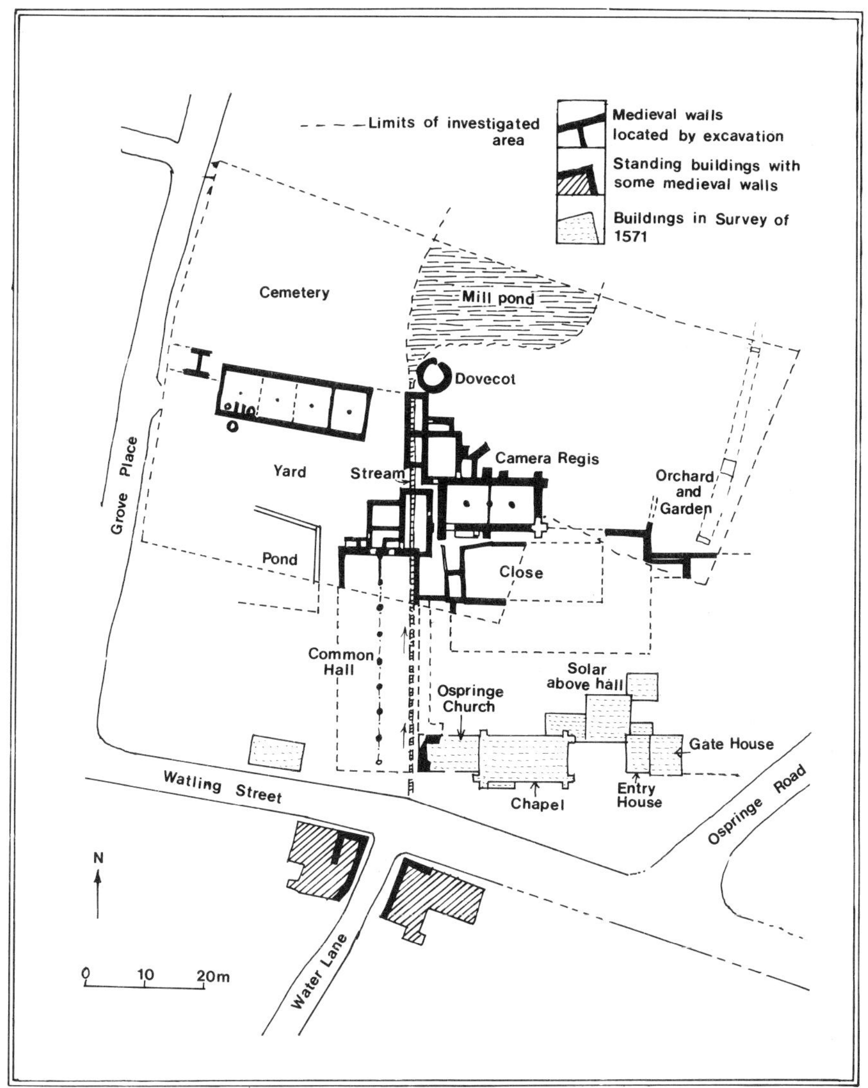

116 *Maison Dieu, Ospringe (Kent). A plan of the excavations and standing buildings.* (After Smith, 1979.)

ashlar' painting and motifs including trefoils. Painted window glass was also found. Another chamber with undercroft, decorated with painted plaster, painted glass and tiles, was built adjoining. Henry III, Edward I and Edward II all stayed at Ospringe. They also sent their old servants to take up residence there on their retirement. In 1277 Juliana, 'sometime damsel of Queen Eleanor, the king's mother', was among the sisters dwelling in the hospital. In 1292 Edward I sent letters to the master asking him to find suitable maintenance for Ralph le Bedel, who had been in the service of the king's mother. Thereafter a succession of recommendations follow. As one old servant dies, he is replaced by another.

Education

The English monarchy had early distinguished itself by founding monasteries but it was not until the beginning of the fourteenth century

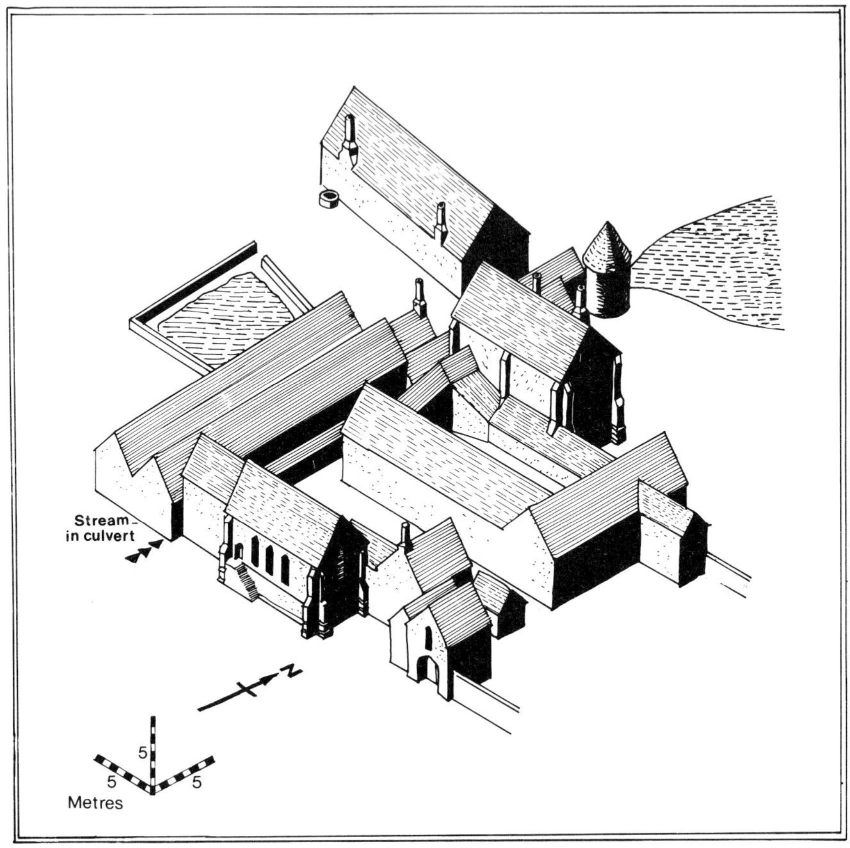

117 Maison Dieu, Ospringe (Kent). Reconstruction of the buildings of the medieval hospital north of Watling Street. (After Smith, 1979.)

that kings began to interest themselves in purely educational institutions. A powerful reason for this was that more care was now being taken with the education and upbringing of the English princes (Orme 1973, 23). It became customary for the heir to the throne to be removed from his nurse in about his seventh year and handed over to the care of a responsible and experienced knight, described as his *magister* or *preceptor*. He was taught good manners and disciplined; an attempt was also made to transmit ideas of virtue, justice and statecraft and to inject an abhorrence of tyranny. Medieval English kings from about 1200 were likely to be literate; until then the fact that a king like Henry I could read (it is uncertain whether he could write) was a cause for comment and congratulation. Edward I enjoyed Arthurian legends. The book learning of Edward II might be suggested by the purchase of a primer, or elementary prayer book in Latin, for the considerable sum of £2 in 1300 when he was still Prince of Wales. He is known to have owned other books but there is no proof that he could read; he could have had them read to him or, if they were in Latin or French, translated for him, or he could have simply looked at the pictures and left them unread (Johnstone 1946). The books owned by kings from John to Richard II have been recently studied (Cavanaugh 1988). It seems from this that English kings and their queens and families were using and enjoying books from an early date.

King's Hall, Cambridge

Edward II's undoubted involvement in the foundation of a society of king's scholars in the University of Cambridge is not really a reflection of his own proven interest of learning. On 7 July 1317, he issued a writ to the sheriff of Cambridgeshire ordering him to pay from his revenues money necessary for the maintenance of John de Baggeshote, clerk, and 12 children of the chapel royal whom the king had sent to be educated at Cambridge (Cobban 1969, 9). One of the aims of the king was apparently the provision of a reservoir of educated personnel from which the Crown might draw to meet its particular requirements. King's Hall was seen as a long-term 'investment' aimed at buttressing the waning power of the Crown by increasing the number of educated clerks. Edward III decided in 1337 to stabilize its rather uncertain financial provision by setting it up as an endowed college, and 11 successive kings from the time of the founder considered it worthwhile to maintain it from the Exchequer revenues. It was by far the largest of the Cambridge colleges in the fourteenth century, having a complement of 32 or more fellows, and it accounted for the production of about one fifth of that university's total output of legists. It is likely that the result was to 'nourish a climate of legal thought generally favourable to the accentuation of the more theocratic aspects of kingship' (Cobban 1969, 302).

King's Hall can lay claim to being one of the most innovatory of the colleges in medieval Cambridge. It was the first English college to make regular provision for the admission of undergraduates, so constituting the earliest prototype of those mixed collegiate societies which were to characterize post-Reformation Oxford and Cambridge.

Such a large-scale institution required ample space and buildings. It developed from the land and house of Robert of Croyland, presumed to have stood immediately north of Kings' Childer Lane and close, west of the present Great Gate of Trinity college. By 1351 all the land further north to the hospital of St John (now St John's College), north-east to the High Street and west to the river Cam had been acquired. A series of ranges, a chapel and two impressive gatehouses were built (RCHM 1988, ii, 210). These buildings, together with the neighbouring college of Michaelhouse, were assimilated into Henry VIII's new foundation of Trinity College in 1546.

Despite the reshaping on a much larger scale of the buildings of Trinity College, substantial fragments of the late medieval buildings of King's Hall can still be seen. The lower part of Great Gate and the flanking sections of the east range were under construction shortly before 1490. The gateway itself was completed rapidly and a new door is recorded in 1497–8. The upper parts of the tower took a further 30 years to build and the floors of the four turrets, completing the building, were not paid for until 1535. A heraldic gallery is carved above the entrance archways – the royal arms of old France and England, with lion supporters and a small shield of the arms of John Blyth, Master of King's Hall 1488–98, Henry VII's chaplain. The arms are those of the sons of Edward III. Above that, an insertion of *c.*1600, is a statue of the new founder Henry VIII, in impressive and characteristic pose as far as his upper body is concerned but standing on rather shrunk shanks. The second gatehouse, known as King Edward's Tower, now adjoins the college chapel to the west; formerly it stood some 27m (90ft) further south, facing King's Hall Lane where it was predecessor to Great Gate and served as the principal entrance to the college. It was begun in 1428 and completed in 1435, when the principal mason carved King Edward's statue, and colours were bought to paint it (Willis and Clark 1886, 445–6). It was removed from its first site in 1599–1600, the stonework being carefully stored. When re-erected, however, compression was necessary for it to fit into the constricted space between the chapel and the old library; the vault was left out and the north turrets were superimposed. Later additions such as the clock (1726–7) and the bell turret (nineteenth century) have further altered its appearance, but it still remains a remarkable architectural expression of the late medieval splendour of King's Hall.

If Edward III's literary interests were undoubted, they are thrown into the shade by those of his grandson, Richard II. Richard, born in Bordeaux, had a Frenchwoman as nurse (who married his tailor!). He was brought up by three masters, including Sir Simon Burley who carried the young prince on his shoulder to the fatiguing experience of his coronation in 1377. Burley owned a 'book of the government of kings and princes' in French in 1387–8. The king evidently spoke and read French and 19 of his books are mentioned between 1385 and 1388; the fact that one was written in Latin 'for the solace of King Richard' suggests that he could read Latin as well as French. His regular practice of attesting documents with his signature or 'sign manual' is further indication of royal literacy (Orme 1984).

The three Lancastrian kings all shared a more than average interest in learning and literature. Henry IV had a study built for himself at Eltham Palace. The room was furnished with two desks, a small one and a large one of two stages 'to keep the king's books in'. Such a receptacle was common in medieval libraries and preceded book presses (Brown, Colvin and Taylor 1963, ii, 935–6). The fact that, on his visit to Bardney Abbey in 1406, he spent an afternoon in the monks library 'reading for as long as he wished' does not prove that his reading was habitual, but he was able to write in both French and English. Henry V's irregular youth, made notorious by Shakespeare's characterization of Prince Hal, was not entirely misspent. He was tutored in grammar and is said by John Rouse to have continued his studies at the Queen's College, Oxford, under the direction of his uncle Henry Beaufort, the chancellor of the University; 'the chamber which he occupied was above the entrance gate of the college' (Hodgkin 1949, 42). In later life he wrote in both French and English. His conversion, which turned him into a pious fanatic, was politically convenient. Through his religious foundations he buttressed the shaky Lancastrian dynasty and they provided a channel of unceasing prayers for his soul, even if they were endowed by 'plunder and illegality'. It is said that he also intended to found a college for arts men and theologians in the castle at Oxford, to which the whole of the rest of the property of the alien priories was meant to go (Wylie 1914, I, 229).

His son Henry VI, famed for his munificent and long-lasting foundations at Eton and King's College, Cambridge, was thus not the first English monarch to interest himself in education. In 1424, when two years old, the boy-king solemnly granted permission in council for his nurse to teach him courtesy and chastise him reasonably from time to time. The Earl of Warwick, the king's tutor several years later, was accorded similar powers but when his charge was ten years old the Earl reported that the king had so grown in stature and knowledge of his high estate that he resented being disciplined. As a boy of 12 Henry and his court had lived with the monks of St Edmundsbury for several months while the council was passing through a period of financial crisis, but a recent biographer argues against the traditional view that Henry VI was uniquely addicted to prayer and private meditation (Wolffe 1981, 9). He considers that Henry, to mark the attainment of his majority at the age of 18, founded Eton College as a distinctive commemorative act and a gift to God.

Eton College

His foundation at Eton was to be a powerhouse of prayer: 25 paupers and enfeebled men were attached to the clergy whose purpose was to pray for Henry, for the souls of his parents, his forebears and all the faithful departed. He fixed on the old parish church of Eton, proposing to raise it from poverty to distinction, partly because it was next door to his birthplace, Windsor Castle, and partly because it was already dedicated to the Assumption of the Blessed Virgin Mary, his favourite saint. Initially, Wolffe points out, Henry did not envisage Eton's development as principally an educational institution (Wolffe 1983, 137). His prime concern for several years was to wrest every possible privilege and immunity from the papacy for the appropriated church. This included giving the maximum quota of indulgence and power to the provost of the new establishment to hear confessions. What Henry hoped for was a huge concourse of pilgrims to his collegiate church, attracted by the lure of the indulgences. In 1445 the college hired 30 beds for confessors and other servants in hopeful anticipation of this influx. Another indication that educational provision was not his prime concern is the final Eton statute he enacted when financial stringency struck. This guaranteed the upkeep of four chaplains, four clerks (one of whom was to be skilled at playing the organ) and eight choristers; the 400 marks per annum for the building fund was to be spent on completing the minster-church. The school had dropped out of the royal calculations for the time being.

So much for Henry VI's priorities. The second point to notice is that there is no evidence of a link between Eton and King's College, Cambridge in the initial foundation of 1440–1. It has been suggested that when Waynflete, installed as Provost of Eton on 21 December 1443, swore to keep the statutes, they made future provision for scholars at Oxford not

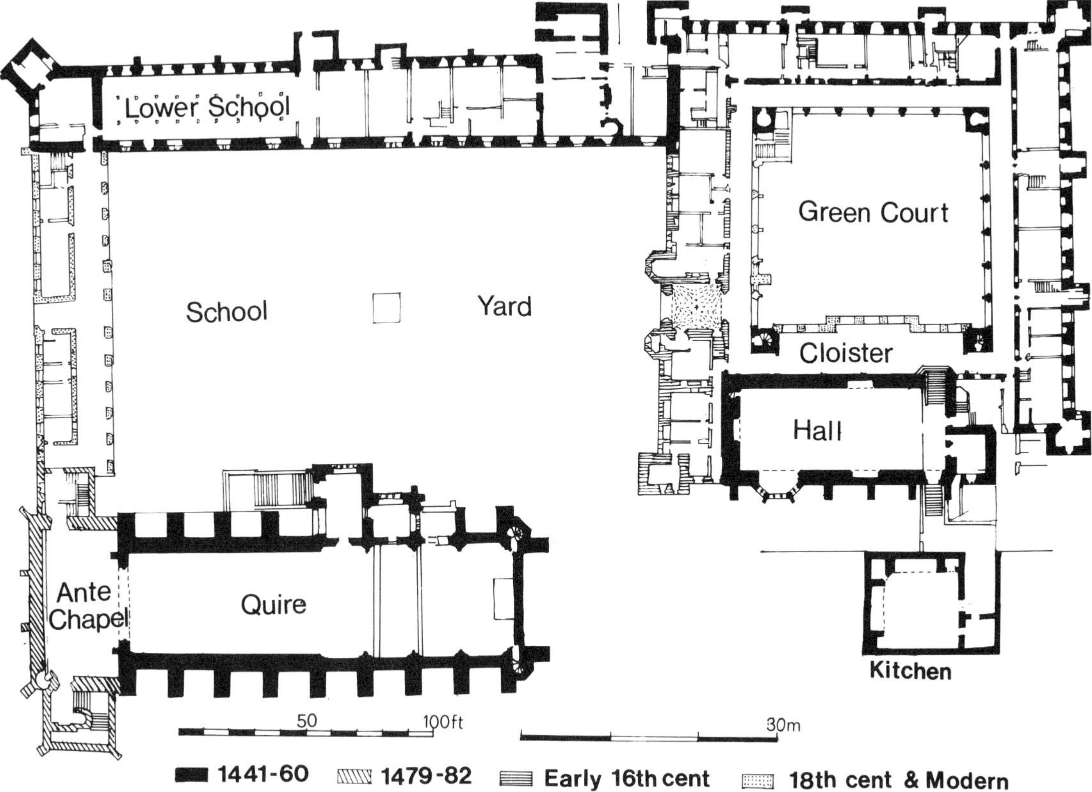

118 Eton College (Buckinghamshire). A plan of the college with dates of the buildings. (After RCHM Bucks.)

Cambridge. Only when the king had made the first of many visits to Winchester (in 1441, and subsequently in 1444, 1445, 1446, 1447, 1449 (twice), 1451 and 1452) did the idea take root that Eton and King's could perhaps be transformed by imitating the Wykehamist pattern. The similarities in plan between Wykeham's twin foundations at Winchester and New College, Oxford are obvious. A central entrance gateway with warden's lodging over opened into a quadrangle with staircases giving access to the accommodation ranges. Along one side in each case was a first-floor hall built end-on to a chapel, an economical use of space. In both there is a detached cloister for meditation and exercise and a detached bell tower. The layouts of both Eton and King's College owe a great deal to these senior foundations of Wykeham but because they were not completed according to Henry VI's intentions the extent of the imitation involved is masked. In each case a detached cloister with a free-standing bell tower was planned but not executed (Fig. 118). At Eton and King's, however, the chapels were each given much greater prominence and built on a greater scale; each ultimately occupied a full side of a quadrangle.

Indecision amounting to incapacity was the hallmark of the king's approach to building both his royal foundations. There is ample proof of this in both the documentary and the archaeological record. As planned in the foundation charter of 11 October 1440, Eton was to be a secular college with a school and almshouse attached. There were to be a provost, ten fellows, four clerks and six choristers to undertake the divine office, 25 poor men to live in an almshouse, 25 poor scholars, with a master to instruct them, to be boarded and schooled. The schoolmaster was also to teach grammar for nothing to anyone else who came to him. During the 1440s Henry became more ambitious, attempting to rival the Wykehamist foundation. He secured the services of William Waynflete as provost; he bought more land round the constricted site of the parish church; his statutes of 1447 considerably augmented the liturgical and educational functions of the college. The school now became the size of Winchester, with 70 poor scholars and an usher supporting the teaching of his master. The master was to be paid £16 a year, compared with the Winchester master's £10. The scholars were to be chosen from the natives of parishes in which King's or Eton had property. That a landlord who exacted rents and services from his tenants should feel he had equal responsibilities to protect and patronize them was one of the characteristic strengths of medieval society. Clearly, the school was now emerging as a more important element in the institution.

The building programme at Eton made spasmodic progress, mainly as a result of the king's inability to pursue a consistent policy. The driving force for the first campaign came from the joint leadership of William Waynflete and the Marquess (later Duke) of Suffolk. Waynflete saw that the funds largely derived from the Duchy of Lancaster were delivered, while Suffolk supervised their spending and made a suitable personal contribution. The master mason, Robert Westerly, was given authority to impress as many masons as he needed. Smyth, Thirsk and Clerk, successively, were in charge of the design and the labour force which implemented it. Stone supplies during the first nine years depended heavily on imports from Caen, Normandy. Later the deteriorating military situation in France dictated a switch to the white magnesian limestone quarries of Yorkshire at Huddleston and Stapleton. Water transport was used extensively: the stone was taken to Cawood on the Ouse and thence shipped to London and so to Eton via the Thames. Taynton (West Oxfordshire) was the source of a darker orange stone which had already been used in quantity at Windsor. It was brought by wagon to Culham and shipped down river to Eton. Later, owing to weirs and other obstructions, Taynton stone was carried by land as far as Henley before being put on barges (Davis 1973, 264).

The accommodation ranges at Eton were built largely of brick despite the fact it appears to have been regarded as an inferior building material to be avoided in the collegiate church itself. A piece of ground was rented at Slough and a brick kiln built upon it. William Veysey (a Dutch-sounding name) was employed on this in 1442–3; it is calculated that on average about 300,000 bricks a year were brought to the college between 1442 and 1451. William de la Pole's general superintendence may have been connected with this because his family were used to building in brick at Hull and in Suffolk; during these years his own almshouse, school and palace, largely of brick, were under construction at Ewelme in the neighbouring county of Oxfordshire.

The fundamental problem, which Henry VI proved unable to resolve, was the scale to be adopted for the collegiate church. The first version was well advanced by 1448, since provisions were being made to roof it and to fit the stalls. There is some doubt about the size of this first attempt but it is clear that the king made drastic revisions in his own 'avyse' and was prepared to order the demolition of the brand-new structure and virtually start afresh. This has been taken to indicate that he was already suffering from bouts of insanity, but Colvin suggests that structural defects may have developed and cites as evidence the king's very detailed instructions concerning the foundations.

Curiously, the footings were not to be disturbed but were to be augmented ('so that the groundes were to be takyn be syde the oold growndes for the enlargeyng of the seid qwere'). Also, the use of chalk, brick and Reigate stone was forbidden. Another clue to the problem lies in the elaborate precautions taken for 'enhancing' or artificially raising the ground levels (Willis and Clark 1886, 363–4). But the most startling change was that the church was now to be of cathedral-like proportions, with a total length of 97m (318ft) compared with previous drafts in the so-called 'Will' of 72.2m (237ft) and 63m (207ft). That Henry was striving after architectural grandeur seems an understatement: his master of the works had visited the cathedral churches of Salisbury and Winchester to measure them. Emulation of Wykeham's work at both Winchester and Oxford was doubtless a constant spur.

The end result was that time was lost, and political disaster overwhelmed the Lancastrian monarchy before the college could be com-

119 Eton College (Buckinghamshire), the south side of College Hall. Truncated buttresses and windows are half in stone and finished off in brick, a less imposing building material. This shows evidence for stop-start in Henry VI's educational foundation. (Photograph: RCHM England.)

pleted. Thanks to Waynflete's determination, the works were pushed on in the late 1460s and 1470s (though at a greatly reduced rate) despite the drying up of funds and the positive hostility of the new Yorkist dynasty. What the documents indicate, archaeology demonstrates (Fig. 119). Political uncertainty and economic indigence have left their mark on the buildings of Eton. Stones, maybe reused from the earlier chapel pulled down in 1448, were bodged into the head of the east window. Inferior clunch or ragstone appears in the arch-mould of the windows on the south side. Brick is used in the upper and internal parts of the stair turrets and parapets, and in the ante-chapel which Waynflete substituted for the nave after the king's deposition.

The timber roof to the chapel may itself have been a substitute for the stone vault that appears to have been intended. The hall, moreover, was never completed according to its original design. On the south side the exterior displays truncated buttresses and windows chopped off and finished in brick. Despite the supreme importance of the church to Henry's vision, in the long run it was the educational aspect of the foundation which had greater potential for the future.

King's College, Cambridge

A similar history of royal indecision involving order, counter-order and disorder marked the building of King's College, Cambridge. On 14 September 1440 royal commissioners were authorized to acquire land for Henry immediately to the west and north of the schools, with a main entrance from Milne Street (now Trinity Lane). It was to be used for a college to be called the Royal College of St Nicholas devoted to the extirpation of heresy, the augmentation of the priesthood and the adornment of holy mother Church. There was no mention at this stage of any connection with Eton. The buildings on this difficult and congested site were already well advanced when Henry had second thoughts. He bought up houses and gardens for a new site, six or seven times the area of the original; this necessitated the clearance of buildings and the closing of roads. By

120 King's College chapel, Cambridge, the north side. The so-called 'wedge of cheese' in which white Huddleston stone is used in the lower courses, a profile built up from a number of horizontal layers, each slightly shorter westward than its predecessor. (Photograph: J. M. Steane.)

1445 Henry was planning a replacement, an unprecedentedly large college for Cambridge, not for 12 but 70 scholars. The rector was renamed the provost and an usher was appointed to assist the schoolmaster. In addition, there were to be ten extra priests, six more clerks and ten more boy choristers, but a reduction from 25 almsmen to 13 weak single old men. The foundation stone of the new chapel was laid on 25 July 1446. The magnificent scale of college buildings the king had in mind was outlined in a document known as the 'Will'. Willis and Clark printed this and Colvin has reconstructed the plan (Willis and Clark 1886, 368–70; Brown, Colvin, Taylor 1963, 270, Fig. 29). There was to be a mighty chapel occupying the whole north side of a 'quadrant closyng unto both endes of the same chirche the est pane whereof shal conteyne CCXXX fete in lengthe'. The south and east ranges were to be used for accommodation. The hall and library were to be housed end-on in the western side with, under the library, 'a large hous for redyng and dispotacions'. The hall was to be on the first floor, 'in length C fete, upon a vaulte of xii fete high, ordeigned for the Celer and Boterie'. The other features have already been mentioned – a cloister and a tower to the west between the main complex and the river Cam.

So much for the vision; the reality is that in the end only the chapel was built. The latest study of the building (albeit by an architectural historian) reckons that the fabric of the chapel can be read like a book, though admittedly many of the early pages are missing (Woodman 1986). Its progress was halting and haphazard; the masons entered the site in 1448 but the structure was not completed until 1515. It began, says Woodman, as an act of piety and deep religious conviction and ended as an object of artistic splendour and dynastic propaganda. The design, despite its overwhelming sense of unifying power, went through considerable changes. This was only to be expected given that control was vested in four successive master masons over a period of 70 years, in which English Perpendicular developed and changed. Financial support from four successive kings was wavering and unreliable.

Henry VI proposed a long unaisled building, divided roughly into two halves: a choir or chapel proper, unencumbered with additions other than a vestry to the north-east, and an ante-chapel. The latter was to be flanked with eight side chapels or 'closets' as they were called. The disappearance of all the fifteenth-century building accounts forces us to examine the fabric of the chapel closely to establish its architectural history. It has been realized from Willis's time onwards that the use of different building materials may hold the key to the progression of the structure. In 1447 the king had obtained from Henry Vavasour the use of a quarry of white magnesian limestone in Thevesdale, in the lordship of Hazlewood near Tadcaster (Yorkshire), plus the right of carriage over his estate to the river Wharfe, whence it was possible to carry the stone to Cambridge by water.

Woodman has observed that the division between this white Yorkshire limestone and the brown oolite from Northamptonshire is less clear-cut than previously thought. He notices that the Yorkshire stone was neither the first nor the only material in use at King's before 1460. Recent cleaning of the interior shown that the expensive Huddleston stone was reserved from early on for use in prominent areas such as the walls round the high altar. It was also kept for major external features such as the base-course plinth mouldings of the great buttresses. Woodman does not agree that its use in the lower parts means that the building was laid out in its entirety before 1461; instead, he plausibly suggests that it was stockpiled and used gradually as the building progressed in the 1470s. It seems to have been getting short by the time the builders had completed the lower half of the windows in the north-east corner. He interestingly suggests that the main lateral window tracery was inserted from top to bottom, the tracery head having been built first as a suspended structure. The work of successive master masons can be plotted by studying (among other features) the mullion mouldings; Clark, for instance, abandoned the wedge-shaped profile of the exterior mullions in favour of a more decorative form. As at Eton, a good deal of brick was used in the upper works at King's, completely masked by the external stone skins. It is not generally realized that the uppermost 2.84m (9ft 4in) of the elevation below the sixteenth-century battlements consists of two parallel brick walls flanking a longitudinal passage which runs unbroken between the stair turrets in the corner towers.

King's College chapel is a vivid example of the disruption caused by civil war and multiple changes in dynasty in late medieval England. At the deposition of Henry VI in 1461, and for 15 years thereafter, little was done except to thatch the unfinished wall-tops and to pay off creditors with the greatly depleted resources available to the college. Edward IV cut off the funds, partly as a vengeful act against his predecessor, partly because he had little interest in architecture at this insecure stage in his reign. A resumption of royal support (1000 marks over three years) enabled the college to push ahead in 1479. The five eastern bays were now ready to be roofed. By the time the overthrow of Richard III had brought the work again to an abrupt halt, these five bays, though lacking a vault and open to a timber roof, were completed and two of the side-chapels finished and glazed. There again followed a long period when precious little was done, until 23 April 1506 when Henry VII kept the feast of St George at King's College, Cambridge. The Provost and Fellows impressed on the king the necessity of completing their great chapel and Henry promised royal resources for the purpose. In March 1509 he instructed that £5000 should be paid 'for the building and making the said church'. His unfortunate executors were obliged to match this sum before the job could be finished.

The Tudor programme of works at King's is remarkable for the survival of an account dating from 1508–15, plus a series of contracts which give a clear picture of the welter of architectural activity during these final years. The ante-chapel was rapidly completed and the whole crowned with master mason Wastell's fan-vaulting. That there were political strings attached to the royal grants is suggested by the sculptured display of great heraldic beasts and ciphers relating to Henry VII. The lower part of the chapel, inside and out, is liberally sprinkled with these emblems of the Tudor dynasty – exquisitely executed, it must be admitted, but contrasting vaingloriously in their elaboration with the ascetic lines of Henry VI's east end (Fig. 121). They symbolize the political interests which mingles with education and religious

aspirations in royal thinking throughout the Middle Ages.

Henry VIII's reputation for learning is partly based on the fact that he was the first English king to write, publish and print a book. He read certain books compulsively, annotating them vigorously, in sharp contrast to the picture books belonging to Edward IV (who liked to be read to). He also collected books, accumulating 329 of them, housing them in a specially built 'highest library' on the second floor of the new wing of his palace at Greenwich, begun in 1519. His reading interests, however, were partly fuelled by a desire to find grounds for his divorce, and his libraries at Greenwich, Whitehall and Hampton Court were supplied with transfusions of books from monastic plunder. Even Leland's greatest itineraries of monastic libraries ultimately developed into a salvaging expedition rather than a disinterested search for materials to further the cause of British history (Starkey 1991, 155).

Henry VIII never fulfilled the mighty plans that Wolsey had for Cardinal College, Oxford. By encompassing the fall of his great minister he deprived Oxford of a splendid chapel which might well have rivalled that of King's College, Cambridge as one of the greatest Gothic buildings of the age (Colvin 1983, 6).

121 King's College chapel, Cambridge, windows and buttresses at the west end. The ostentatious support of the foundation by the Tudor dynasty at this later stage of the building is demonstrated by the display of heraldry. (Photograph: J. M. Steane.)

References

ALEXANDER, J. and BINSKI, P., 1987, *Age of Chivalry: Art in Plantagenet England, 1200–1400*, Royal Academy, London.

ALLEN, D. F., 1951, *A Catalogue of English Coins in the British Museum, Henry II: cross and crosslets type*, London.

AMBROSE, T., 1980, *The Bishop's Palace, Lincoln*, Lincolnshire Museum, Information Sheet.

ANDERSON, M. D., 1971, *History and Imagery in British Churches*, London.

ARIÈS, P., 1976, *Western Attitudes towards Death from the Middle Ages to the Present*, London.

ARIÈS, P., 1981, *The Hour of our Death*, London.

ASTLE, T., 1786, 'An account of the events produced in England by the grant of the Kingdom of Sicily to Prince Edmund, second son of King Henry the third', *Archaeologia* 4, 195–211.

AYLOFFE, J., 1786, 'An account of the body of King Edward the First as it appeared in opening his tomb in the year 1774', *Archaeologia* 3, 376–413.

BAILLIE, H. M., 1967, 'Etiquette and the Planning of the State Apartments in Baroque Palaces', *Archaeologia* 101, 169–200.

BAINES, F., 1914, *Westminster Hall*, Report to the first commissioners of H.M.'s works on the condition of the roof timbering, Westminster Hall, HMSO, London.

BAKER, D., 1973, 'Bedford Castle: some preliminary results from rescue excavations', *Château Gaillard Studies, VI*, 1972.

BAKER, D., BAKER, E., HASSALL, J. and SIMCO, A., 1979, 'Excavations in Bedford 1967–77', *Bedfordshire Archaeological Journal.*

BAKER, E., 1981, 'The medieval travelling candlestick from Grove Priory, Bedfordshire', *Antiquaries Journal* 91, part 2, 336–8.

BALDWIN, D., 1986, 'King Richard's grave at Leicester', *Leicestershire Archaeological and Historical Society Transactions* LX, 1986, 21–4.

BARKER, S., 1977, 'A Collection of Pilgrim Signs and other Badges in Bristol City Museum', *Transactions of the Bristol and Gloucester Archaeological Society*, 47–50.

BARRACLOUGH, G., 1957, *History in a Changing World*, Oxford.

BARTON, K. J. and ALLEN, D., 1985, '*Odiham Castle Excavations, 1984*', Hampshire County Council.

BAUML, F. H., 1969, *Medieval Civilization in Germany, 800–1273*, London.

BEARD, C. R., 1933, *The Romance of Treasure Trove*, London.

BENTLEY, S., 1831, *Excerpta Historica or Illustrations of English History*, London.

BIDDLE, M., 1961, 'Nonsuch Palace 1959–60', *Surrey Archaeological Collections* LVIII, 1–20.

BIDDLE, M., 1961, 'The Vanished Gardens of Nonsuch', *Country Life* Oct. 26, 1008–10.

BIDDLE, M., 1976, *Winchester in the Early Middle Ages*, Oxford.

BIDDLE, M., 1986, 'Seasonal Festivals and Residence: Winchester, Westminster and Gloucester in the Tenth to Twelfth Centuries', in BROWN, A. R. (ed.), *Anglo Norman Studies* VIII, Woodbridge, 51–2.

BIDDLE, M. and BIDDLE, B., 1989, 'The Repton Stone', *Anglo-Saxon England* 14, 233–92.

BIDDLE, M., 1990, *Object and Economy in Medieval Winchester – Winchester Studies*, 7 ii, *Artifacts from Medieval Winchester*, Oxford.

BIDDLE, M., (forthcoming) *The Round Table of Winchester Castle.*

BINSKI, P., 1986, *The Painted Chamber at Westminster*, Society of Antiquaries of London Occasional Paper (NS) IX, London.

BLACKMORE, H. L., *The Armouries of the Tower of London, I, Ordnance*, London.

BLACKMORE, H. L., 1987, 'The Boxted Bombard', *Antiquaries Journal*, LXVII, 86–96.

BLAYLOCK, S. R. and HENDERSON, C. G., 1987, *Exeter Archaeology, 1985/6*, Exeter.

BLOCH, M., 1973, *The Royal Touch*, London.

BOASE, T. S. R., 1971, 'Fontévrault and the Plantagenets', *Journal of the British Archaeological Association* 3rd ser. XXIV, 1–10.

BOND, J. and TILLER, K., 1987, *Blenheim, Landscape for a Palace*, Oxford.

BONY, J., 1983, *French Gothic Architecture of the Twelfth and Thirteenth Centuries*, California.

BORENIUS, T., 1943, 'The Cycle of Images in the Palaces and Castles of Henry III', *Journal of the Warburg and Courtauld Institutes*, vi, 40–50.

BORENIUS, T., 1970, *St Thomas Becket in Art*, London.

BOTFIELD, B. and TURNER, T., 1841, *Manners and Household Expenses of England in the Thirteenth and Fifteenth Centuries*, Roxburgh Club.

BOWKER, J. R. V., 1986, *The Tournament in England, 1100–1400*, Woodbridge.

BRADFORD, A., 1933, *Heart Burial*, London.

BRAUN, H., 1943, *The English Castle*, London.

BRAYLEY, E. W. and BRITTON, J., 1836, *The History of the Ancient Palace and Late Houses of Parliament at Westminster*, London.

BRIEGER, P., 1957, *English Art, 1216–1307*, Oxford.

BROOKE, C. N. L., 1989, *The Medieval Idea of Marriage*, Oxford.

BROOKE, C. N. L., 1989, 'The Central Middle Ages', in LOBEL, M. D., *The City of London, British atlas of historic towns, III*, 30–41.

BROOKE, G. C., 1916, *A Catalogue of English Coins in the British Museum, The Norman Kings*, London.

BROWN, A. R., COLVIN, H. M. and TAYLOR, A J. (eds), 1963, *The History of the King's Works*, London.

BROWN, A. R., 1976, *English Castles*, London.

BROWN, A. R., 1985, *Rochester Castle*, London.

BROWN, E. A. R., 1981, 'Death and the Human Body in the later Middle Ages: The Legislation of Boniface VIII on the Division of the Corpse', *Viator, Medieval and Renaissance Studies* 12, Los Angeles, 221–70.

BROWN, R. C., 1967, 'Observations on the Berkhamstead bow', *The Journal of the Society of Archer Antiquaries*, 10, 12–18.

BROWNBILL, J., 1914, *The Ledger-Book of Vale Royal Abbey*. Record Society of Lancashire and Cheshire, 68.

BUCKTON, D., ENTWISTLE, C. and PRIOR, R., 1984, *The Treasury of San Marco, Venice*, Milan.

BURGES, W., 1863, 'The Shrine of Edward the Confessor', in SCOTT, G. C. (ed.), *Gleanings from Westminster Abbey*, Oxford.

BUTT, R., 1989, *A History of Parliament, the Middle Ages*, London.

BYERLY, B. F. and BYERLY, C. K., 1977, *Records of the Wardrobe and Household 1285–86*, HMSO, London.

CAMPBELL, M., 1988, 'The Shrewsbury Bowl and an Escutcheon of John, Duke of Bedford', *Antiquaries Journal* LXVIII, 312–14.

CANTOR, L., (ed.), 1982, *The English Medieval Landscape*, London.

CARLIN, M., 1985, 'The Reconstruction of Winchester House, Southwark', *London Topographical Record* 25, 33–57.

CARTER, J., 1838, *Specimens of Ancient Sculpture and Painting*, 2 Vols, London 1780–7, second ed.

CAVANOUGH S. H., 1988, 'Royal Books: King John to Richard II', *The Library*, 6th ser. 10, 4.

CAVINESS, M. H., 1981, *The Windows of Christ Church Cathedral, Canterbury*, London.

CHARLTON, J. (ed.), 1978, *The Tower of London; its building and institutions*, London.

CHERRY, B. and PEVSNER, N., 1984, *The Buildings of England, London 2, South*, Harmondsworth.

CHERRY, J., 1969, 'The Dunstable Swan Jewel', *Journal of the British Archaeological Association*, 38–53.

CHERRY, J. C., 1987, 'Late 14th Century Jugs' in ALEXANDER, J. and BINSKI, P. (eds), *Age of Chivalry, Art in Plantagenet England, 1200–1400*, London, 524–5.

CHETTLE, G. H., CHARLTON, J. and ALLAN, J., 1982, *Hampton Court Palace, Greater London*, HMSO London.

CLAPHAM, A. W., 1934, *English Romanesque Architecture after the Conquest*, Oxford.

CLARK, G., 1986, *Symbols of Excellence*, Cambridge.

CLAYTON, P. B., 1912, 'The Inlaid Tiles of Westminster Abbey', *Archaeological Journal* LXIX, 36–73.

COAD, J. G., 1984, *Battle Abbey*, HMSO London.

COBBAN, A. B., 1969, *The Kings' Hall within the University of Cambridge, in the later middle Ages*, Cambridge.

COCKERELL, C. R., 1851, *Iconography of the West Front of Wells Cathedral*, Oxford and London.

COLDSTREAM, N., 1981, 'Art and Architecture', in METCALF, S. (ed.), *The Later Middle Ages*, London, 172–225.

COLVIN, H. M. (ed.), 1971, *The Building Accounts of Henry III*, Oxford.

COLVIN, H. M., RANSOME, D. R. and SUMMERSON, J., 1975, *The History of the Kings' Works* Vol. III, 1485–1660, Part 1.

COLVIN, H. M., 1982, COLVIN, H. M., SUMMERSON, J., BIDDLE, M., HALE, J. R. and MERRIMAN, M., *History of the Kings' Works* Vol. IV, 1485–1660, Part II. London.

CONTAMINE, P., 1986, *War in the Middle Ages*, London.

COOK, G. H., 1948, *Medieval Chantries and Chantry Chapels*, London.

COOPER, I. M., 1937, 'Westminster Hall', *Journal of the British Archaeological Association*, 3rd ser, 1, 168–223.

COOPER, I. M., 1938, 'The Meeting Places of Parliament in the Ancient Palace of Westminster', *Journal of the British Archaeological Association*, 3rd ser, III, 97–138.

COURTENAY, L. T. and MARK, R., 1987, 'The Westminster Hall Roof, an historiographic and structural study', *Journal of Society of Architectural Historians* (of America) XLVI, 374–93.

COURTENAY, L. T., 1990, 'The Westminster Hall Roof: A New Archaeological Source', *Journal of the British Archaeological Association*, CXLIII, 95–111.

CROWTHER, M., Dec. 1987, 'The Miracle of the Retable', *Landscape*, 51–5.

CRUDEN S., 1981, *The Scottish Castle*, Edinburgh.

CRUICKSHANK, 1971, *The English Occupation of Tournai, 1513–19*, Oxford.

CUNLIFFE, B. and MUNBY, J., 1985, *Excavations at Portchester Castle Volume IV Medieval. The Inner Bailey*, Society of Antiquaries Research Report.

CURNOW, P. E., 1977, 'The Wakefield Tower, Tower of London', in APTED, M. K., GILYARD-BEER, R. and SAUNDERS, A. D., *Ancient Monuments and their Interpretation*, Chichester.

CUTTINO, G. P. and LYMAN, T. W., 1978, 'Where is Edward II?', *Speculum*, 522–43.

DALLAWAY, J., 1803, 'An Account of the Walls of Constantinople', *Archaeologia* XIV, 231–43.

DALTON, O. M., 1924, *The Royal Gold Cup in the British Museum*, London.

DAVIS, R. H. C., 1973, 'The Ford, the river and the City', *Oxoniensia*, 38, 258–267.

DAVIS, R. H. C., 1989, *The Medieval Warhorse*, London.

DAWSON, G. J., 1976, *The Black Prince's Palace at Kennington, Surrey, British Archaeological Reports* 26, Oxford.

DEER, B., 1989, 'Carnivore King and the Main Course of History', *Sunday Times*, 3 Sept.

DENHOLM-YOUNG, N., 1947, *Richard of Cornwall*, Oxford.

DENT, J., 1962, *The Quest for Nonsuch*, London.

DICKINSON, J. C., 1956, *The Shrine of Our Lady of Walsingham*, Cambridge.

DILLANGE, M., 1985, *The Sainte-Chapelle*, Paris.

DILLON, VISCOUNT, and ST JOHN HOPE, W. H., 1914, *Pageant of Birth, Life and Death of Richard Beauchamp, 1389–1439*, London.

DOUGLAS, D. C., 1964, *William the Conqueror*, London.

DOUIE, D. L. and FARMER, H. (eds), 1961, *Magna Vita Sancti Hugonis*, Vol. I. London.

DRAKE, C. H., 1914, 'The Hospital of St Mary of Ospringe, commonly called Maison Dieu', *Archaeologia Cantiana* XXX, 35–78.

DUGDALE, W., 1846, *Monasticon Anglicanum* VI, Part 3, London.

DUNNING, G. C., 1958, 'A Norman Pit at Pevensey Castle and its Contents', *Antiquaries Journal* XXXVIII, 205–17.

DUNNING, G. C., 1965, 'Heraldic and Decorated Metalwork and other Finds from Rievaulx Abbey, Yorkshire', *Antiquaries Journal* XLV, 53–63.

DURHAM, B., 1991, The Infirmary and Hall of the Medieval Hospital of St John the Baptist in Oxford, *Oxoniensia*, LVI, 17–76.

DYER, C., 1989, *Standards of Living in the Later Middle Ages*, Cambridge.

DYSON, T., 1989, *The Medieval London Waterfront*, annual archaeology lecture, Museum of London.

EAMES, E., 1965, 'The Royal Apartments at Clarendon Palace in the Reign of Henry III', *Journal of the British Archaeological Association*, 3rd ser., XXVIII, 57–85.

EAMES, E., 1980, *Catalogue of Medieval Tiles in the British Museum*, British Museum, London.

EAMES, P., 1977, *Furniture in England, France and the Netherlands from the twelfth to the fifteenth century*, Furniture History Society, London.

EGAN, G. and PRITCHARD, F., 1991. *Dress Accessories c.1150–1450*, London.

ELIAS, E. R. D., 1984, *The Anglo-Gallic Coins*, Paris.

EMERY, A., 1958, 'Dartington Hall, Devonshire', *Archaeological Journal* CXV, 184–202.

ERLANDE-BRANDENBURG, 1968, 'Le Tombeau de Saint Louis', *Bulletin Monumental* CXXVI, I, 7–36.

ERLANDE-BRANDENBURG, 1984, *The Royal Tombs, the Abbey Church of St Denis*, Paris.

EVANS, J., 1881, 'Edmund Langley and his Tomb', *Archaeologia* 46, 297–328.

FAULKNER, P., 1975, 'The Surviving Medieval Buildings', in PLATT, C. and COLEMAN-SMITH, R., *Excavations in Medieval Southampton 1953–1969*, Leicester, 56–124.

FAWCETT, R., 1990, *Stirling Castle*, Edinburgh.

FINUCANE, R. C., 1977, *Miracles and Pilgrims*, London.

FLETCHER, J., 1974, 'Tree Ring Dates for Some Panel Paintings in England', *The Burlington Magazine* CXVI, 250–8.

FLETCHER, J. M., 1924, 'The SS Collar in Dorset and Elsewhere', *Proceedings of Dorset Natural History and Antiquarian Field Club* XLV, 81–100.

FLEURY, M. and KRUTA, V., 1989, *The Medieval Castle of the Louvre*, Paris.

FOSS, E., 'Hackington, or St Stephen's Canterbury, Collar of SS', *Archaeologia Cantiana*, 73–93.

FOSTER, R., 1990, *The Great Pavement of Westminster Abbey*, London.

FOSTER, R., 1991, *Patterns of Thought*, London.

GAIRDNER, J., 1861, 1863, *Letter and Papers Illustrative of the Reigns of Richard III and Henry VII*, Rolls Series, 24.

GANZ, P., 1950, *Holbein*, London.

GARDNER, A., 1940, *Alabaster Tombs of the Pre-Reformation Period in England*, Cambridge.

GARDNER, J. S. and EAMES, E., 1954, 'A Tile Kiln at Chertsey Abbey', *Journal of the British Archaeological Association*, 3rd ser., XVII, 24–42.

GEE, E., 1987, 'Heating in the Late Middle Ages', *Trans. of Ancient Monuments Society*, NS, 31, 88–105.

GILLINGHAM, J., 1984, 'Richard I and the Science of War in the Middle Ages' in GILLINGHAM, J. and HOLT J. C., *War and Government in the Middle Ages*, Cambridge.

GIVEN WILSON, C., 1986, *The Royal Household and the King's Affinity*, Yale.

GIVEN WILSON, C., 1988, *The Royal Bastards of Medieval England*, London.

GOODALL, I. H., 1980, *Ironwork in Medieval Britain: an archaeological study*, unpublished Ph.D. thesis, University of Cardiff.

GOUGH, H., 1900, *Itinerary of Edward I, 1272–1307*, Paisley.

GRANT, A., 1984, 'Medieval Animal Husbandry: the archaeozoological evidence', in GRIGSON, C. and CLUTTON-BROCK, J., *Animals and Archaeology* 4, Husbandry in Europe, BAR International Series 227, 179–86.

GRANT, A., 1985, 'The Large Mammals', in CUNLIFFE, B. and MUNBY, J., *Excavations at Portchester Castle. Vol. IV. Medieval. The Inner Bailey*, Society of Antiquaries Research Report, London.

GRANT, A., 1988, 'Animal Resources', in ASTILL, G. and GRANT, A., (eds), *The Countryside of Medieval England*, Oxford, 149–85.

GREEN, C. and WHITTINGHAM, A. B., 1968, 'Excavations at Walsingham Priory, Norfolk, 1961', *Archaeological Journal* CXXV, 255–89.

GREEN, H. J. M. and THURLEY, S. J., 1987, 'Excavations on the west side of Whitehall, 1960–2, Part 1, *Transactions of London and Middlesex Arch. Soc.*, 59–130.

GRIFFITH, N. J. L., HALSTEAD, P. L. J., MACLEAN, A. and ROWLEY-CONWY, P. A., 1983, 'Faunal Remains and Economy', in MAYES, P. and BUTLER, L. A. S., *Sandal Castle Excavations, 1964–73*, Wakefield, 341–8.

GUNTHER, R. T., 'On the Architecture of the Hospital of St John' in SALTER, H. E. *A Cartulary of the Hospital of St John the Baptist, III, Oxford Historical Society*, 393–434.

HAHNLOSER, H. R., 1972, *Villard de Honnecourt*, Graz.

HALLAM, E. M., 1977, 'Henry II as a Founder of Monasteries', *Journal of Ecclesiastical History*, 28, 2, April, 113–37.

HALLAM, E. M., 1990, 'The Eleanor Crosses and Royal Burial Customs', in PARSONS D., 1990, *Eleanor of Castile 1290–1990*, Stamford, 9–22.

HALLET, C., 1902, 'The Tombs of our Angevin Kings', *The Nineteenth Century*, Aug., 265–81.

HAMMOND, P., 1978, *Royal Fortress. The Tower of London through Nine Centuries*, London.

HARDY, T. D., 1829, 'Itinerarium Johannis Regis Angliae', *Archaeologia* XXII, 124–60.

HARTING, J. E., 1883, *Essays on Sport and Natural History*, London.

HARTSHORNE, C. H., 1862, 'Illustrations of Domestic Manners during the Reign of Edward I', *Journal of the British Archaeological Association*, XVIII.

HARTSHORNE, C. H., 1862, 'An Itinerary of Edward I', in *Collectanea Archaeologica*, British Archaeological Association, II. London.

HARVEY, B., 1977, *Westminster Abbey and its Estates in the Middle Ages*, Oxford.

HARVEY, J. H., 1943, 'The Building Works of Cardinal Wolsey', *Journal of British Archaeological Association*, 3rd ser., VIII, 50–9.

HARVEY, J. H., 1944, *Henry Yevele*, London.

HARVEY, J. H., 1984, *English Medieval Architects – A biographical dictionary down to 1550*, Gloucester.

HASTINGS, M., 1955, *St Stephen's Chapel and its Place in the Development of Perpendicular Style in England*, Cambridge.

HEPBURN, F., 1986, *Portraits of the Later Plantagenets*, Woodbridge.

HESLOP, T. A., 1980, 'Seals from the mid-Ninth Century to 1100', *Journal of the British Archaeological Association* CXXXIII, 1–17.

HESLOP, T. A., 1984, 'Seals', in ZARNECKI, G., HOLT, J. and HOLLAND, T. (eds), *English Romanesque Art, 1066–1200*, Hayward Gallery, London.

HESLOP, T. A., 1987, 'English Seals in the Thirteenth and Fourteenth Centuries' in ALEXANDER, J. and BINSKI, P., *Age of Chivalry, Art in Plantagenet England, 1200–1400*, Royal Academy, London.

HIGGINS, A., Sept. 1894, 'On the Work of Florentine Sculptors in England in the Early Part of the Fifteenth Century', *Archaeological Journal*, LI, 129–220.

HINDLE, B. P., 1976, 'The Road Network of Medieval England', *Journal of Historical Geography* 2, 3, 207–21.

HINDLE, B. P., 1978, 'Seasonal Variations in Travel in Medieval England', *Journal of Transport History* 4 (3), 170–8.

HODGKIN, R. H., *Six Centuries of an Oxford College*, Oxford.

HOGG, O. F. G., 1963, *English Artillery, 1326–1716*, London.

HOLMES, M. R., 1937, 'The Crowns of England', *Archaeologia* 86, 73–90.

HOLMES, M. R., 1959, 'New Light on St Edward's Crown', *Archaeologia* 97, 213–23.

HORN, W. and BORN, E., 1965, *The barns of the abbey of Beaulieu at its granges of Great Coxwell and Beaulieu St Leonards*, Berkeley.

HORSMAN, V. and DAVISON, B., 1989, 'The New Palace Yard and its fountains: excavations in the Palace of Westminster, 1972–4', *Antiquaries Journal* LXIX Part II, 279–97.

HOWELL, M., 1962, *Regalian Right in Medieval England*, London.

HOWGRAVE-GRAHAM, R. P., 1961, The Earlier Royal Funeral Effigies', *Archaeologia* 98, 159–82.

HUNTER, J., 1842, 'On the Death of Eleanor of Castile, Consort of King Edward and the Honours Paid to her memory', *Archaeologia* 29, 167–91.

HUTCHINSON, F. E., 1949, *Medieval Glass at All Souls College*, London.

IVENS, R. J., 1984, 'De Arte Venandi cum Avibus', *Cake and Cockhorse* 9, 5, 130–7.

JACOB, E. F., 1961, *The Fifteenth Century, 1399–1485*, Oxford.

JAMES, M. K., 1971, *Studies in the Medieval Wine Trade*, Oxford.

JAMES, M. R. (ed.), 1983, *Walter Map, De Nugis Curialium*, Oxford.

JAMES, T. B. and ROBINSON, A. M., 1988, *Clarendon Palace. The History and Archaeology of a medieval palace and hunting lodge near Salisbury, Wiltshire*, Report of Research Committee of Society of Antiquaries XLV.

JAMES, T. B., 1990, *The Palaces of Medieval England*, London.

JOHNSON, C. (ed.), 1950, *Dialogus de Scaccario*, London.

JOHNSTONE, H., 1922–3, 'The Wardrobe and Household of Henry, Son of Edward I', *Bulletin of John Ryland's Library* 7.

JOHNSTONE, H., 1929, 'Poor Relief in the Royal Households of Thirteenth Century England, *Speculum*, 149–67.

JOHNSTONE, H., 1946, *Edward of Caernarvon, 1284–1307*, Manchester.

JONES-BAKER, D., 1984, 'Graffito of Medieval Music in the Tresaunt, Windsor Castle', *Antiquaries Journal* LXIV, 373–6.

KANTOROWICZ, E. H., 1958, *Laudes Regiae. A Study in Liturgical Acclamations and Medieval Ruler Worship*, Berkeley and Los Angeles.

KEELEY, H. C. M., 1987, *Environmental Archaeology, A Regional Review*, Vol. II, Historic Buildings and Monuments Commission for England Occasional Papers No. 1.

KEEN, M., 1984, *Chivalry*, London.

KENDALL, J. M., 1923, 'The Siege of Berkhamstead Castle in 1216', *Antiquaries Journal*, III, 1923, 37–48.

KENYON, J. R., 1981, 'Early Artillery Fortification in England and Wales', *Archaeological Journal*, 138, 1981, 205–40.

KERR, B., 1992, Lecture on Windsor Castle excavations.

KIMBALL, E. G., 1936, *Serjeanty tenure in Medieval England*, Newhaven.

KINGSFORD, C. L., 1915, *The Grey Friars of London*, Aberdeen.

KNOWLES, D. and ST JOSEPH, J. K. S., 1952, *Monastic Sites from the Air*, Cambridge.

KNOWLES, J. A., 1936, *The York School of Glass Painting*, London.

KYBETT, S. M., 1989, 'Henry VIII, a Malnourished King?', *History Today*, 39, 19–25.

LAW, E., 1926, *Hampton Court Gardens*, London.

LE PATOUREL, H. E. J., 1968, 'Documentary Evidence and the Medieval Pottery Industry', *Medieval Archaeology* 12, 101–26.

LETHABY, W. R., 1906, *Westminster Abbey: The Kings' Craftsmen*, London.

LEWIS, J. M., 1986, 'The Oxwich Brooch', *Archaeologia Cambrensis* CXXXV, 203–4.

LEWIS, J. M., BROWNSWORD, R. and PITT, E. E. H., 1987, 'Medieval "Bronze" Tripod Ewers from Wales', *Medieval Archaeology* XXXI, 80–93.

LEYSER, K. J., 1982, *Medieval Germany and its Neighbours, 900–1250*, London.

LEYSER, K. J., 1989, *Rule and Conflict in an Early Medieval Society*, Oxford.

LIGHTBOWN, R., 1989, 'The Kings Regalia, Insignia and Jewellery', in MACGREGOR A., 1989, *The Late Kings Goods*, Oxford, 257–75.

LINDLEY, P., 1986, 'The Imagery of the Octagon at Ely', *Journal of the British Archaeological Association* CXXXIX, 75–99.

LIST and INDEX SOCIETY, 1974, Vol. 103, *Itinerary of Edward I*, Part 1, 1272–90.

LONGFORD, E., 1989, *The Oxford Book of Royal Anecdotes*, Oxford.

LOOMIS, R. S., 1938, *Arthurian Legends in Medieval Art*, New York.

LOOMIS, R. S., 1953, 'Edward I, Arthurian Enthusiast', *Speculum* XXVIII.

LYSONS, S. (ed.), 1806, 'Extracts from the Rotulus Familiae in the Eighteenth Year of the Reign of King Edward I', *Archaeologia* XV, 350–62.

LYSONS, S. (ed.), 1812, 'Copy of a Roll of the Expenses of King Edward the First at Rhuddlan Castle in the tenth and eleventh years of his reign', *Archaeologia* XVI.

MACGREGOR, A., 1983, *Tradescant's Rarities, A Catalogue of Early Collection in the Ashmolean Museum*, Oxford.

MACGREGOR, P., 1983, *Odiham Castle, 1200–1500*, Gloucester.

MACKENZIE, F., 1844, *The Architectural Antiquities of the Collegiate Chapel of St Stephen's*, London.

MCFARLANE, K. B., 1973, *The Nobility of Later Medieval England*, Oxford.

MCLEAN, T., 1981, *Medieval English Gardens*, London.

MCNIVEN, P., 1985, 'The Problems of Henry IV's Health, 1405–13', *English Historical Review*, 747–72.

MADDICOTT, J. R., 1989, 'Trade, Industry and the Wealth of King Alfred', *Past and Present*, 123, May 1989, 3–51.

MÂLE, E., 1972, *The Gothic Image. Religious Art in France of the Thirteenth Century*, New York.

MANN, J. G., 1942, 'Two Fourteenth Centuries Gauntlets from Ripon Cathedral', *Antiquaries Journal* XXII, 113–22.

MARKS, R., 1978, 'The Glazing of Fotheringhay Church and College', *Journal of the British Archaeological Association*, 131.

MARSDEN, P., 1973, 'Baynard's Castle', *Note in Medieval Archaeology* XVII, 162–3, Fig. 60.

MAYR-HARTING H. M. and MOORE, R. I., 1985, *Studies in Medieval History presented to R. H. C. Davis*, London.

MILLAR, F., 1977, *The Emperor in the Roman World*, London.

MITCHINER, M., 1986, *Medieval Pilgrims and Secular Badges*, Sanderstead.

MOORE, S. A., 1888, 'Documents relating to the death and burial of Edward II', *Archaeologia* L, 215–26.

MOORHOUSE, S., 1983, 'Documentary Evidence and its Potential for Understanding the Inland Movement of Medieval Pottery', *Medieval Ceramics* 7, 45–88.

MOORMAN, J. R. H., 1952, 'Edward I at Lanercost Priory', *English Historical Review* 67, 161–74.

MORRIS, J. E., 1901, *The Welsh Wars of Edward I*, Oxford.

MUSTY, J., ALGAR, D. J. and EWENCE, P. F., 1969, 'The Medieval Pottery Kilns at Laverstock, near Salisbury, Wiltshire', *Archaeologia* CII, 83–150.

MYERS, A. R., 1959, *The Black Book of the Household of Edward IV*, Manchester.

NEAL, D. S., 1973, 'Excavations at the Palace and Priory at King's Langley 1970', *Hertfordshire Archaeology*, 31–72.

NICOLAS, N. H., 1828, *The Siege of Caerlaverock*, London.

NICHOLS, J. G., 1842, 'Observations on the Heraldic Devices discovered on the Effigies of Richard II and his Queen in Westminster Abbey', *Archaeologia* 29, 32–59.

NOPPEN, J. G., 1931, 'A Tomb and Effigy of Hennequin of Liège', *Burlington Magazine* LIX, 114–7.

NOPPEN, J. G., 1949, 'Building by King Henry III and Edward, the Son of Odo', *Antiquaries Journal* XXIX, 13–25.

O'NEILLY, J. G. and TANNER, L. E., 1966, 'The Shrine of St Edward the Confessor', *Archaeologia* 100 (2nd ser., 50), 129–54.

ORME, N., 1973, *English Schools in the Middle Ages*, London.

ORME, N., 1984, *From Childhood to Chivalry. The Educating of the English Kings and Aristocracy, 1066–1530*, London.

ORMEROD, W. M., 1990, 'The Personal Religion of Edward III', *Speculum*, 64, 850–77.

OSCHINSKY, D. (ed.), 1971, *Walter of Henley and Other Treatises on Estate Management and Accounts*, Oxford.

OXLEY, J., 1986, *Excavations at Southampton Castle*, Southampton.

PACKE, M., 1983, *King Edward III*, London.

PAFFORD, J. H. F., 1958, 'King John's Tomb in Worcester Cathedral', *Transactions of the Worcestershire Archaeological Society* NS XXXV, 58–60.

PALMER, W., 1953, *The Coronation Chair*, London.

PARSONS, D., 1990, *Eleanor of Castile 1290–1990*, Stamford.

PARSONS, J. C., 1977, *The Court and Household of Eleanor of Castile in 1290*, Toronto.

PARSONS, J. C., 1990, 'Eleanor of Castile, 1241–90, Legend and Reality through seven centuries', in PARSONS, D., 1990, 23–54.

PAUL, J. B., 1903–6, 'Royal Pilgrimages in Scotland', *Transactions of the Scottish Ecclesiological Society* I, 147–55.

PERCIVAL-PRESCOTT, W., 1957, *The Coronation Chair: An historical and technical enquiry*, London.

PERKINS, J., 1938. *Westminster Abbey, Its Worship and Ornaments*, Alcuin Club XXXIII, Oxford.

PHILLIPS, T., 1834, 'Survey of the Manor and Forest of Clarendon, Wilts., in 1272', *Archaeologia* 25, 151–8.

PINCHES, J. H., 1974, *The Royal Heraldry of England*, London.

PLATT, C. and COLEMAN-SMITH, R., 1975, *Excavations in Medieval Southampton, 1953–1969*, Leicester.

PLENDERLEITH, H. J. and MARYON, H., 1959, 'The Royal Bronze Effigies in Westminster Abbey', *Antiquaries Journal* 39, 87–90.

PONSFORD, M. W., 1979, *Bristol Castle. Archaeology and History of a Royal Fortress*, Unpublished M.Litt. thesis, University of Bristol.

POOLE, R. L., 1919–20, 'Seals and Documents', *Proceedings of British Academy*, 319–39.

PORTAL, M., 1899, *The Great Hall, Winchester Castle*, Winchester.

POWICKE, F. M., 1953, *The Thirteenth Century*, Oxford.

PRESTWICH, M., 1984, 'The Piety of Edward I', in ORMROD, W. M. (ed.) *England in the Thirteenth Century*, proceedings of the 1984 Harlaxton Symposium.

PRESTWICH, M., 1988, *Edward I*, London.

Queen Eleanor's Garden, Great Hall, Winchester Castle. No date. No author.

RACKHAM, O., 1980, *Ancient Woodland*, London.

RACKHAM, O., 1986, *The History of the Countryside*, London.

RACKHAM, O., 1989, *The Last Forest, The Story of Hatfield Forest*, London.

RACKHAM, R. B., 1909–10, 'The Nave of Westminster', *Proceedings of British Academy*, 33–96.

RADY, J., TATTON BROWN T. and BOWEN, J., 1991, 'The Archbishops Palace, Canterbury', *Journal of the British Archaeological Association* 1–60.

RAHTZ, P. A., 1969, *Excavations at King John's Hunting Lodge, Writtle, Essex, 1955–7*, Society for Medieval Archaeology Monograph Series 3, London.

RAHTZ, P. A., 1979, *The Saxon and Medieval Palaces at Cheddar*, British Archaeological Reports, 65, Oxford.

REES, W., 1961, 'Gower and the March of the Wales', *Archaeologia Cambrensis* CX, 1–29.

RICHARDSON, H. G., 1965. Review of *The Kings Works*, vols i and ii, *English Historical Review*, XXX, 555.

RICKERT, M., 1954, *Painting in Britain. The Middle Ages*, Pelican History of Art, Harmondsworth.

RIGOLD, S. E., 1976, *The Chapter House and Pyx Chamber*, HMSO Guide.

RIGOLD, S. E., 1979, 'Additional Documentation', in SMITH, G. H., *The Excavation of the Hospital of St Mary at Ospringe, commonly called Maison Dieu, Archaeologia Cantiana* XCV.

ROBERTS, E., 1986, 'The Bishop of Winchester's Fishponds in Hampshire, 1150–1400', *Proceedings of Hampshire Field Club and Archaeological Society* 42, 125–38.

Royal Commission on Ancient and Historical Monuments in Wales and Monmouthshire, 1956, *Caernarvonshire* Vol. I.

Royal Commission on Ancient and Historical Monuments in Wales and Monmouthshire, 1960, *Caernarvonshire* Vol. II.

Royal Commission on Historical Monuments, 1924, *An Inventory of the Historical Monuments of London I, Westminster Abbey*, HMSO, London.

Royal Commission on Historical Monuments, 1925, *London, West*, HMSO, London.

Royal Commission on Historical Monuments (England), 1930, *London, East*, HMSO, London.

Royal Commission on Historical Monuments (England), 1960, 'Excavations in the West Bailey of Corfe Castle', *Medieval Archaeology* IV, 29–55.

Royal Commission Historical Monuments (England), 1970, *Dorset II, South-East*, Part 1, HMSO, London.

Royal Commission on Historical Monuments (England), 1984, *County of Northampton* VI, HMSO, London.

Royal Commission on Historical Monuments (England), 1988, *City of Cambridge*, HMSO, London.

RUBIN, M., 1987, *Charity and Community in Medieval Cambridge*, Cambridge.

RUSHFORTH, G. MCN., 1936, *Medieval Christian Imagery*, Oxford.

SALTER, H. E., 1917, *A Cartulary of the Hospital of St John the Baptist*, Oxfordshire Record Society III.

SALZMAN, L. F., 1926–1927, 'The Glazing of St Stephen's Chapel, Westminster', *Journal of British Society of Master Glass Painters*, April 14–17 and October 31–6 (1926), April 38–42 (1927).

SALZMAN, L. F., 1952, *Building in England down to 1540*, Oxford.

ST CLAIR BADDELEY, W., 1908, *A Cotteswold Shrine, being a Contribution to the History of Hailes*, Gloucester.

ST JOHN HOPE, W. H., 1901, *The Stall Plates of the Knights of the Order of the Garter, 1348–1485*, Westminster.

ST JOHN HOPE, W. H., 1906, 'The Loss of King John's Baggage Train in the Wellstream in Oct. 1216', *Archaeologia* 60, 93–110.

ST JOHN HOPE, W. H., 1911, 'The Discovery of the Remains of King Henry VI in St George's Chapel, Windsor Castle', *Archaeologia* 12 (2nd ser.) 533–42.

ST JOHN HOPE, W. H., 1913, 'Windsor Castle', *Country Life*.

ST JOHN HOPE, W. H., 1914, 'The Funeral Monument and Chantry Chapel of King Henry the Fifth', *Archaeoelogia* 15 (2nd ser.).

SANDFORD, F., 1677, *A Genealogical History of the Kings of England*, London.

SASS, L., 1976, *To the King's Taste, Richard II's book of feasts and recipes*, London.

SAUNDERS, A., 1985, 'Cow Tower Norwich', *Medieval Archaeology* XXVX, 109–19.

SAUNDERS, P. and SAUNDERS, E., 1991, *Medieval Catalogue, Salisbury and South Wiltshire Museum*, Part 1.

SCARISBRICK, J. J., 1988, *Henry VIII*, London.

SCHOFIELD, J., 1984, *The Building of London*, London.

SCHRAMM, P., 1937, *The History of the English Coronation*, Oxford.

SCOTT, G. C., 1863, *Gleanings from Westminster Abbey*, Oxford.

SCOTT, R. F., 1914–5 'On the Contracts for the Tomb of Lady Margaret Beaufort', *Archaeologia* LXVI, 365–76.

SHARP, M. (ed.), 1982, 'Account of Constables of Bristol Castle in the Thirteenth and Early Fourteenth Centuries', *Bristol Record Society*, vol. 34.

SHORTT, H. DE S., 1958–9, 'The Early Episcopal Tombs in Salisbury Cathedral', *Wiltshire Archaeological and Natural History Magazine*, 57, 217–9.

SIMPSON, W. S., 1874, 'On the Pilgrimage to Bromholm in Norfolk', *Journal of the British Archaeological Association* XXX, 52–61.

SMIRKE, S., 1834, 'Notices of the Palace of Whitehall', *Archaeologia* XXV, 113–8.

SMITH, G. H., 1979, 'The Excavation of the hospital of St Mary of Ospringe, commonly called Maison Dieu', *Archaeologia Cantiana*, 95, 81–184.

SMITH, J. T., 1807, *Antiquities of Westminster, The Old Palace, St Stephen's Chapel*, London.

SMITH, N., 1988, 'The Eleanor Cross, Geddington', *English Heritage Conservation Bulletin* 5, 8–10.

SPENCER, B., 1978, 'King Henry of Windsor and the London Pilgrim', in BIRD, J., CHAPMAN, H. and CLARK, J., *Collectanea Londiniensia*, London and Middlesex Archaeological Society, 235–64.

SPENCER, B., 1985, 'Fifteenth Century Collar of SS and Hoard of False Dice', *Antiquaries Journal* LXV, Part II, 449–53.

STANILAND, K., 1978, 'Clothing and Textiles at the Court of Edward III, 1342–52', in BIRD, J., CHAPMAN, H. and CLARK, J., *Collectanea Londiniensia*, London and Middlesex Archaeological Society, 223–34.

STANLEY, A. P., 1880, 'On an Examination of the Tombs of Richard II and Henry III in Westminster Abbey', *Archaeologia* XLV, 309–27.

STANLEY, A. P., 1911, *Historical Memorials of Westminster Abbey*, London.

STARKEY, D. (ed.), 1991, *Henry VIII, A European Court in England*, London.

STEANE, J. M., 1975, 'The Medieval parks of Northamptonshire', *Northants Past and Present*, Vol. 3, 211–34.

STEANE, J. M., 1984, *The Archaeology of Medieval England and Wales*, London.

STEANE, J. M., 1988, 'The Royal Fishponds of Medieval England', in ASTON, M., *Medieval Fish, Fisheries and Fishponds in England*, British Archaeological Reports, British Series 182 (i).

STEANE, J. M., 1989, 'Renaissance Gardens and Parks', in FORD, B., *Cambridge Guide to Arts in Britain, 3, Renaissance and Reformation*, 208–21.

STEANE, M. A., 1986, *Charlemagnes' Architecture at Aachen*, an unpublished diploma dissertation presented to Cambridge University Faculty of History of Art and Architecture.

STEVENSON, W. H., 1888, 'The Death of Queen Eleanor of Castile', *English Historical Review* III, 315–21.

STEVENSON, W., 1899, 'The Death of Queen Eleanor of Castile in Nottinghamshire', *Transactions of the Thoroton Society*, Supplement 1–15.

STOCKER, D., 1991, '*St Mary's Guildhall, Lincoln*', The Archaeology of Lincoln vol XII-I. Lincoln.

STODDARD, W. S., 1966, *Monastery and Cathedral in France*, Middletown.

STONE, L., 1955, *Sculpture in Britain. The Middle Ages*, Pelican, Harmondsworth.

STOTHARD, C. A., 1817, *The Monumental Effigies of Great Britain*, London.

STRAKEN, E., 1931, *Wealden Iron*, London.

STRETTON, G., 1933–6, 'The Travelling Household in the Middle Ages', *Journal of the British Archaeological Association* NS XXXIX-XLI.

STRONG, D. E., 1978, *Eltham Palace, London*, HMSO, London.

STRONG, R. C., 1983, *Portraits of Queen Elizabeth I*, Oxford.

STRONG, R. C., 1990, *Lost Treasures of Britain*, London.

SUTHERLAND, C. H. V., 1973, *English Coinage, 600–1900*, London.

TANNER, J. D., 1953, 'Tombs of Royal Babies in Westminster Abbey', *Journal of British Archaeological Association* 3rd ser. XVI, 25–40.

TANNER, L. E. and WRIGHT, W., 1935, 'Recent Investigations Regarding the Fate of the Princes in the Tower', *Archaeologia* 34, 1–26.

TANNER, L. E., 1969, *Recollections of a Westminster Antiquary*, 153–65, London.

TATTON-BROWN, T. and SPARKS, M., 1984, *St Augustine's Abbey and the Royal Palace*, Canterbury Archaeological Trust.

TAYLOR, A. J., 1952, 'The Date of Caernarvon Castle', *Antiquity*, 25–34.

TAYLOR, A. J., 1985, 'Castle Building in thirteenth Century Wales and Savoy', in TAYLOR, A. J., (ed.), *Studies in Castle Building*, London.

TAYLOR, A. J., 'Edward I and the Shrine of St Thomas of Canterbury', in TAYLOR, A. J. (ed.), *Studies in Castles and Castle Building*, 291–7, London.

TAYLOR, A. J., 1985, The Building of Flint: a postscript in TAYLOR, A. J., (ed.) *Studies in Castles and Castle Building*, 165–72, London.

TAYLOR, A. J., 1985, 'Royal Alms and Oblations in the Later Thirteenth Century', in TAYLOR, A. J., (ed.), *Studies in Castles and Castle Building*, 257–89, London.

TAYLOR, A. J., 1985, *Beaumaris Castle*, Cadw, Welsh Historic Monuments, Cardiff.

THOMPSON, M. W., 1964, 'Reclamation of Waste ground for the Pleasance at Kenilworth Castle, Warwickshire', *Medieval Archaeology*, VIII, 222–3.

THOMPSON, M. W., 1985, *Pickering Castle*, HMSO, London.

TOMLINSON, A., 1974, *The Medieval Face*, National Portrait Gallery.

THURLEY, S., 1990, 'The Sixteenth-Century Kitchens at Hampton Court', *Journal of the British Archaeological Association* CXLIII, 1–28.

TOPHAM, J., 1795–1811, *Some account of the Collegiate Chapel of St Stephen, Westminster* with drawings by John Carter, Richard Smirke and Richard Dixon, Society of Antiquaries, London.

TOUT, T. F., 1934, *Collected Papers*, iii, 249–75.

TRISTRAM, E. W., 1955, *English Wall Painting in the 14th Century*, London.

TUDOR CRAIG, P., 1957, 'The Painted Chamber at Westminster', *Archaeological Journal* CXIV, 104–5.

TUDOR CRAIG, P., 1973, *Richard III*, National Portrait Gallery, London.

TUDOR CRAIG, P., *et al.*, 1986, *Westminster Abbey*, London.

TUDOR CRAIG, P., 1989, 'Henry VIII and King David', in WILLIAMS, D. (ed.), *Early Tudor England*, Proceedings of the 1987 Harlaxton Symposium.

TUMMERS, H. A., 1980, *Early Secular Effigies in England. The Thirteenth Century*, Leiden.

TURNER, E., 1785, 'Description of an ancient castle, Rouen in Normandy, called Le Château du Vieux Palais built by Henry V, King of England', *Archaeoelogia* VII, 232–5.

TWINING, LORD, 1960, *A History of the Crown Jewels of Europe*, London.

VALE, J., 1982, *Edward III and Chivalry*, Woodbridge.

VICTORIA and ALBERT MUSEUM, 1927, *Catalogue of carvings in Ivory*, London.

VINCE, A., 1990, *Saxon London*, London.

WAGNER, A. R., 1959, 'The Swan Badge and the Swan Knight', *Archaeologia* XCVII, 127–38.

WARREN, W. L., 1964, *King John*, London.

WARREN, W. L., 1973, *Henry II*, London.

WATERHOUSE, E., 1953, *Painting in Britain 1530–1790*, Harmondsworth.

WAY, A., 1842, 'Effigy of King Richard, Coeur de Lion, in the Cathedral at Rouen', *Archaeologia* 29, 202–16.

WEBB, G., 1949, 'The Decorative Character of Westminster Abbey', *Journal of the Warburg and Courtauld Institutes* 12, 12–20.

WHITE, G. H., 1948, 'The Household of the Norman Kings', *Transactions of the Royal History Society*, 4th ser. XXX, 127–156.

WHITE, G. H., 1959, 'The Princes in the Tower', *Complete Peerage* XII, Part II, Appendix J., 32–9.

WHITTINGHAM, S., 1971, 'The Chronology of the Portraits of Richard II', *Burlington Magazine* CXIII, 12–21.

WHITTINGHAM, S., 1974, *Realism in Medieval Portraiture*, unpublished Ph.D. thesis, University of Manchester.

WICKHAM-LEGG, L. G., 1901, *English Coronation Records*, London.

WICKHAM-LEGG, L. G., 1938, 'Windsor Castle; New College, Oxford; and Winchester College', *Journal of the British Archaeological Association* 3rd ser, III, 83–96.

WILCOX, R. P., 1981, *Timber and Iron Reinforcement in Early Buildings*, Society of Antiquaries, London.

WILLIAMSON, J., 1929–30, 'Benefactors Shields of Arms in the Nave of Westminster Abbey', *London and Middlesex Archaeological Society Transactions* VI, 146–53.

WILLARD, J. F., 1926, 'Inland Transportation in England during the Fourteenth Century', *Speculum* I, 361–74.

WILLIS, R. and CLARK, J. W., 1886, *The Architectural History of the University of Cambridge and of the Colleges of Cambridge and Eton*, Cambridge.

WILLIS, R., 1846, 'On the History of the Great Seals of England, especially those of Edward III', *Archaeologia* II, 14–41.

WILSON, C., 1986, 'The Gothic Abbey Church' in Wilson *et al.*, *Westminster Abbey*, London.

WILSON, D., (ed.), 1985, *The Bayeux Tapestry*, London.

WOLFFE, B. P., 1981, *Henry VI*, London.

WOLFFE, B. P., 1971, *The Royal Demesne in English History*, London.

WOOD, C. A. and FYFE, F. M., 1943, *The Art of Falconry being the De Arte Venandi cum Avibus of Frederick II*, Massachusetts.

WOODMAN, F., 1986, *The Architectural History of Kings College Chapel*, London.

WOODRUFF, C. E., 1932, 'The Financial Aspect of the Cult of St Thomas of Canterbury', *Archaeologia Cantiana* XLIV, 3–32.

WORDSWORTH, C., 1914, 'List of altars in Salisbury Cathedral', *Wiltshire Archaeological and Natural History Magazine* XXXVIII, 557–71.

WORMALD, F., 1937–8, 'The Rood of Bromholm', *Journal of the Warburg Institute* I, 31–46.

WORMALD, F., 1988, *Collected Writings* II, Studies in English and Continental Art of the Later Middle Ages, London.

WYLIE, J. H., 1914, *The Reign of Henry the Fifth*, Cambridge.

WYON, A. B. and WYON, A., 1887, *The Great Seals of England*, London.

ZARNECKI, G., HOLT, J. and HOLLAND, T. (eds), 1984, *English Romanesque Art, 1066–1200*, Hayward Gallery, London.

ZARNECKI, G., 1964, *The Romanesque Sculpture of Lincoln Cathedral*, Lincoln Minster Pamphlets, 2nd series, 2.

Index